ARISA

4

Natsumi Ando

Translated and adapted by
Andria Cheng

Lettered by
North Market Street Graphics

KC
KODANSHA
COMICS

A Kodansha Comics Trade Paperback Original.

Arisa volume 4 copyright © 2010 Natsumi Ando
English translation copyright © 2011 Natsumi Ando

Published in the United States by Kodansha Comics, an imprint of Kodansha USA Publishing, LLC., New York.

Publication rights for this English edition arranged through Kodansha Ltd., Tokyo.

First published in Japan in 2010 by Kodansha Ltd., Tokyo.

ISBN 978-1-935-42918-0

Printed in the United States of America.

www.kodanshacomics.com

2 4 6 8 9 7 5 3 1

Translator/Adapter: Andria Cheng
Lettering: North Market Street Graphics

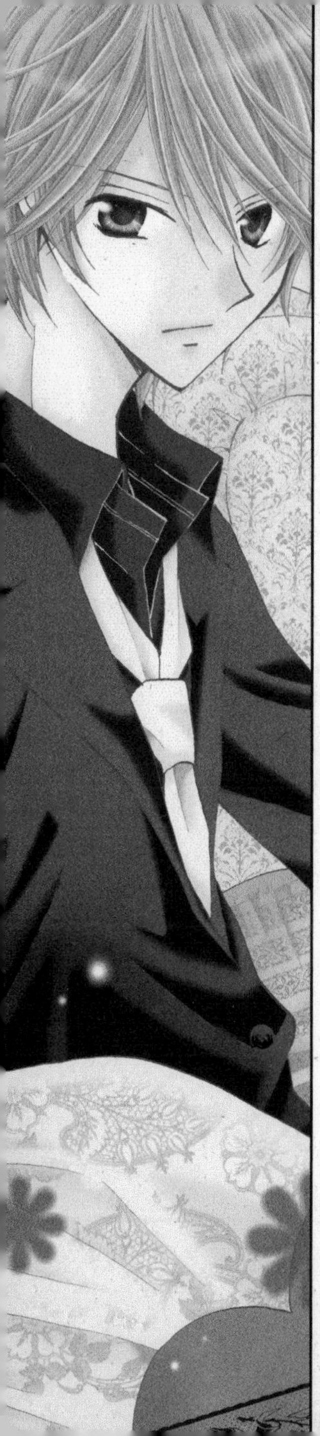

Contents

HONORIFICS EXPLAINED

Throughout the Kodansha Comics books, you will find Japanese honorifics left intact in the translations. For those not familiar with how the Japanese use honorifics and, more important, how they differ from American honorifics, we present this brief overview.

Politeness has always been a critical facet of Japanese culture. Ever since the feudal era, when Japan was a highly stratified society, use of honorifics—which can be defined as polite speech that indicates relationship or status—has played an essential role in the Japanese language. When addressing someone in Japanese, an honorific usually takes the form of a suffix attached to one's name (example: "Asuna-san"), is used as a title at the end of one's name, or appears in place of the name itself (example:

"Negi-sensei," or simply "Sensei!").

Honorifics can be expressions of respect or endearment. In the context of manga and anime, honorifics give insight into the nature of the relationship between characters. Many English translations leave out these important honorifics and therefore distort the feel of the original Japanese. Because Japanese honorifics contain nuances that English honorifics lack, it is our policy at Kodansha Comics not to translate them. Here, instead, is a guide to some of the honorifics you may encounter in Kodansha Comics books.

-san: This is the most common honorific and is equivalent to Mr., Miss, Ms., or Mrs. It is the all-purpose honorific and can be used in any situation where politeness is required.

-sama: This is one level higher than "-san" and is used to confer great respect.

-dono: This comes from the word "tono," which means "lord." It is an even higher level than "-sama" and confers utmost respect.

-kun: This suffix is used at the end of boys' names to express familiarity or endearment. It is also sometimes used by men among friends, or when addressing someone younger or of a lower station.

-chan: This is used to express endearment, mostly toward girls. It is also used for little boys, pets, and even among lovers. It gives a sense of childish cuteness.

Bozu: This is an informal way to refer to a boy, similar to the English terms "kid" and "squirt."

Sempai/ Senpai: This title suggests that the addressee is one's senior in a group or organization. It is most often used in a school setting, where underclassmen refer to their upperclassmen as "sempai." It can also be used in the workplace, such as when a newer employee addresses an employee who has seniority in the company.

Kohai: This is the opposite of "sempai" and is used toward underclassmen in school or newcomers in the workplace. It connotes that the addressee is of a lower station.

Sensei: Literally meaning "one who has come before," this title is used for teachers, doctors, or masters of any profession or art.

-[blank]: This is usually forgotten in these lists, but it is perhaps the most significant difference between Japanese and English. The lack of honorific means that the speaker has permission to address the person in a very intimate way. Usually, only family, spouses, or very close friends have this kind of permission. Known as *yobisute*, it can be gratifying when someone who has earned the intimacy starts to call one by one's name without an honorific. But when that intimacy hasn't been earned, it can be very insulting.

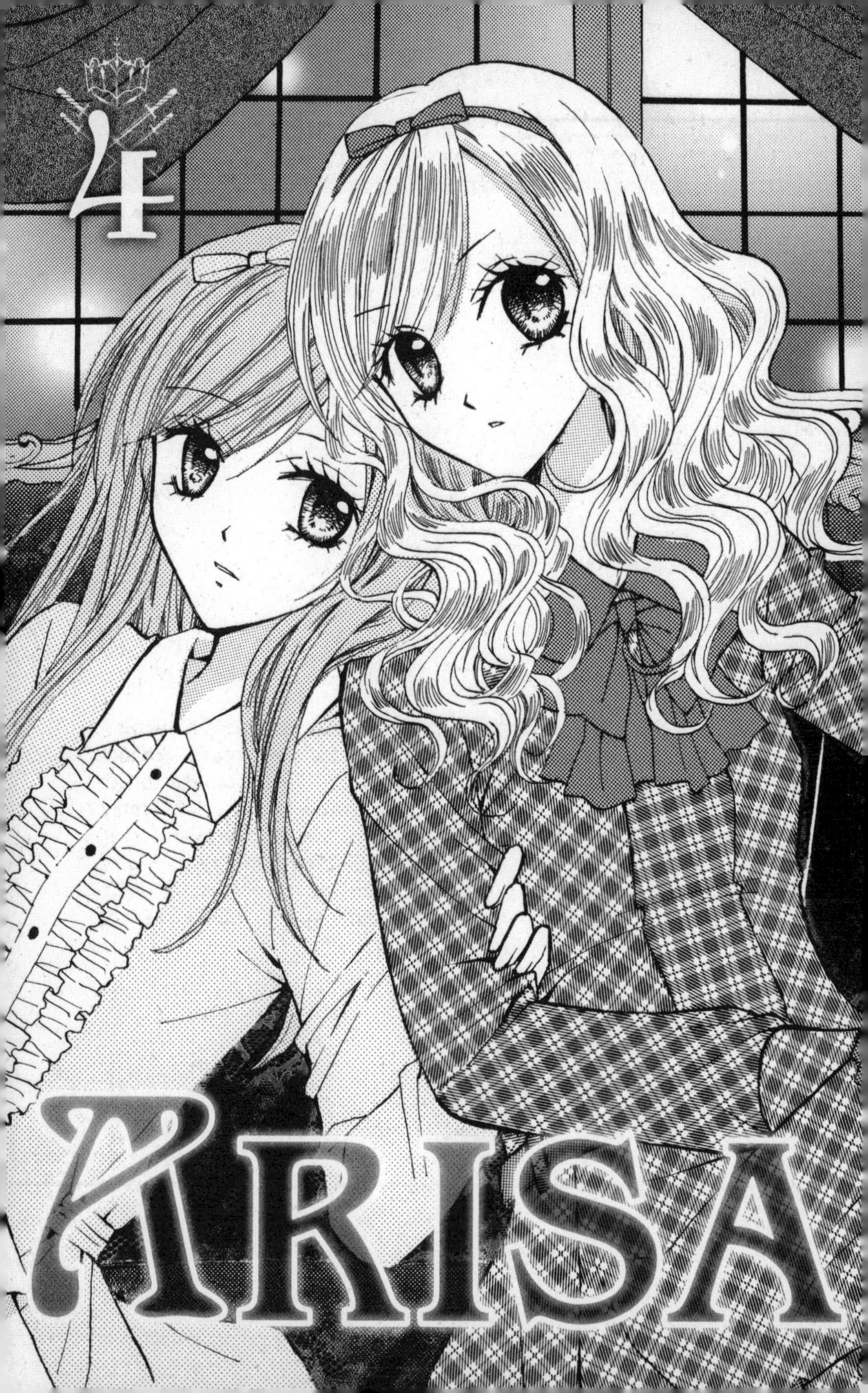
4
ARISA

Contents

ARISA

Secret King's Room

The story so far

Tsubasa and Arisa are twin sisters separated by their parents' divorce. They finally reunited after three years of being apart, but their happy time together came to a sudden end when Arisa jumped out her bedroom window right in front of Tsubasa, leaving behind a mysterious card...

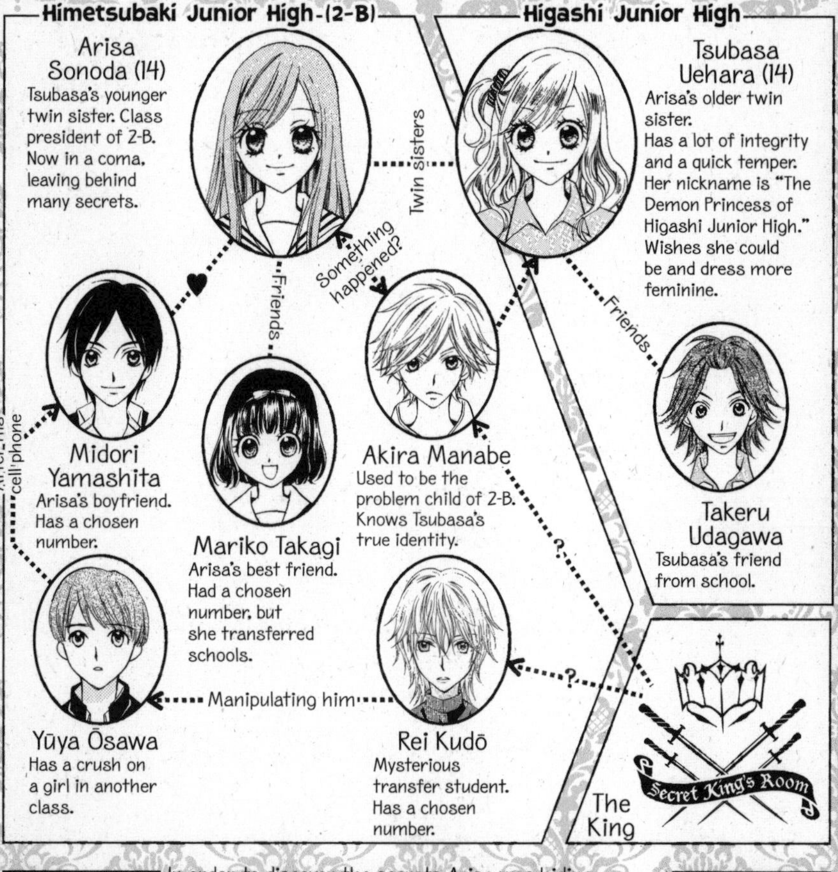

Himetsubaki Junior High-(2-B)
Higashi Junior High
Arisa Sonoda (14)
Tsubasa's younger twin sister. Class president of 2-B. Now in a coma, leaving behind many secrets.
Twin sisters
Tsubasa Uehara (14)
Arisa's older twin sister. Has a lot of integrity and a quick temper. Her nickname is "The Demon Princess of Higashi Junior High." Wishes she could be and dress more feminine.
Friends
Something happened?
Friends
Midori Yamashita
Arisa's boyfriend. Has a chosen number.
Mariko Takagi
Arisa's best friend. Had a chosen number, but she transferred schools.
Akira Manabe
Used to be the problem child of 2-B. Knows Tsubasa's true identity.
Takeru Udagawa
Tsubasa's friend from school.
After his cell phone
?
Manipulating him
?
Yūya Ōsawa
Has a crush on a girl in another class.
Rei Kudō
Mysterious transfer student. Has a chosen number.
Secret King's Room
The King

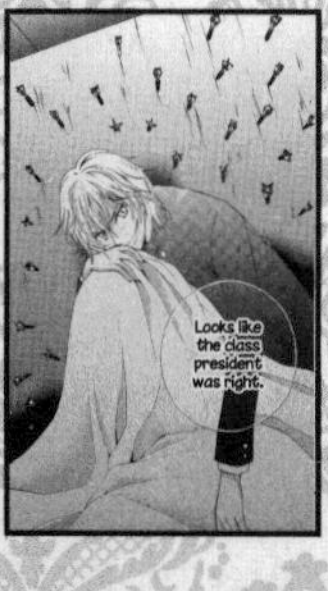

Looks like the class president was right.

In order to discover the secrets Arisa was hiding, Tsubasa pretended to be Arisa and attended Himetsubaki Junior High. In Class 2-B, a mysterious internet presence called "The King" led strange incidents and bullying. It turns out that Arisa was the original "King," but someone else took over in order to control her classmates. Tsubasa decided to team up with Manabe to find the true identity of the "King," but now he will only grant the wishes of five "chosen ones." Mariko told them that one of the chosen ones is the King. And now Kudō is also after the cell phones of the chosen ones.

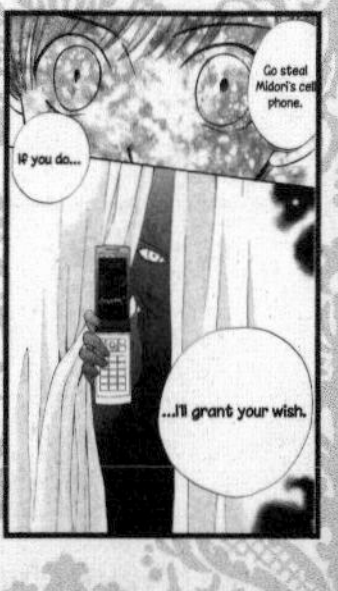

Go steal Midori's cell phone.
If you do...
...I'll grant your wish.

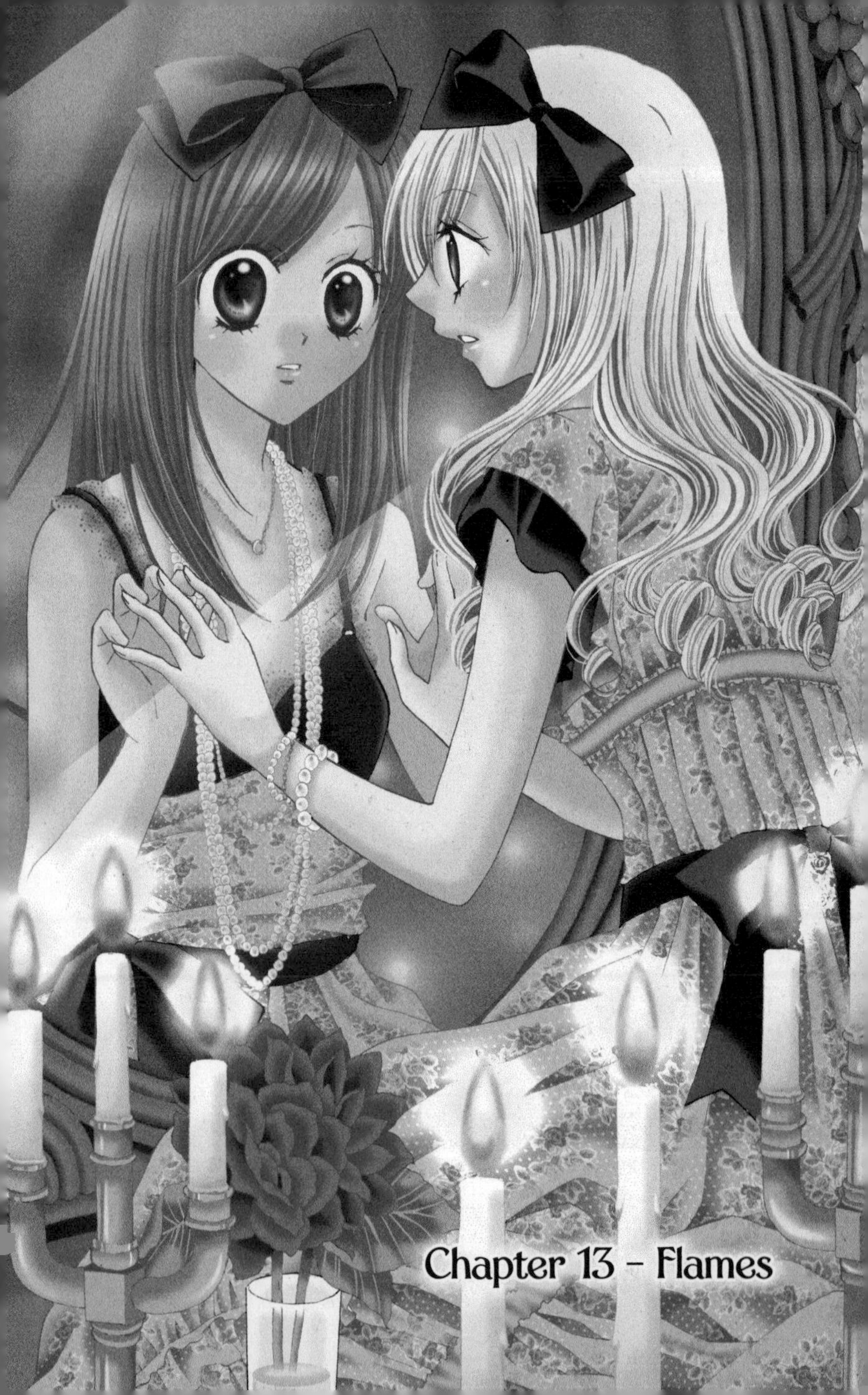
Chapter 13 - Flames

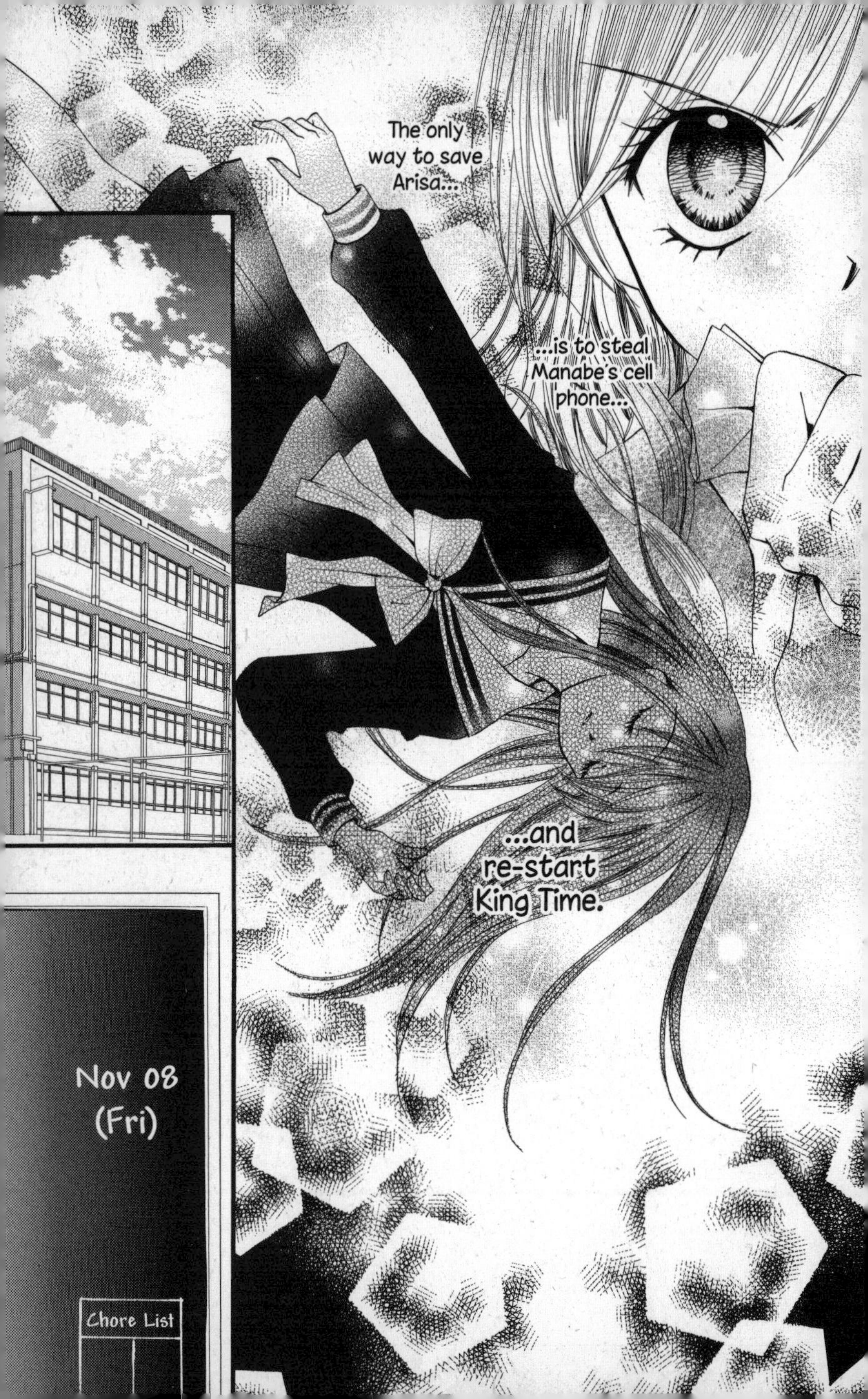
The only way to save Arisa...
...is to steal Manabe's cell phone...
...and re-start King Time.
Nov 08 (Fri)
Chore List

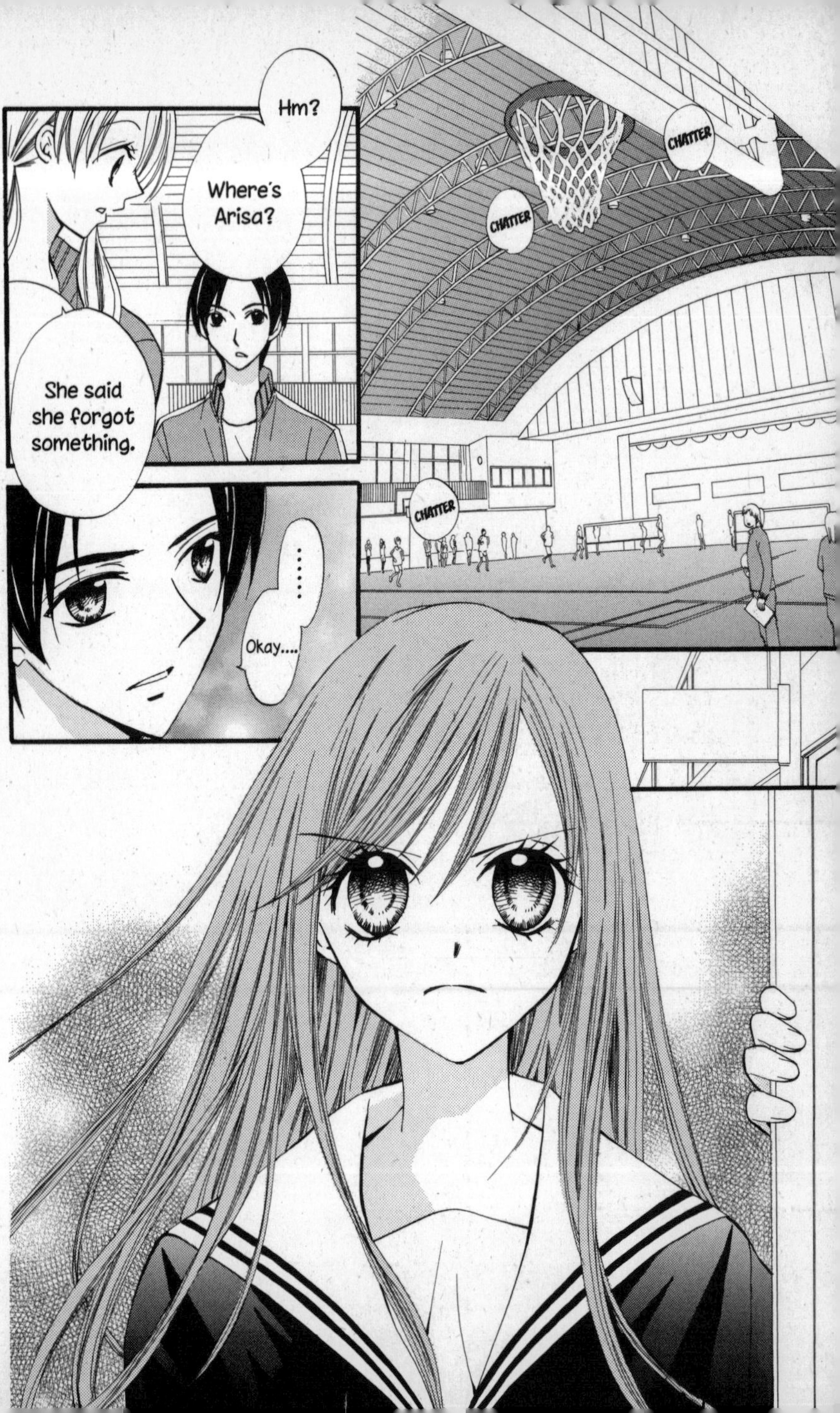
CHATTER
CHATTER
CHATTER
Hm?
Where's Arisa?
She said she forgot something.
......
Okay....

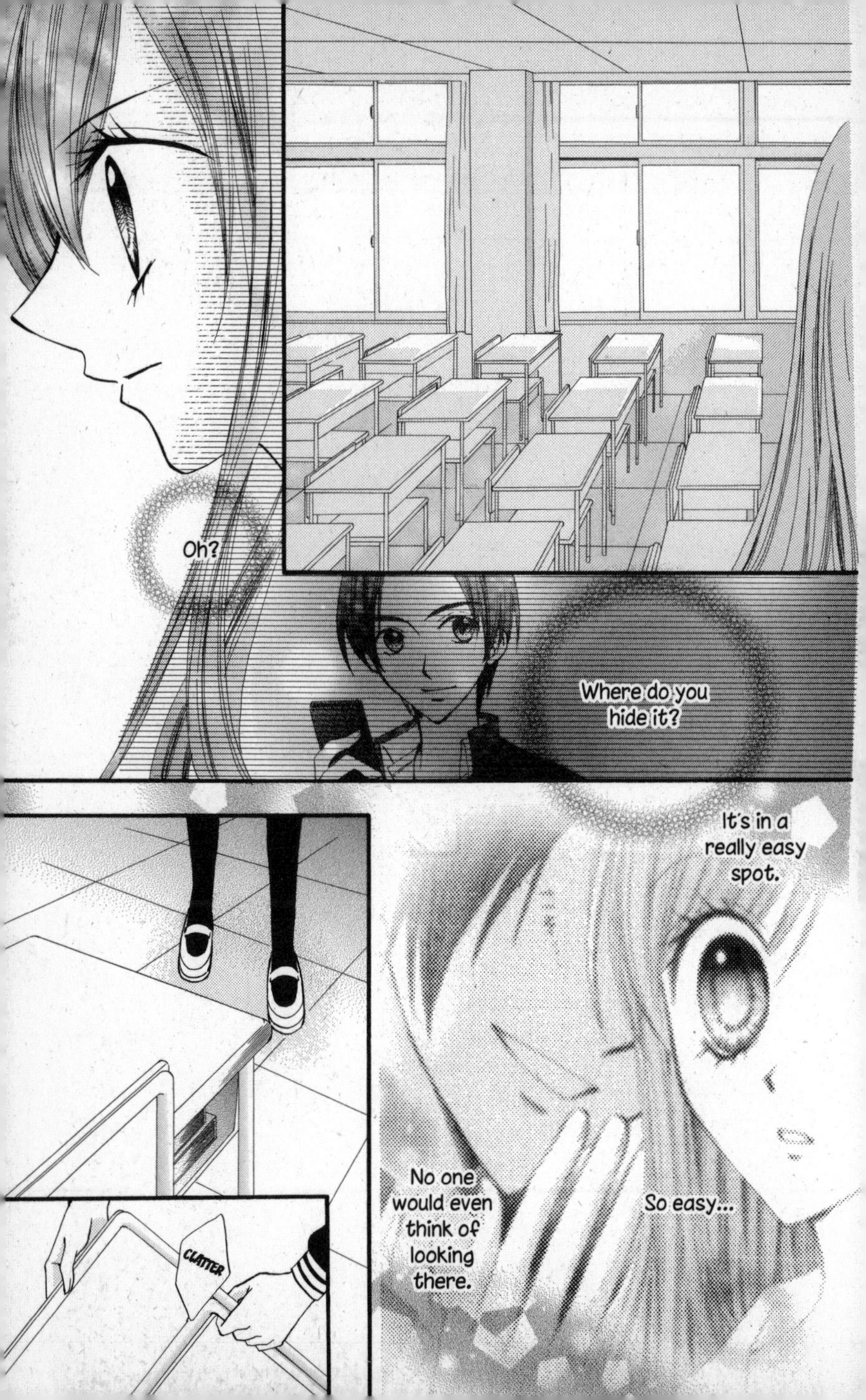
Where do you hide it?
Oh?
It's in a really easy spot.
So easy...
No one would even think of looking there.
CLATTER

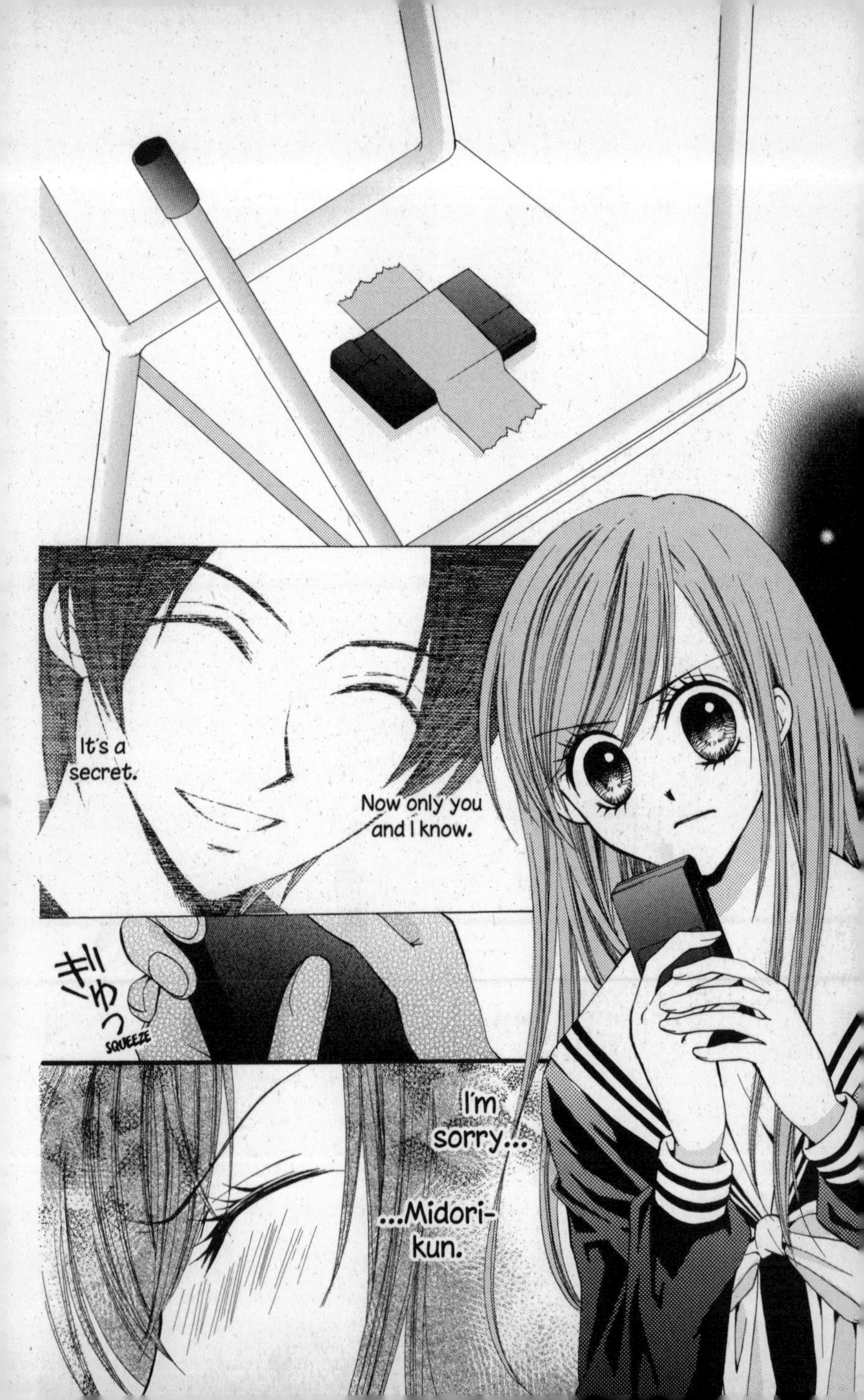
It's a secret.
Now only you and I know.
ぎゅっ
SQUEEZE
I'm sorry...
...Midori-kun.

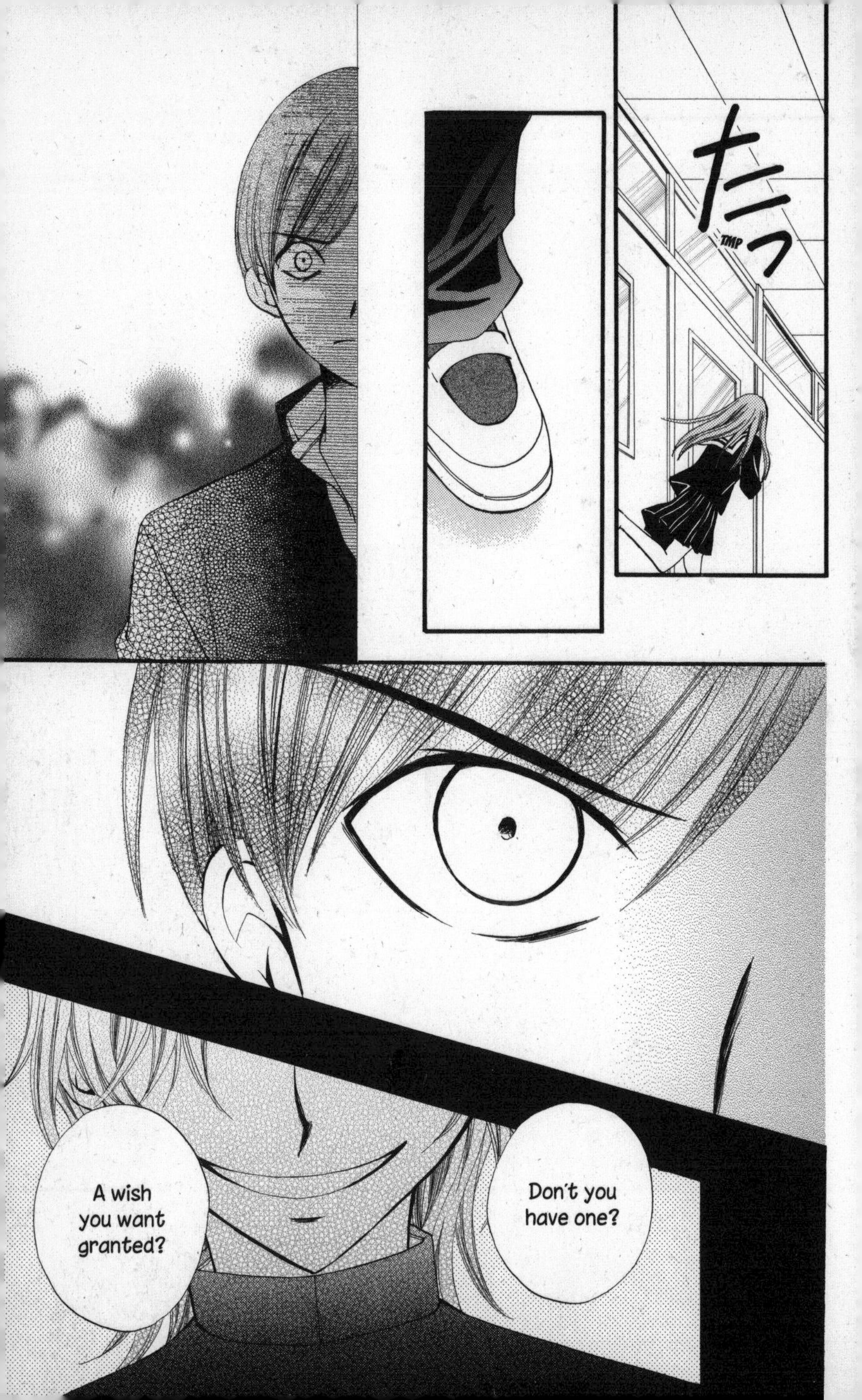
たっ
TMP
Don't you have one?
A wish you want granted?

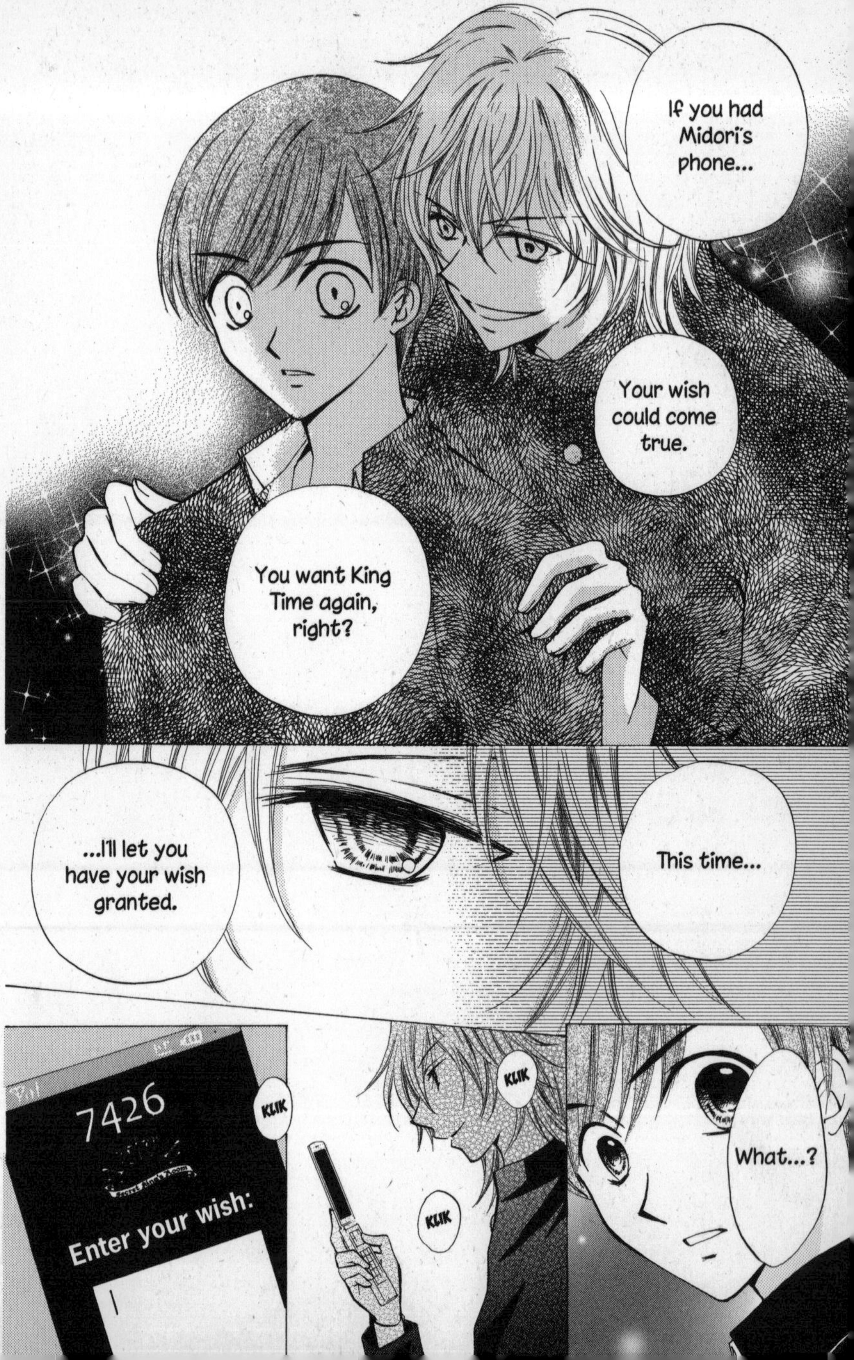
If you had Midori's phone...
Your wish could come true.
You want King Time again, right?
This time...
...I'll let you have your wish granted.
What...?
KLIK
KLIK
KLIK
7426
Enter your wish:

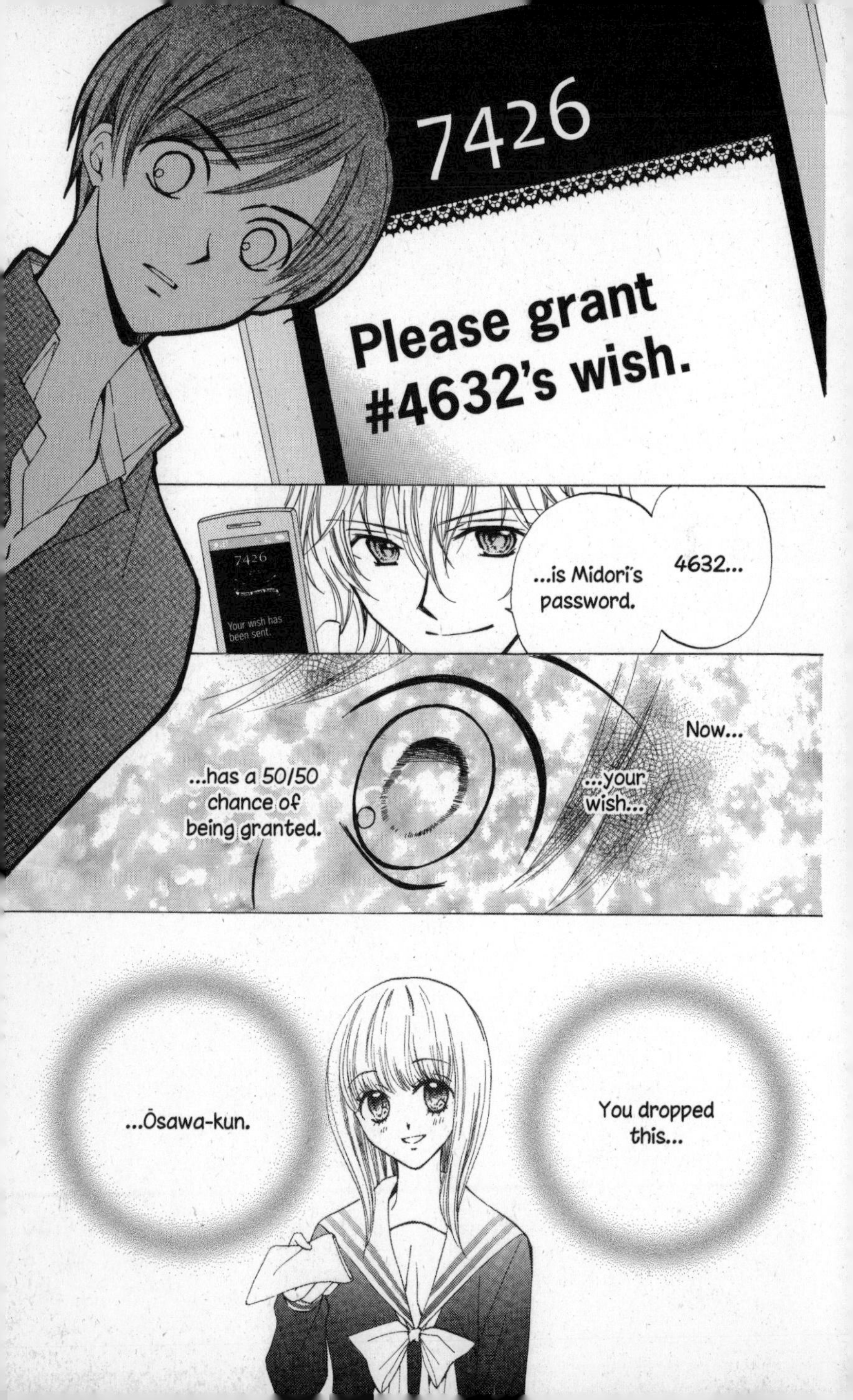
7426
Please grant #4632's wish.
4632...
...is Midori's password.
7426
Your wish has been sent.
Now...
...your wish...
...has a 50/50 chance of being granted.
You dropped this...
...Ōsawa-kun.

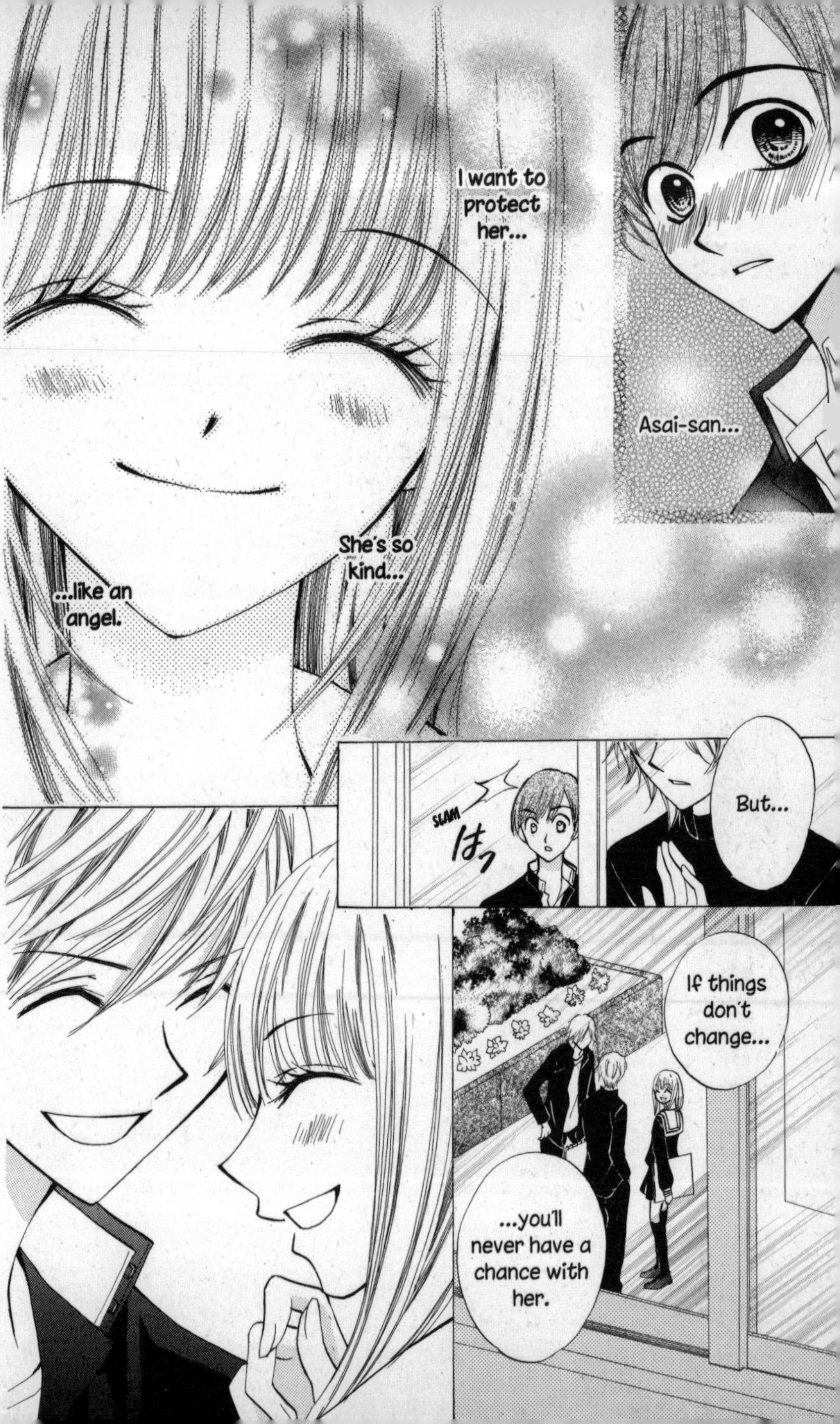
Asai-san...
I want to protect her...
She's so kind...
...like an angel.
But...
SLAM
はっ
If things don't change...
...you'll never have a chance with her.

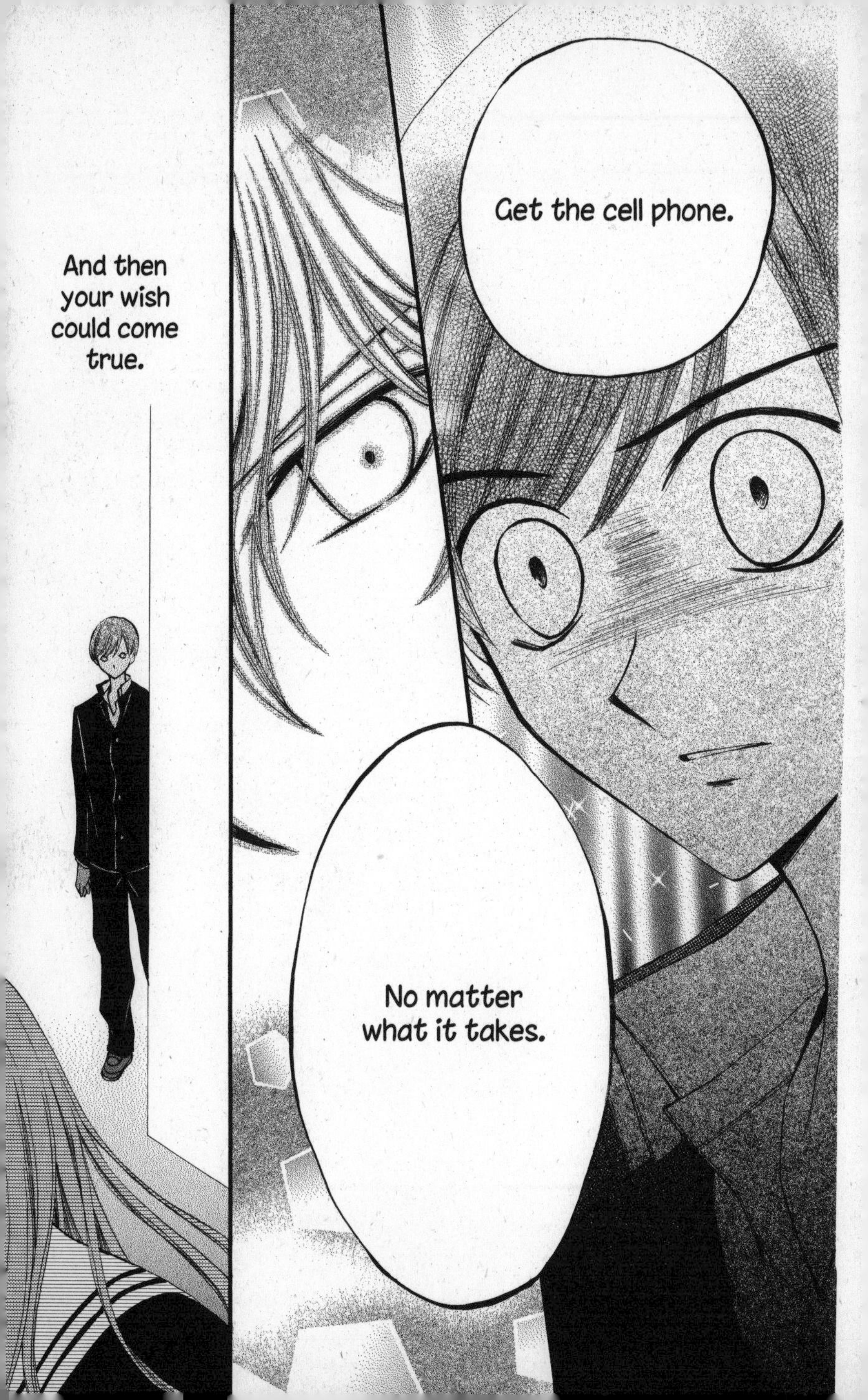
Get the cell phone.
No matter what it takes.
And then your wish could come true.

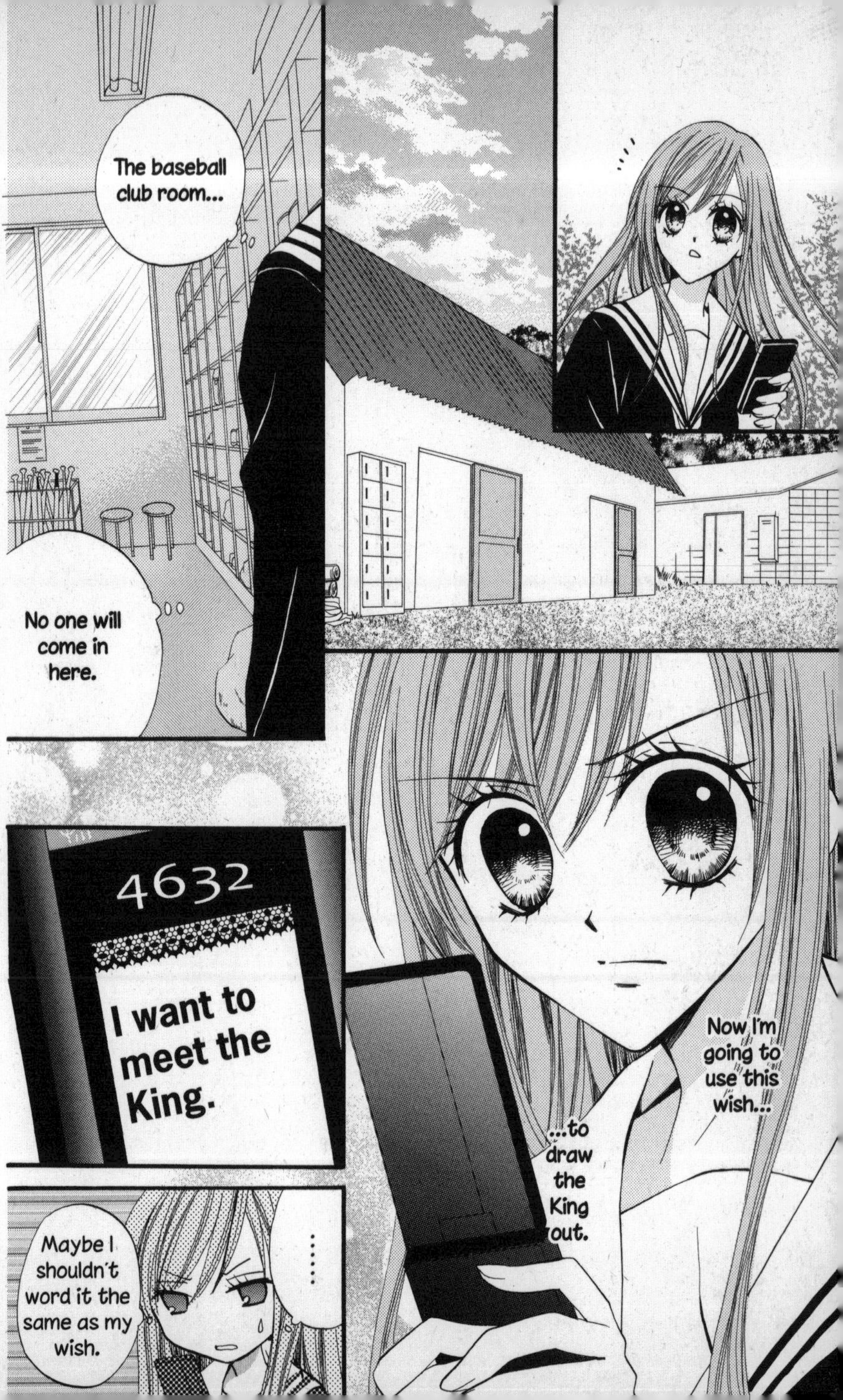
The baseball club room...
No one will come in here.
Now I'm going to use this wish...
...to draw the King out.
4632
I want to meet the King.
......
Maybe I shouldn't word it the same as my wish.

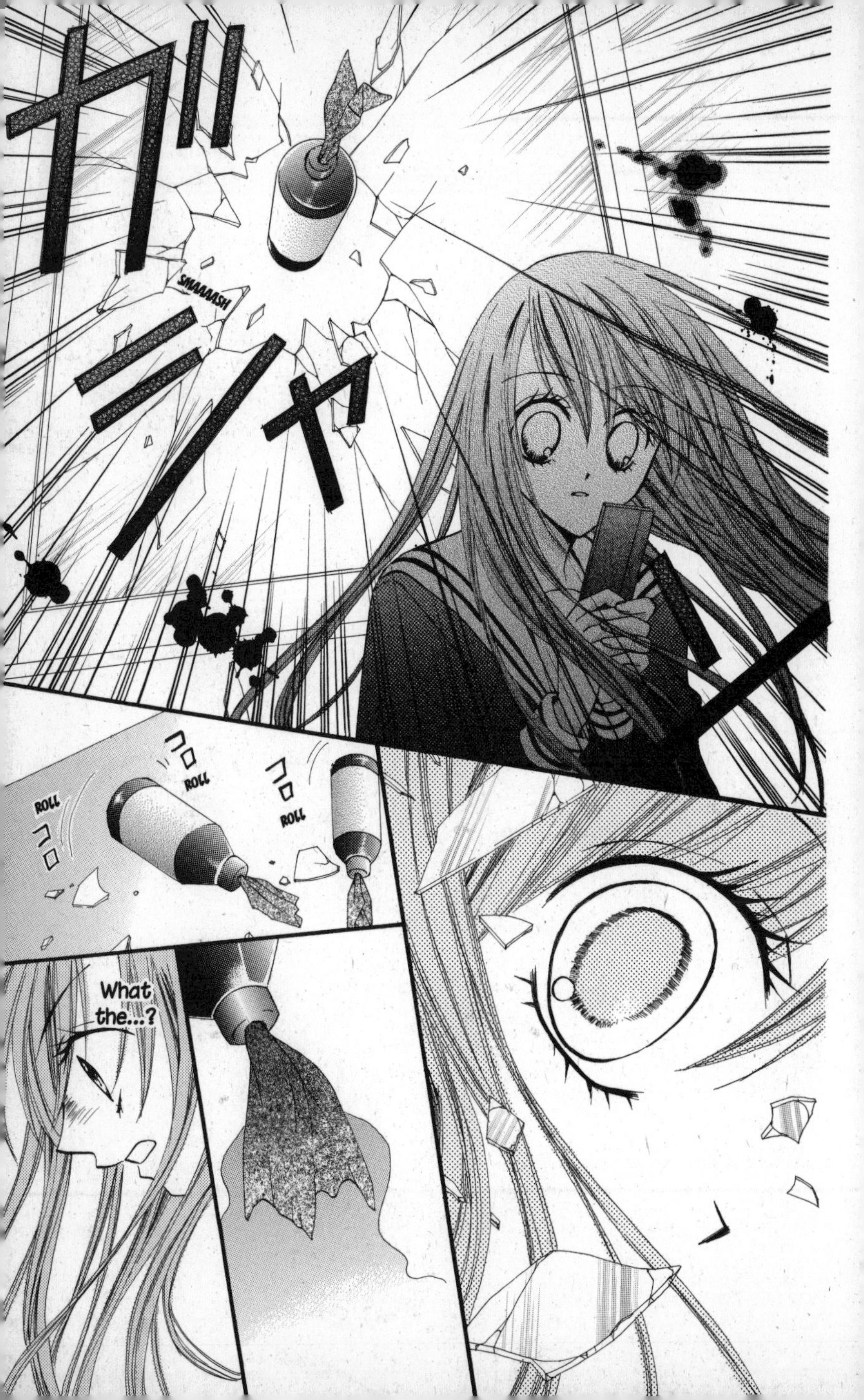
ガシャン
SMAAAASH
コロ
ROLL
コロ
ROLL
ROLL
コロ
What the...?

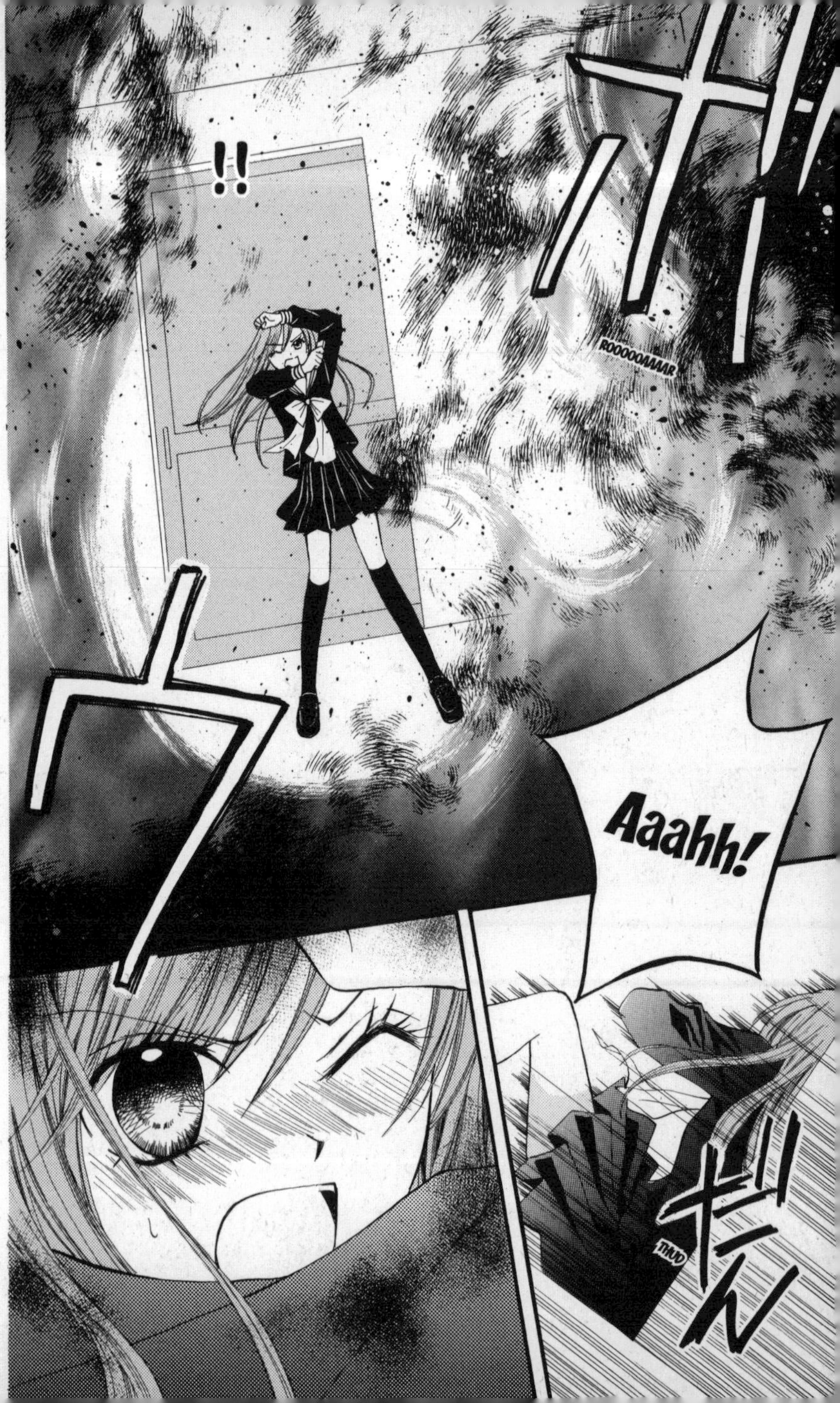
ROOOOOAAAAR
!!
Aaahh!
THUD

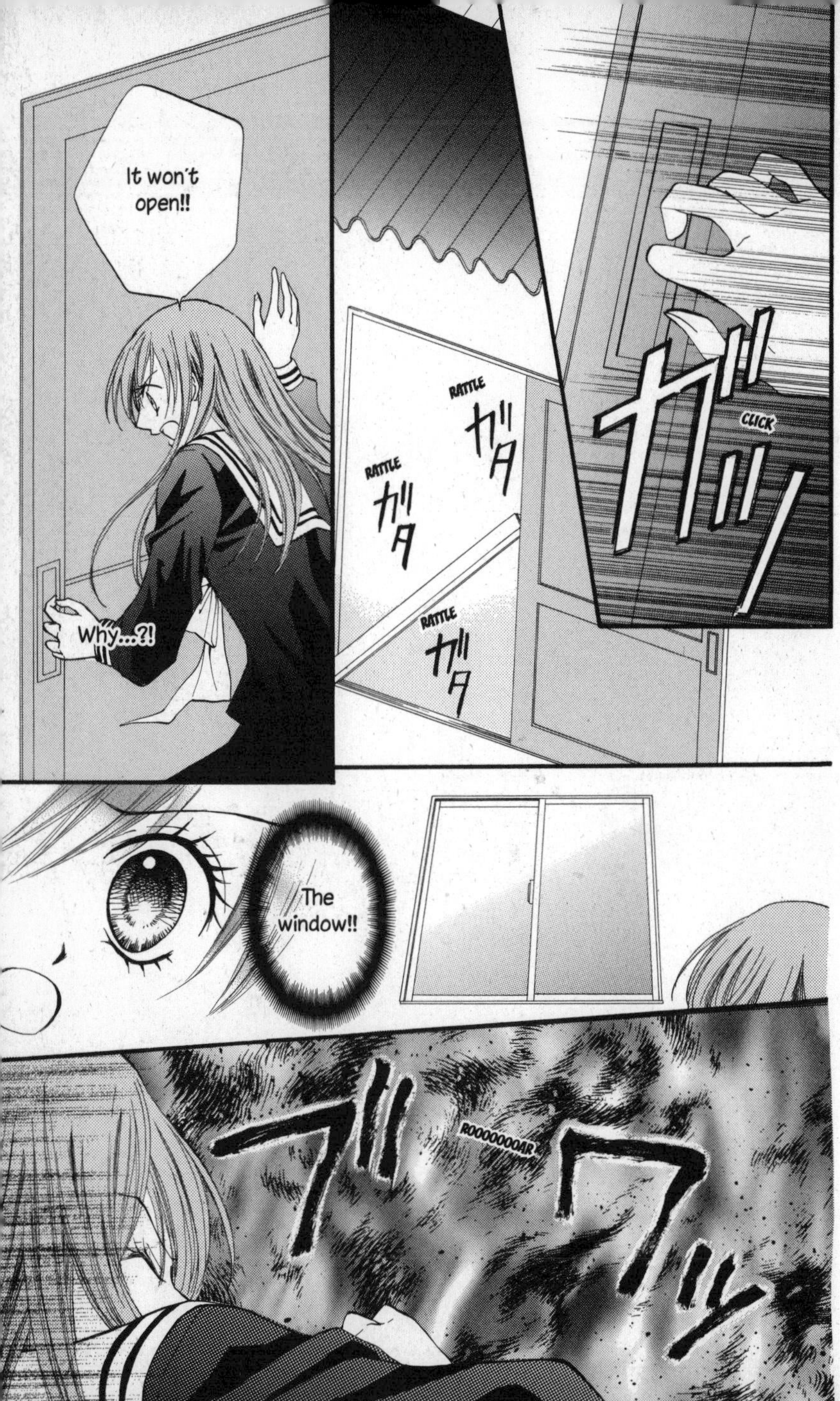
CLICK
ガッ
RATTLE
ガタ
RATTLE
ガタ
RATTLE
ガタ
It won't open!!
Why...?!
The window!!
ROOOOOOOAR
ブワッ

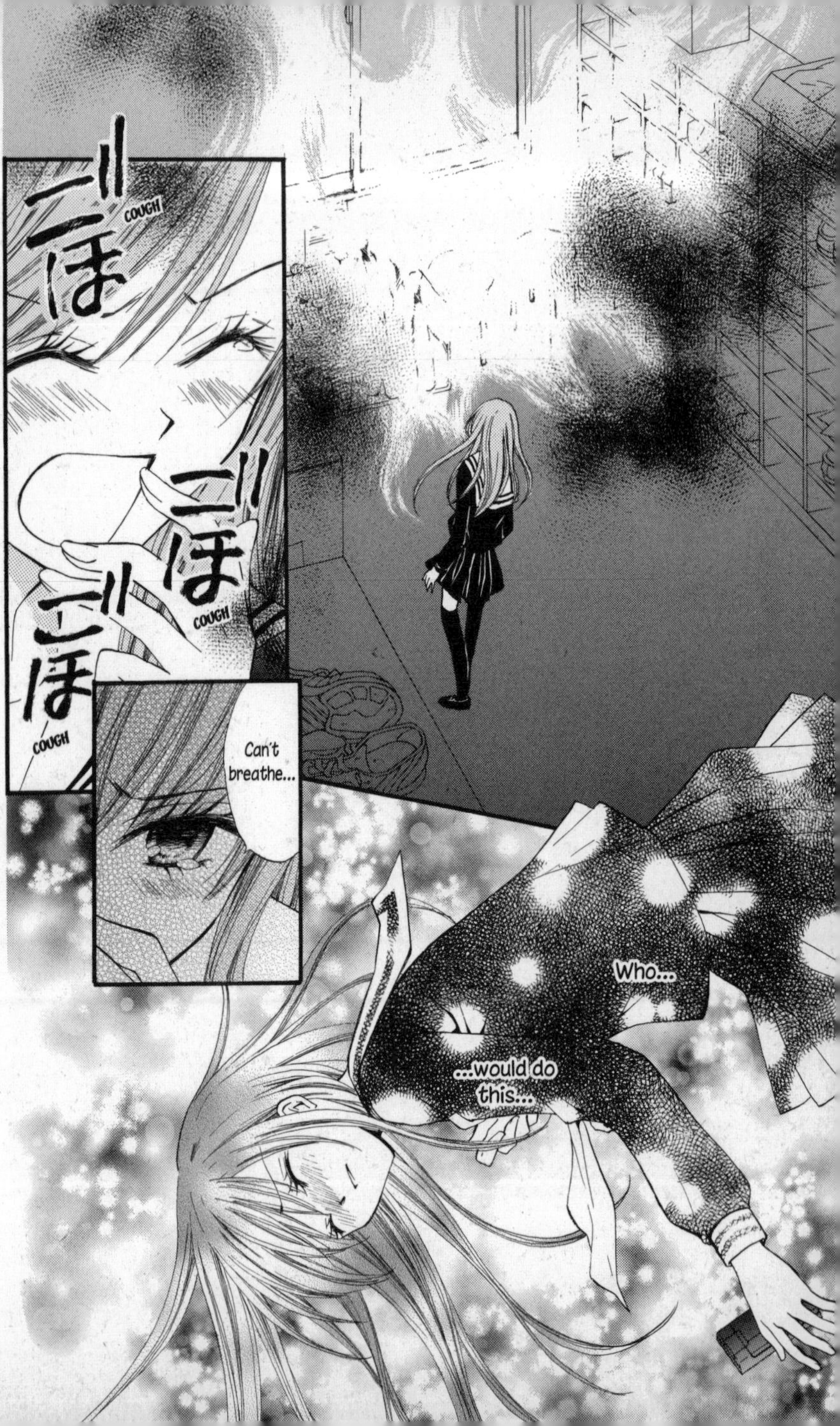
ごほ
COUGH
ごほ
COUGH
ごほ
COUGH
Can't breathe...
Who...
...would do this...

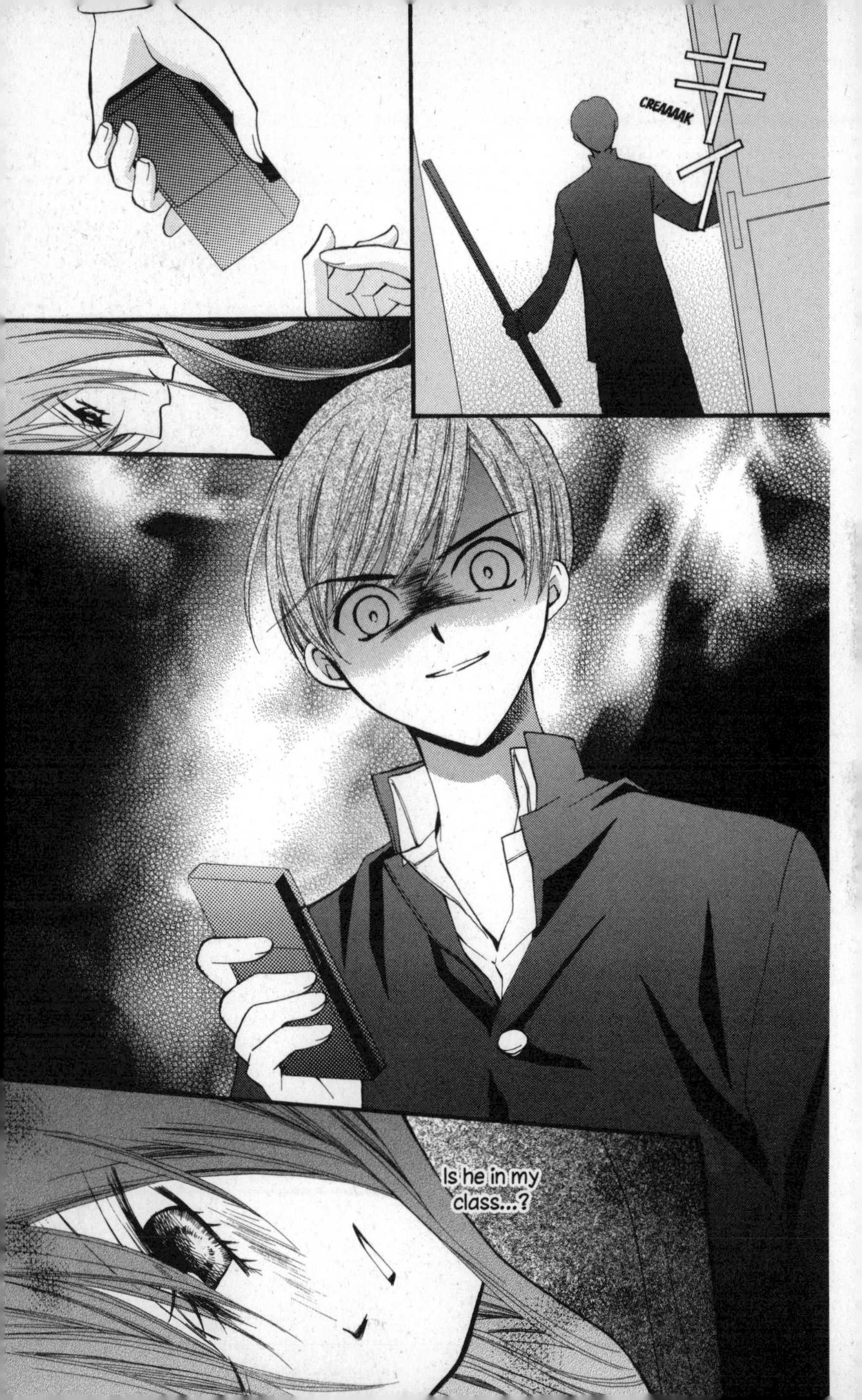
CREAAAAK
Is he in my class...?

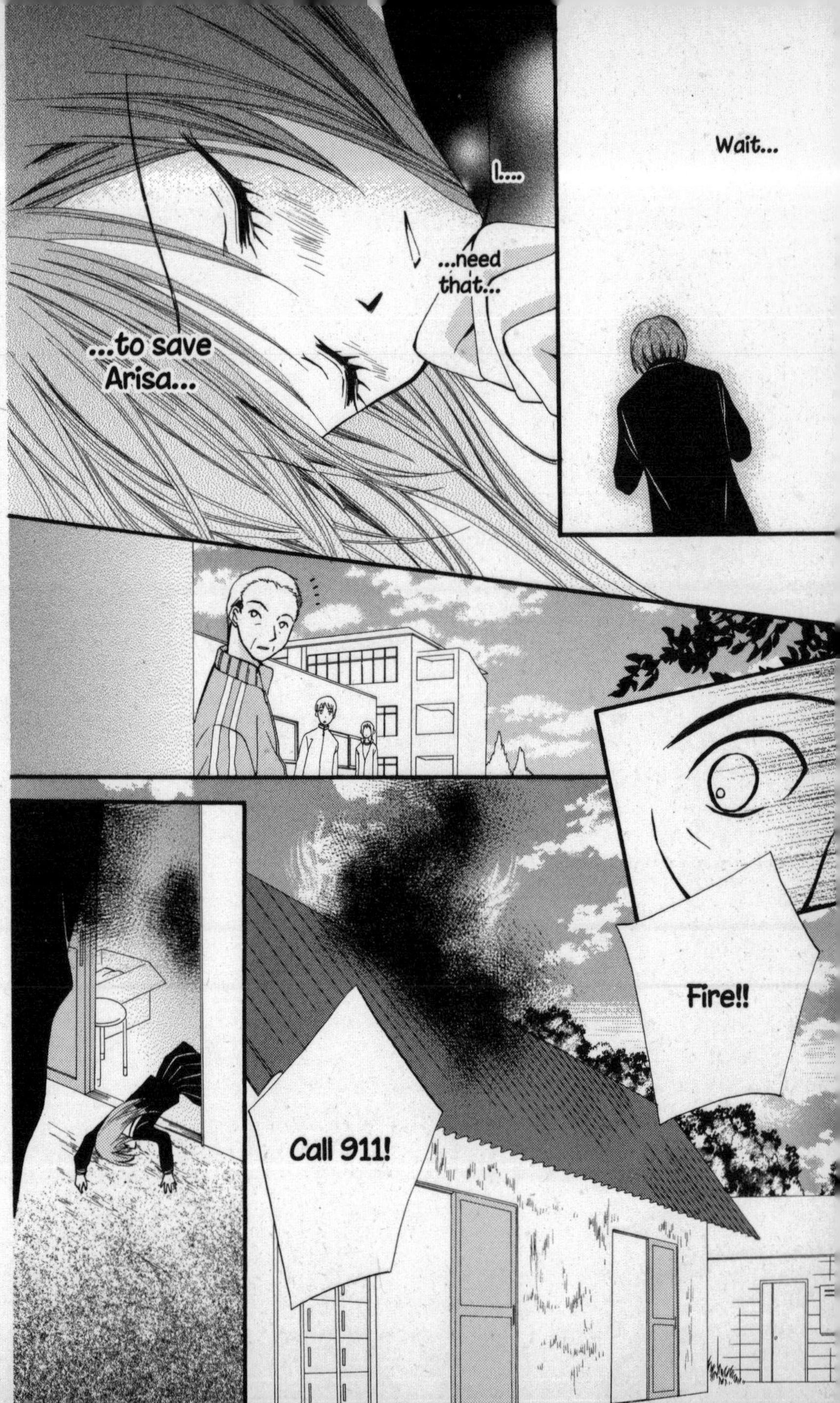
Wait...
I...
...need that...
...to save Arisa...
Fire!!
Call 911!

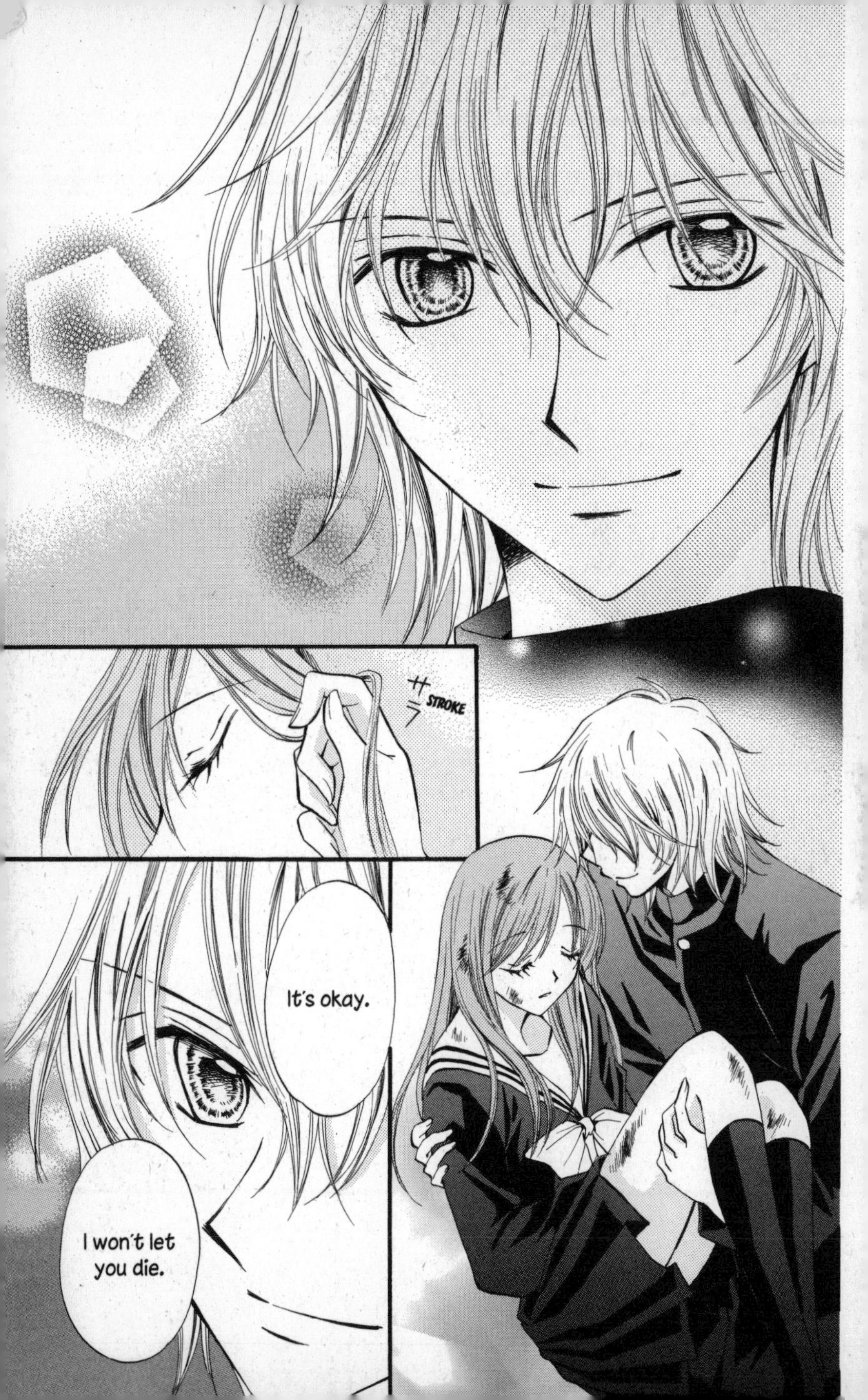
STROKE
It's okay.
I won't let you die.

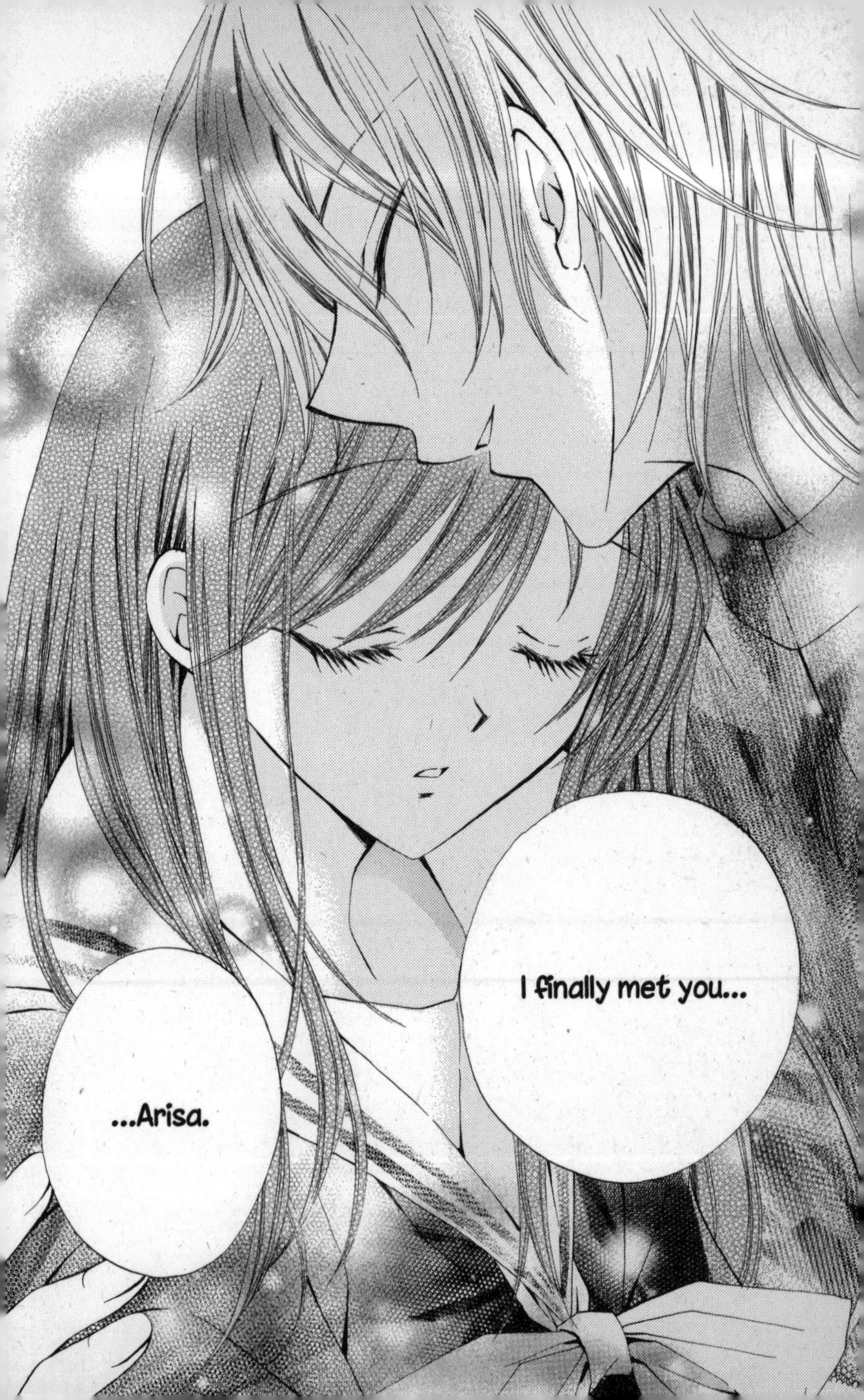
I finally met you...
...Arisa.

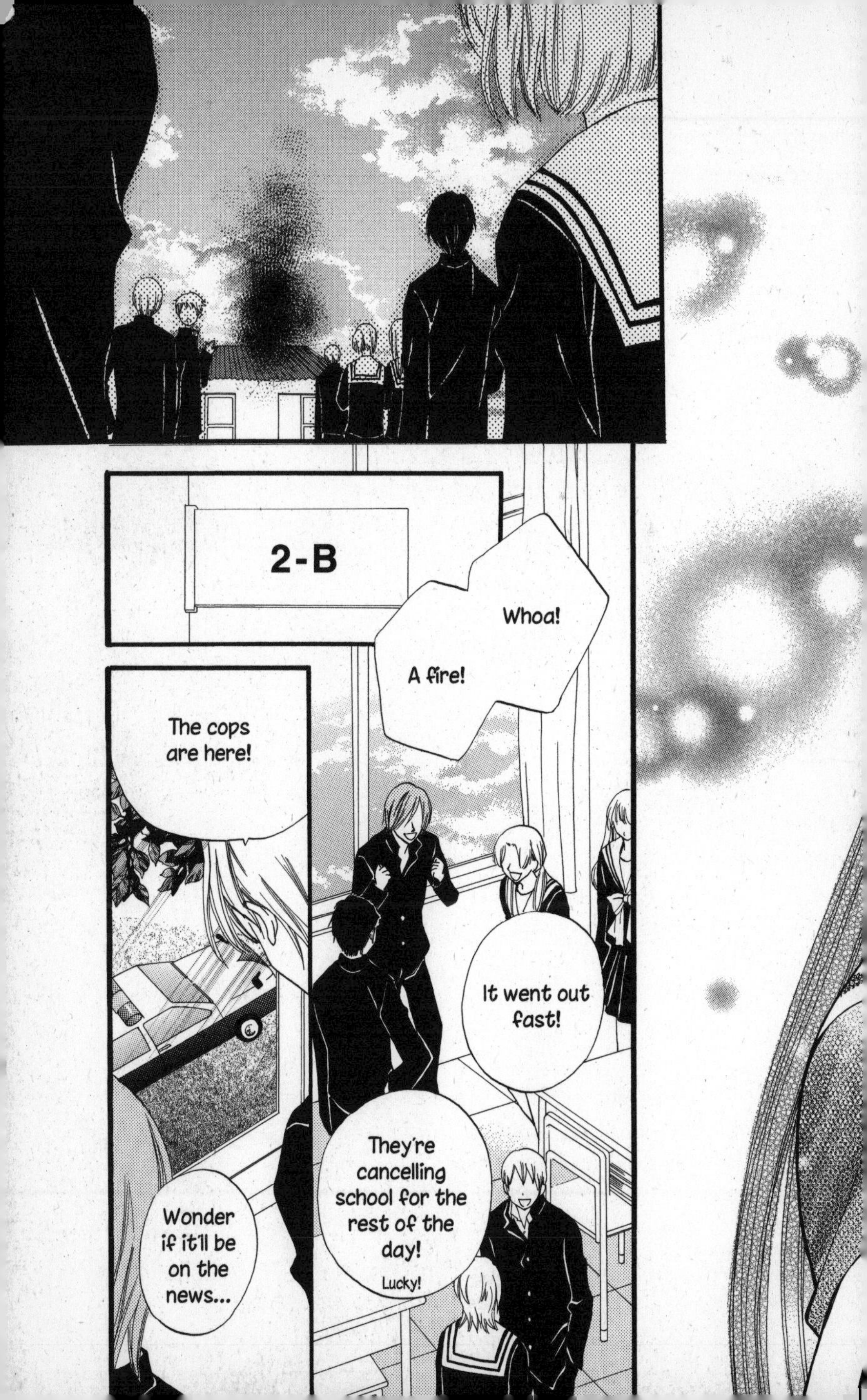
Whoa!
A fire!
It went out fast!
They're cancelling school for the rest of the day!
Lucky!
2-B
The cops are here!
Wonder if it'll be on the news...

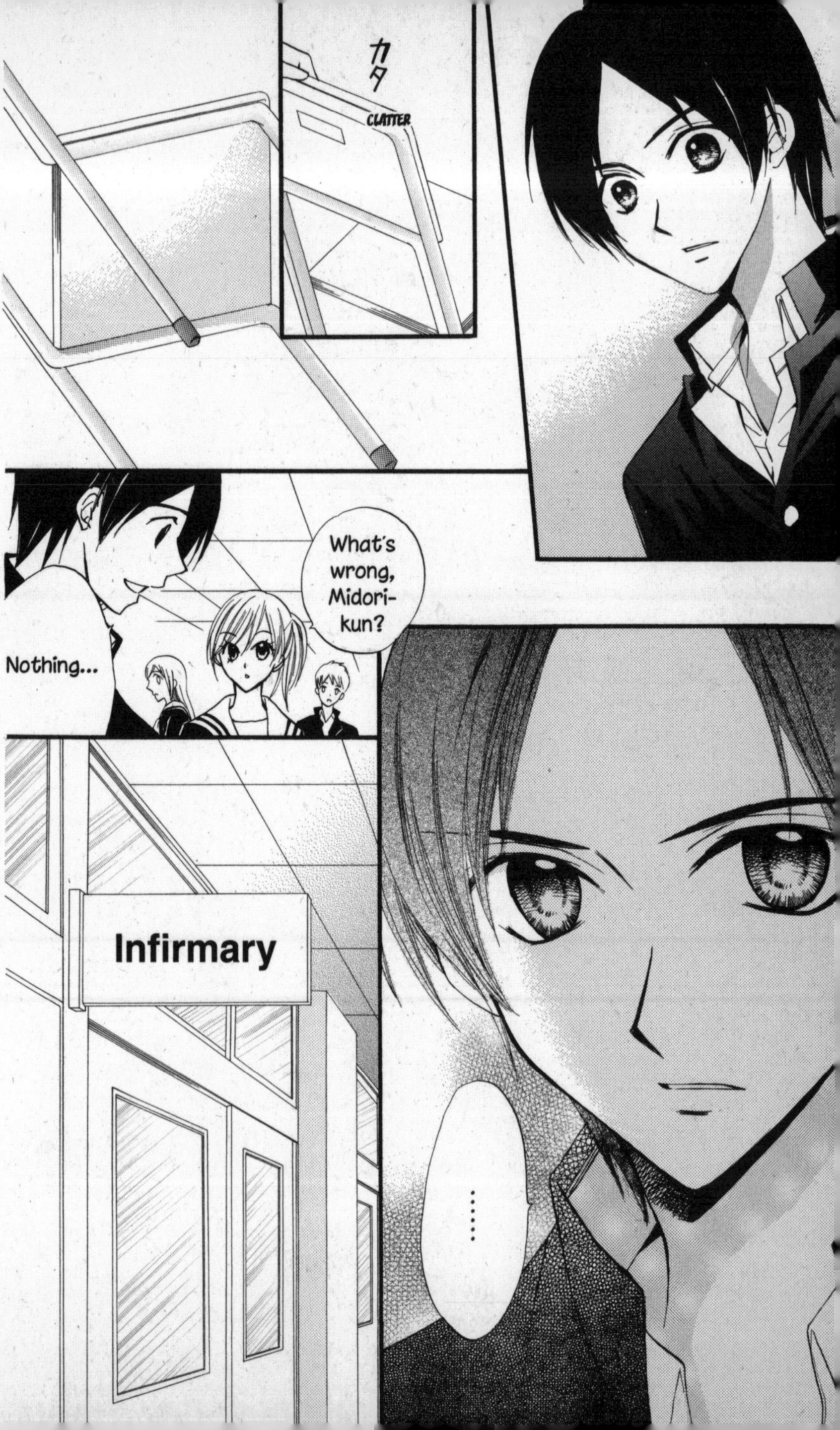

カタ
CLATTER
What's wrong, Midori-kun?
Nothing...
......
Infirmary

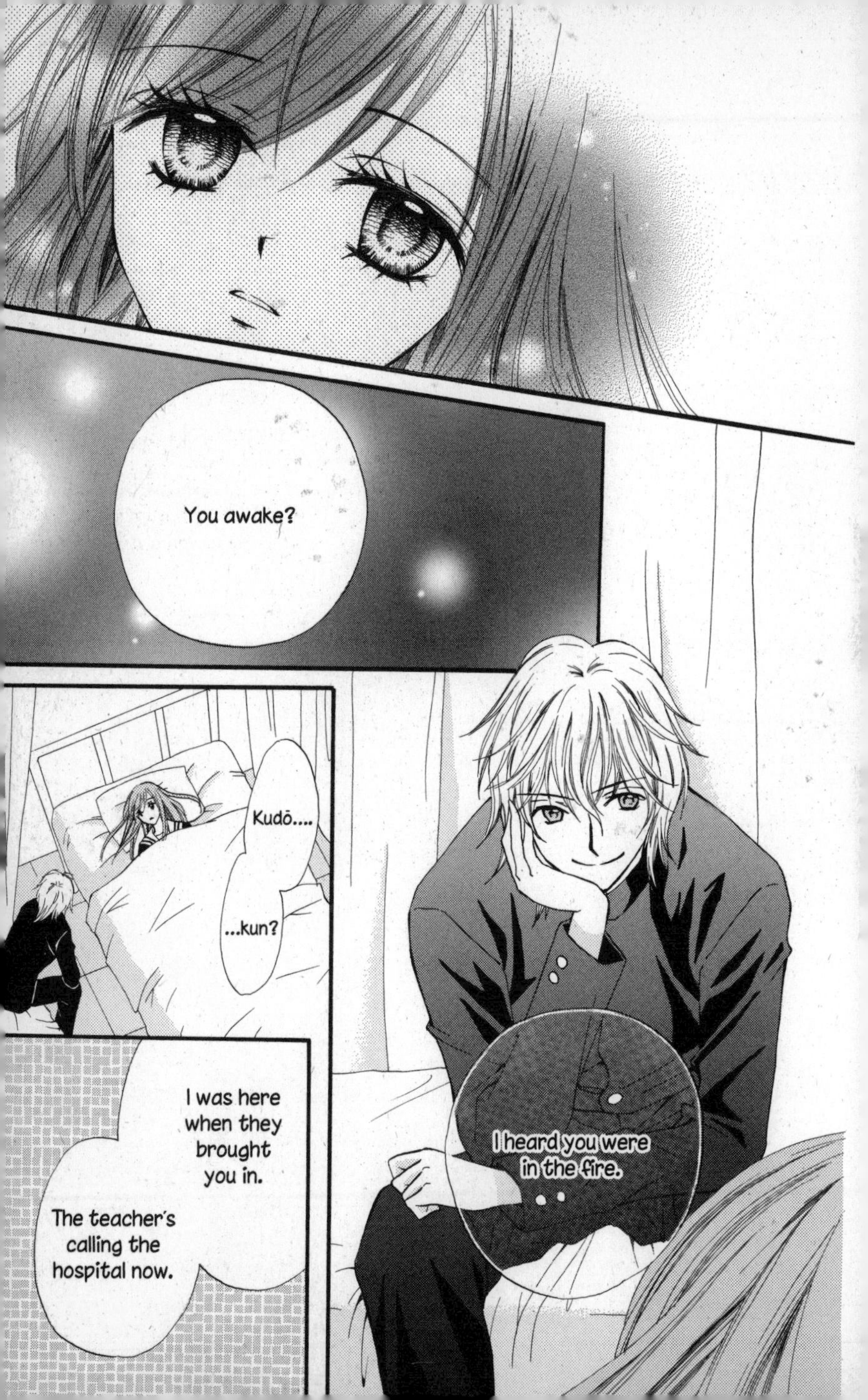

I heard you were in the fire.
You awake?
Kudō....
...kun?
I was here when they brought you in.
The teacher's calling the hospital now.

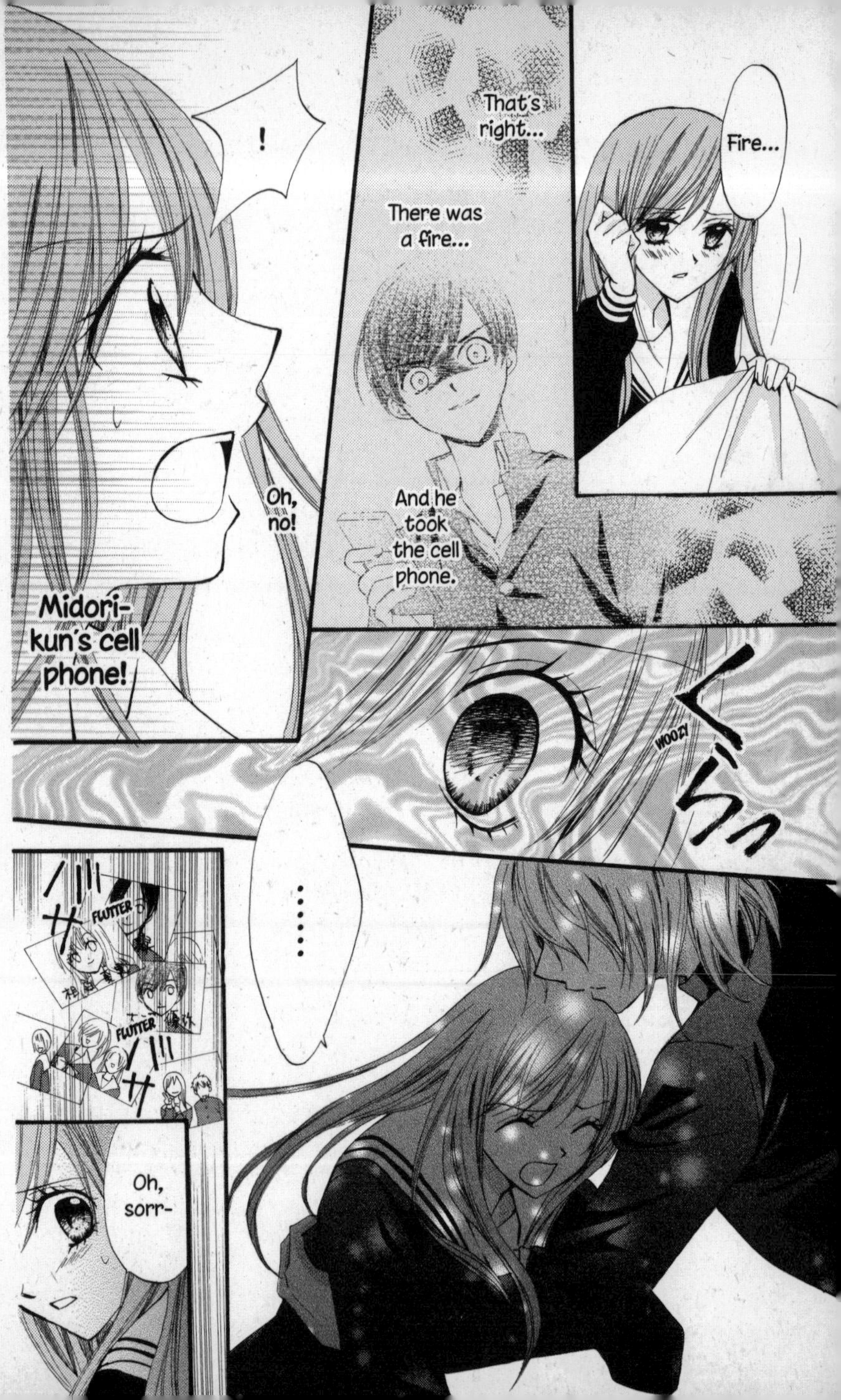
Fire...
That's right...
There was a fire...
And he took the cell phone.
!
Oh, no!
Midori-kun's cell phone!
WOOZY
くらっ
......
FLUTTER
FLUTTER
Oh, sorr-

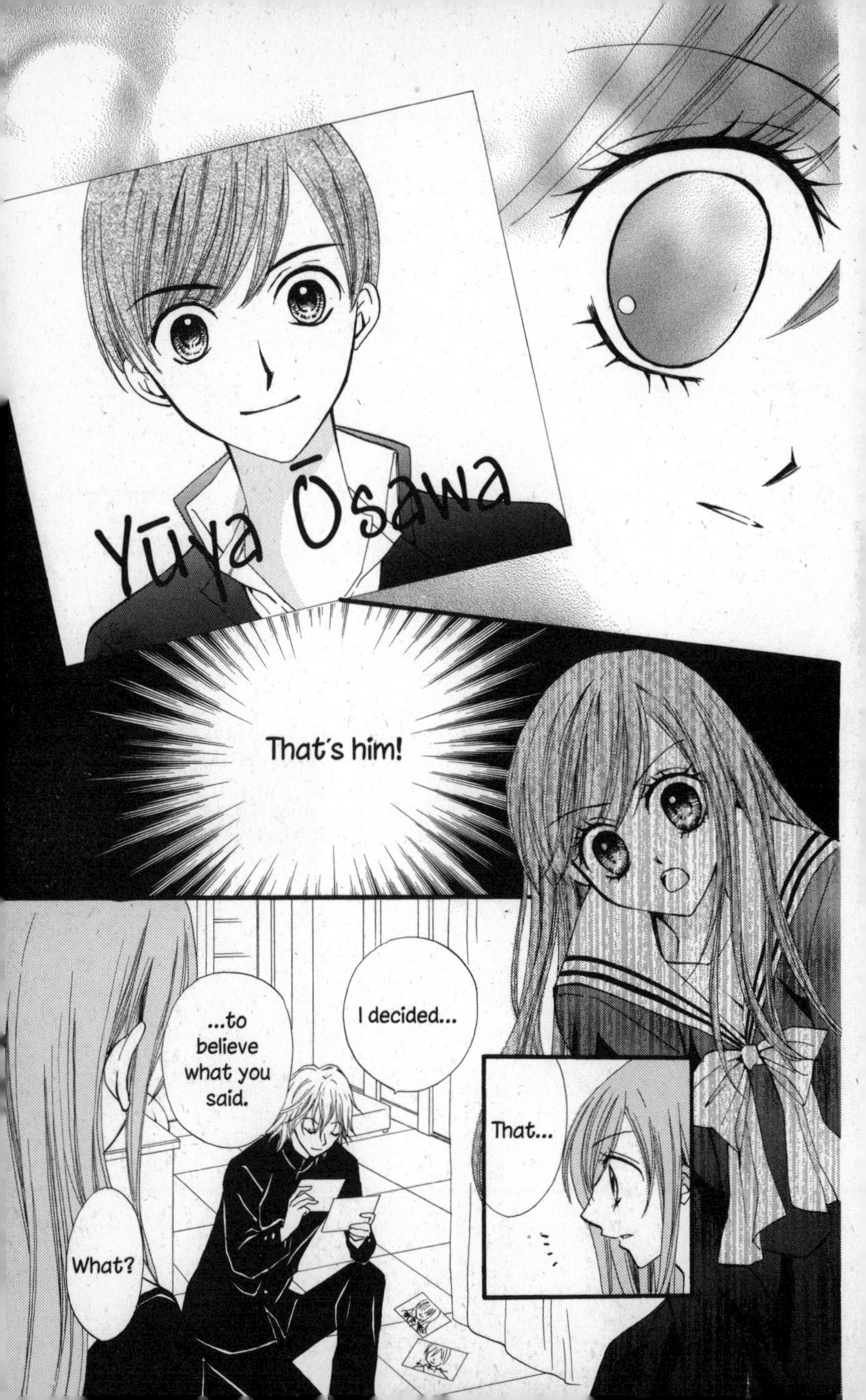
Yūya Ōsawa
That's him!
That...
I decided...
...to believe what you said.
What?

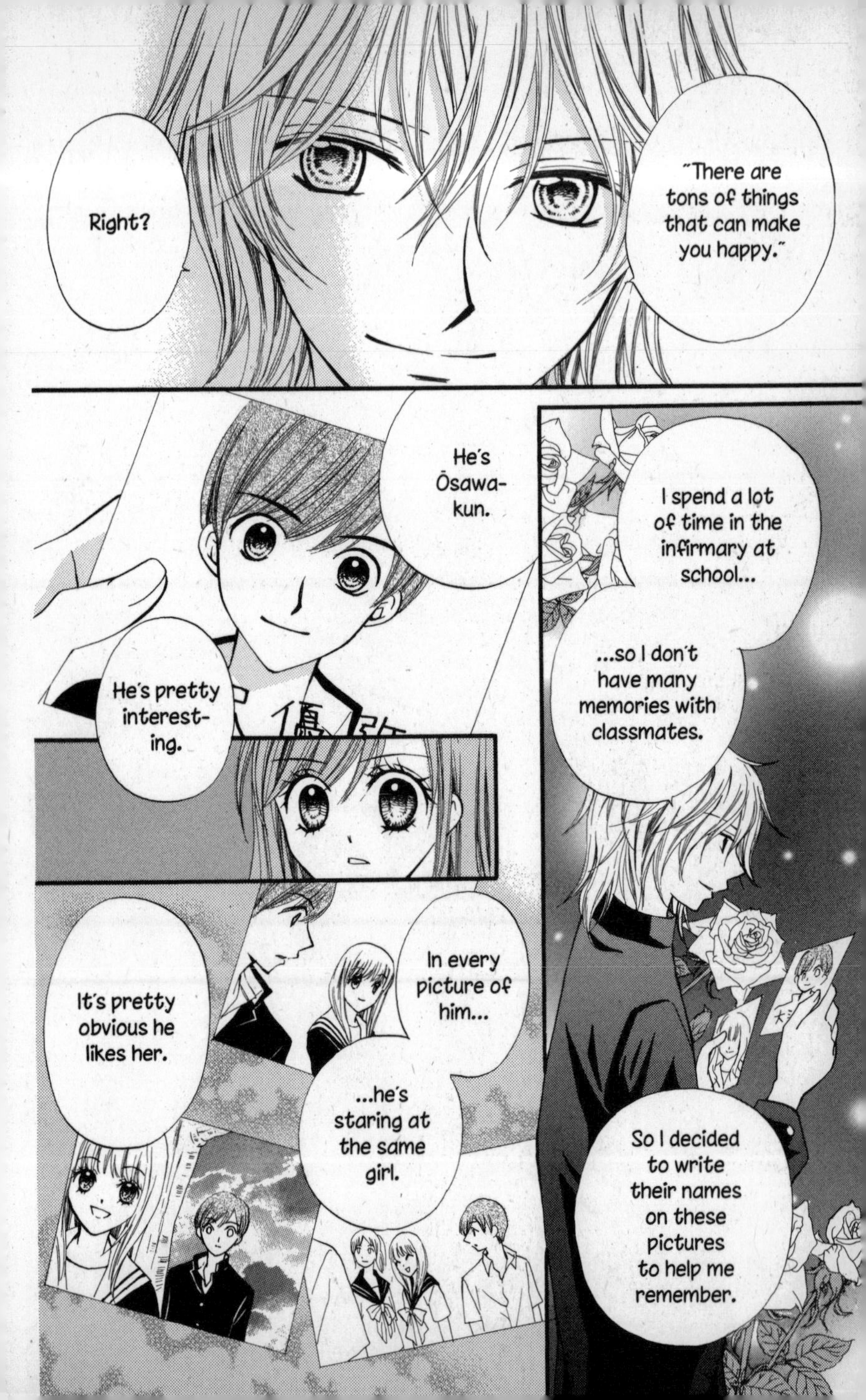
"There are tons of things that can make you happy."
Right?
I spend a lot of time in the infirmary at school...
...so I don't have many memories with classmates.
So I decided to write their names on these pictures to help me remember.
He's Ōsawa-kun.
He's pretty interest-ing.
In every picture of him...
...he's staring at the same girl.
It's pretty obvious he likes her.

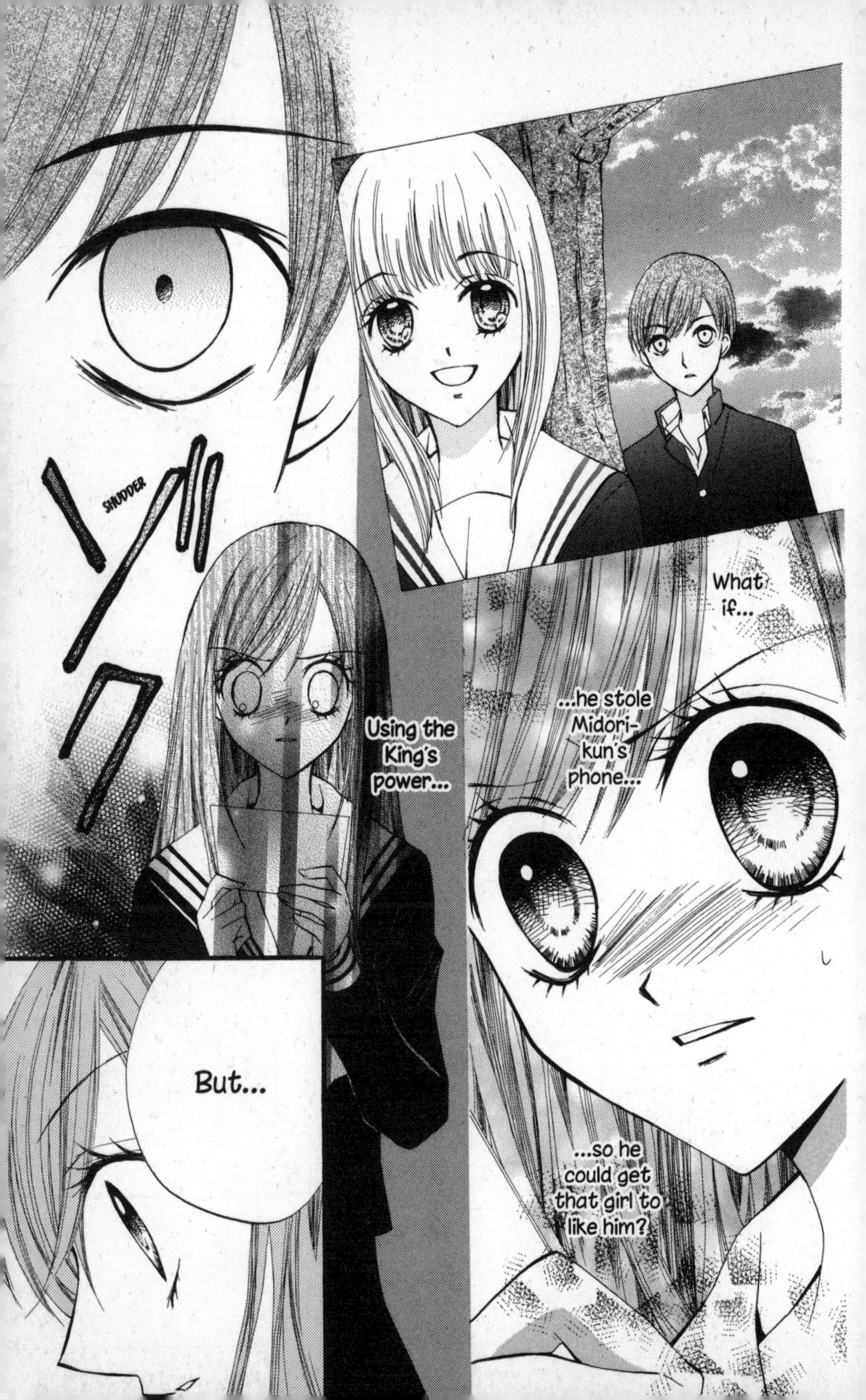

SHUDDER
What if...
...he stole Midori-kun's phone...
Using the King's power...
...so he could get that girl to like him?
But...

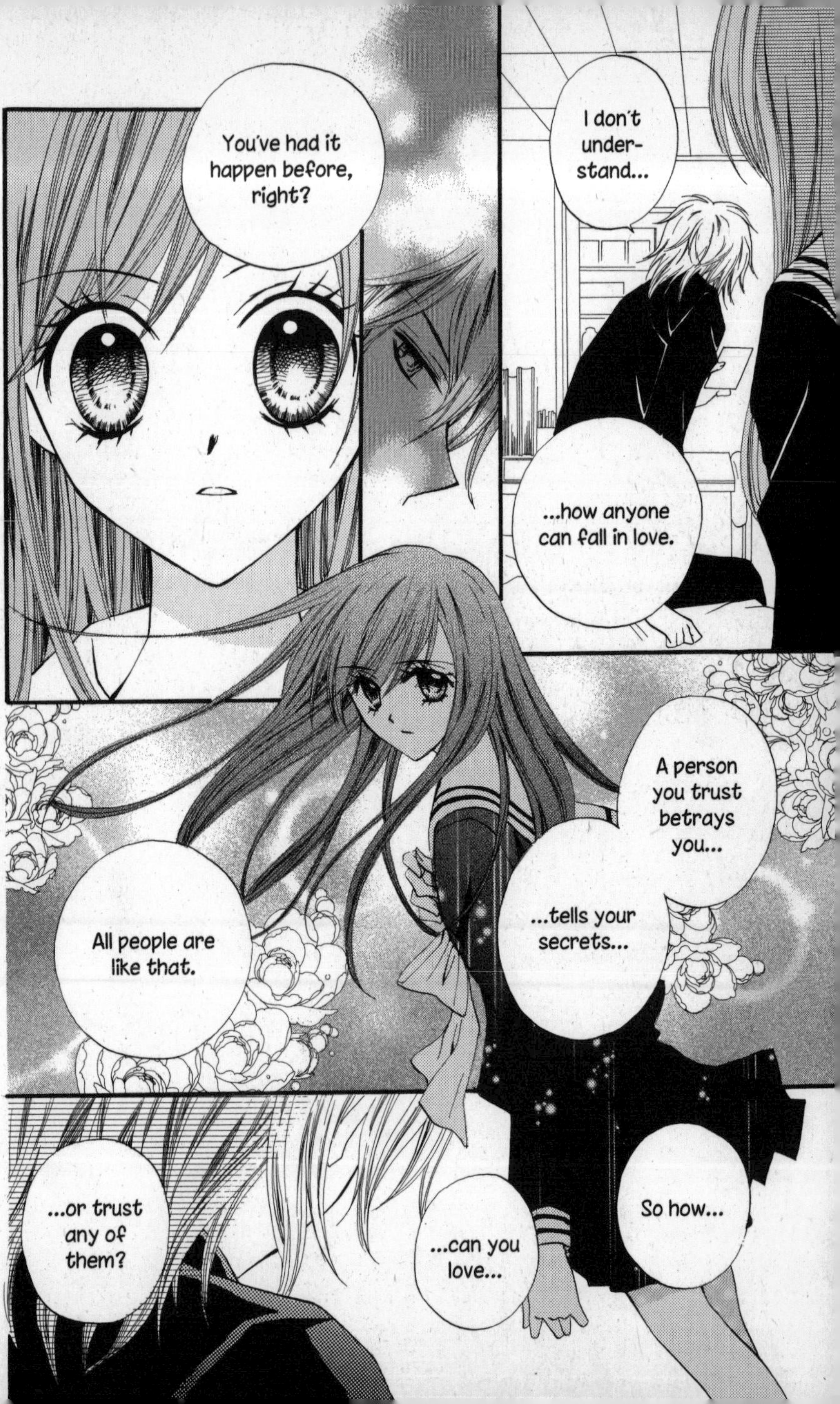
I don't understand...
...how anyone can fall in love.
You've had it happen before, right?
A person you trust betrays you...
...tells your secrets...
All people are like that.
So how...
...can you love...
...or trust any of them?

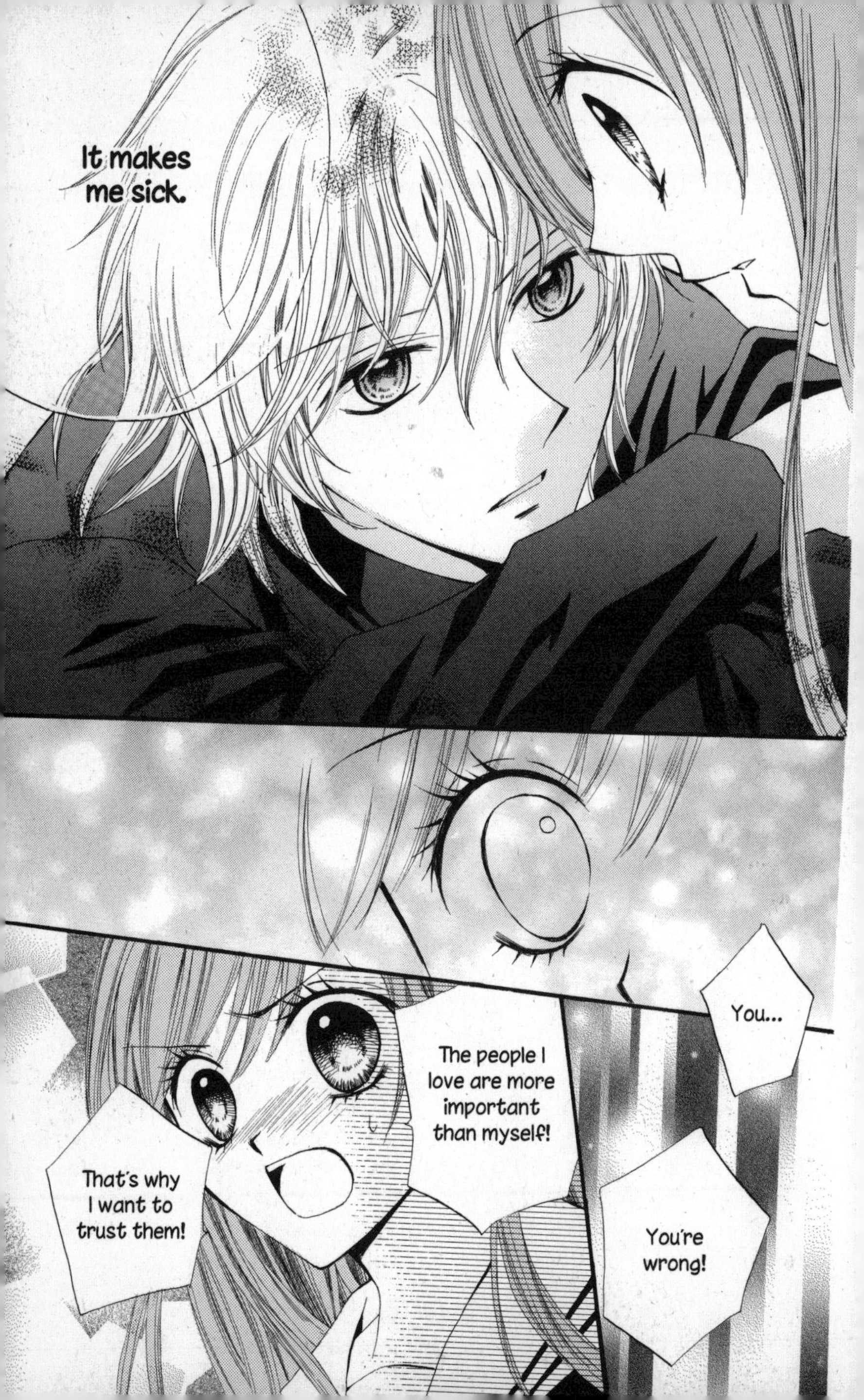
It makes me sick.
You...
You're wrong!
The people I love are more important than myself!
That's why I want to trust them!

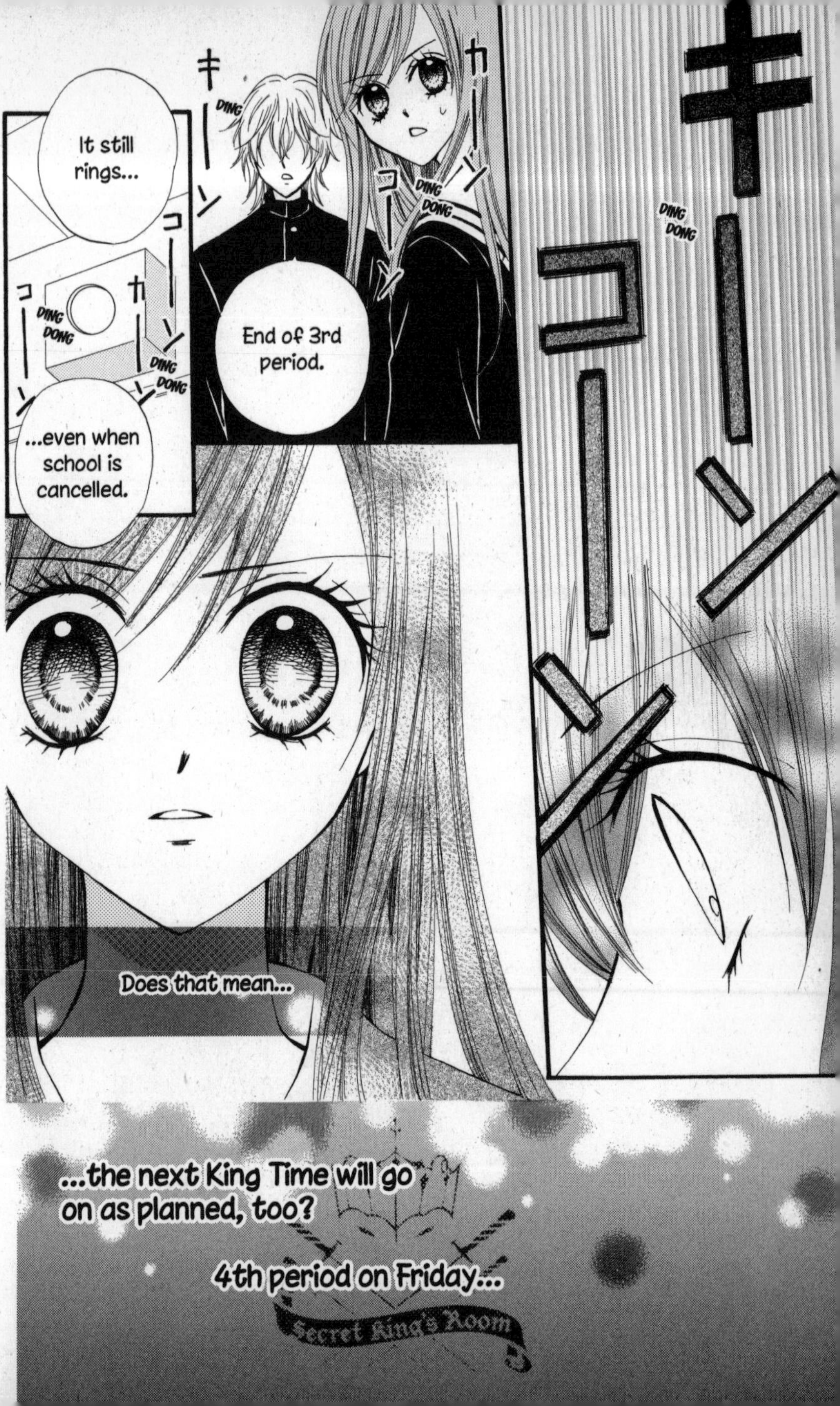
キーンコーン
DING DONG
カーンコーン
DING DONG
End of 3rd period.
キーンコーン
DING
It still rings...
カーンコーン
DING DONG
DING DONG
...even when school is cancelled.
Does that mean...
...the next King Time will go on as planned, too?
4th period on Friday...
Secret King's Room

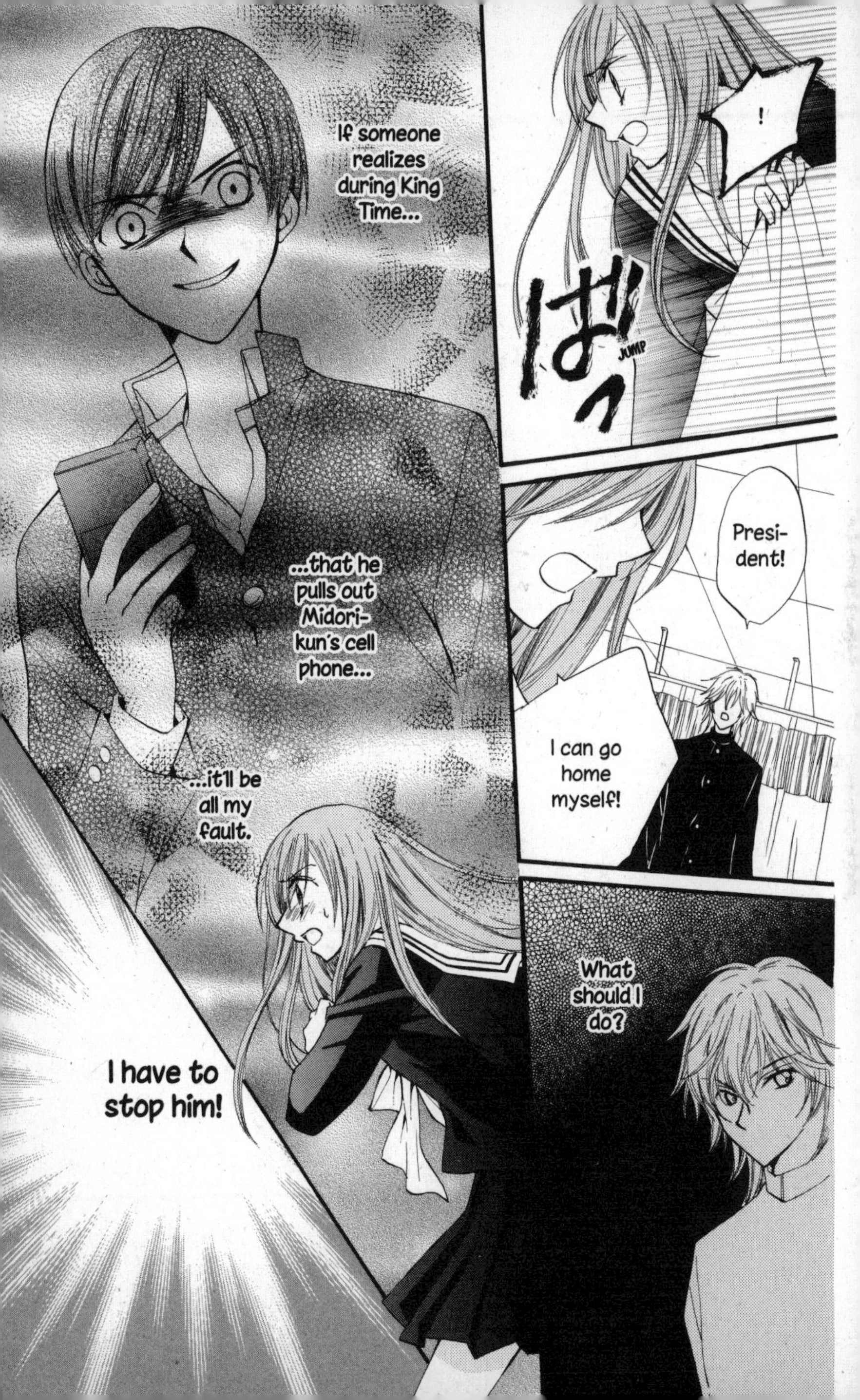
!
ぱっ
JUMP
President!
I can go home myself!
What should I do?
If someone realizes during King Time...
...that he pulls out Midori-kun's cell phone...
...it'll be all my fault.
I have to stop him!

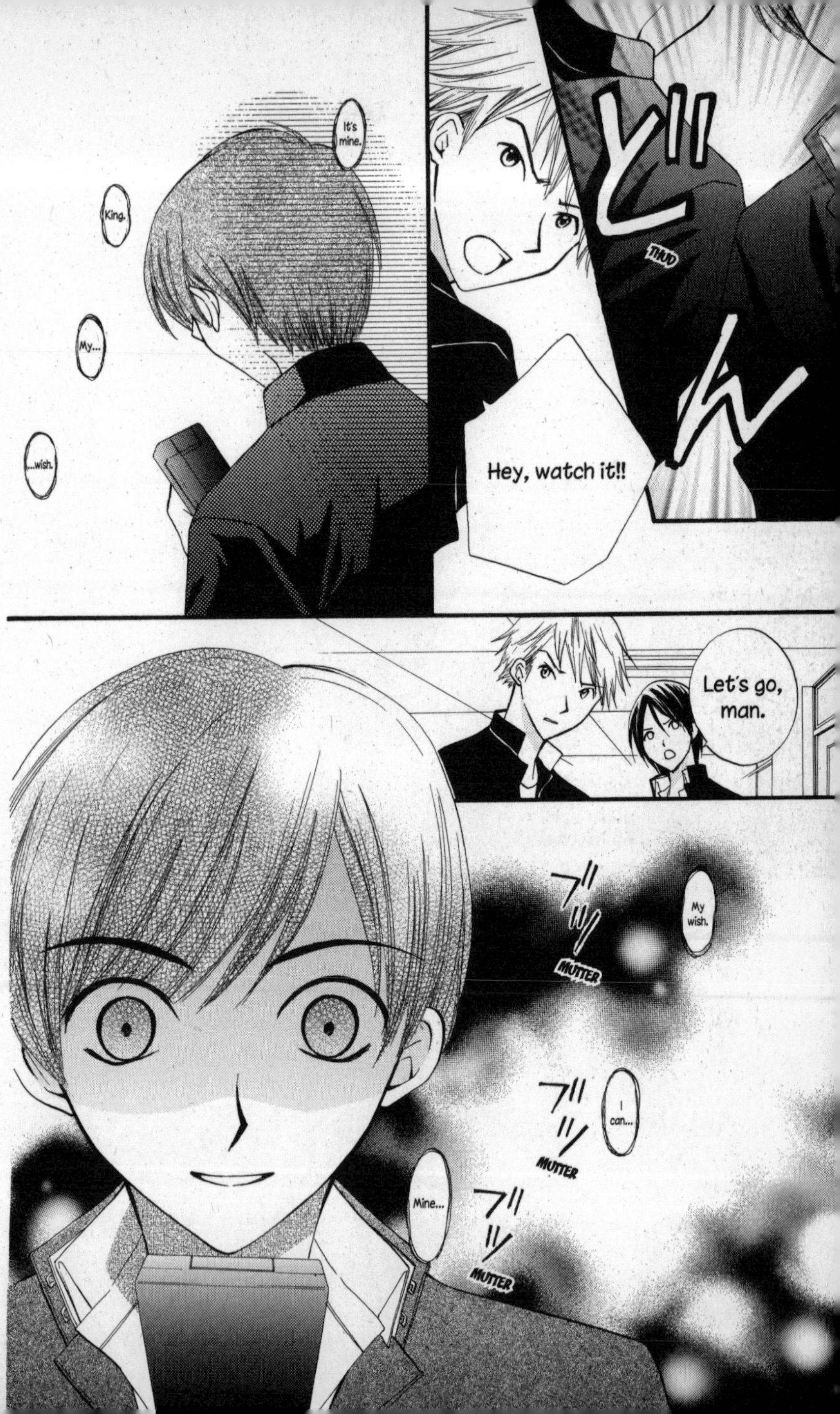
THUD
Hey, watch it!!
It's mine.
King.
My...
...wish.
Let's go, man.
MUTTER
My wish.
MUTTER
I can...
MUTTER
Mine...

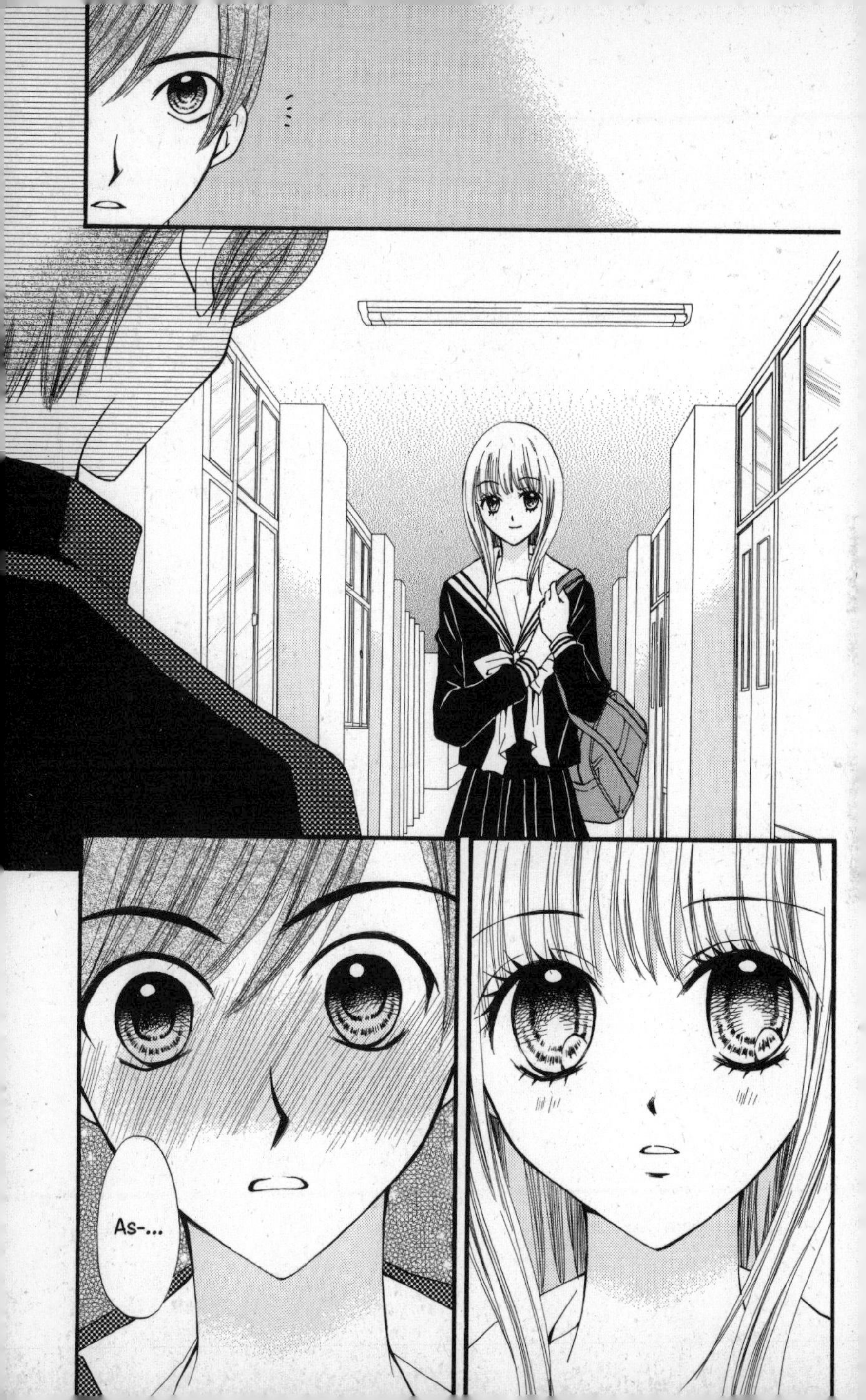
As-...

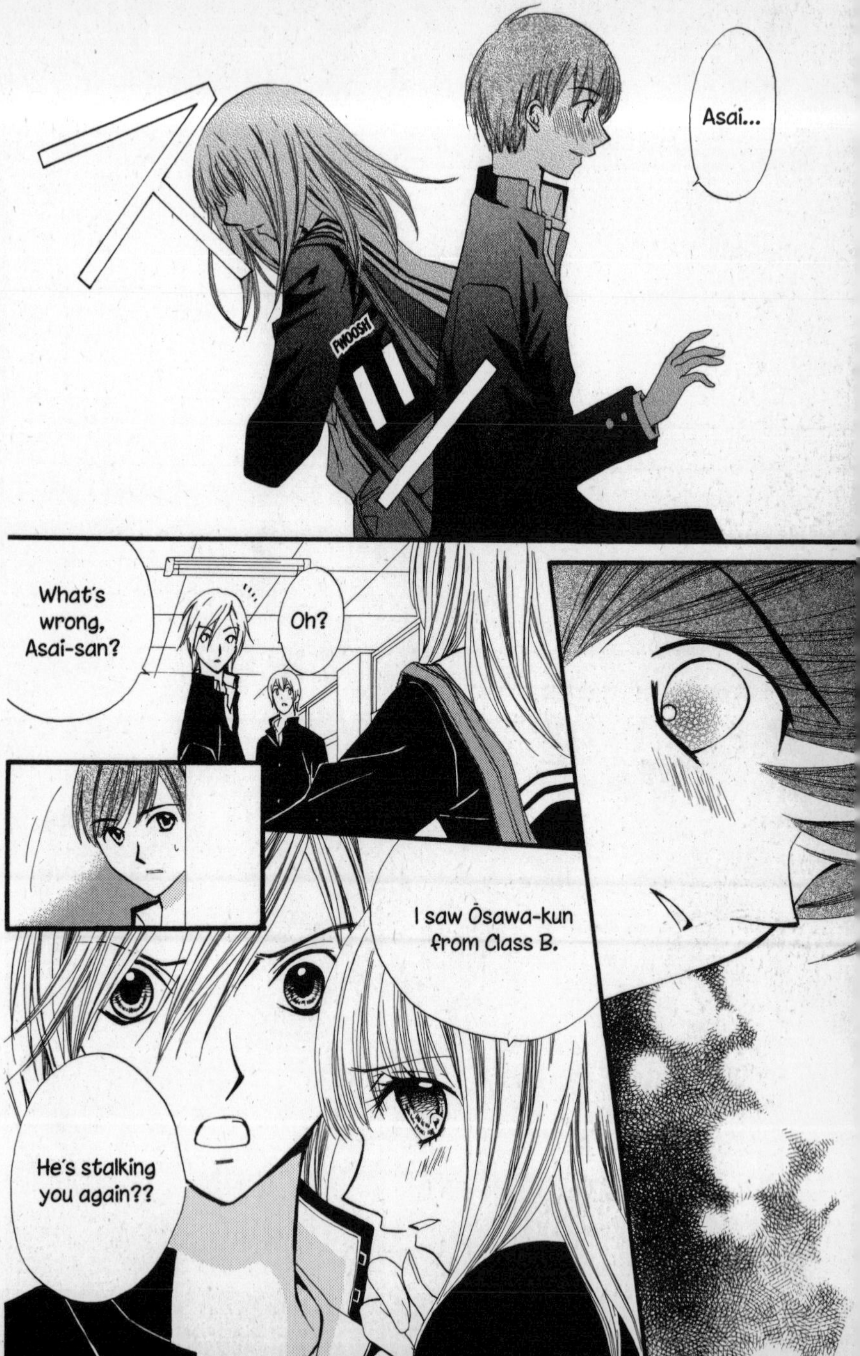
Asai...
PWOOSH
Oh?
What's wrong, Asai-san?
I saw Ōsawa-kun from Class B.
He's stalking you again??

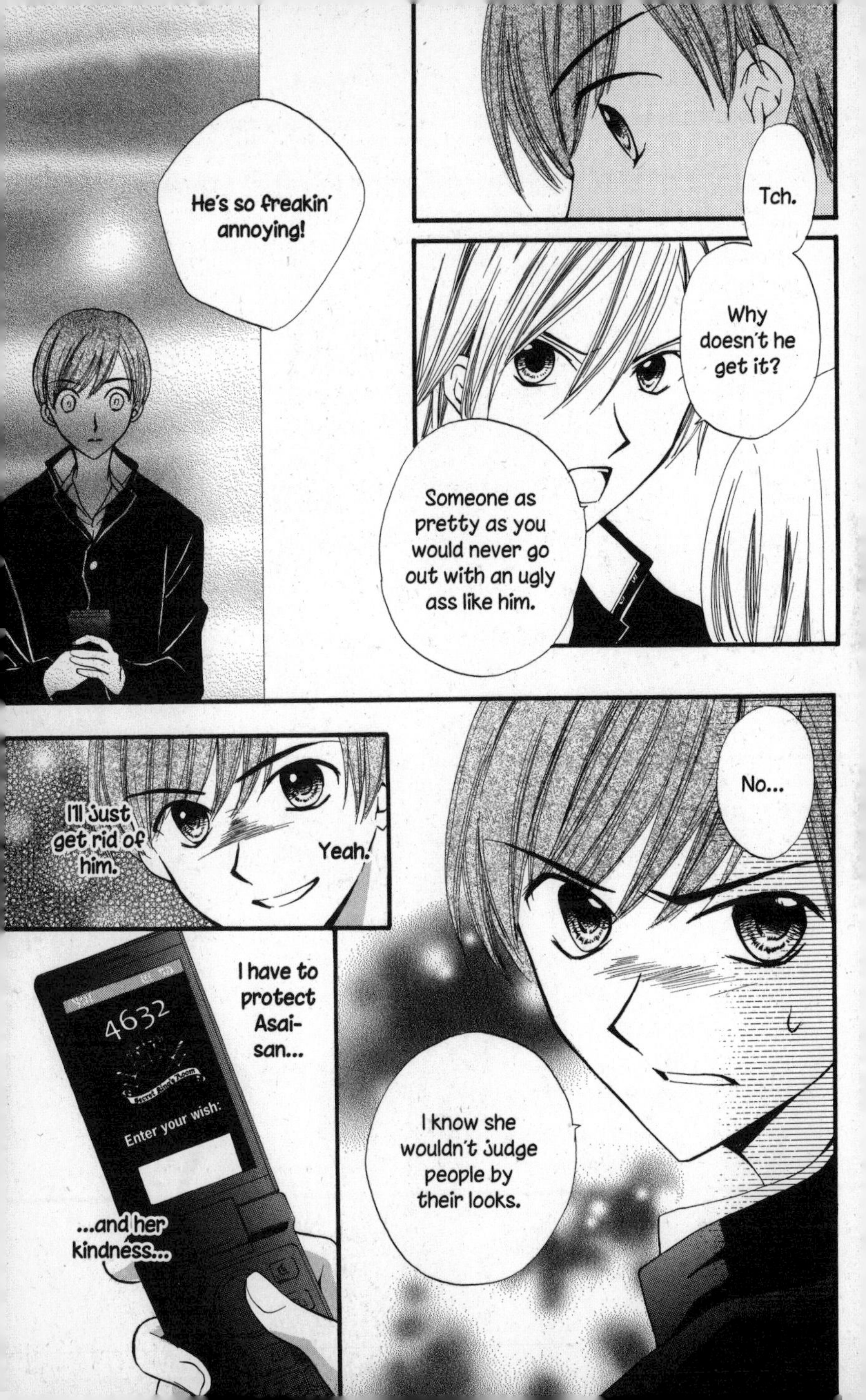
Tch.
Why doesn't he get it?
Someone as pretty as you would never go out with an ugly ass like him.
He's so freakin' annoying!
No...
I know she wouldn't judge people by their looks.
Yeah.
I'll just get rid of him.
I have to protect Asai-san...
4632
Enter your wish:
...and her kindness...

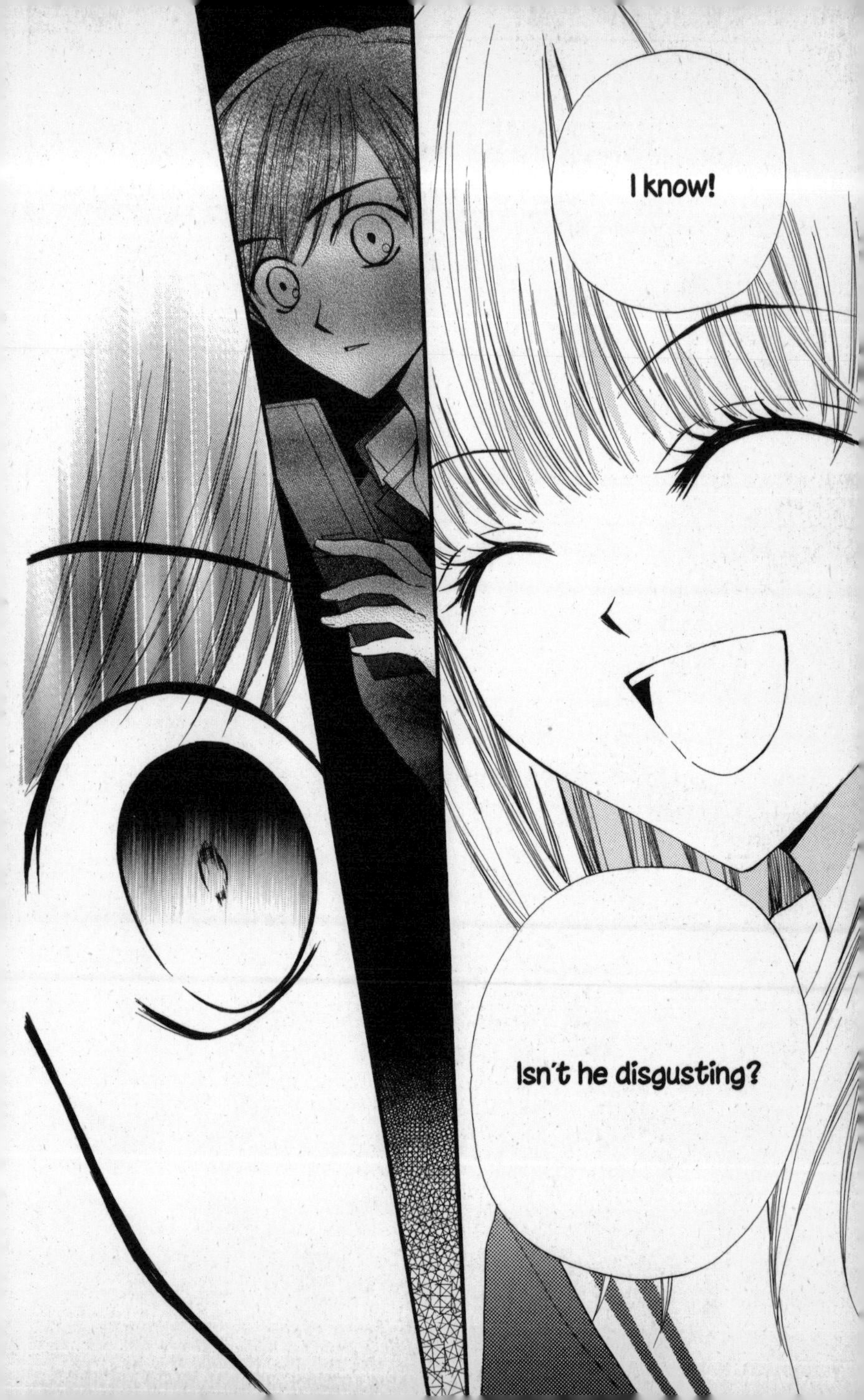
I know!
Isn't he disgusting?

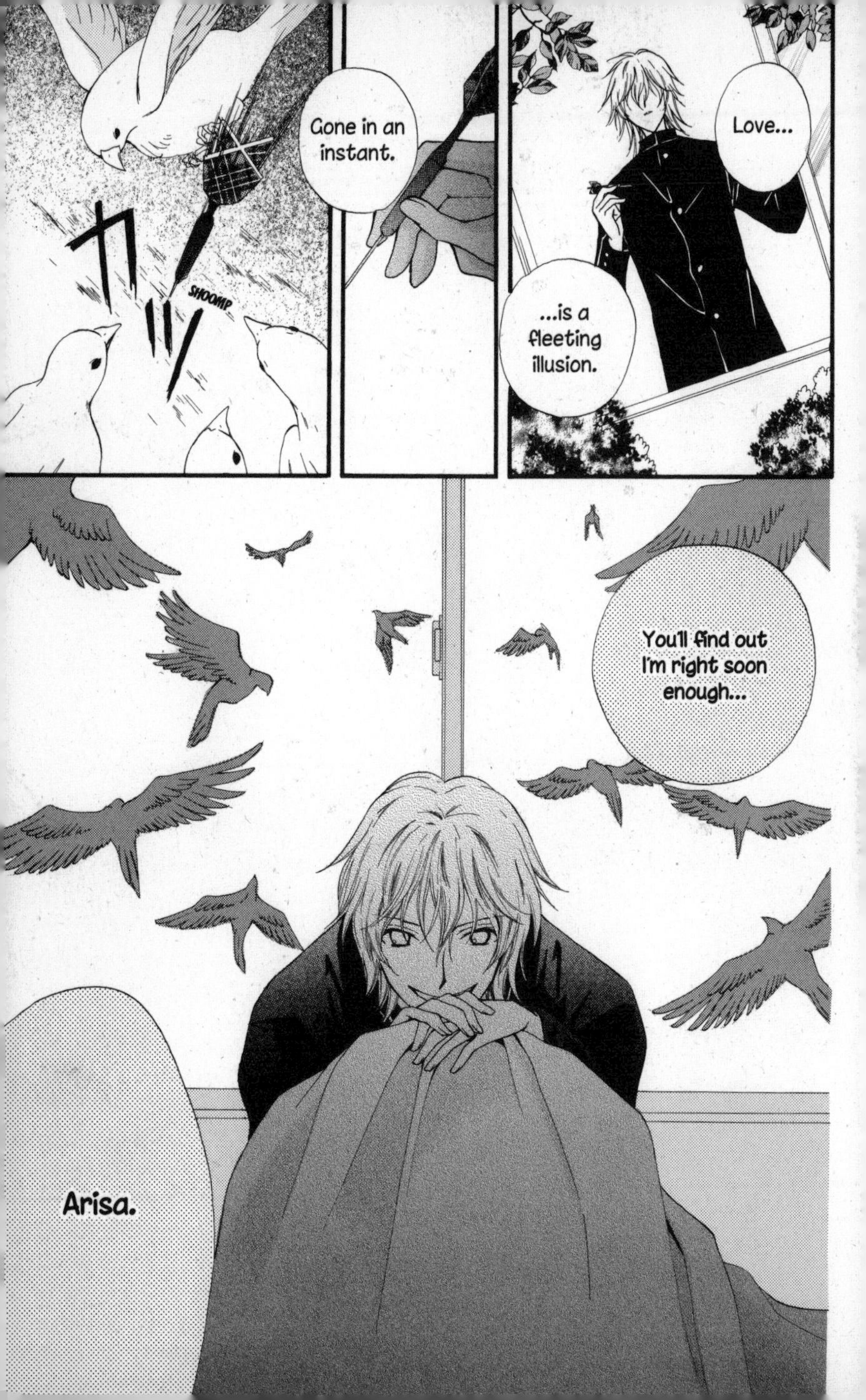
Love...
...is a fleeting illusion.
Gone in an instant.
SHOOMP
You'll find out I'm right soon enough...
Arisa.

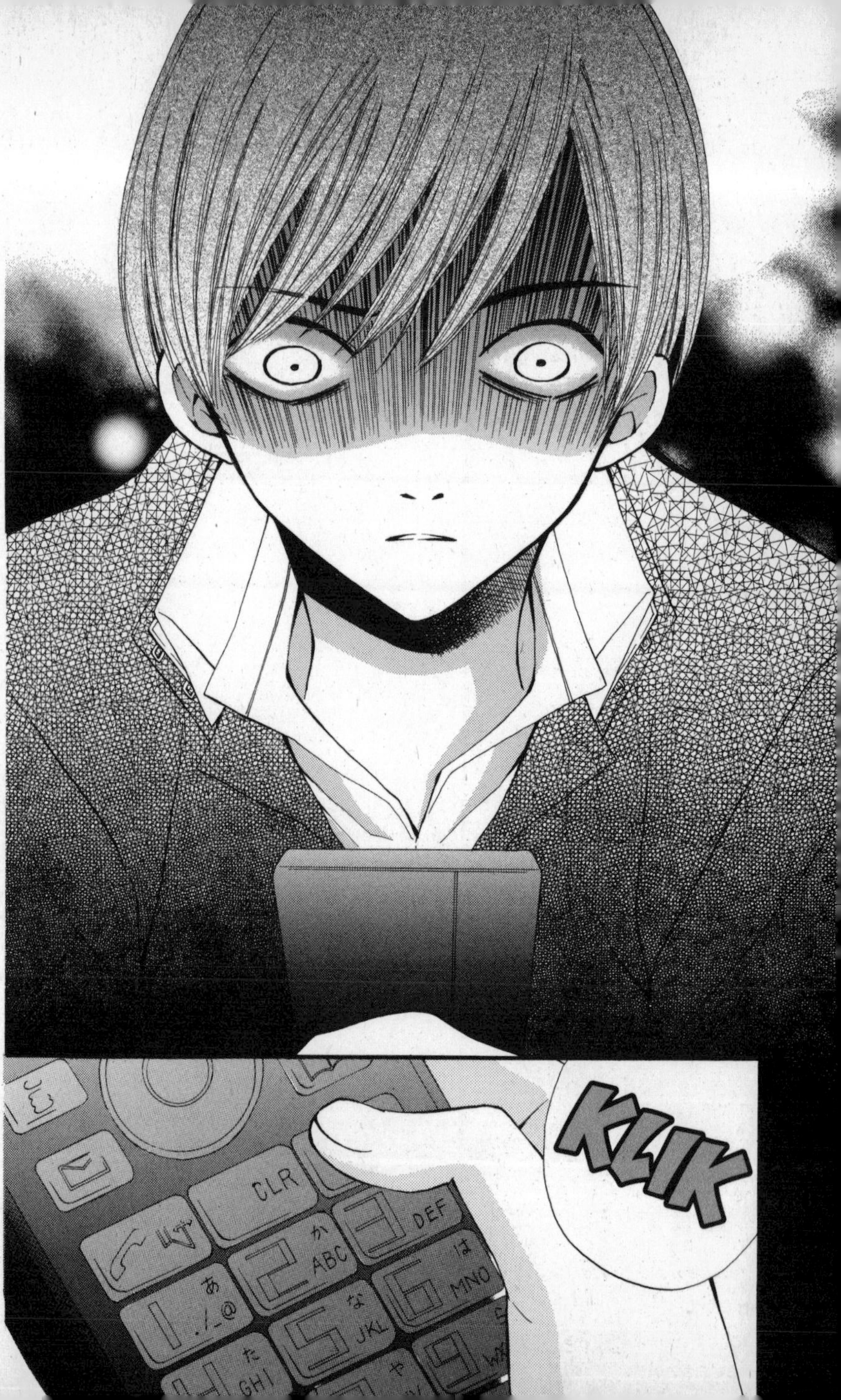
KLIK
CLR
DEF
か ABC
は MNO
あ ./_@
な JKL
た GHI

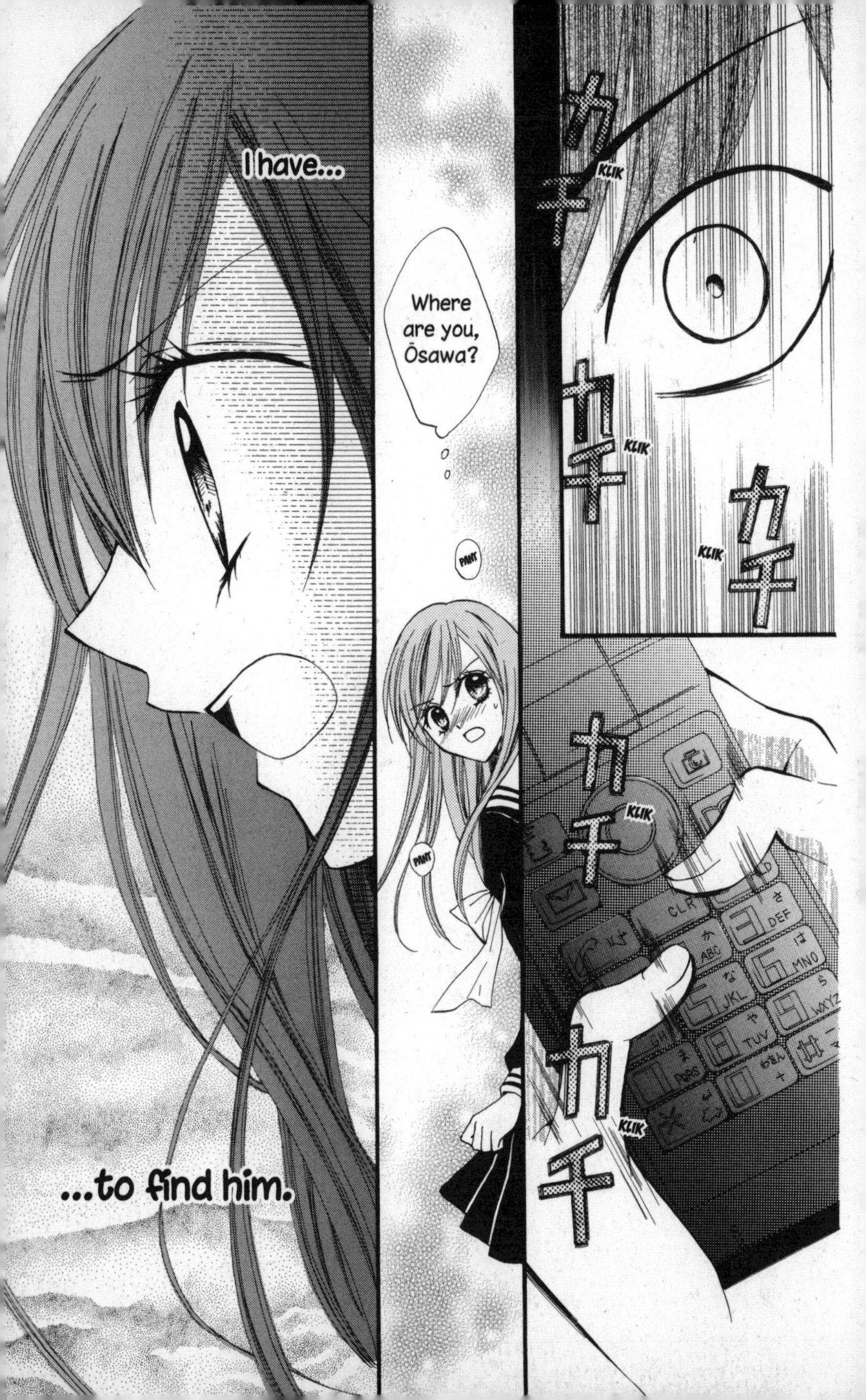

カチ KLIK
カチ KLIK
カチ KLIK
カチ KLIK
カチ KLIK
Where are you, Ōsawa?
PANT
PANT
I have...
...to find him.

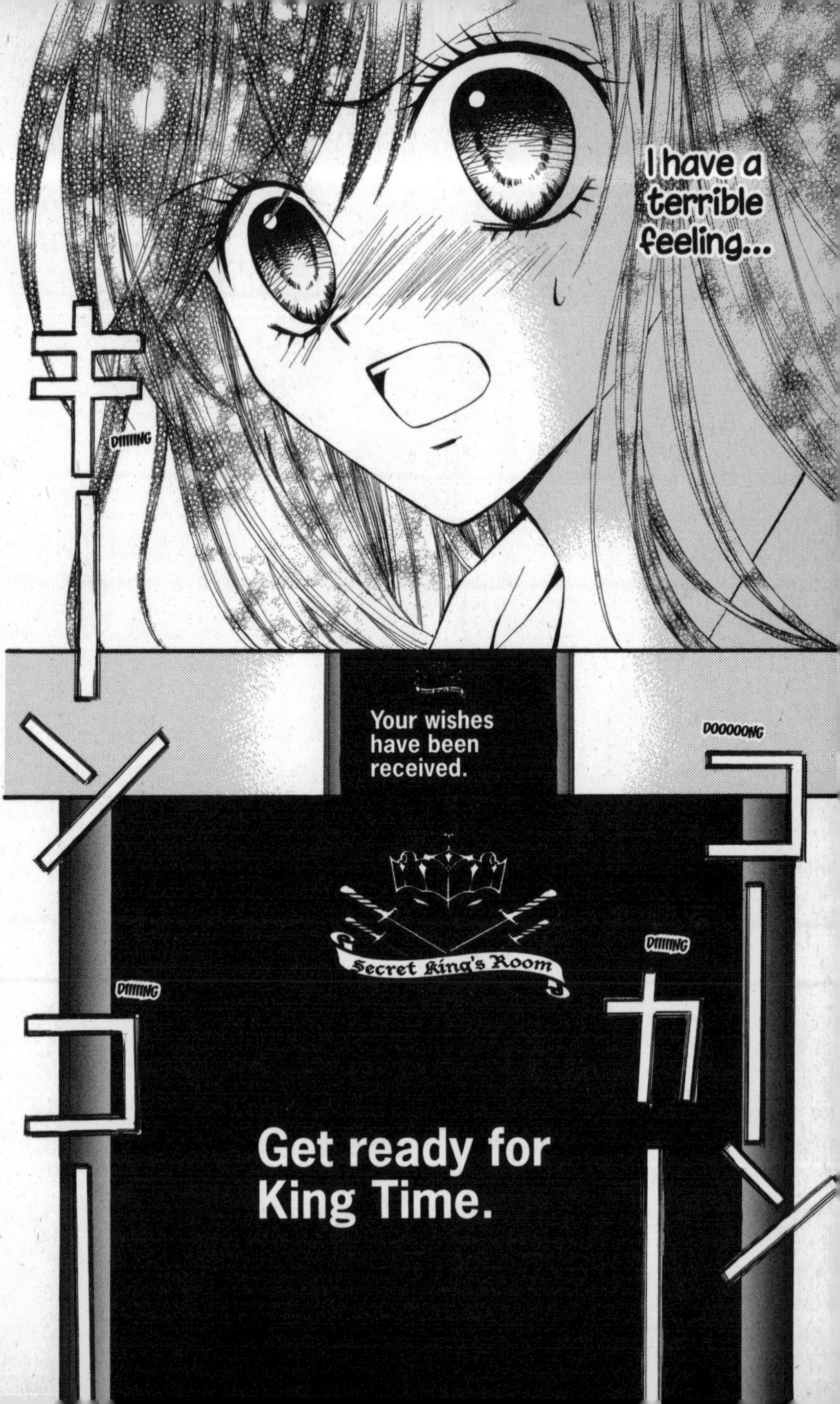
I have a terrible feeling...
DIIIING
Your wishes have been received.
DOOOOONG
Secret King's Room
DIIIING
DIIIING
Get ready for King Time.

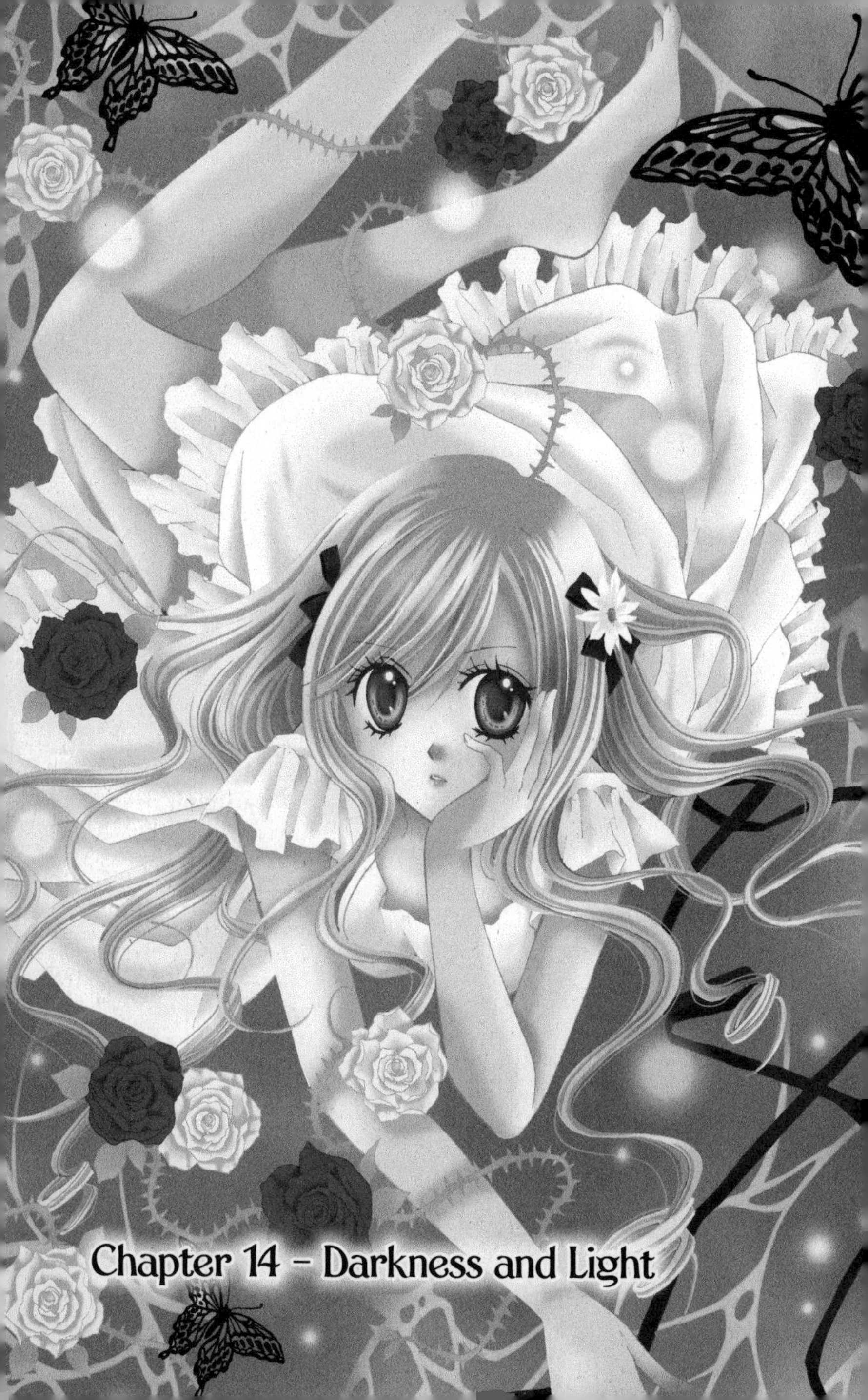

Chapter 14 - Darkness and Light

ARISA

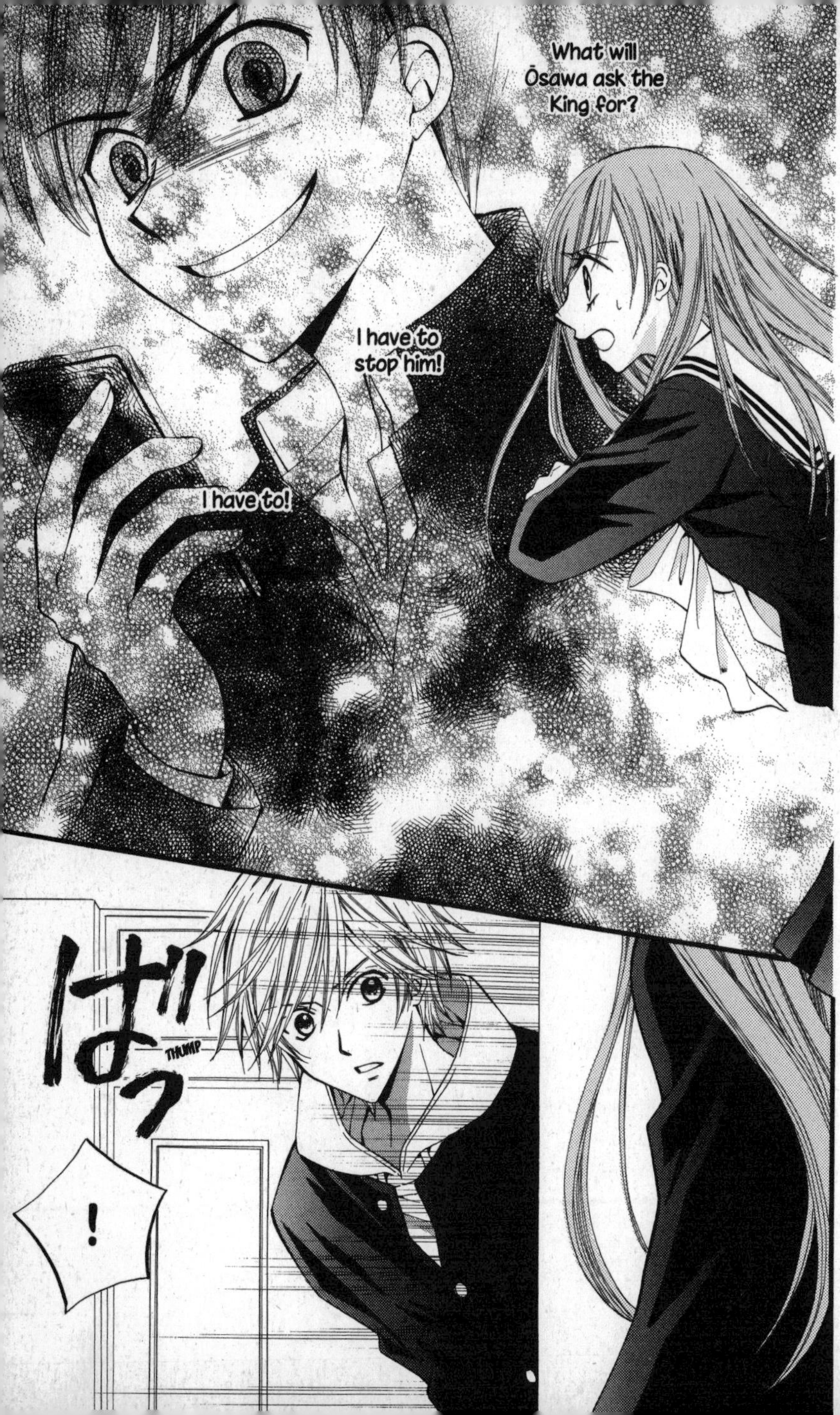
What will Ōsawa ask the King for?
I have to stop him!
I have to!
ぱっ
THUMP
!

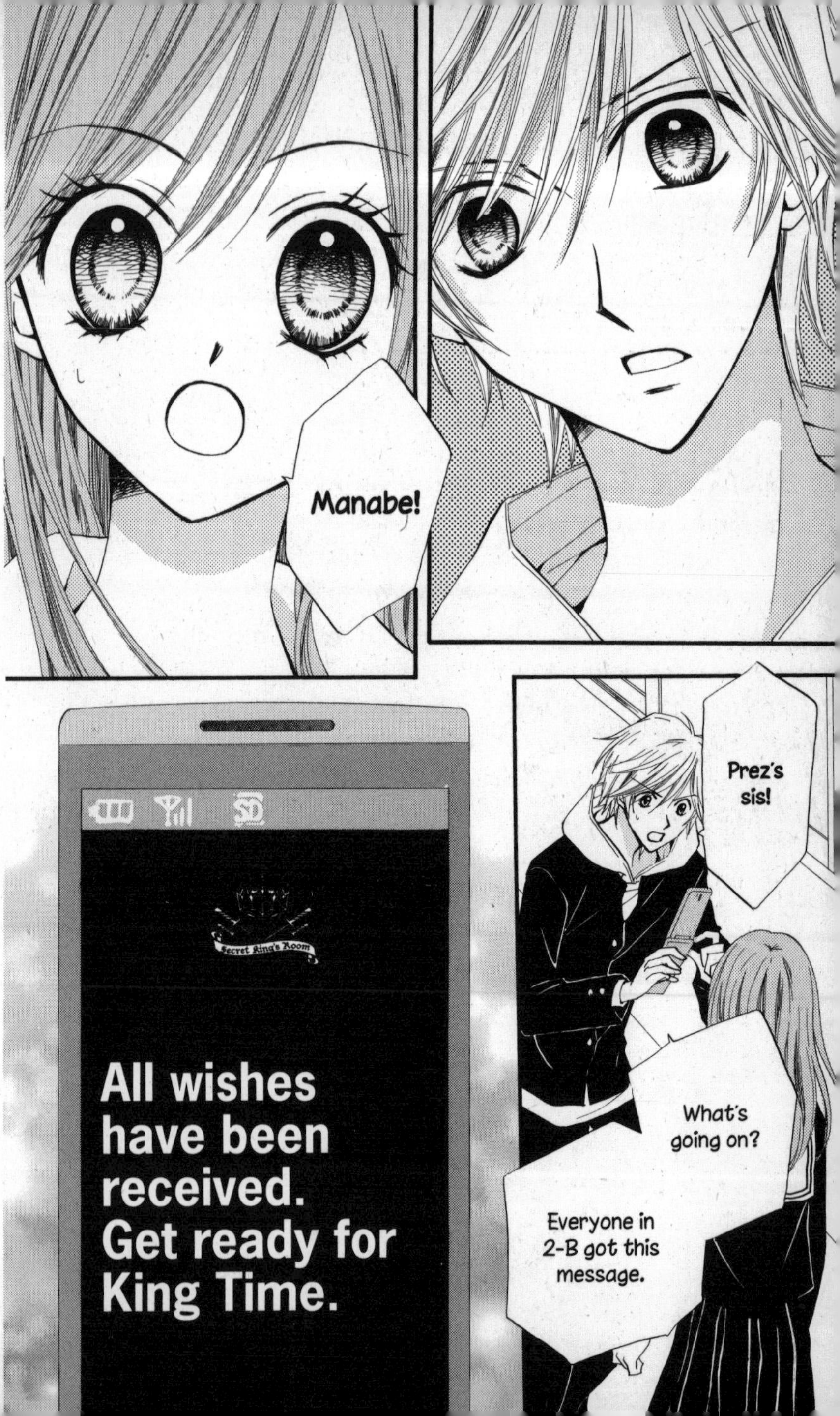
Manabe!
Prez's sis!
What's going on?
Everyone in 2-B got this message.
Secret King's Room
All wishes have been received. Get ready for King Time.

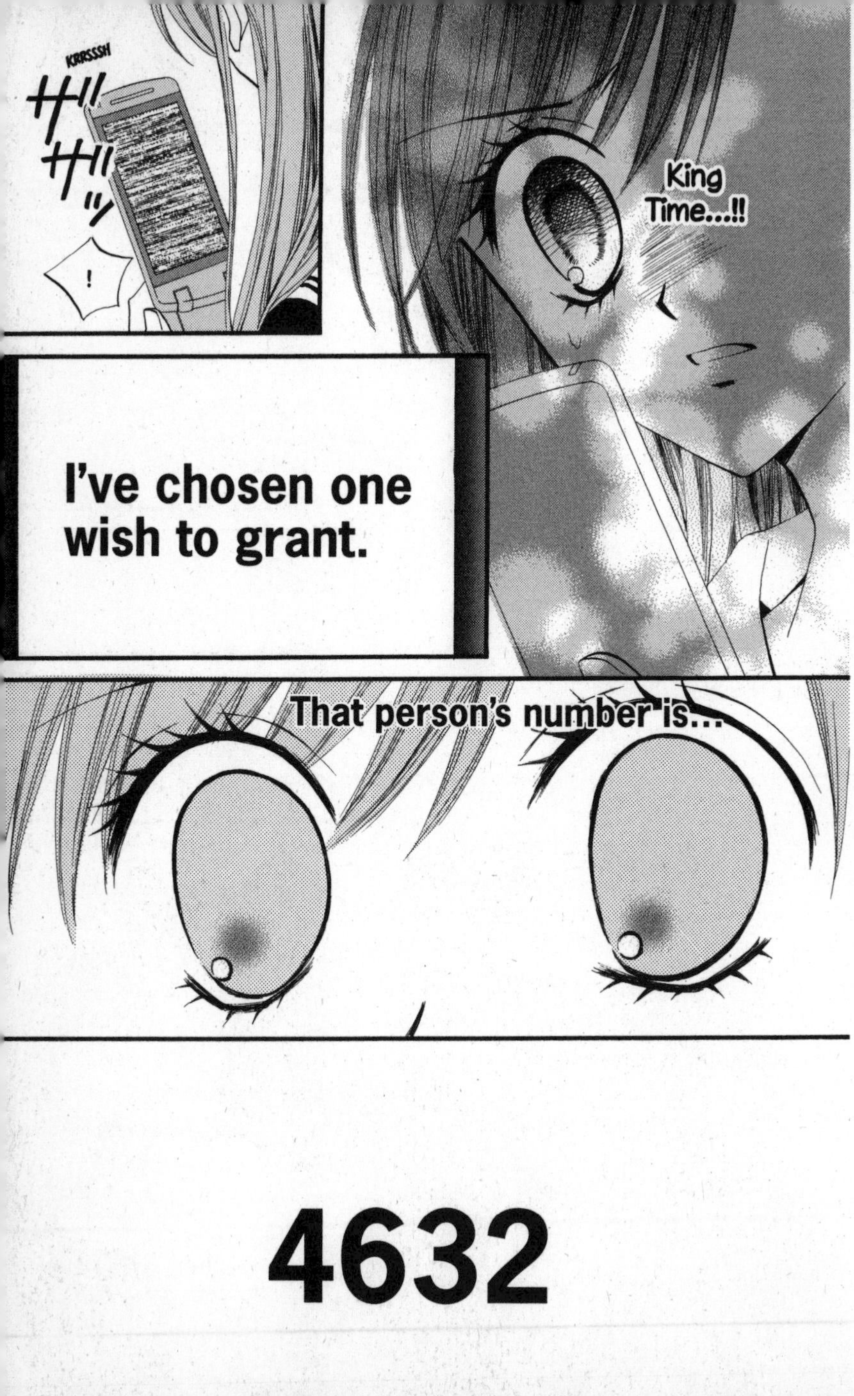
King Time...!!
KRRSSH
!
I've chosen one wish to grant.
That person's number is...
4632

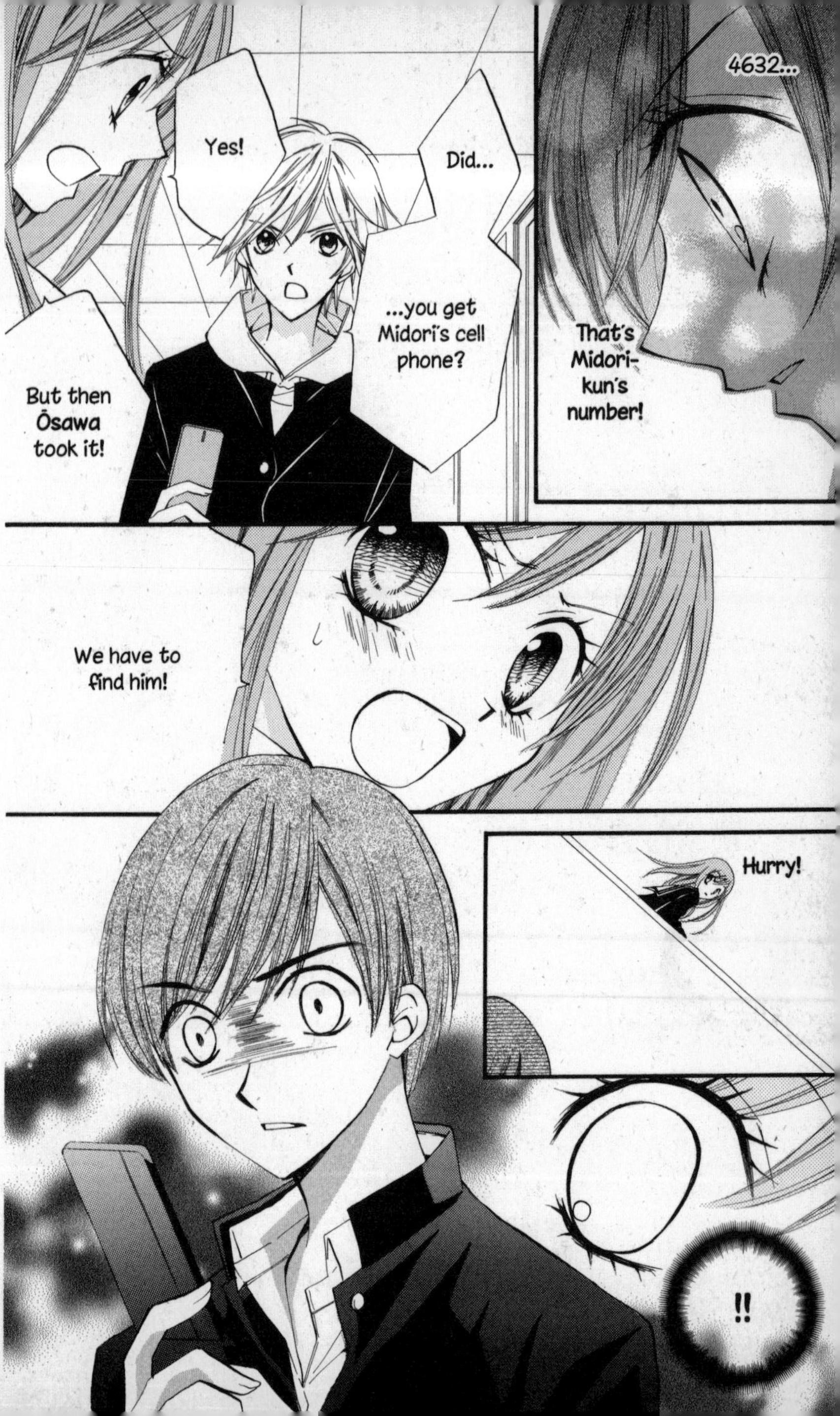
4632...
That's Midori-kun's number!
Did...
...you get Midori's cell phone?
Yes!
But then Ōsawa took it!
We have to find him!
Hurry!
!!

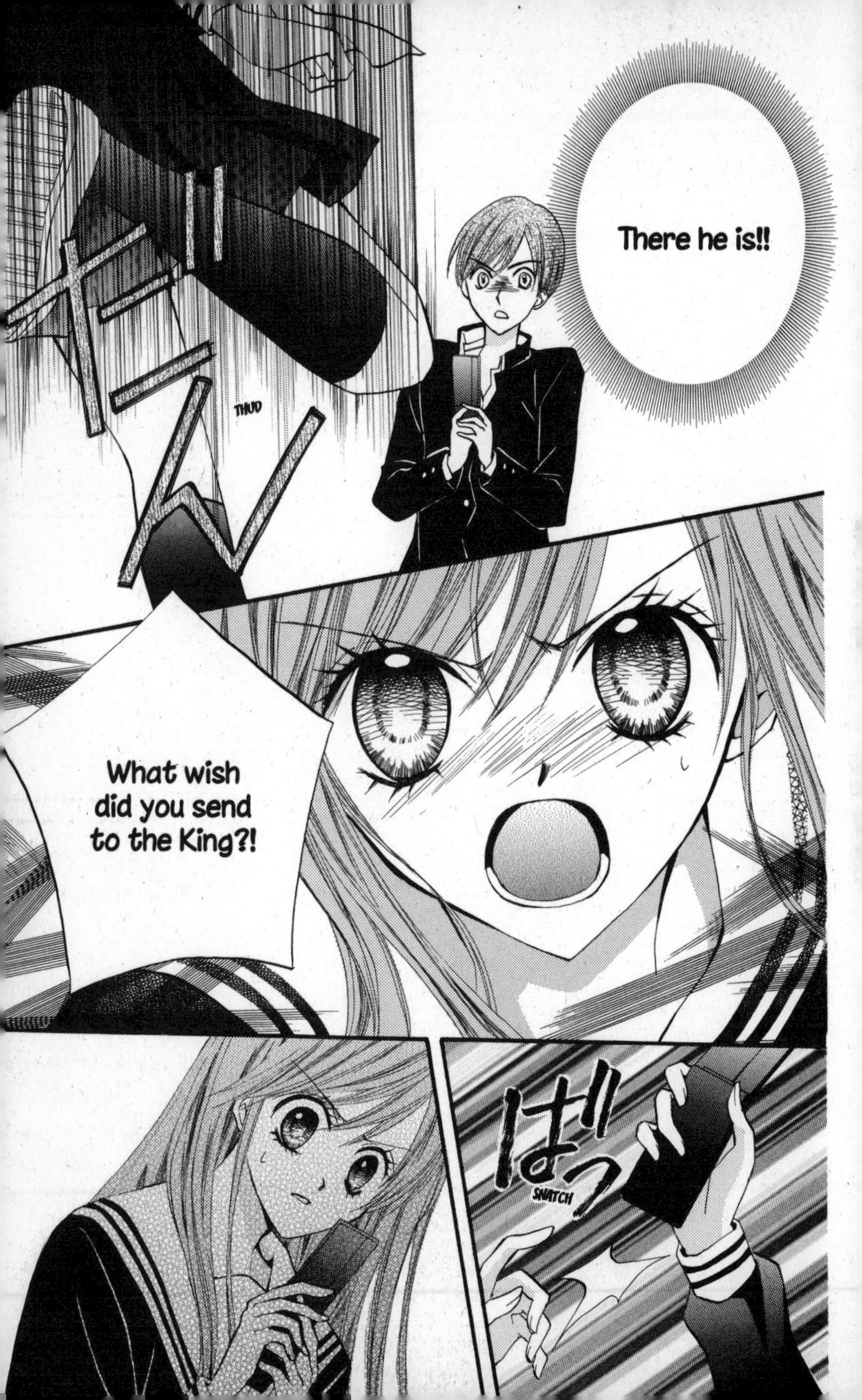
There he is!!
THUD
What wish did you send to the King?!
ばっ
SNATCH

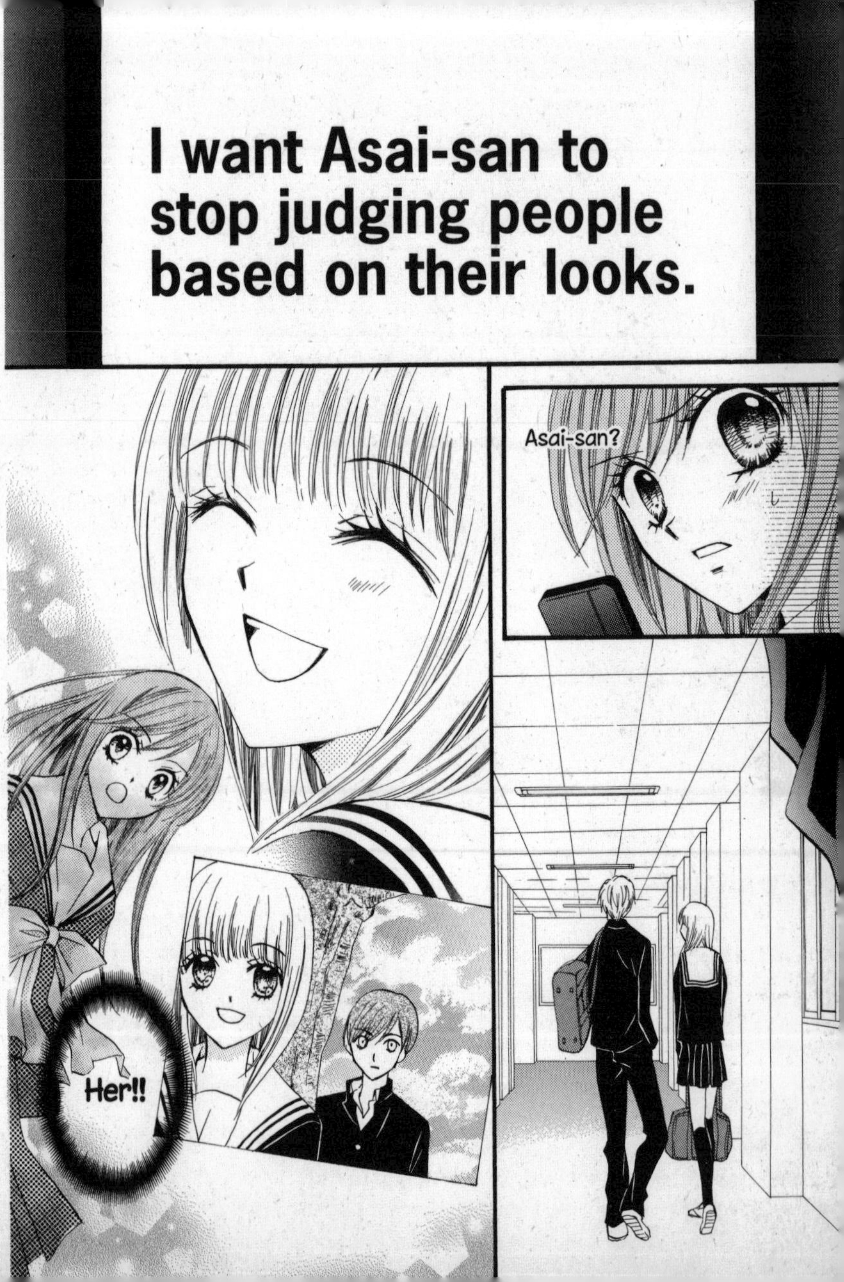
I want Asai-san to stop judging people based on their looks.
Asai-san?
Her!!

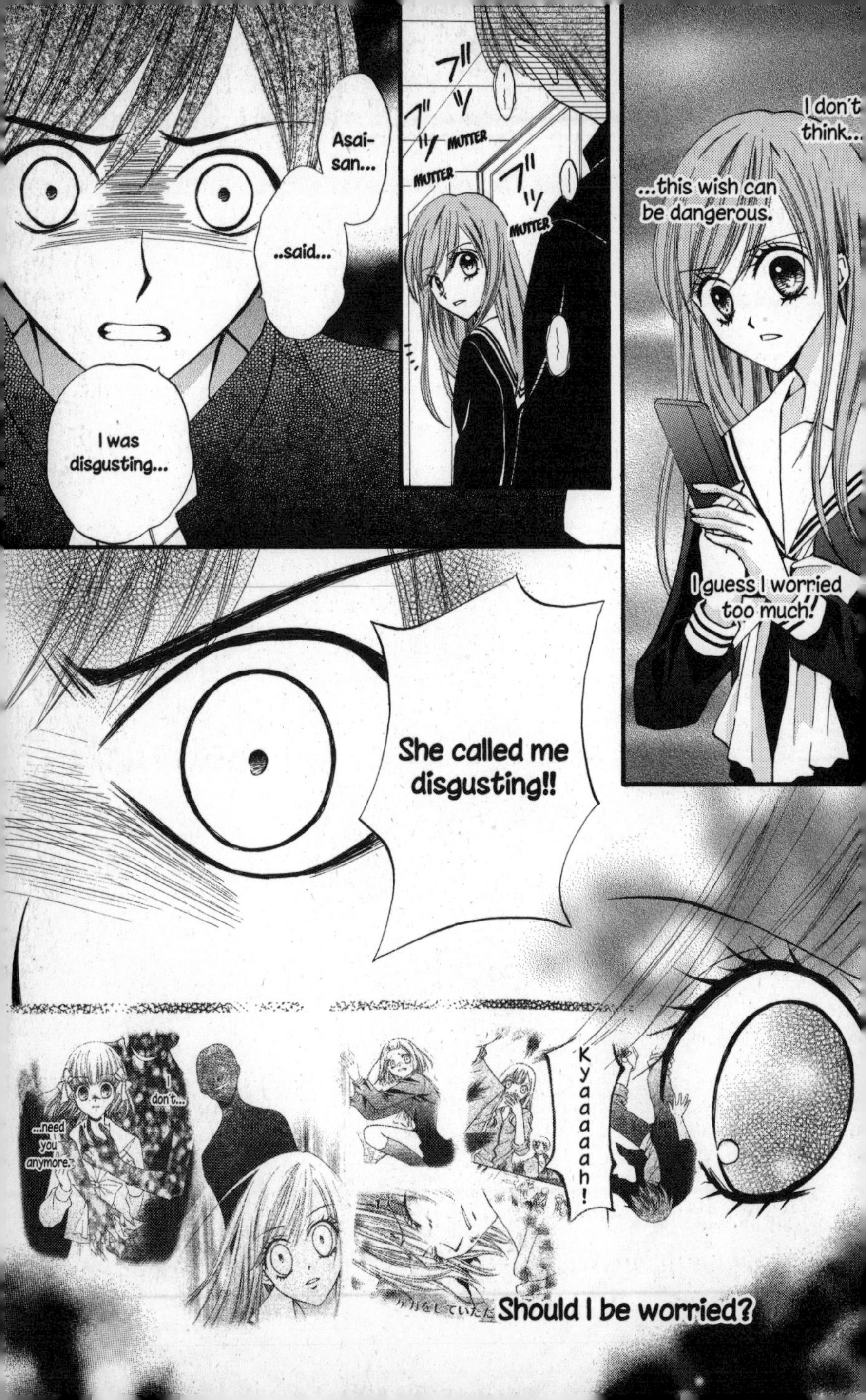
I don't think...
...this wish can be dangerous.
I guess I worried too much!
MUTTER
MUTTER
MUTTER
Asai-san...
..said...
I was disgusting...
She called me disgusting!!
Kyaaaaah!
I don't...
...need you anymore.
Should I be worried?

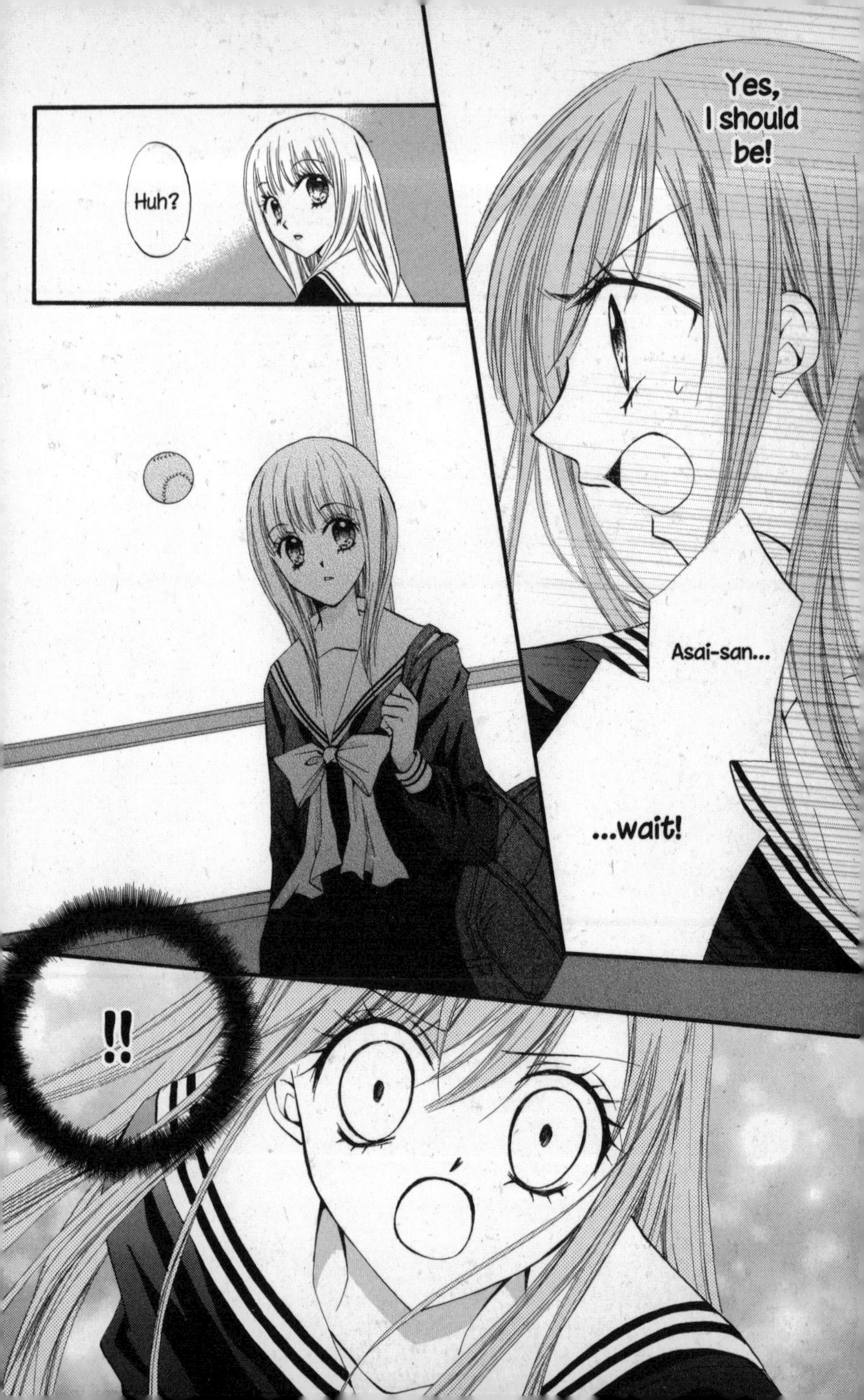
Yes, I should be!
Asai-san...
...wait!
Huh?
!!

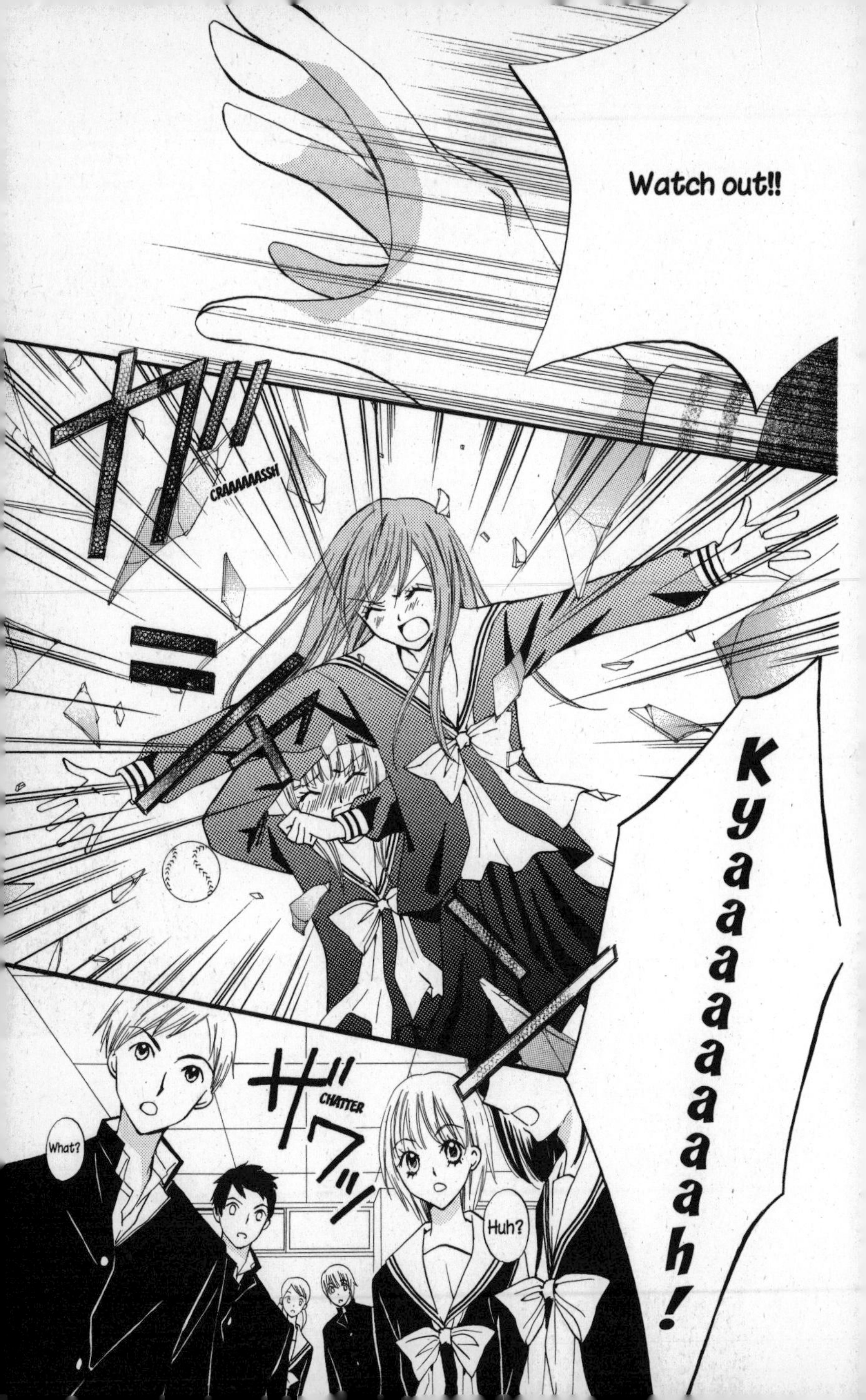
Watch out!!
CRAAAAAASSH
Kyaaaaaaaaaah!
Huh?
CHATTER
What?

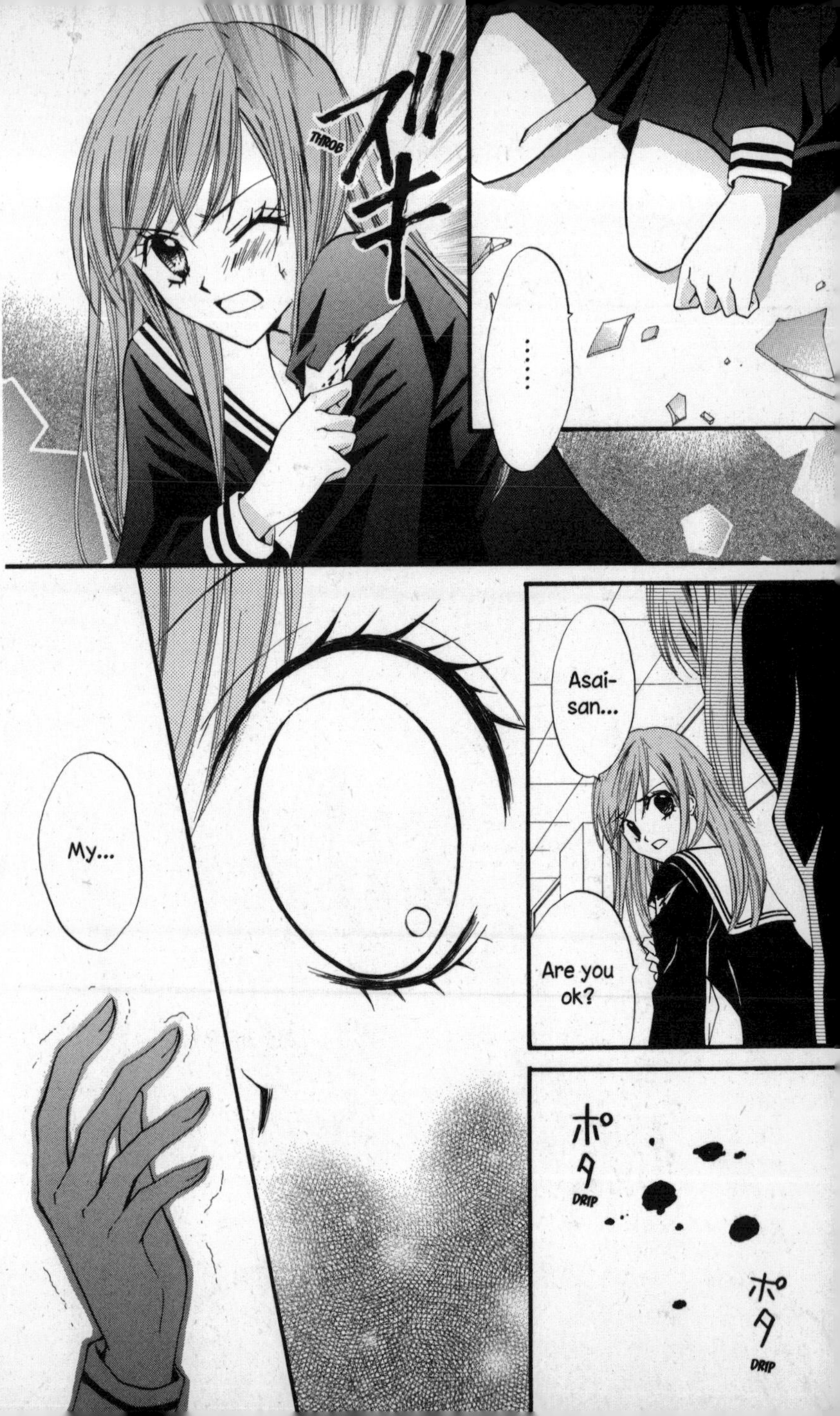
......
ズキ
THROB
Asai-san...
Are you ok?
ポタ
DRIP
ポタ
DRIP
My...

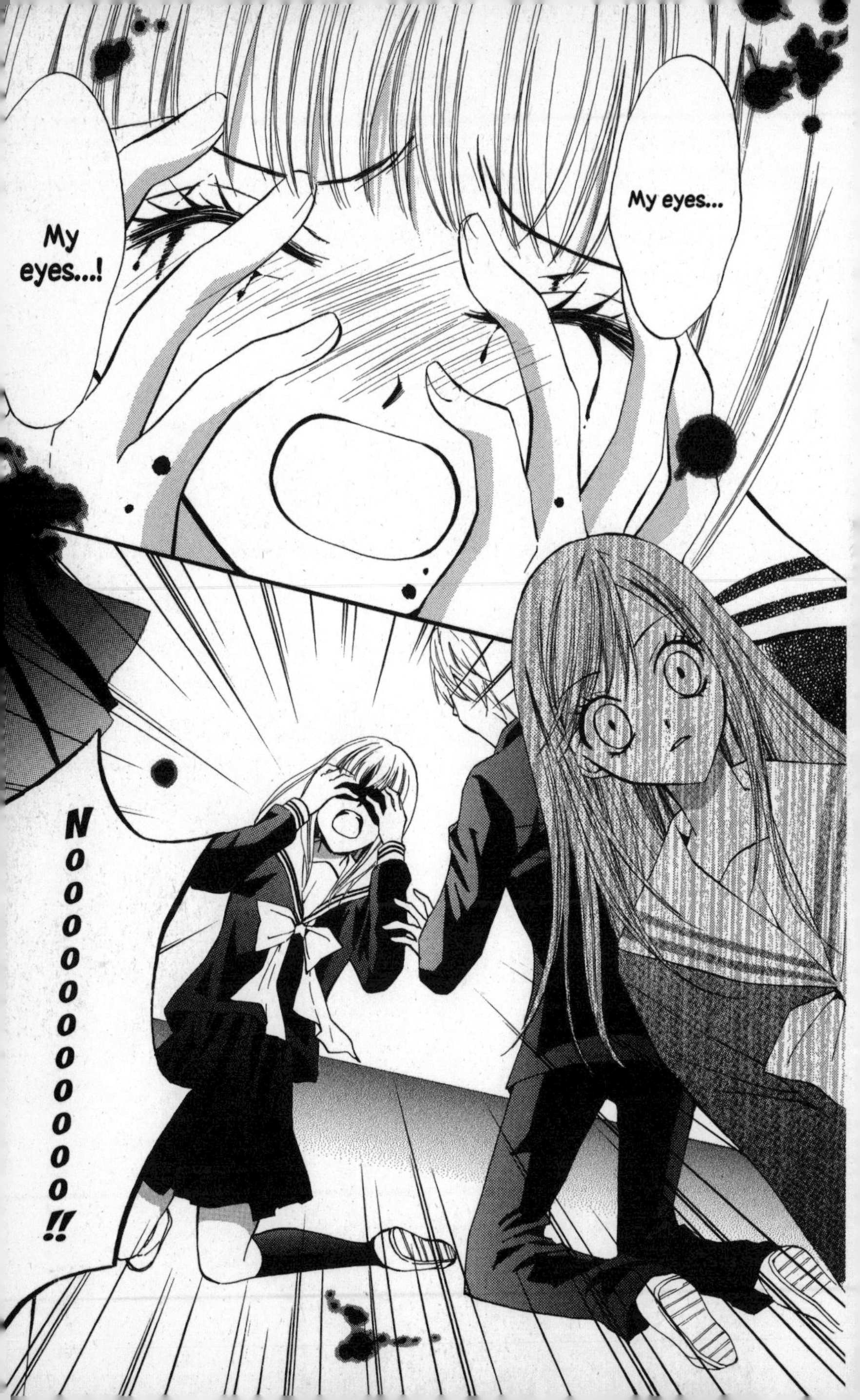
My eyes...
My eyes...!
NOOOOOOOOOOOOOOO!!

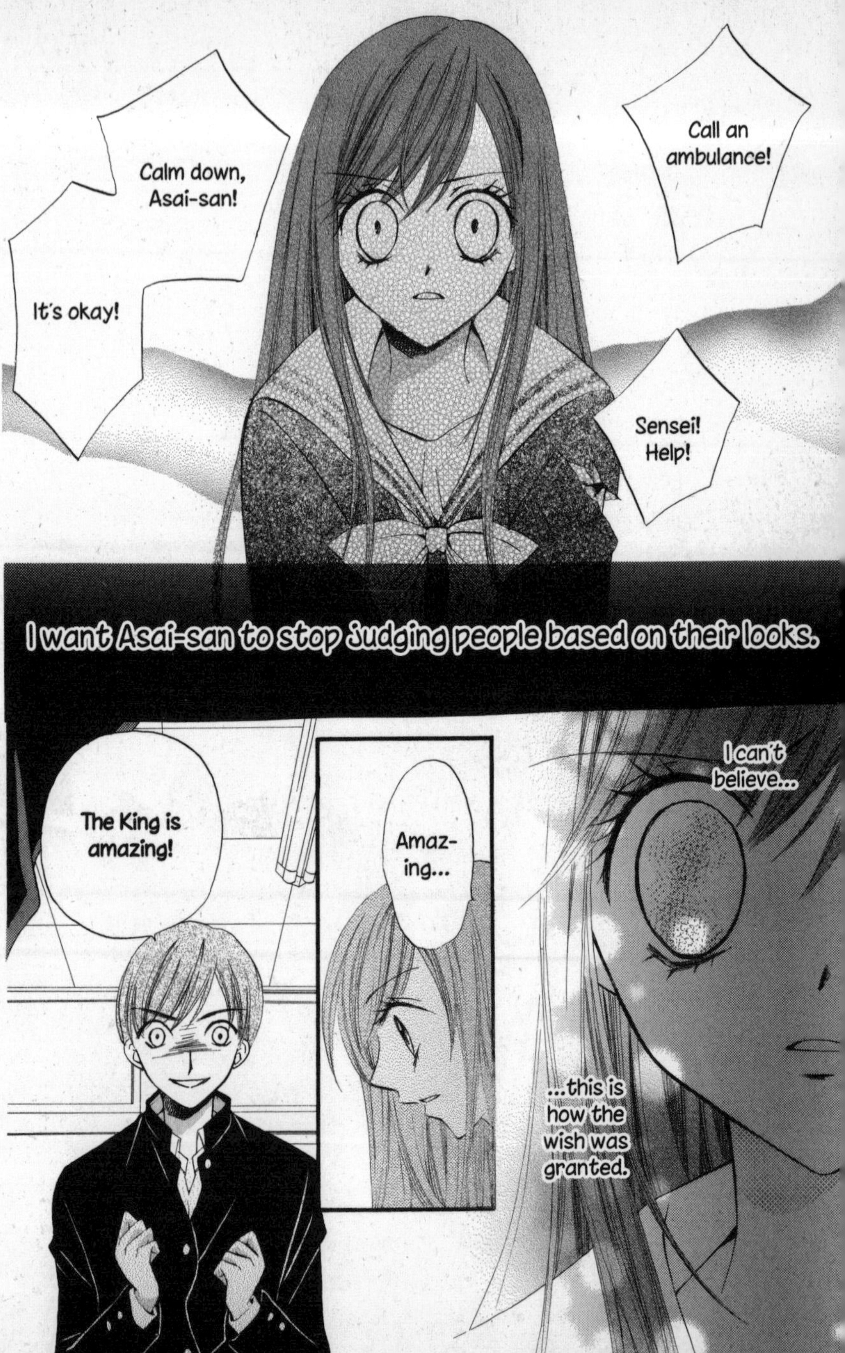
Call an ambulance!
Sensei! Help!
Calm down, Asai-san!
It's okay!
I want Asai-san to stop judging people based on their looks.
I can't believe...
...this is how the wish was granted.
Amaz-ing...
The King is amazing!

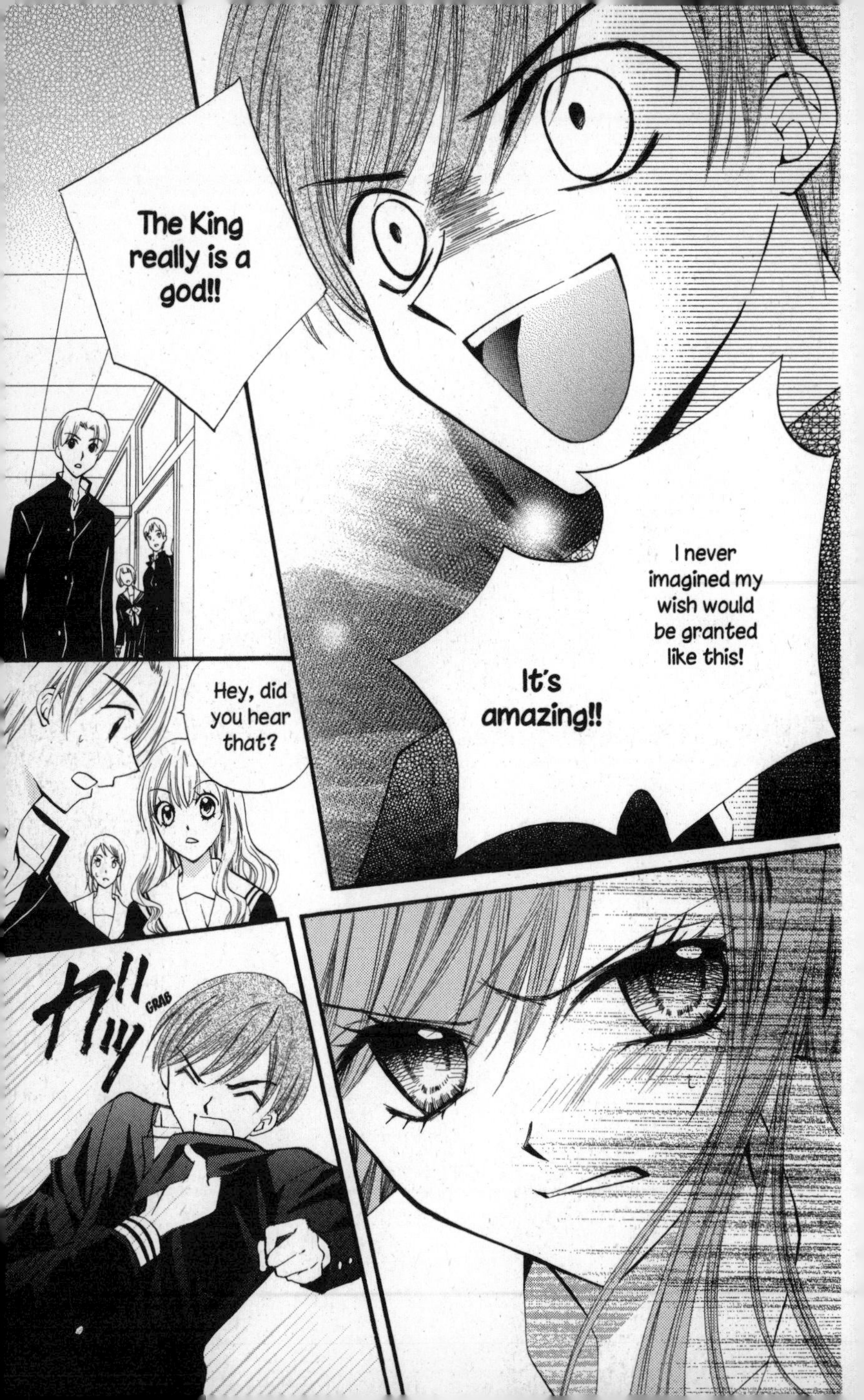

The King really is a god!!
I never imagined my wish would be granted like this!
It's amazing!!
Hey, did you hear that?
GRAB

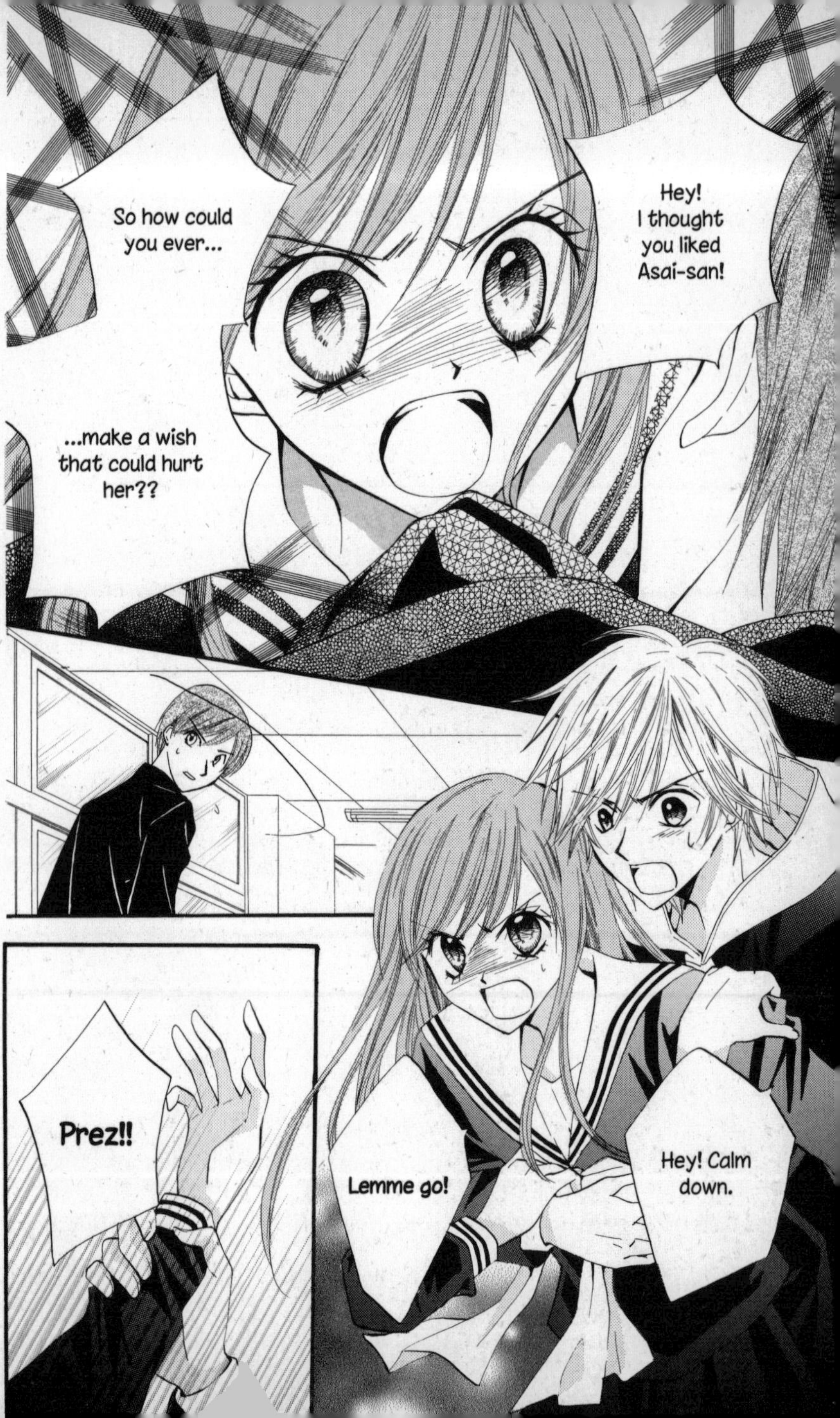
Hey! I thought you liked Asai-san!
So how could you ever...
...make a wish that could hurt her??
Hey! Calm down.
Lemme go!
Prez!!

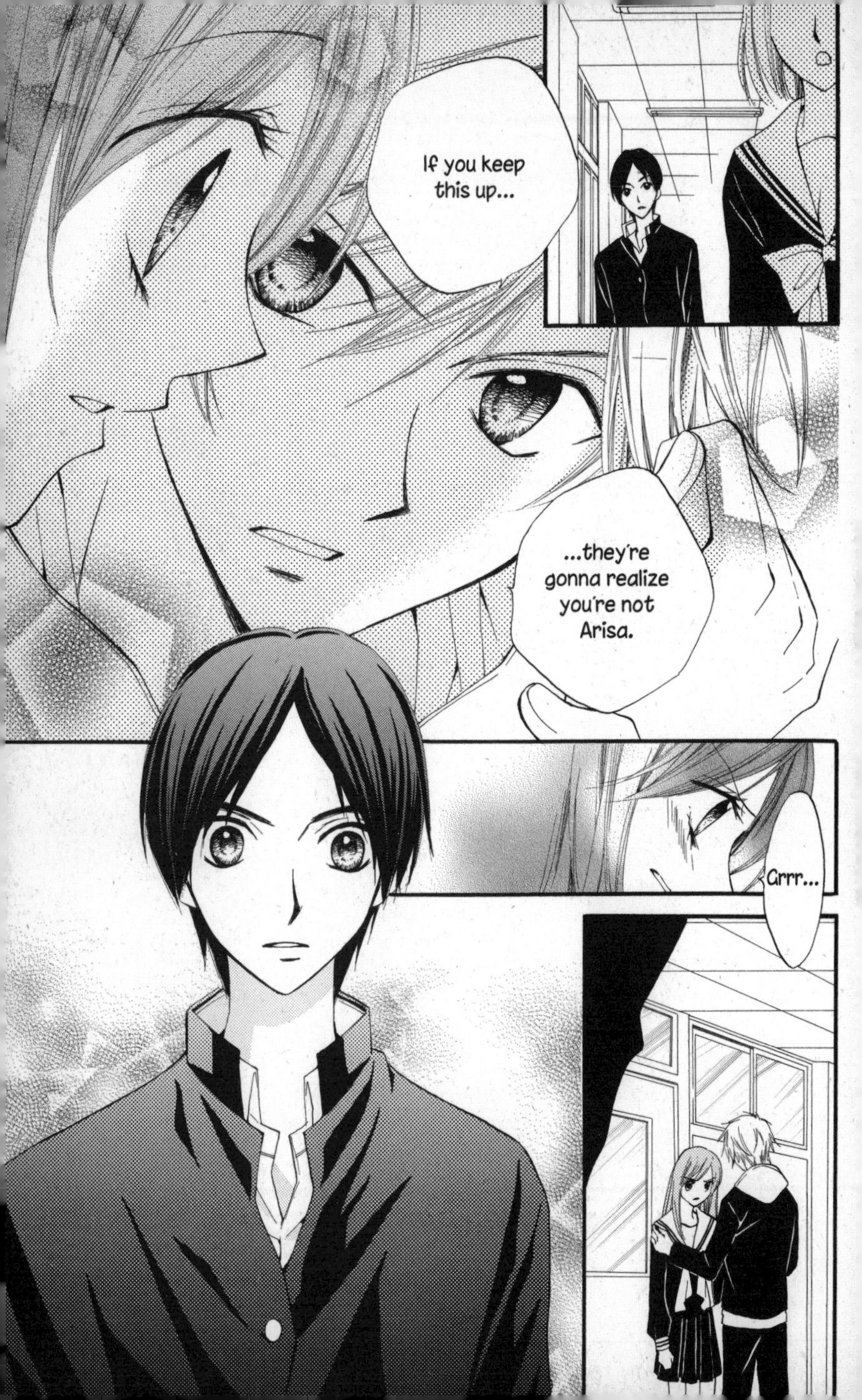
If you keep this up...
...they're gonna realize you're not Arisa.
Grrr...

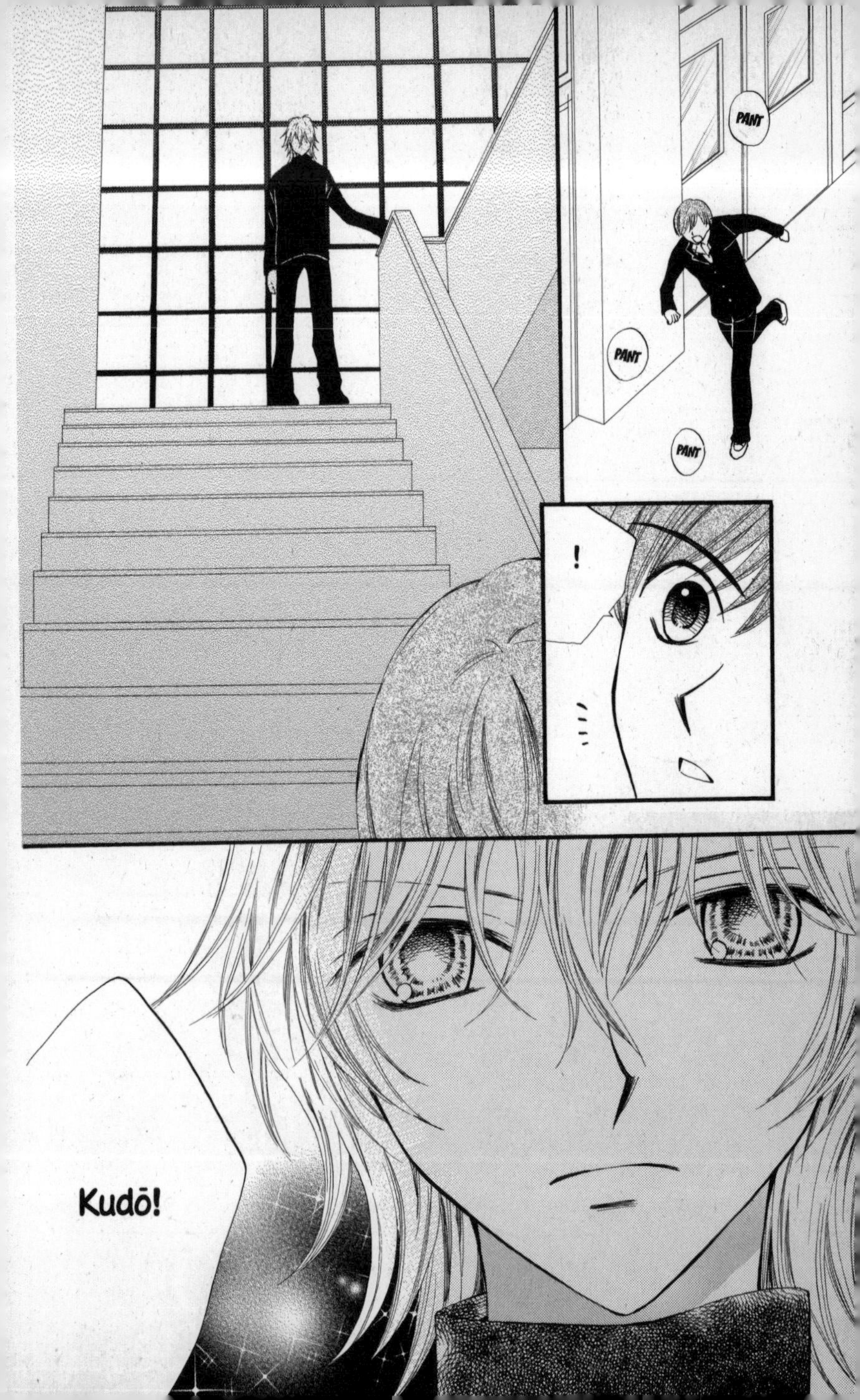
PANT
PANT
PANT
!
Kudō!

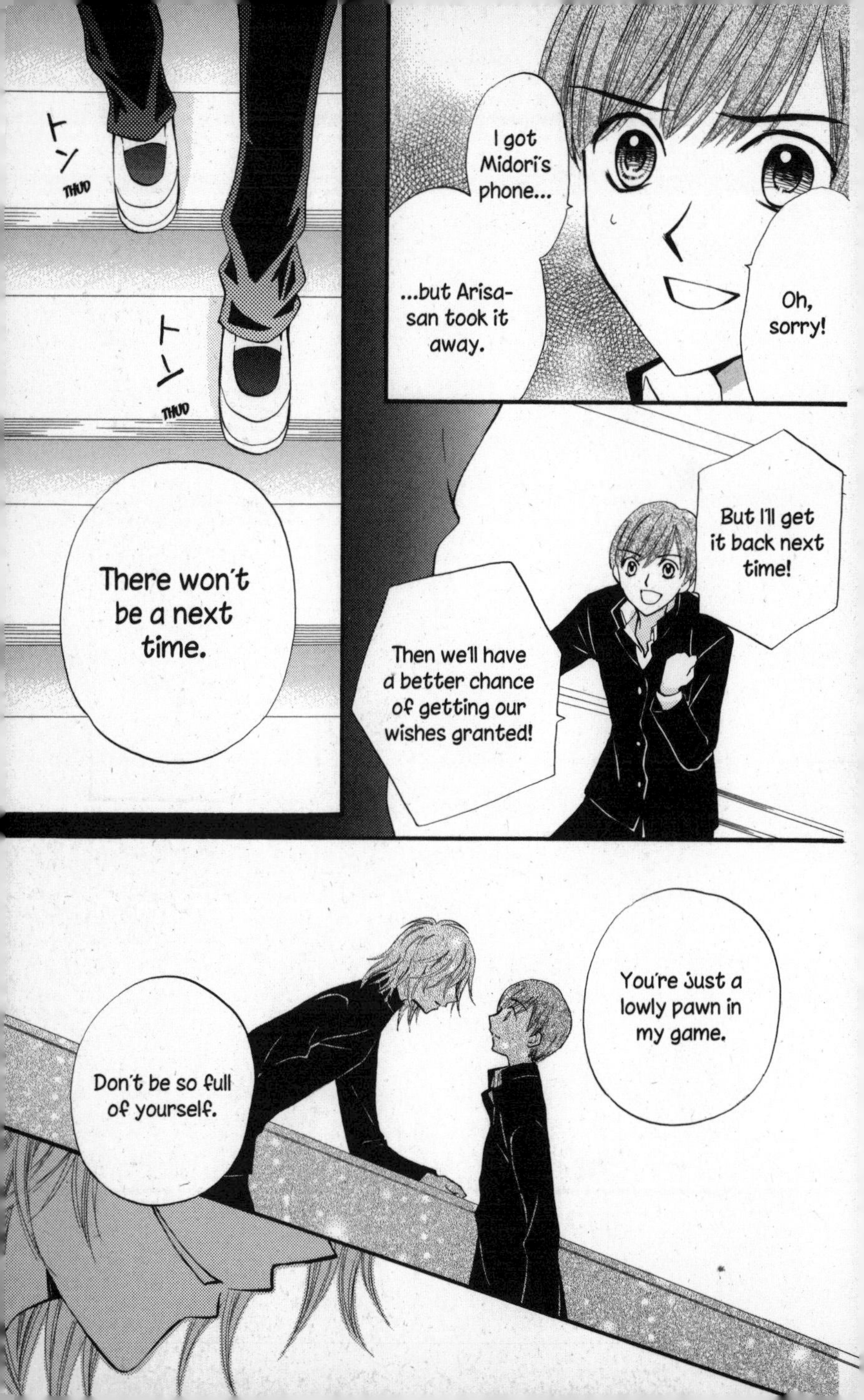
Oh, sorry!
I got Midori's phone...
...but Arisa-san took it away.
But I'll get it back next time!
Then we'll have a better chance of getting our wishes granted!
トン
THUD
トン
THUD
There won't be a next time.
You're just a lowly pawn in my game.
Don't be so full of yourself.

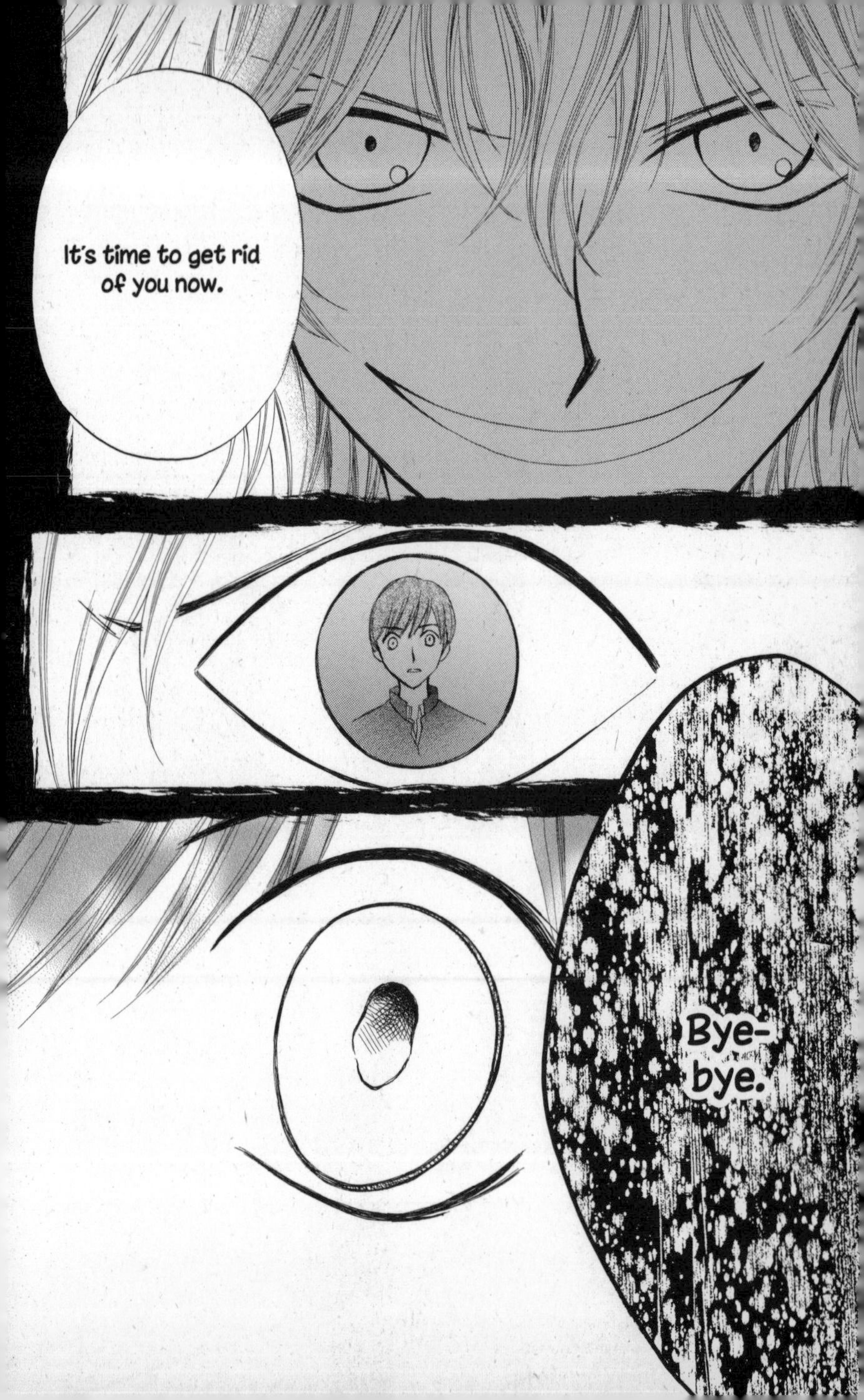
It's time to get rid of you now.
Bye-bye.

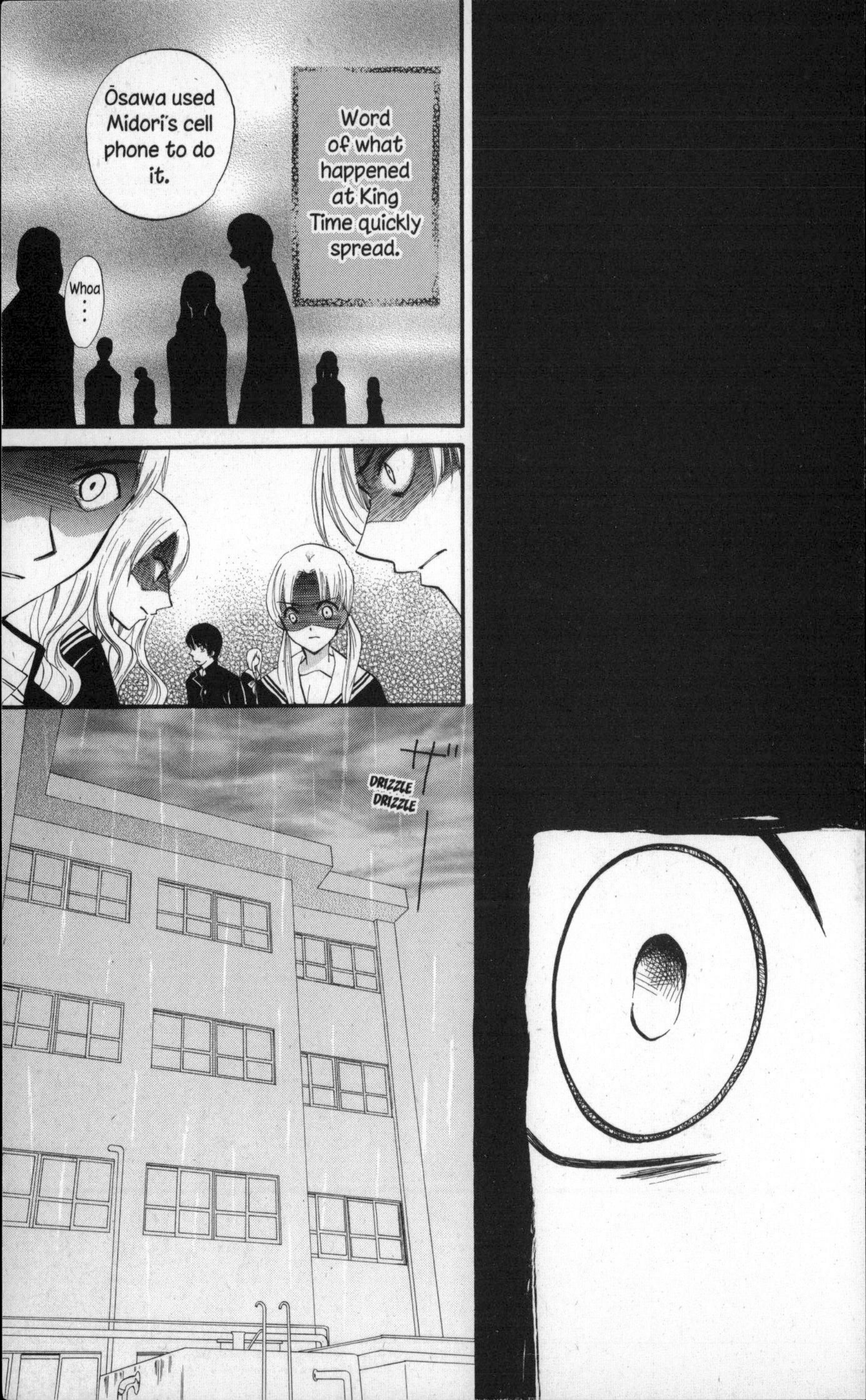
Word of what happened at King Time quickly spread.
Ōsawa used Midori's cell phone to do it.
Whoa...
DRIZZLE DRIZZLE

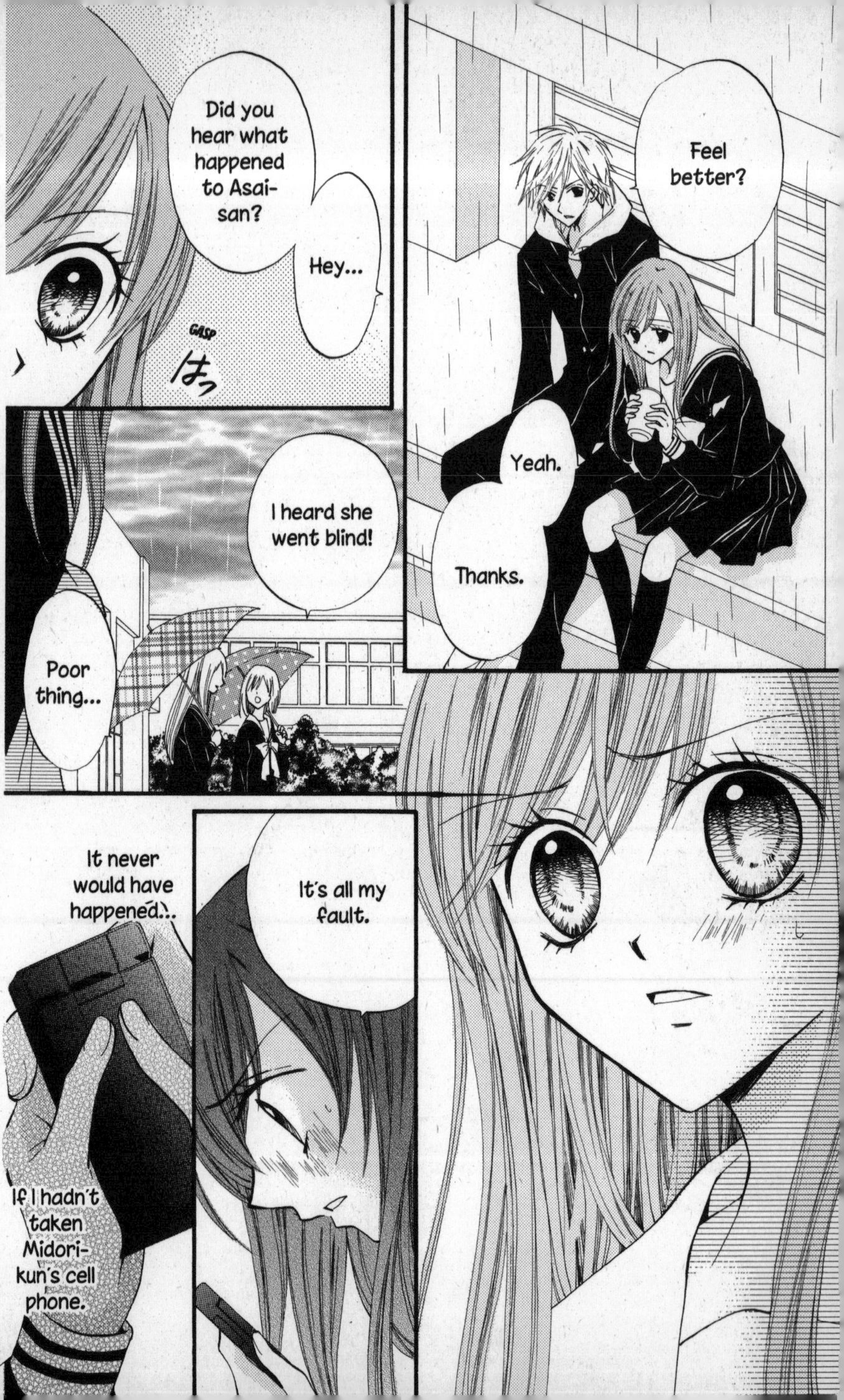
Feel better?
Yeah.
Thanks.
Hey...
Did you hear what happened to Asai-san?
GASP
はっ
I heard she went blind!
Poor thing...
It's all my fault.
It never would have happened...
If I hadn't taken Midori-kun's cell phone.

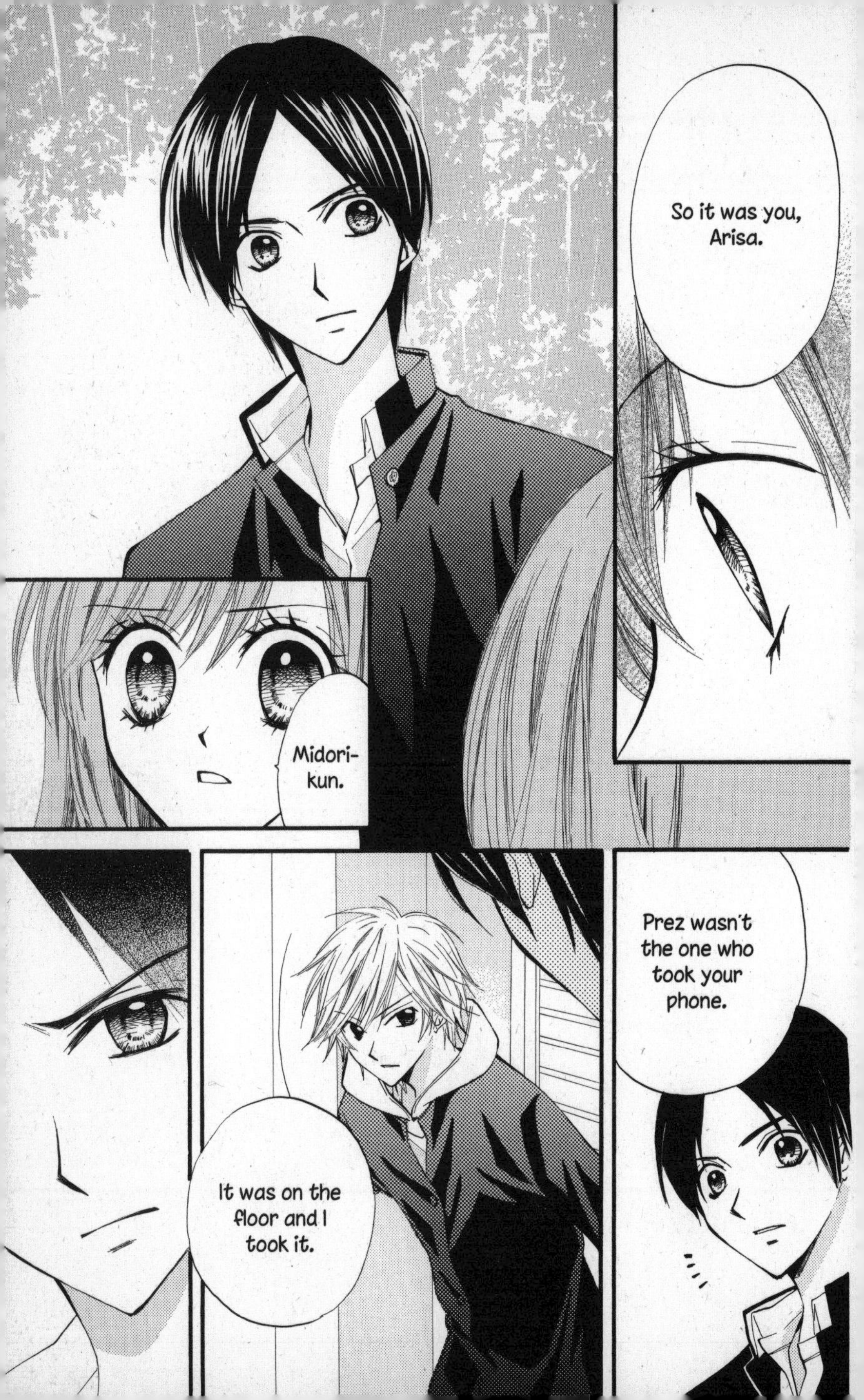
So it was you, Arisa.
Midori-kun.
Prez wasn't the one who took your phone.
...
It was on the floor and I took it.

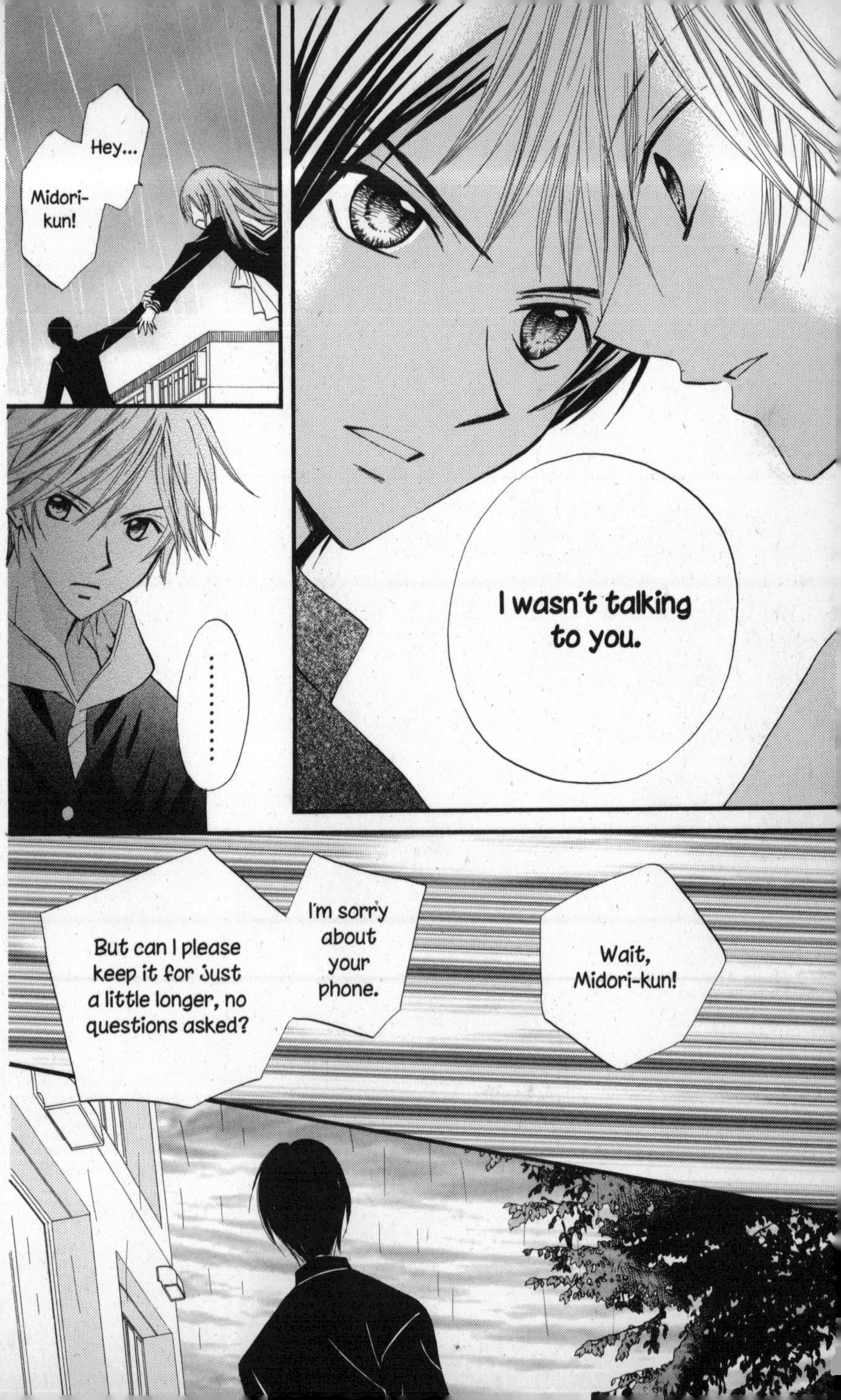
I wasn't talking to you.
Hey...
Midori-kun!
......
Wait, Midori-kun!
I'm sorry about your phone.
But can I please keep it for just a little longer, no questions asked?

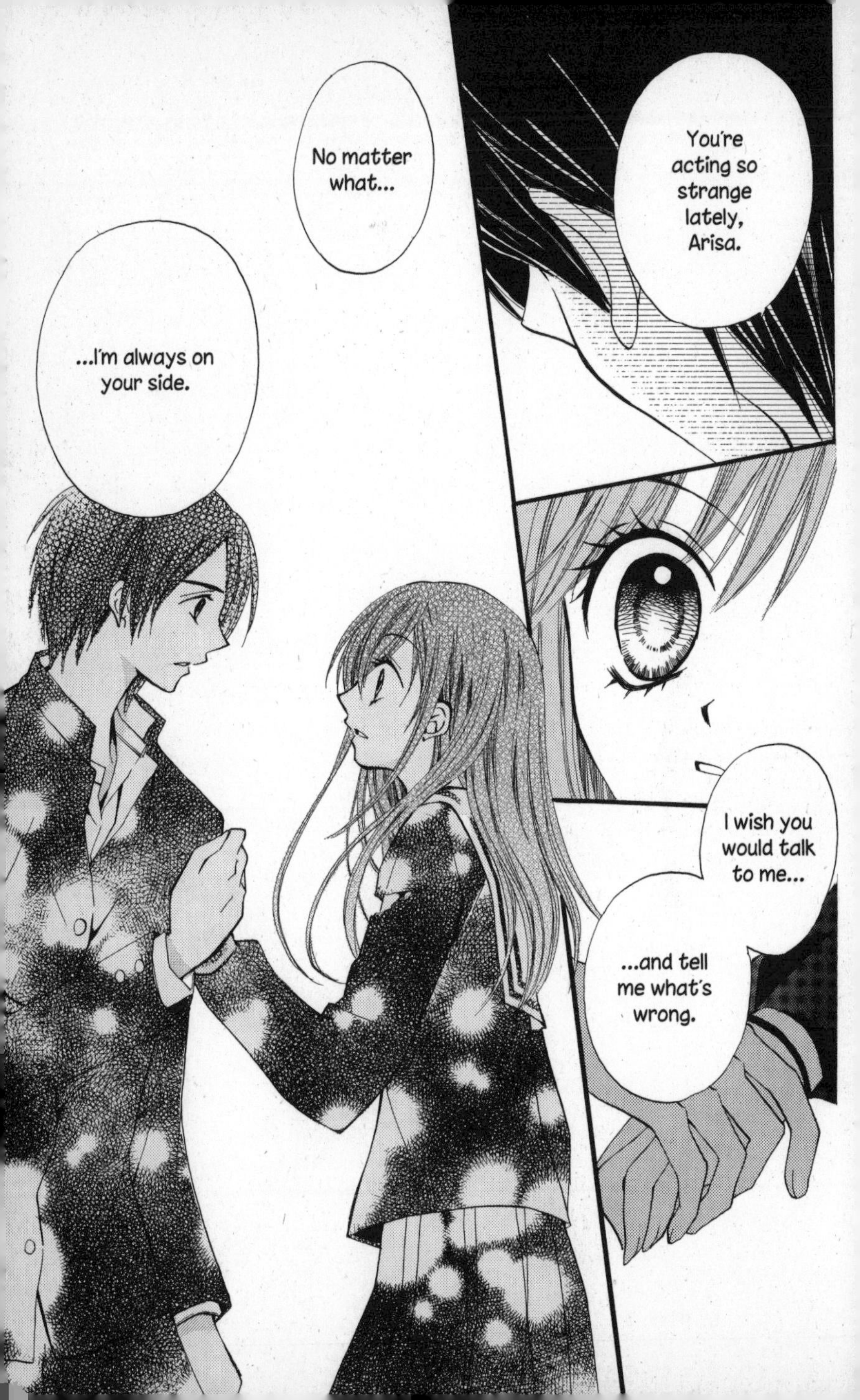
You're acting so strange lately, Arisa.
I wish you would talk to me...
...and tell me what's wrong.
No matter what...
...I'm always on your side.

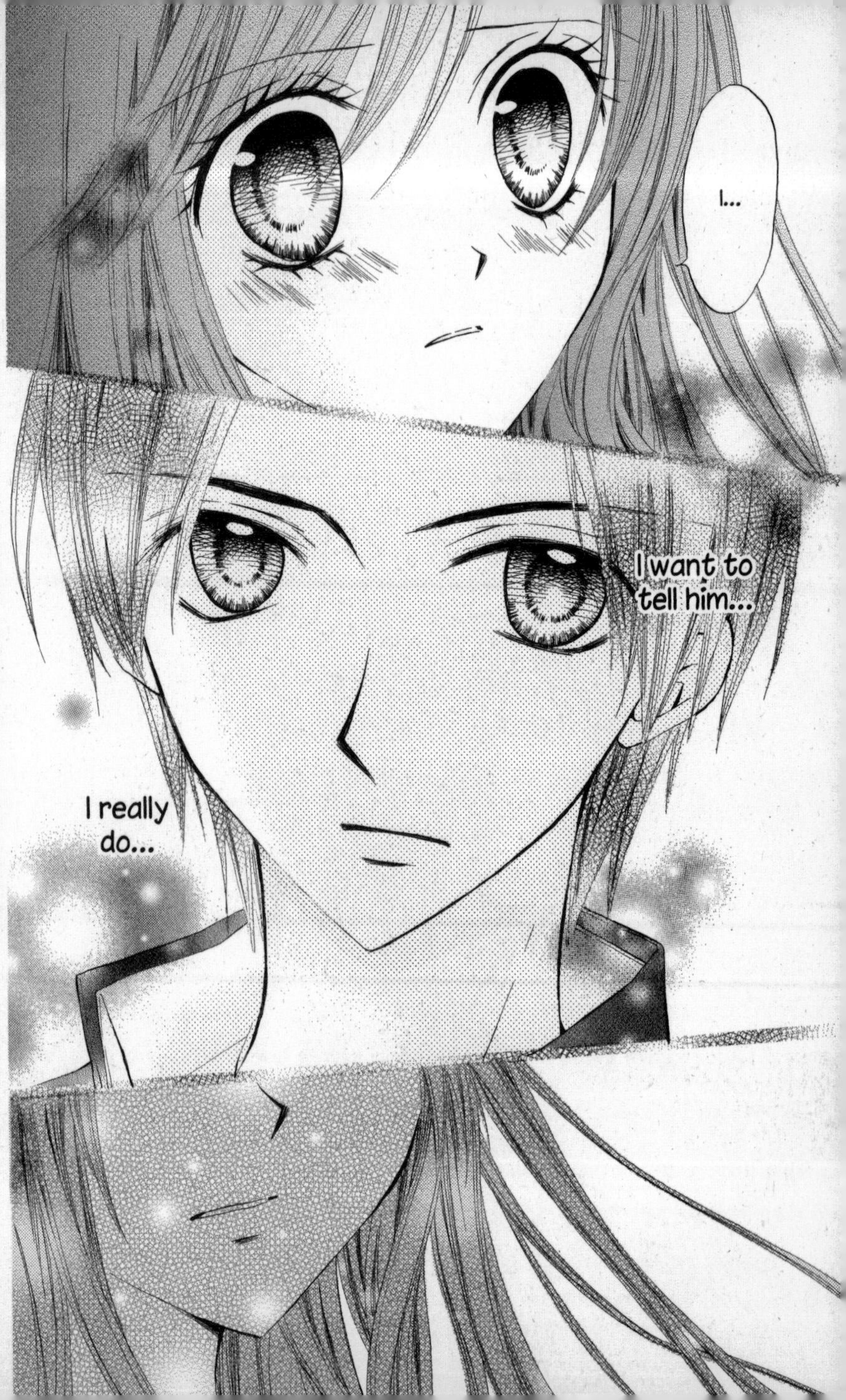
I...
I want to tell him...
I really do...

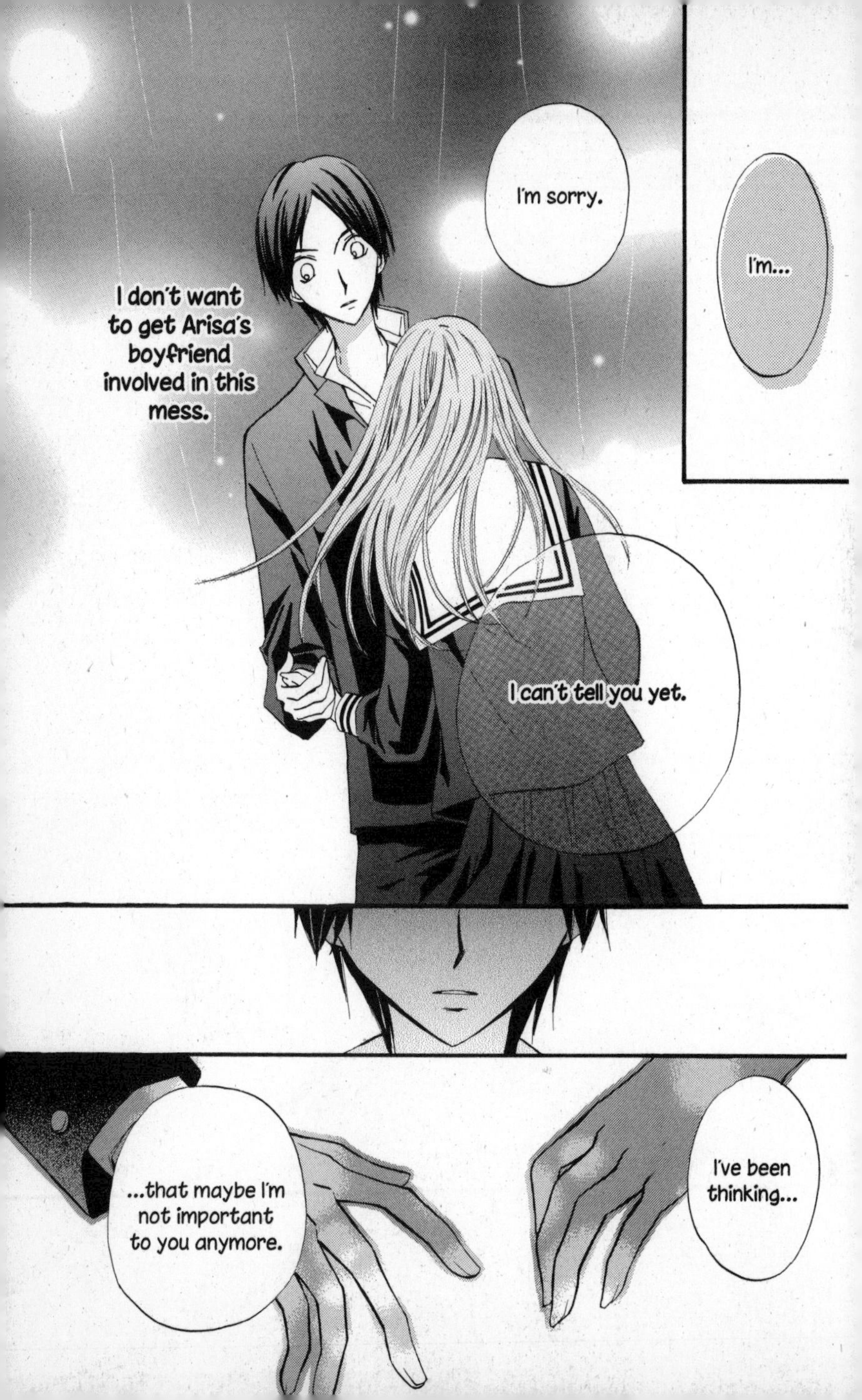
I'm...
I'm sorry.
I can't tell you yet.
I don't want to get Arisa's boyfriend involved in this mess.
I've been thinking...
...that maybe I'm not important to you anymore.

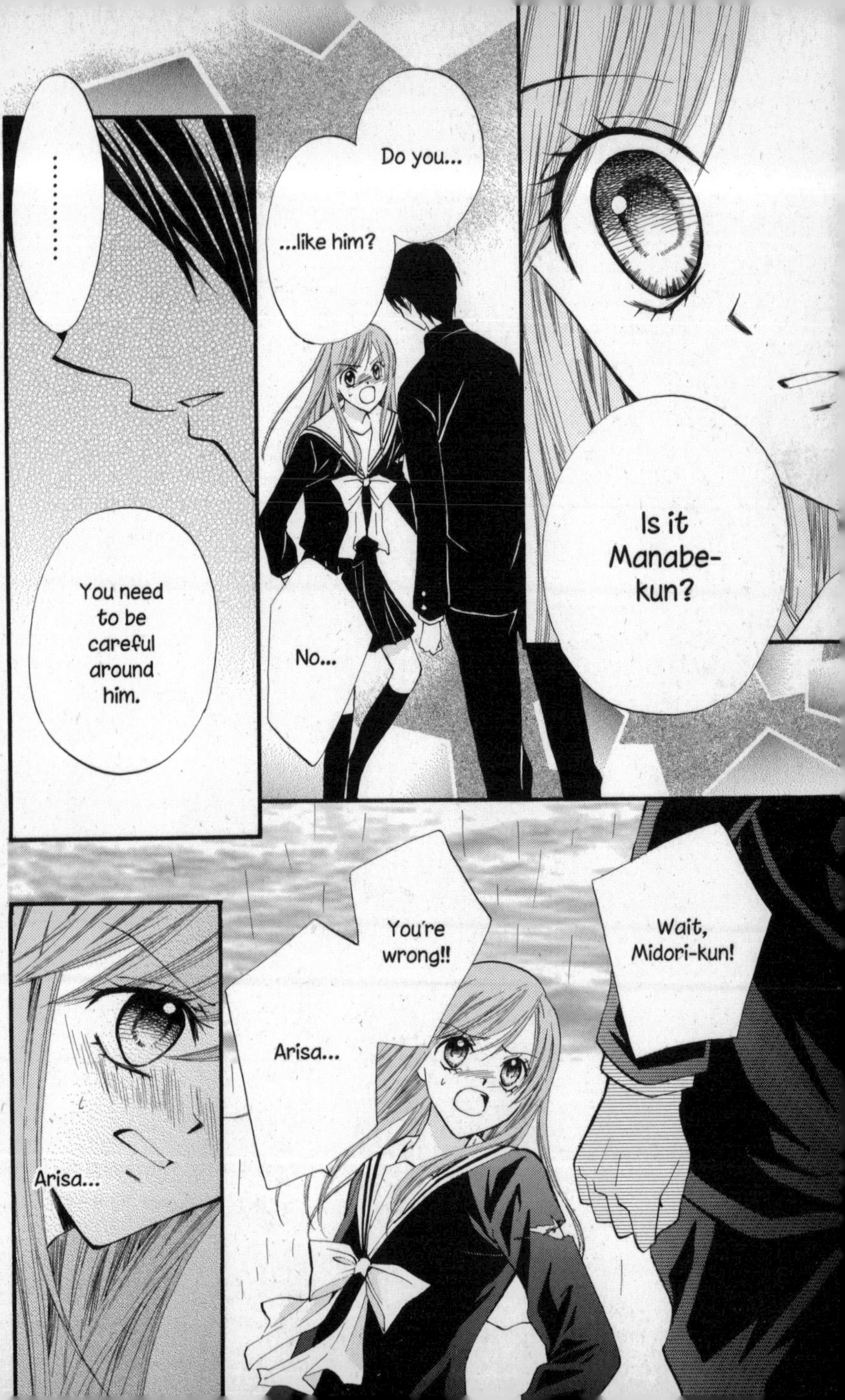

Is it Manabe-kun?
Do you...
...like him?
No...
....
You need to be careful around him.
Wait, Midori-kun!
You're wrong!!
Arisa...
Arisa...

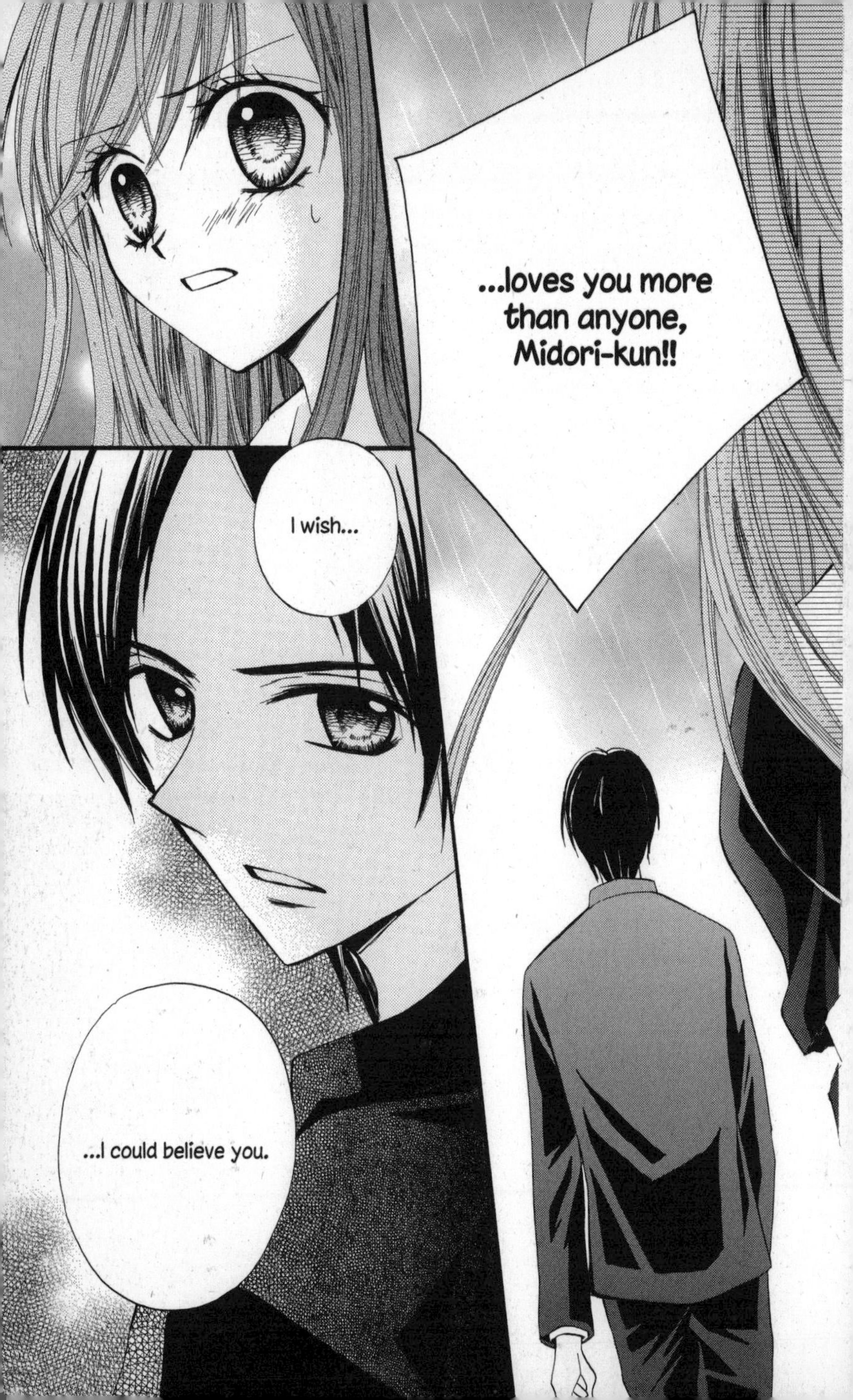
...loves you more than anyone, Midori-kun!!
I wish...
...I could believe you.

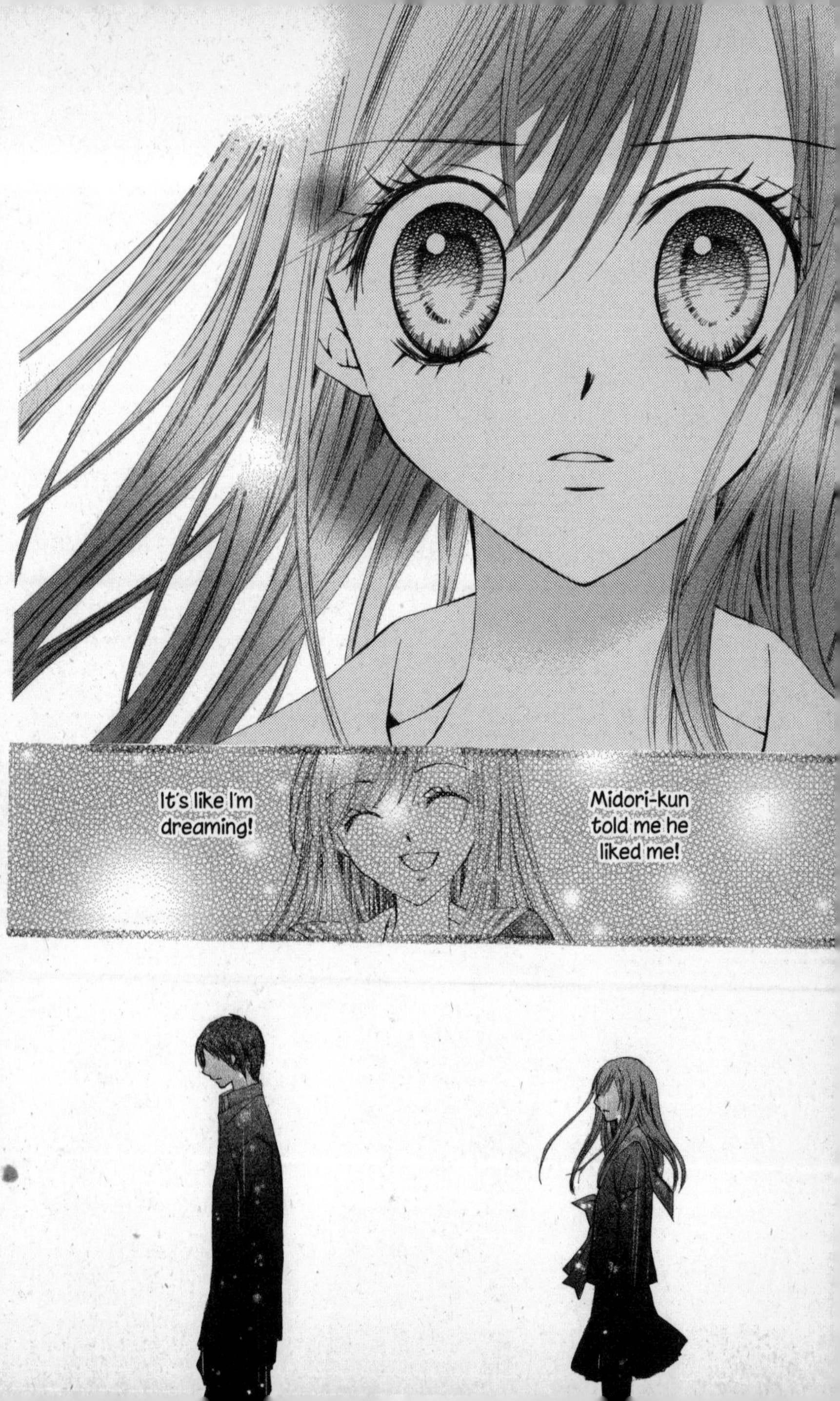
Midori-kun told me he liked me!
It's like I'm dreaming!

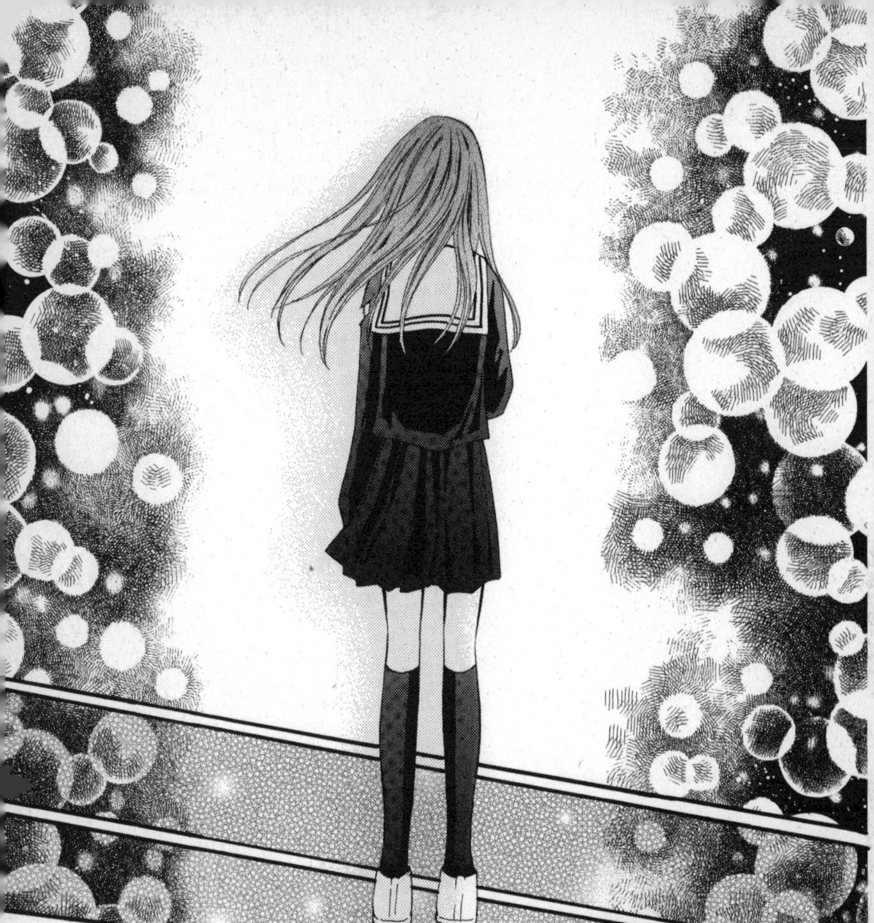

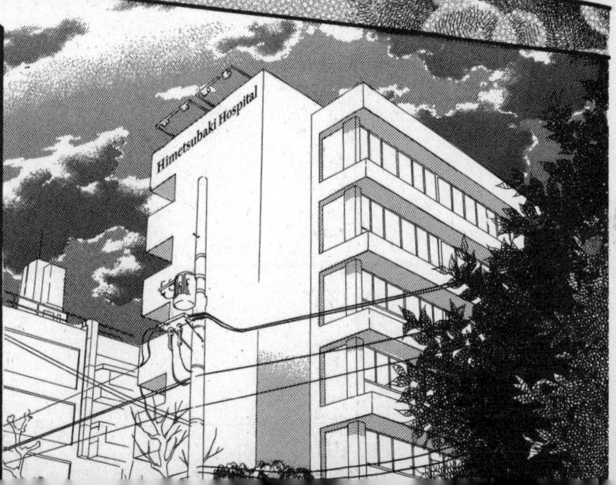
Himetsubaki Hospital

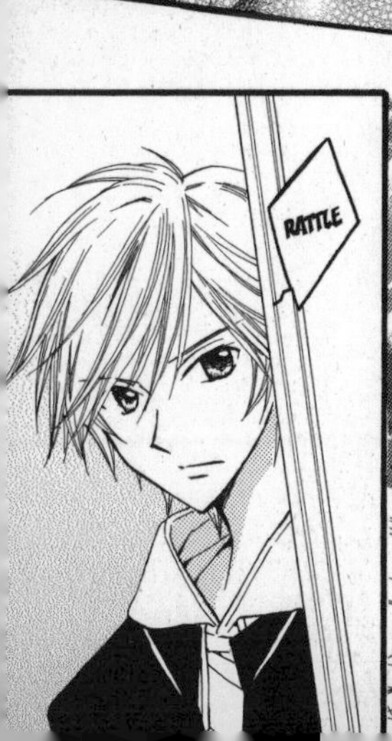
RATTLE

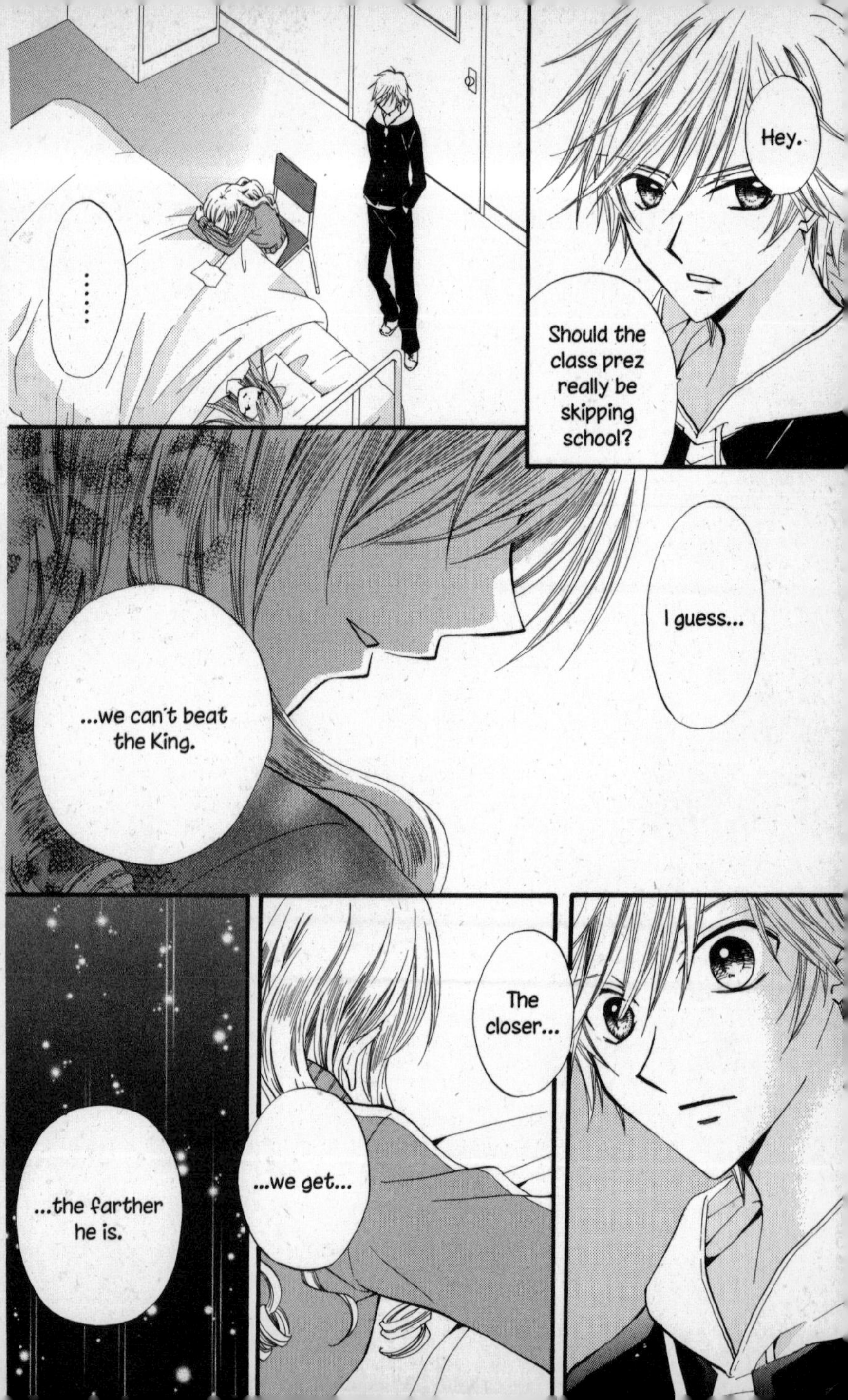
Hey.
Should the class prez really be skipping school?
......
I guess...
...we can't beat the King.
The closer...
...we get...
...the farther he is.

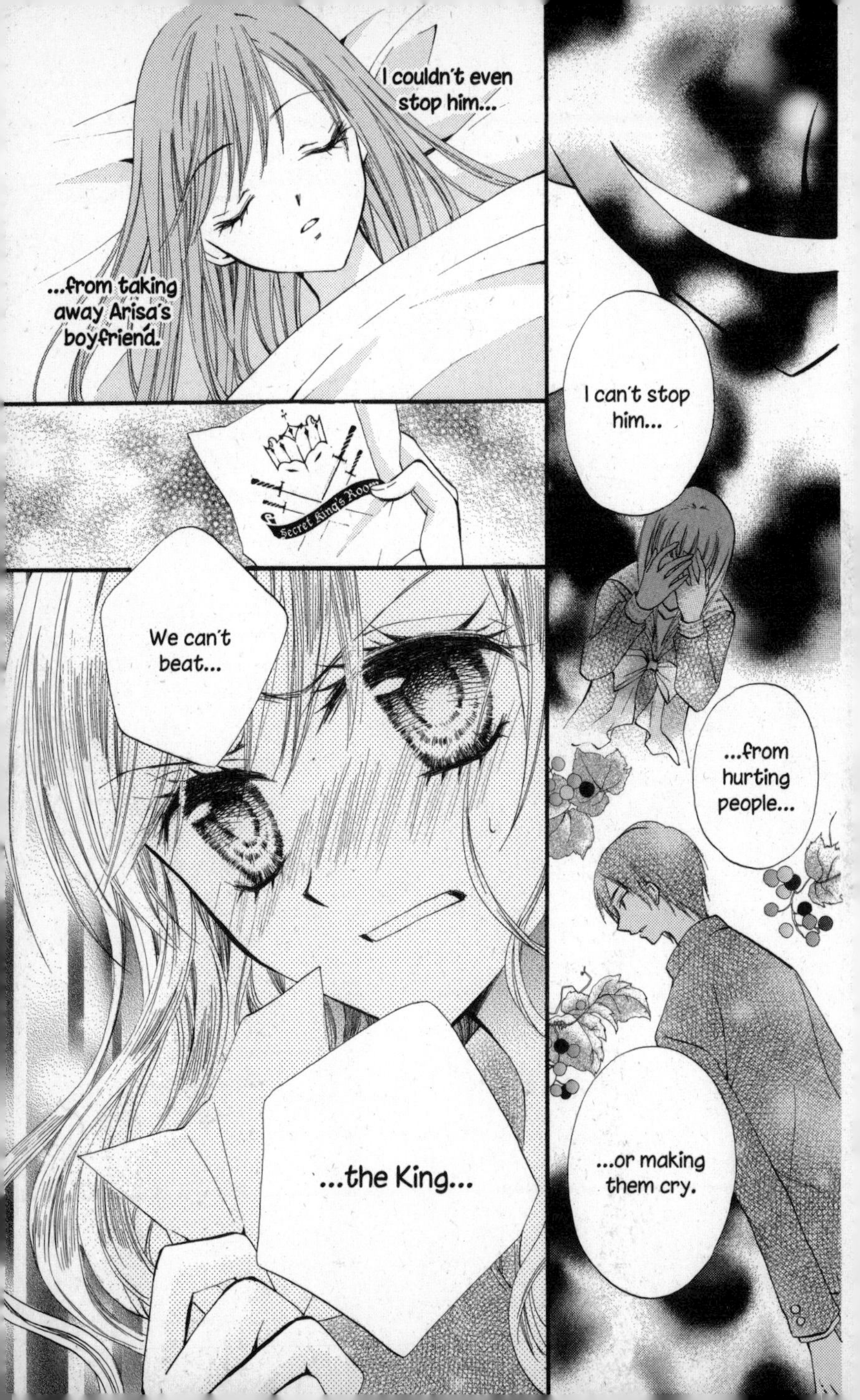

I can't stop him...
...from hurting people...
...or making them cry.
I couldn't even stop him...
...from taking away Arisa's boyfriend.
Secret King's Roo
We can't beat...
...the King...

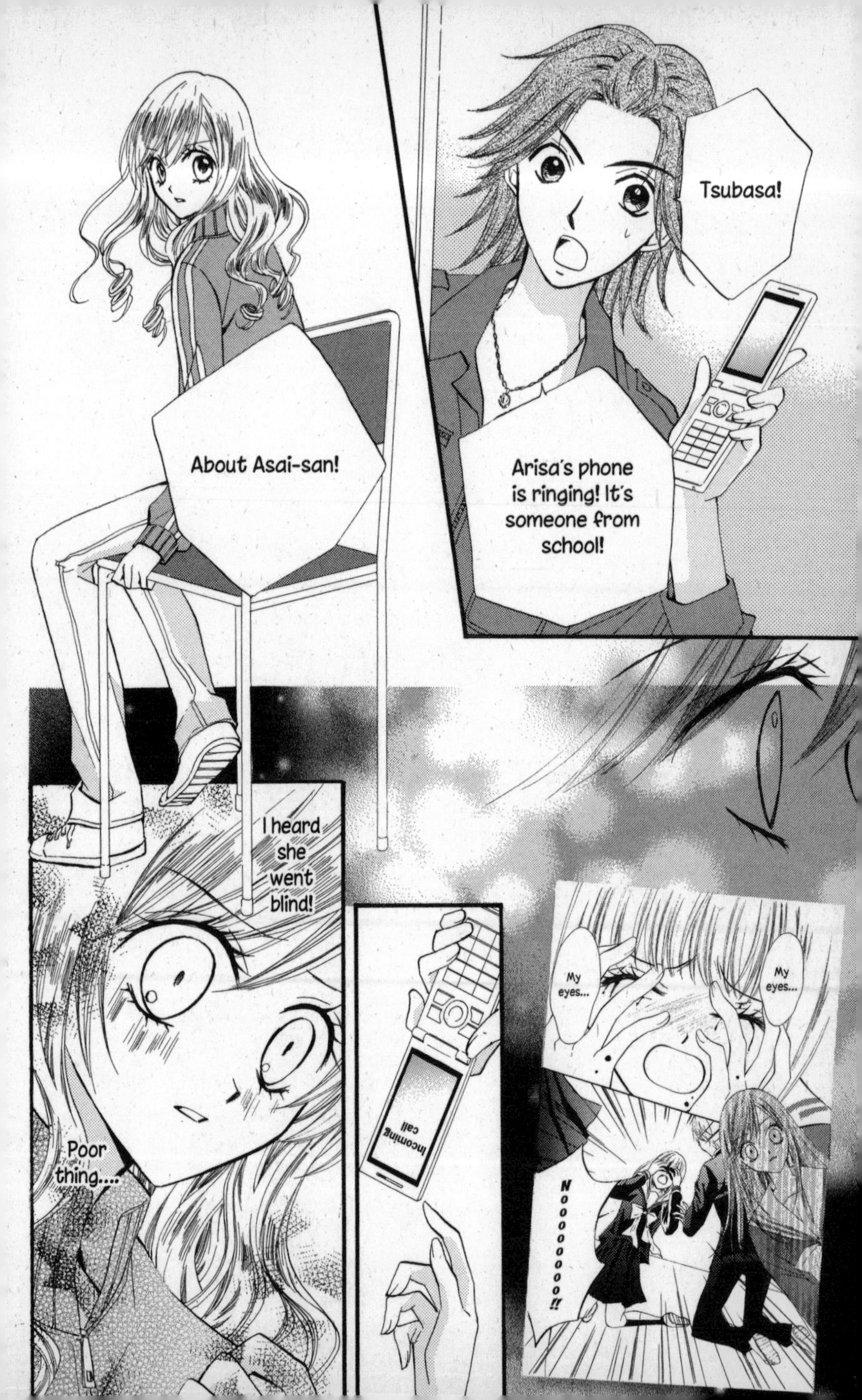
Tsubasa!
Arisa's phone is ringing! It's someone from school!
About Asai-san!
My eyes...
My eyes...
Nooooooooo!!
Incoming call
I heard she went blind!
Poor thing....

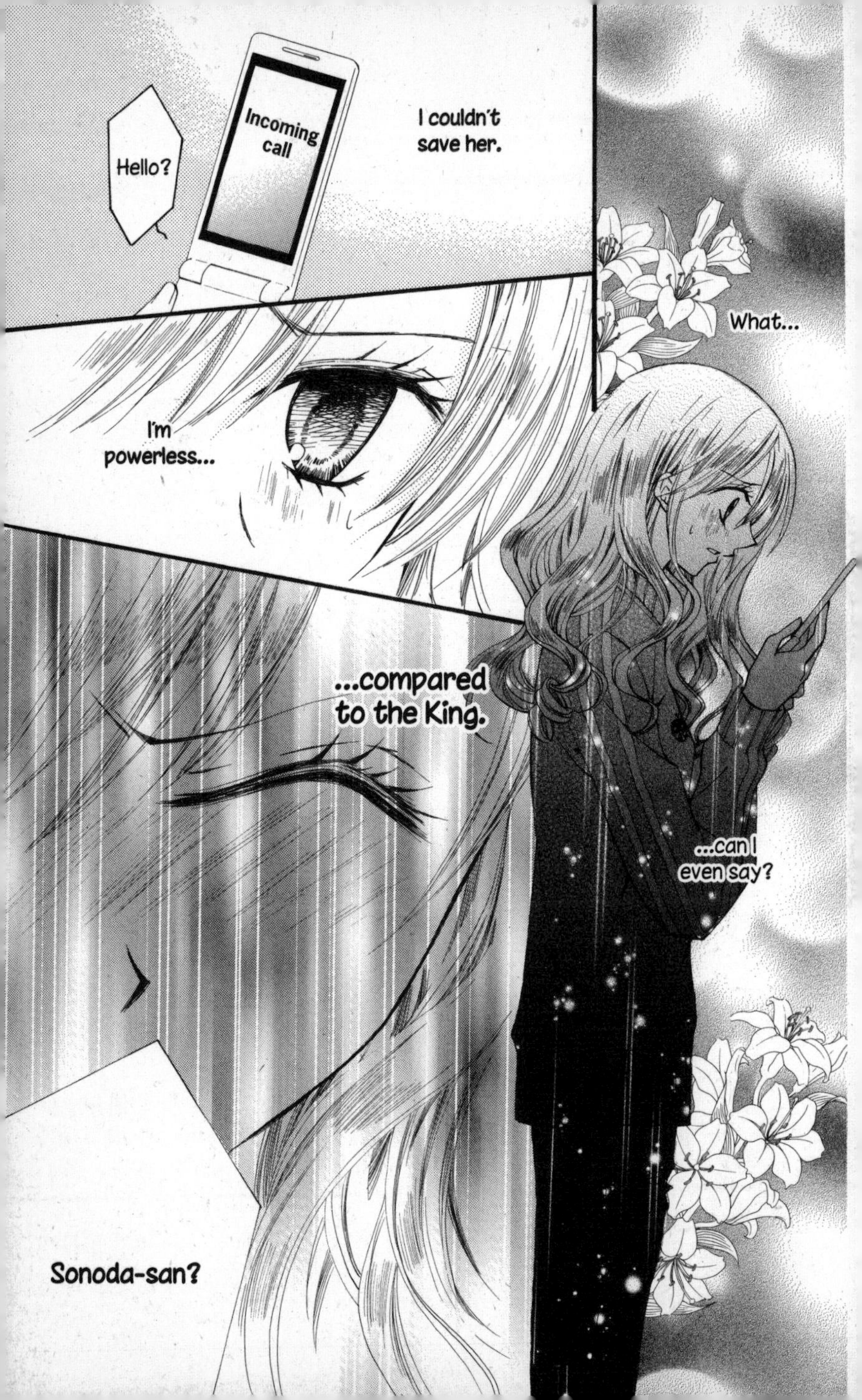
What...
...can I even say?
I couldn't save her.
Incoming call
Hello?
I'm powerless...
...compared to the King.
Sonoda-san?

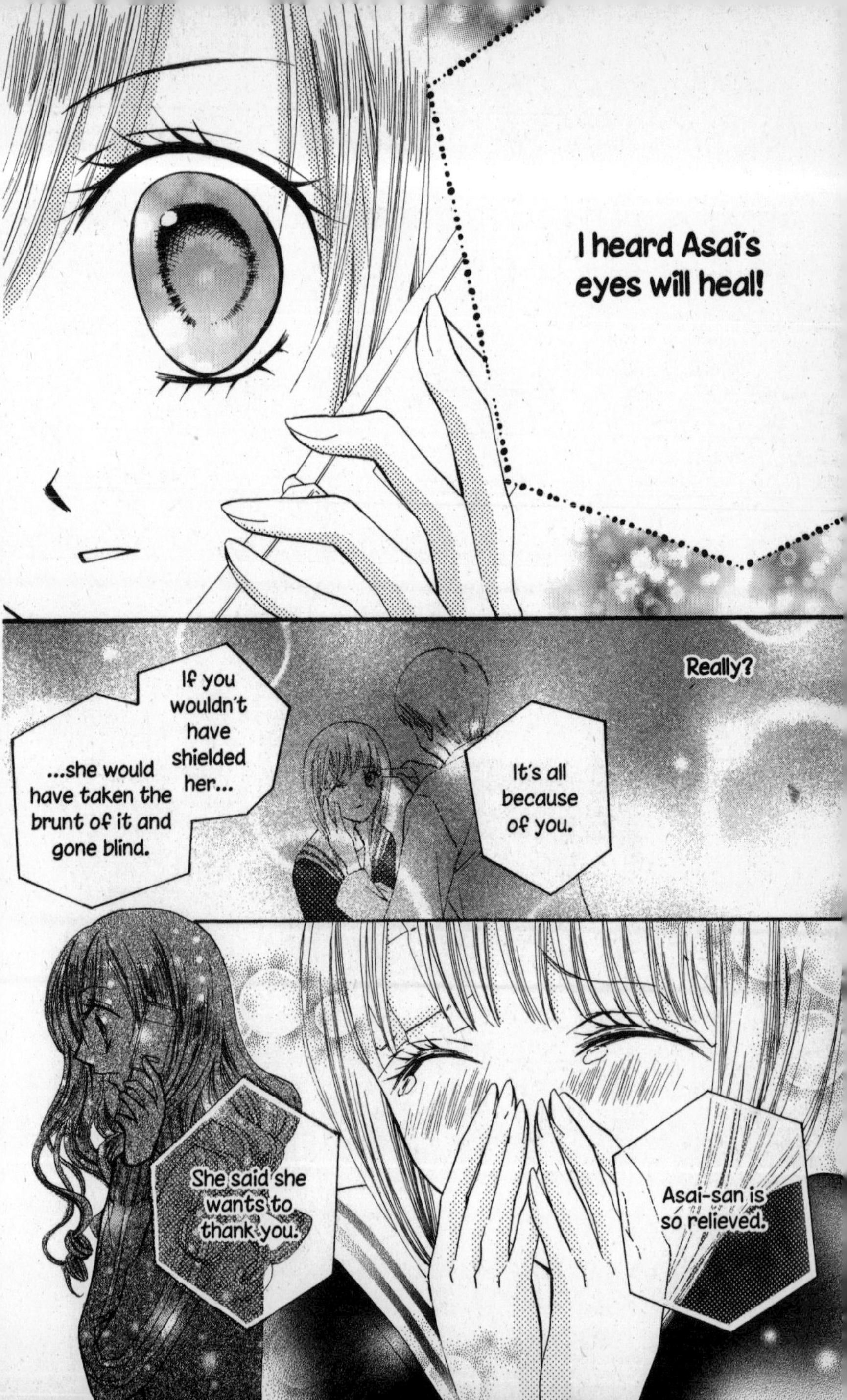
I heard Asai's eyes will heal!
Really?
It's all because of you.
If you wouldn't have shielded her...
...she would have taken the brunt of it and gone blind.
Asai-san is so relieved.
She said she wants to thank you.

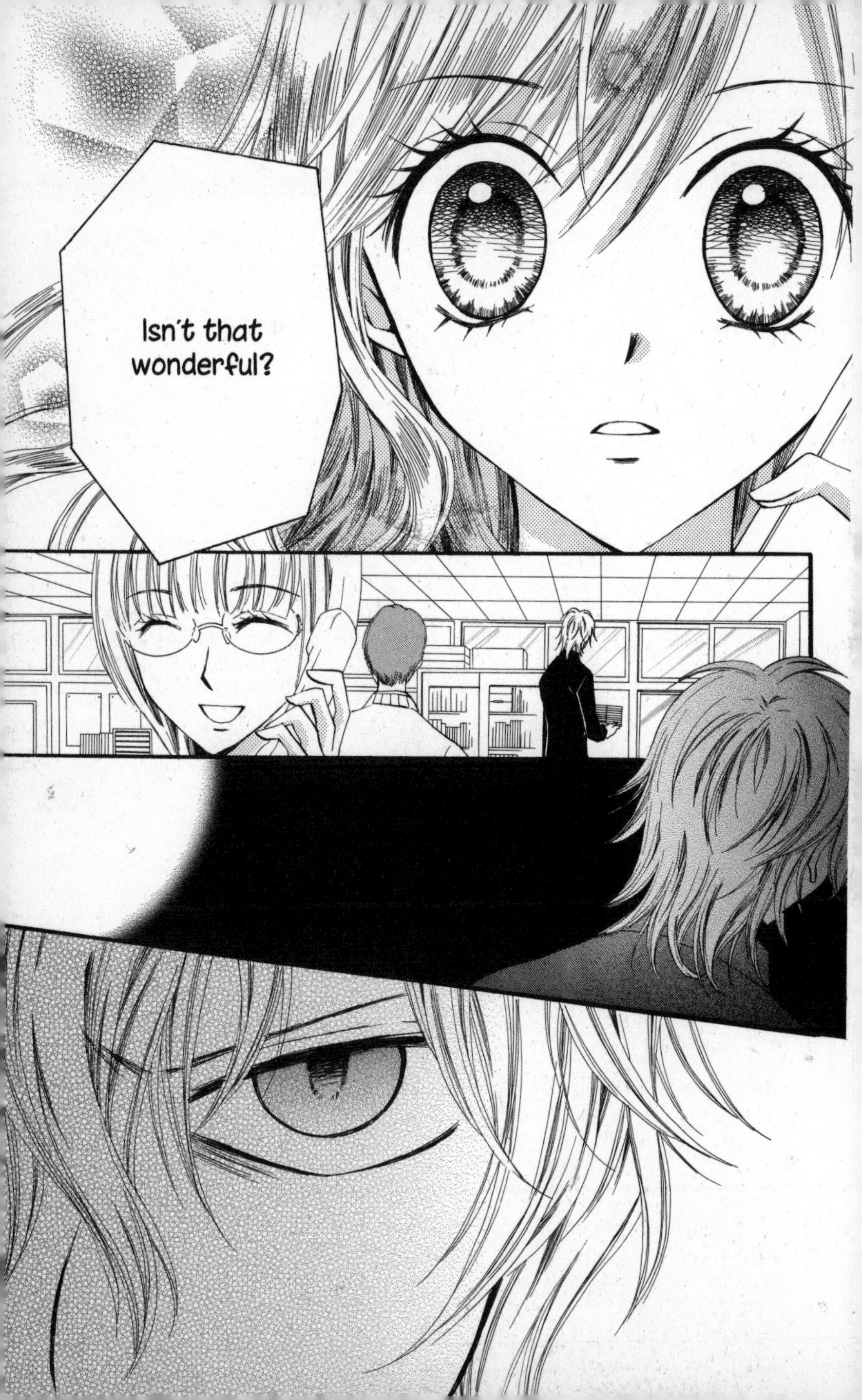
Isn't that wonderful?

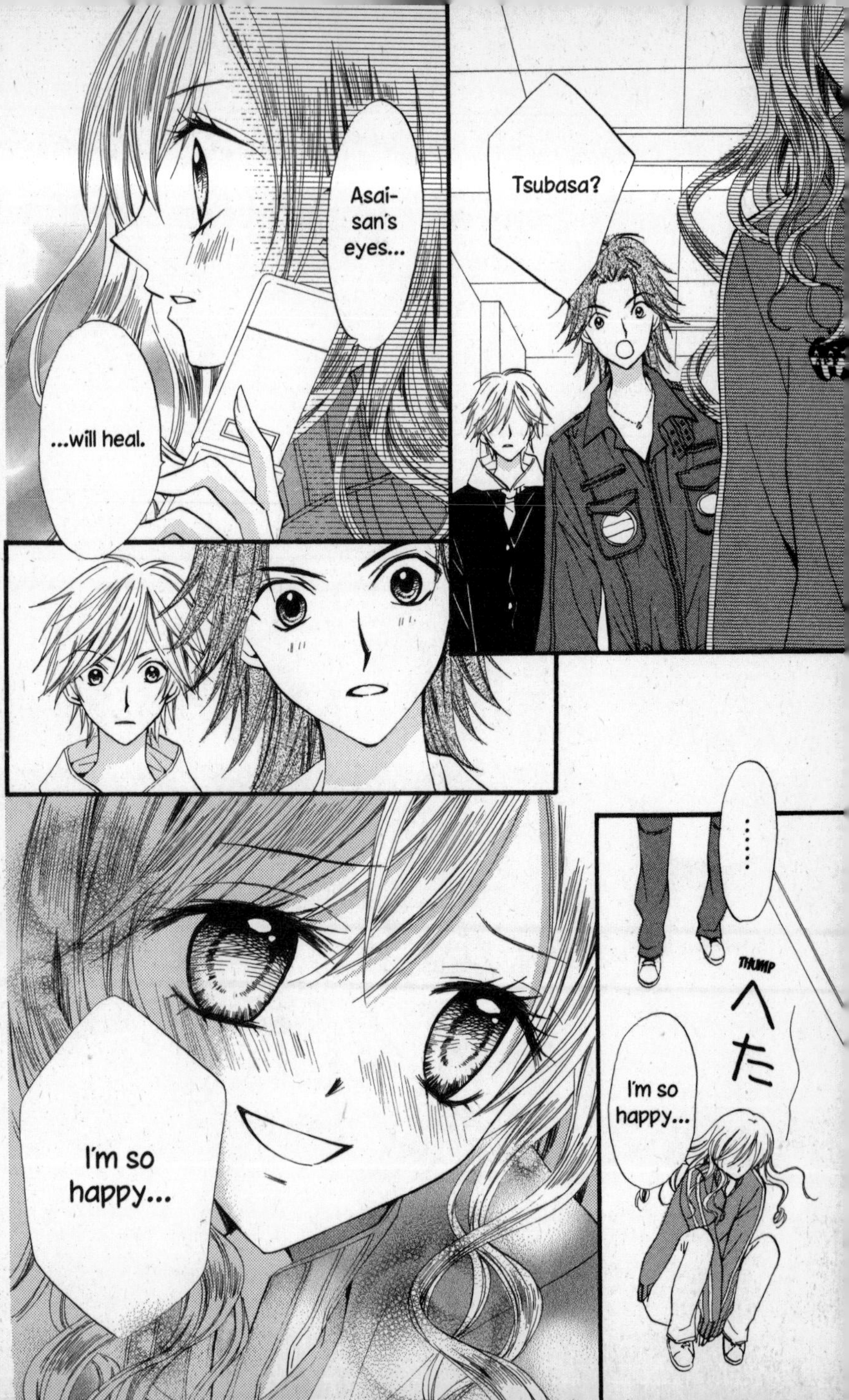
Tsubasa?
Asai-san's eyes...
...will heal.
......
THUMP
へた
I'm so happy...
I'm so happy...

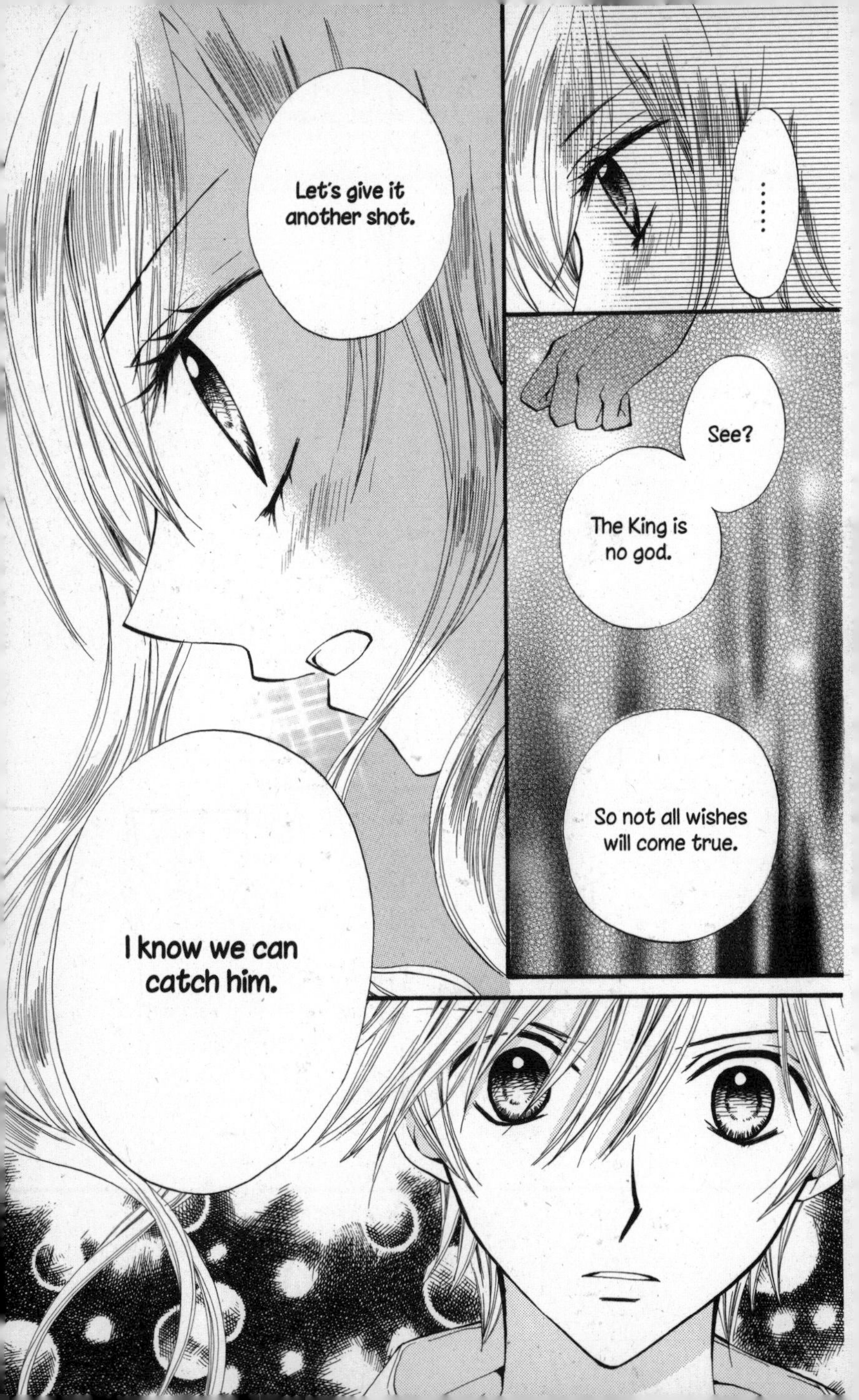
......
See?
The King is no god.
So not all wishes will come true.
Let's give it another shot.
I know we can catch him.

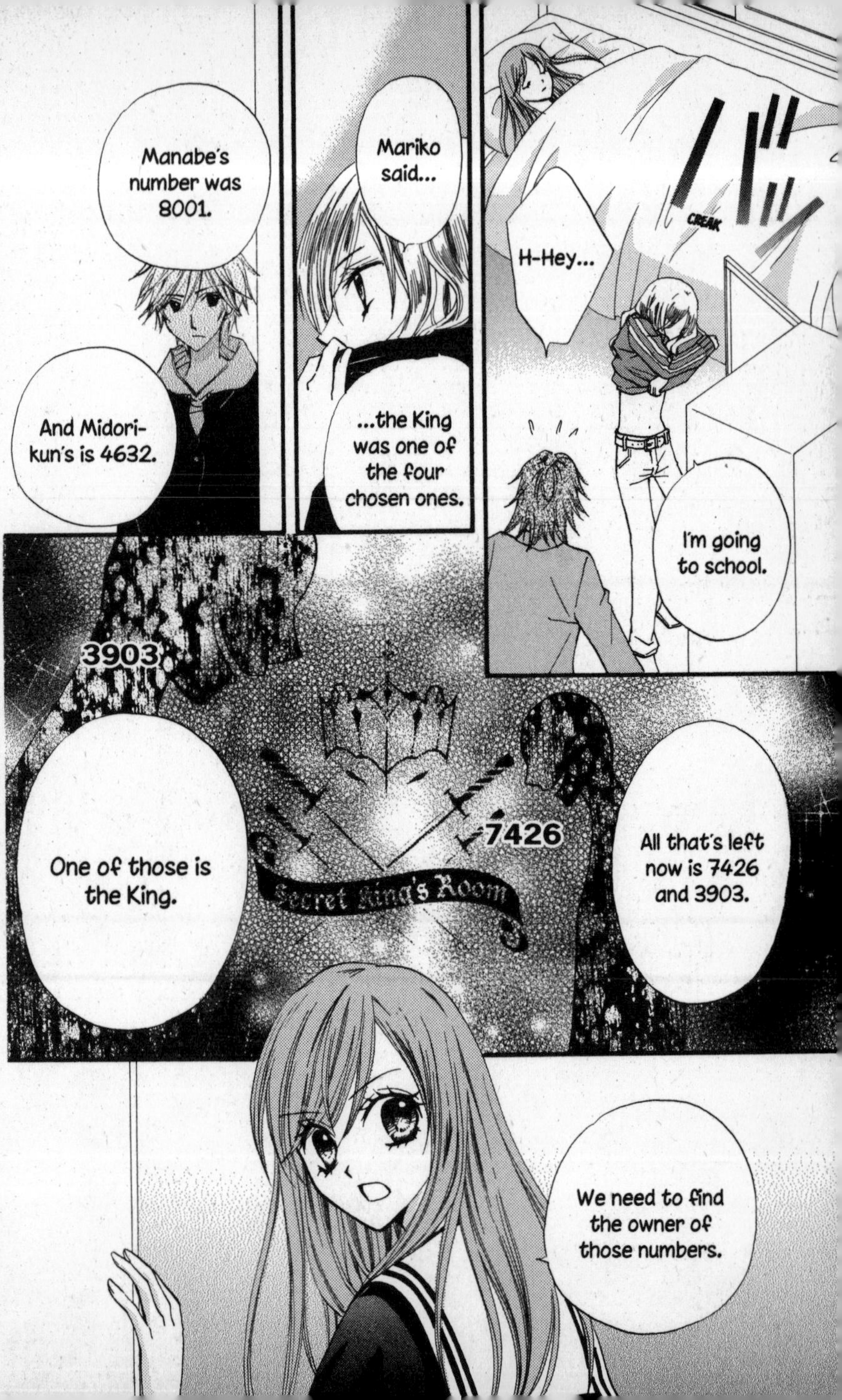
CREAK
H-Hey...
I'm going to school.
Mariko said...
...the King was one of the four chosen ones.
Manabe's number was 8001.
And Midori-kun's is 4632.
All that's left now is 7426 and 3903.
7426
3903
Secret King's Room
One of those is the King.
We need to find the owner of those numbers.

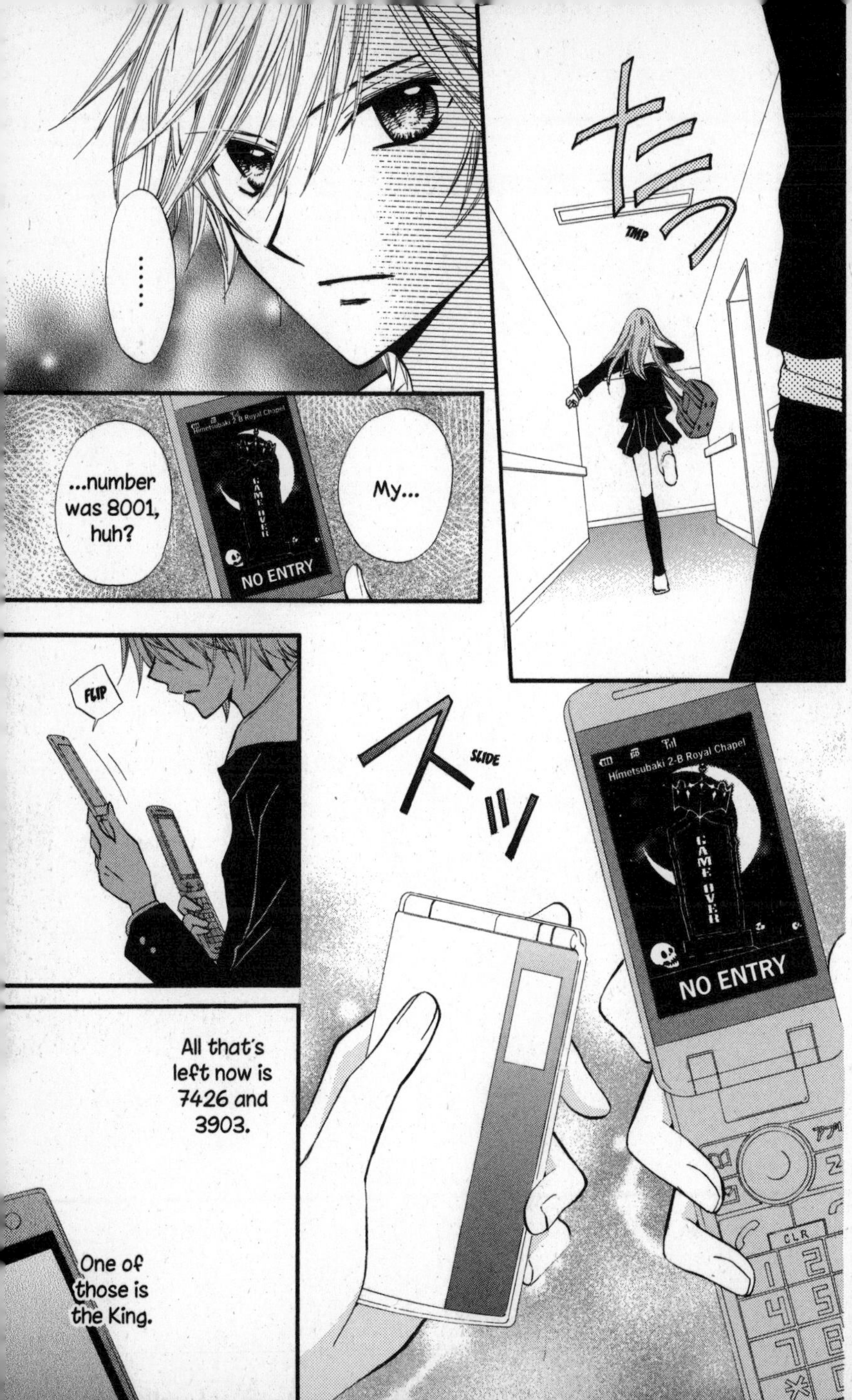
TMP
......
My...
...number was 8001, huh?
Himetsubaki 2-B Royal Chapel
GAME OVER
NO ENTRY
SLIDE
Himetsubaki 2-B Royal Chapel
GAME OVER
NO ENTRY
FLIP
All that's left now is 7426 and 3903.
One of those is the King.

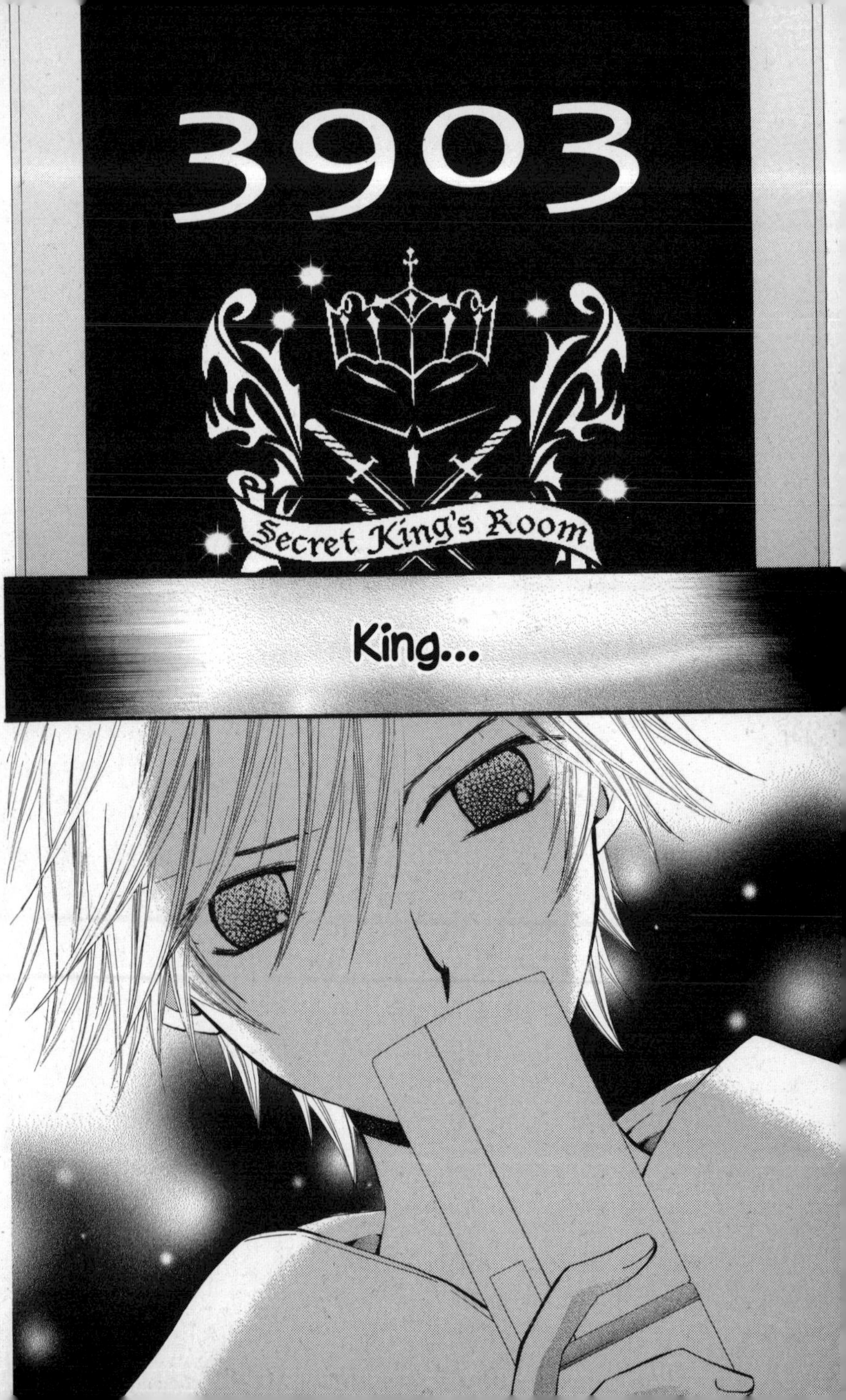
3903
Secret King's Room
King...

Chapter 15

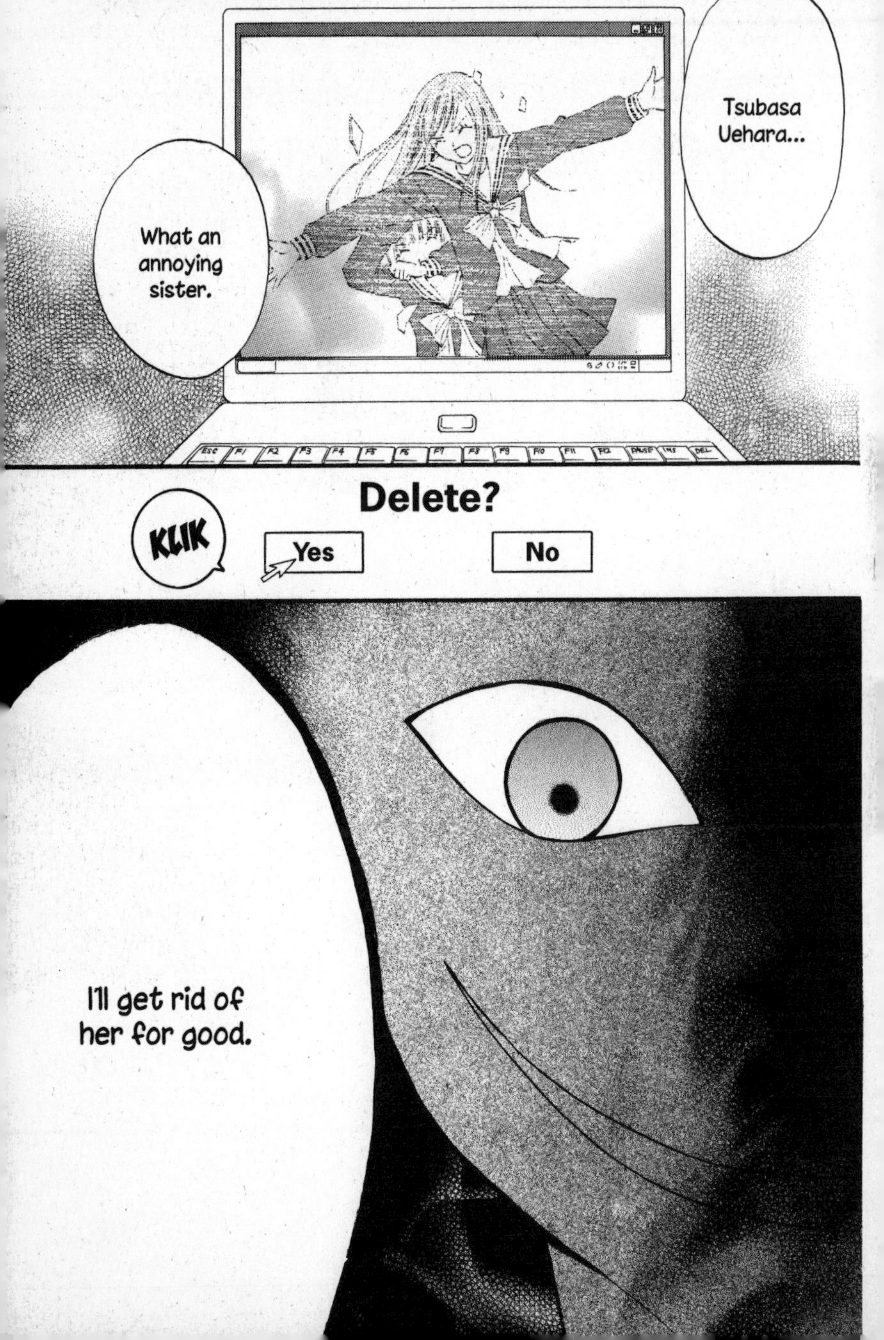

Tsubasa Uehara...
What an annoying sister.
Delete?
No
Yes
KLIK
I'll get rid of her for good.

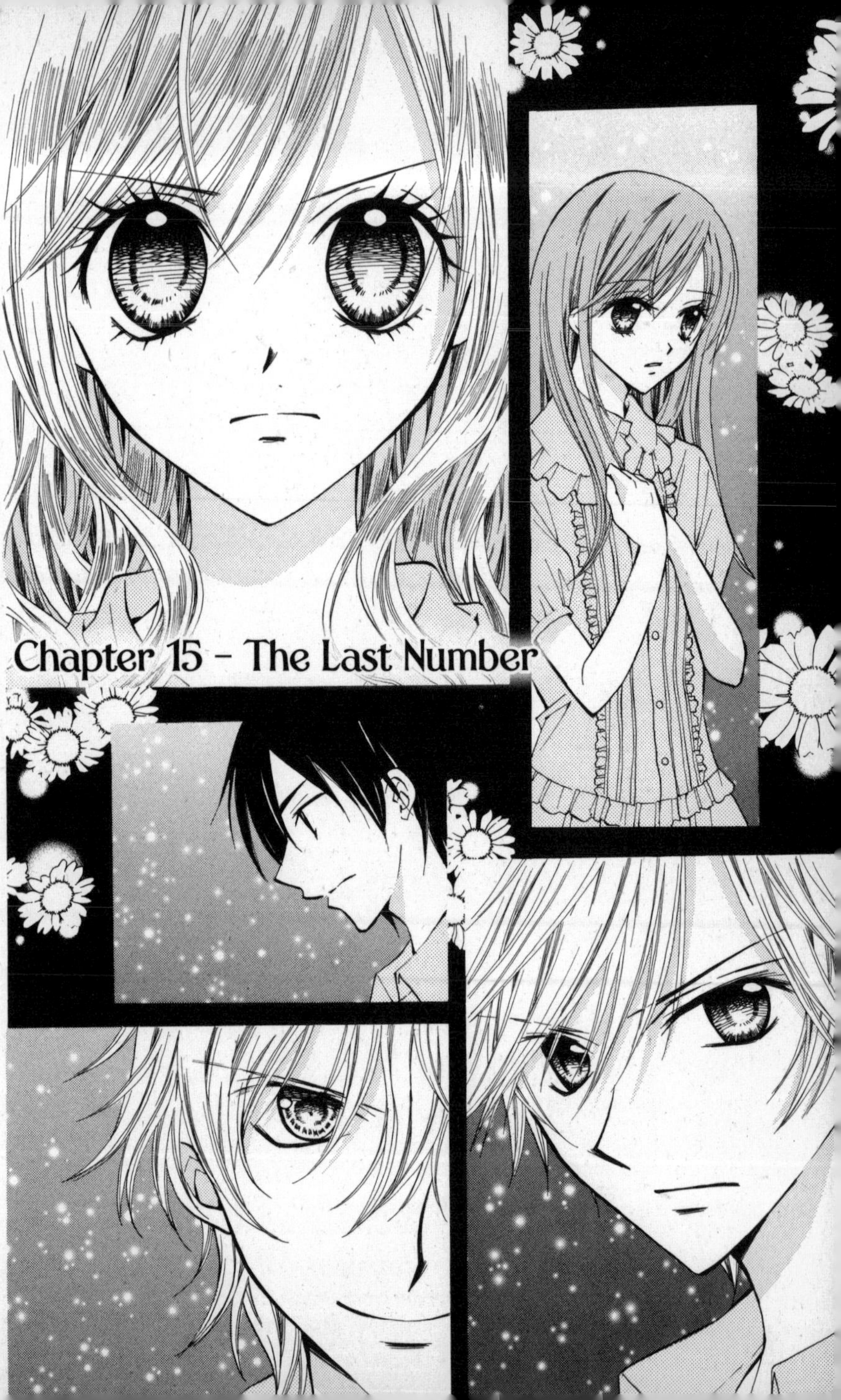
Chapter 15 - The Last Number

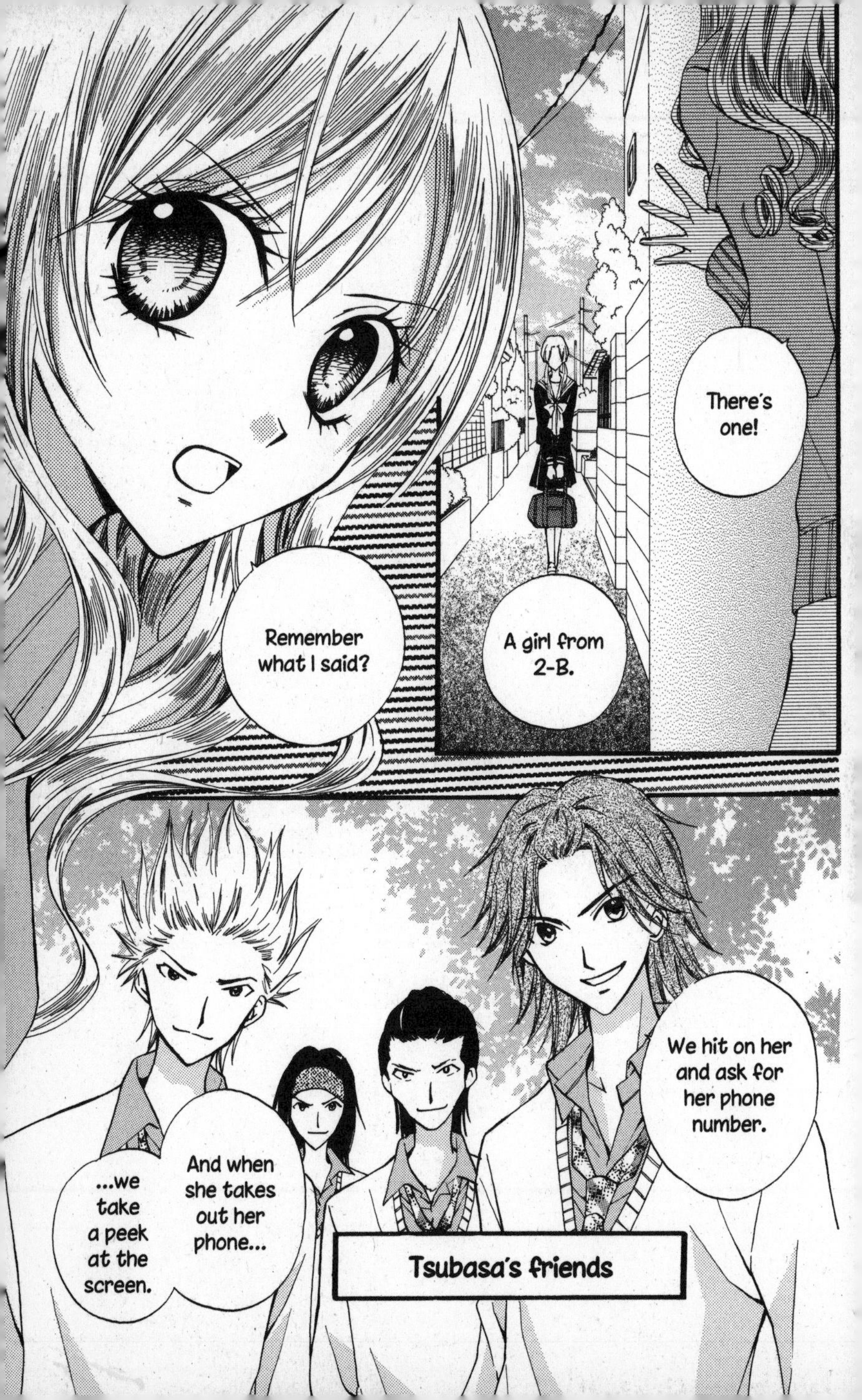
There's one!
A girl from 2-B.
Remember what I said?
We hit on her and ask for her phone number.
And when she takes out her phone...
...we take a peek at the screen.
Tsubasa's friends

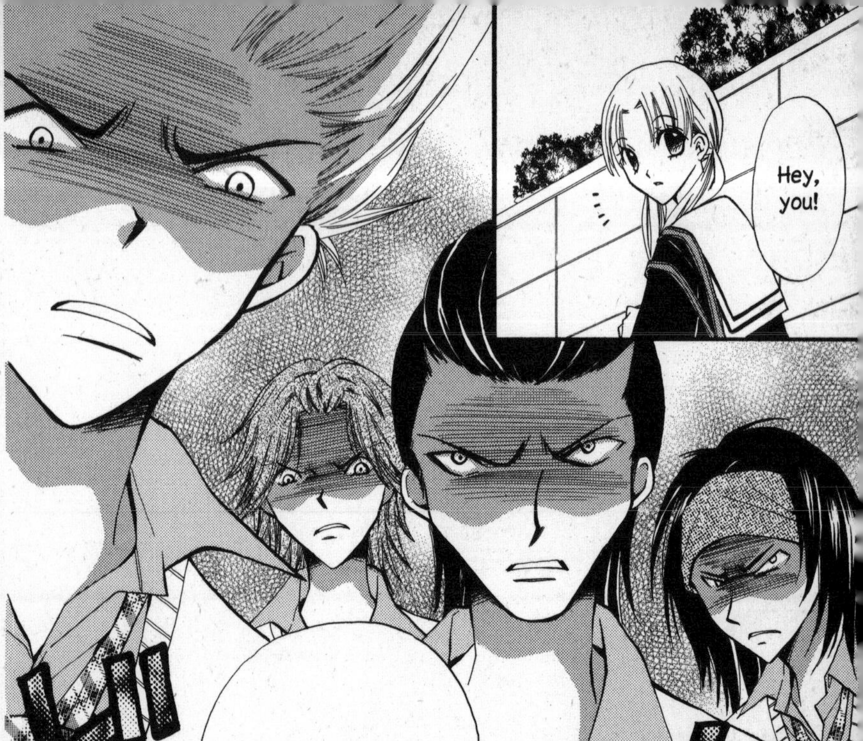
Hey, you!
DUUUNN
You wanna talk?

BEHIND THE SCENES

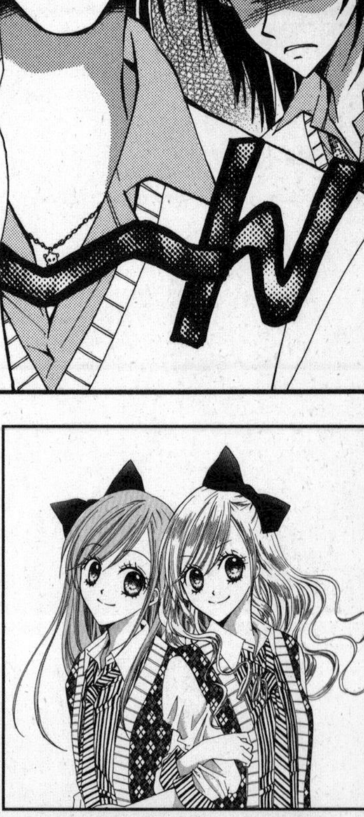

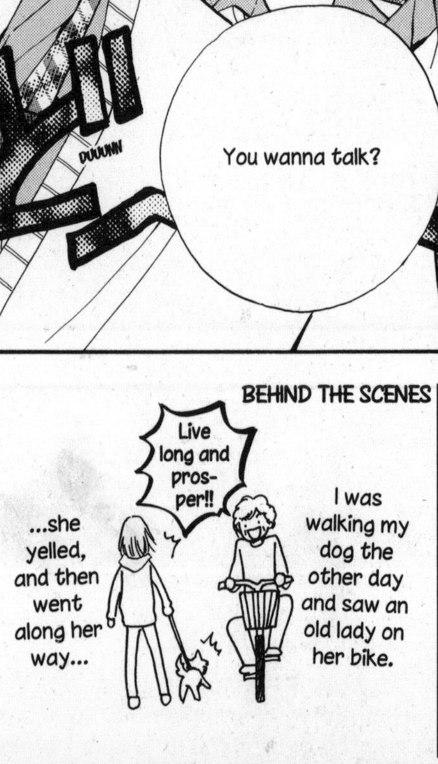
I was walking my dog the other day and saw an old lady on her bike.
Live long and prosper!!
...she yelled, and then went along her way...

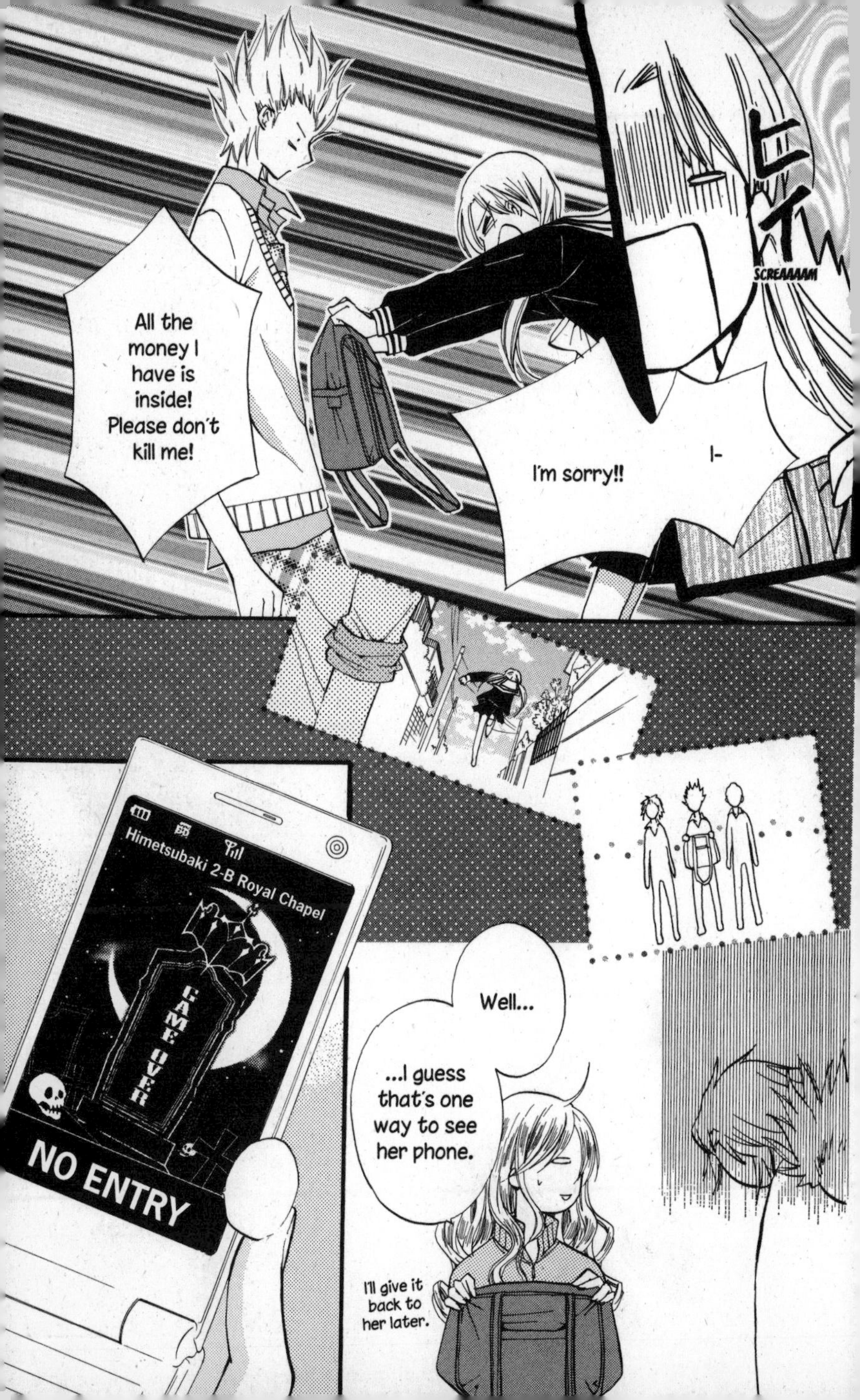
SCREAAAAM
I-
I'm sorry!!
All the money I have is inside! Please don't kill me!
Well...
...I guess that's one way to see her phone.
I'll give it back to her later.
Himetsubaki 2-B Royal Chapel
GAME OVER
NO ENTRY

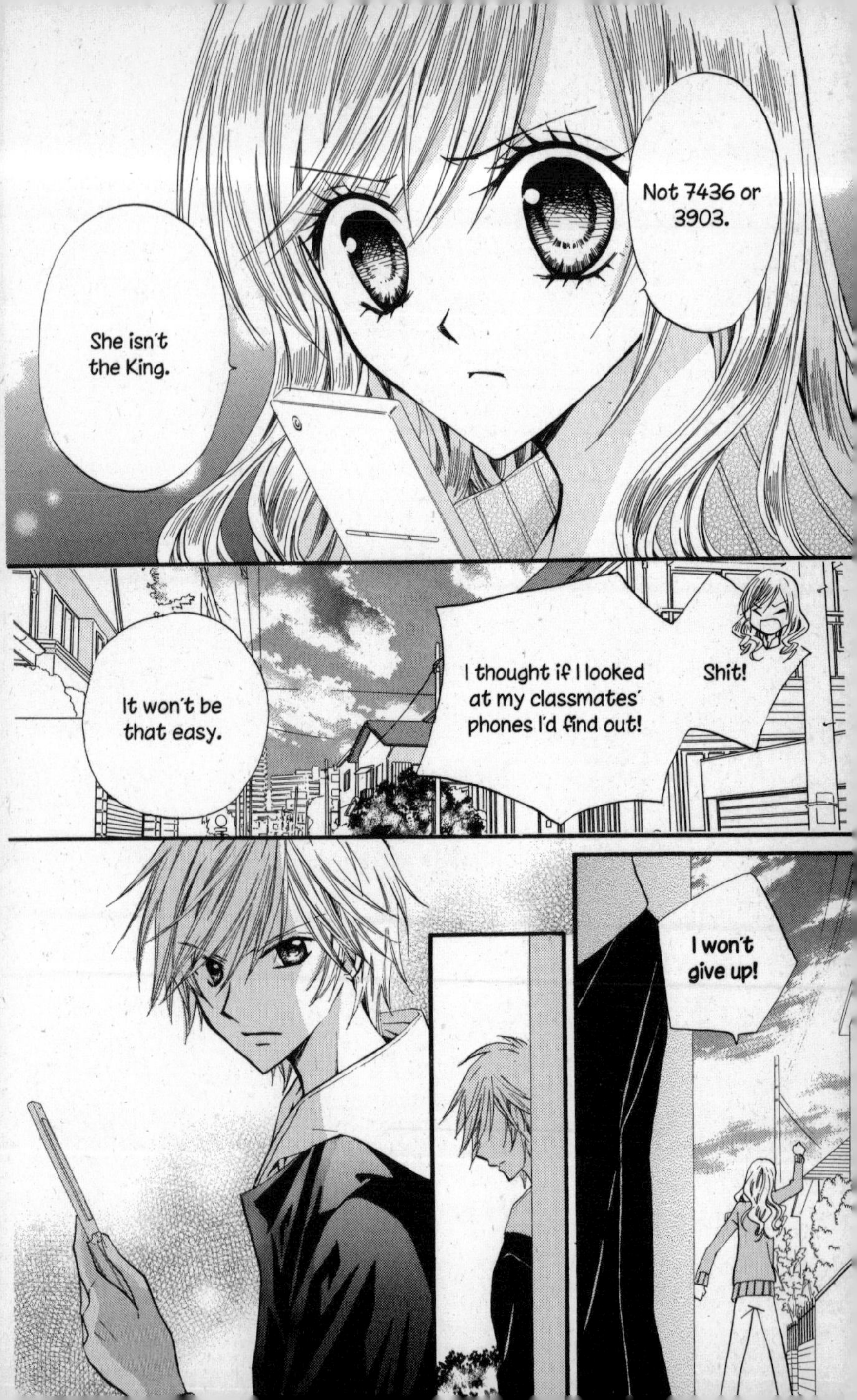
Not 7436 or 3903.
She isn't the King.
Shit!
I thought if I looked at my classmates' phones I'd find out!
It won't be that easy.
I won't give up!

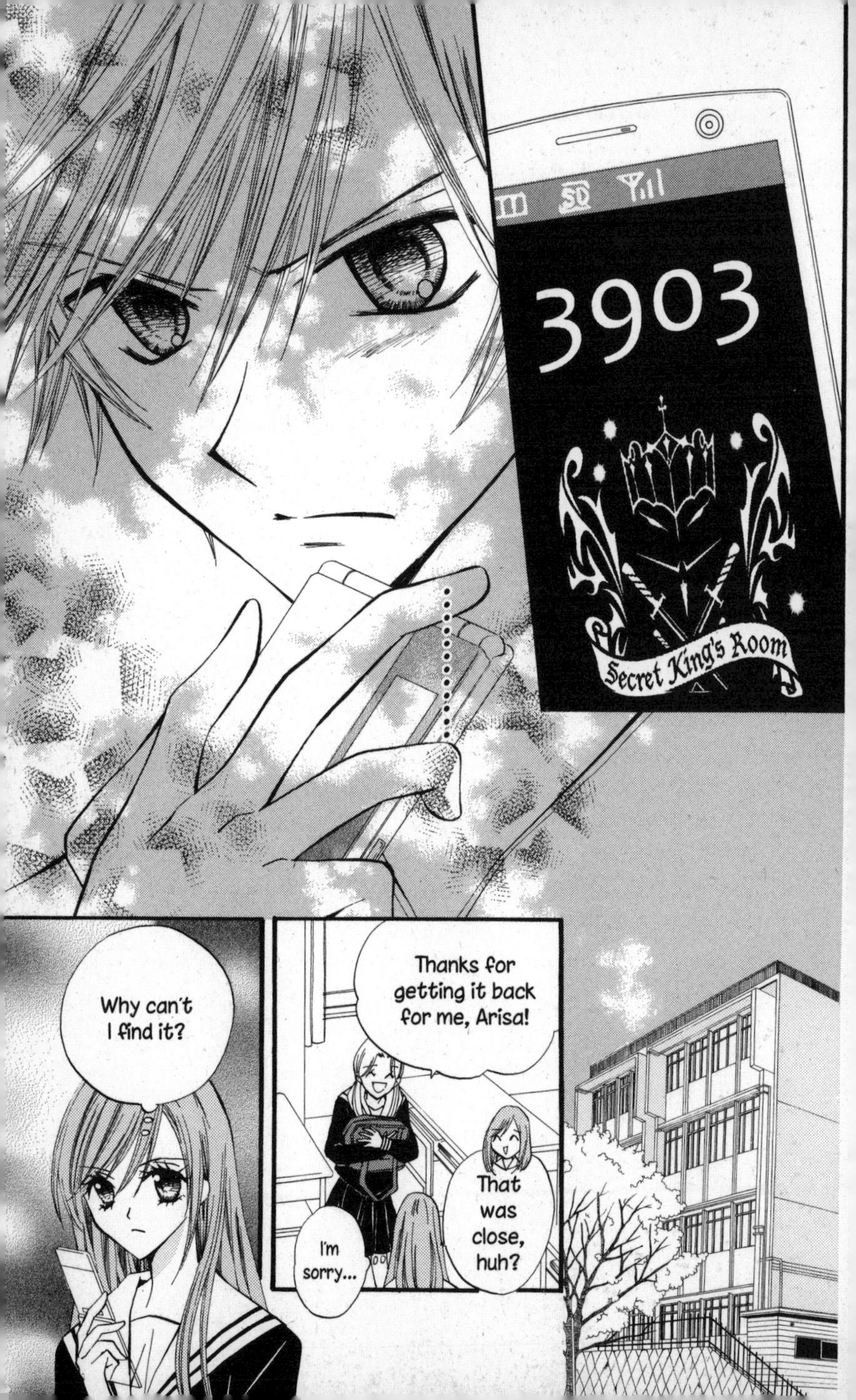
3903
Secret King's Room
Thanks for getting it back for me, Arisa!
That was close, huh?
I'm sorry...
Why can't I find it?

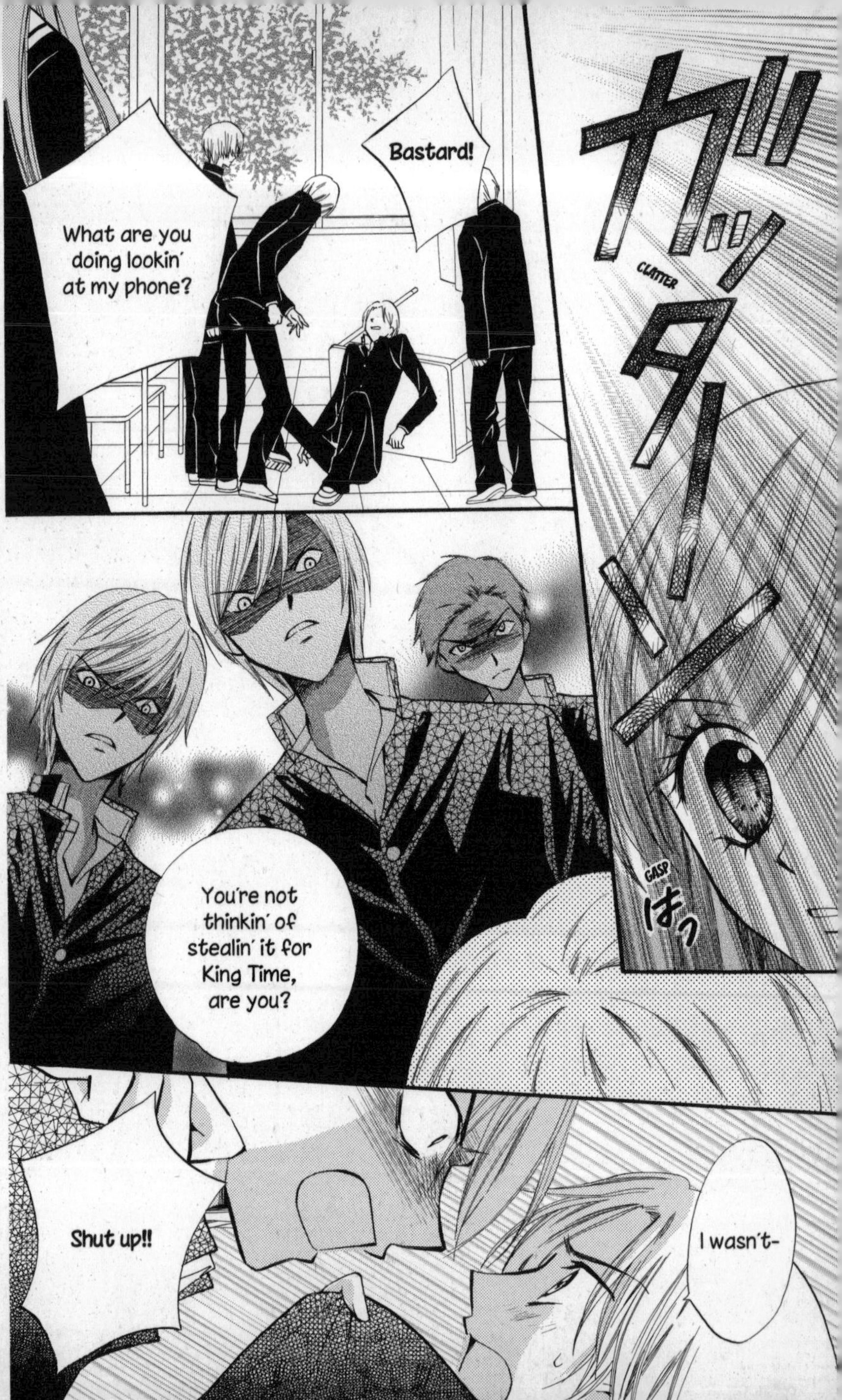
ガタッ
CLATTER
GASP
はっ
Bastard!
What are you doing lookin' at my phone?
You're not thinkin' of stealin' it for King Time, are you?
I wasn't-
Shut up!!

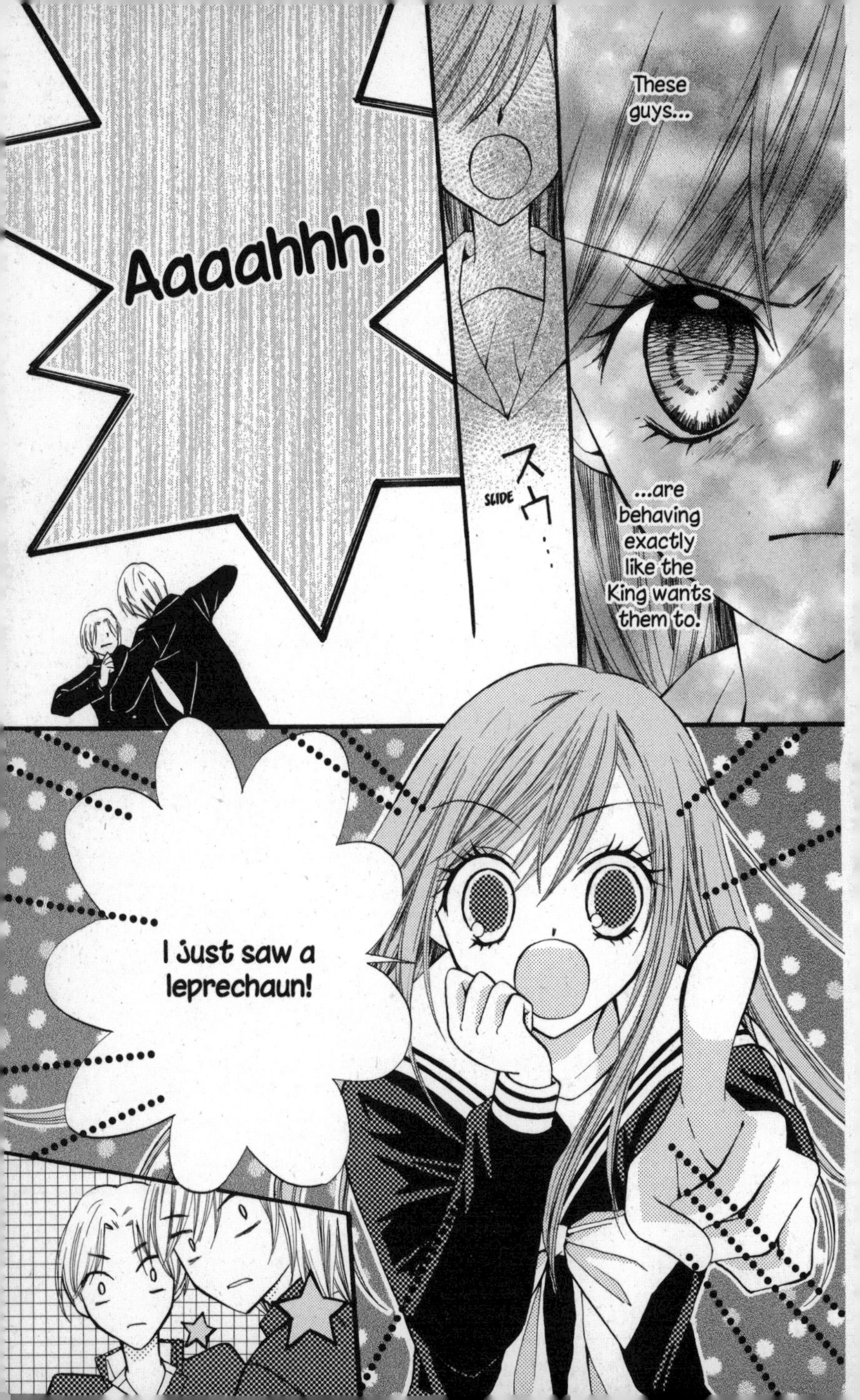
These guys...
...are behaving exactly like the King wants them to.
SLIDE
スゥ…
Aaaahhh!
I just saw a leprechaun!

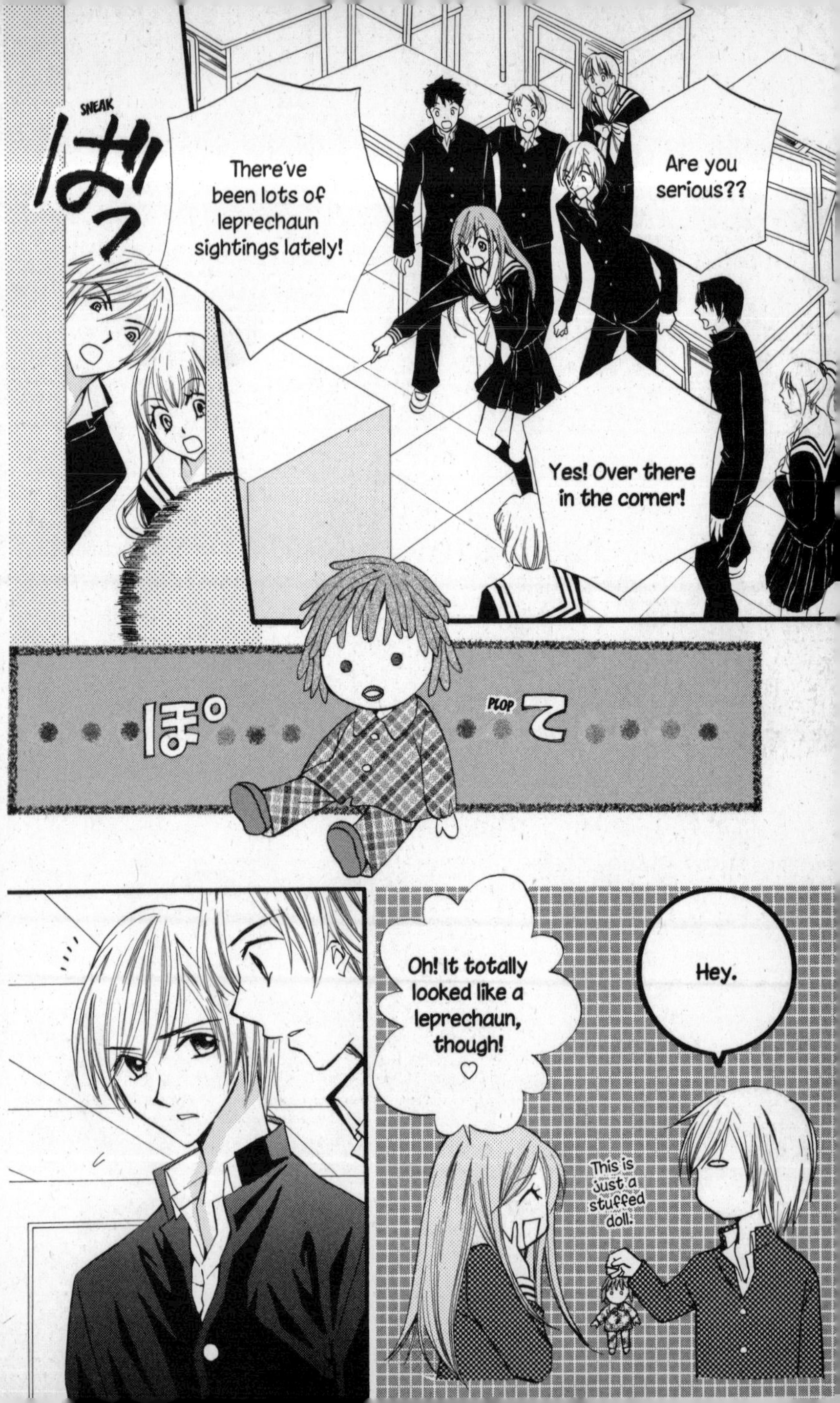
Are you serious??
There've been lots of leprechaun sightings lately!
Yes! Over there in the corner!
SNEAK
ぱっ
・・・ぽ・・・
PLOP
・・て・・・
Hey.
Oh! It totally looked like a leprechaun, though! ♡
This is just a stuffed doll.

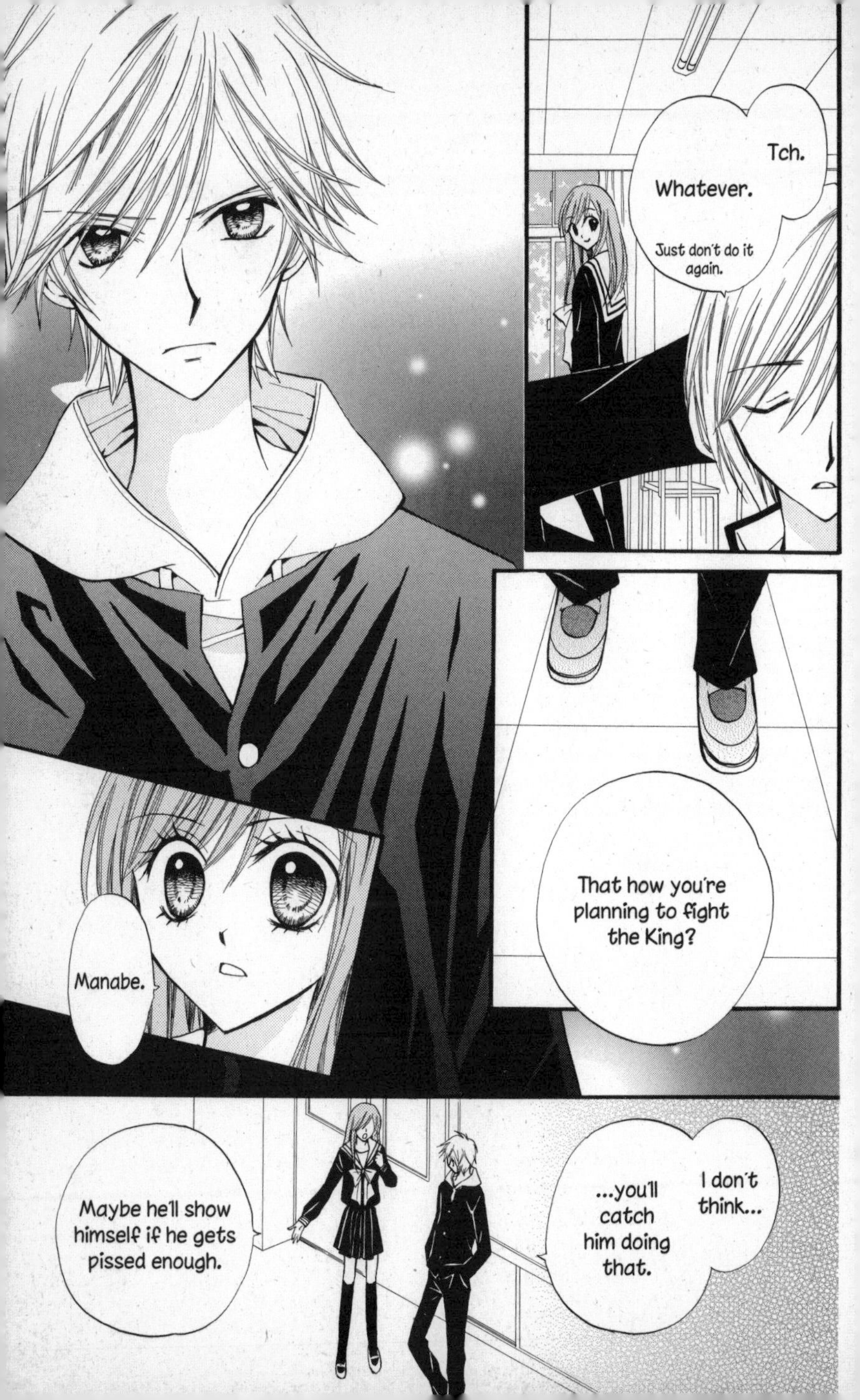

Tch.
Whatever.
Just don't do it again.
That how you're planning to fight the King?
Manabe.
I don't think...
...you'll catch him doing that.
Maybe he'll show himself if he gets pissed enough.

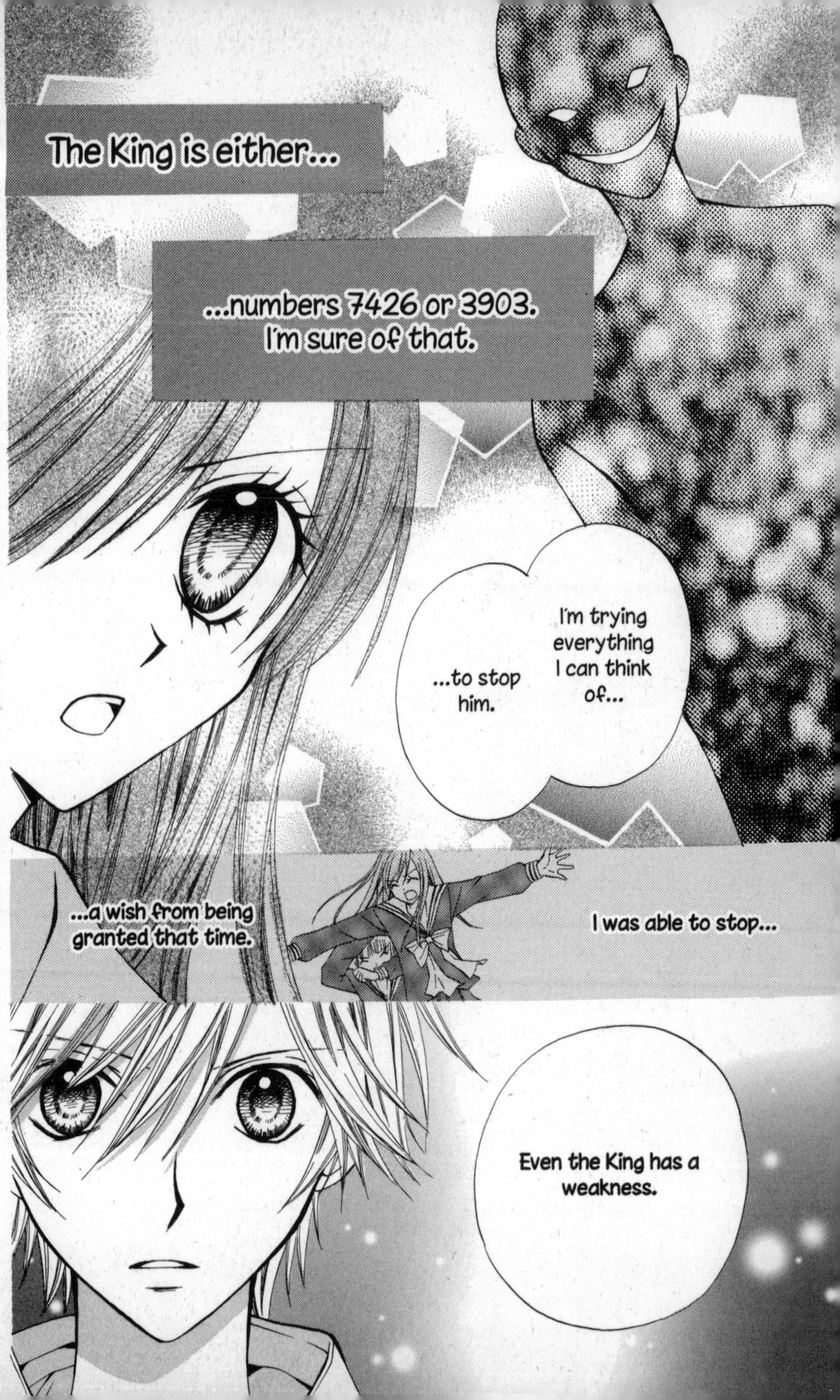
The King is either...
...numbers 7426 or 3903. I'm sure of that.
I'm trying everything I can think of...
...to stop him.
I was able to stop...
...a wish from being granted that time.
Even the King has a weakness.

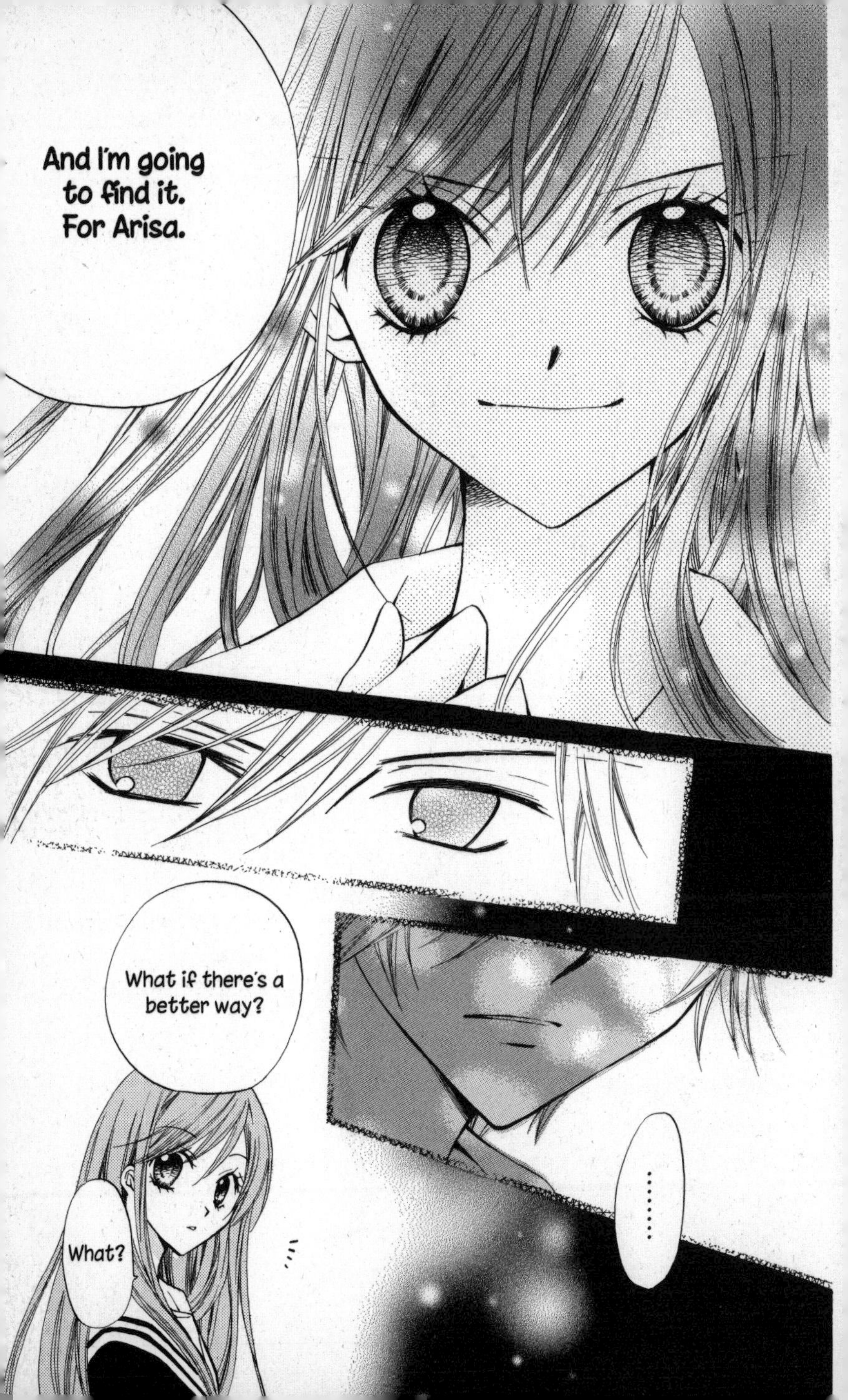
And I'm going to find it. For Arisa.
What if there's a better way?
......
What?

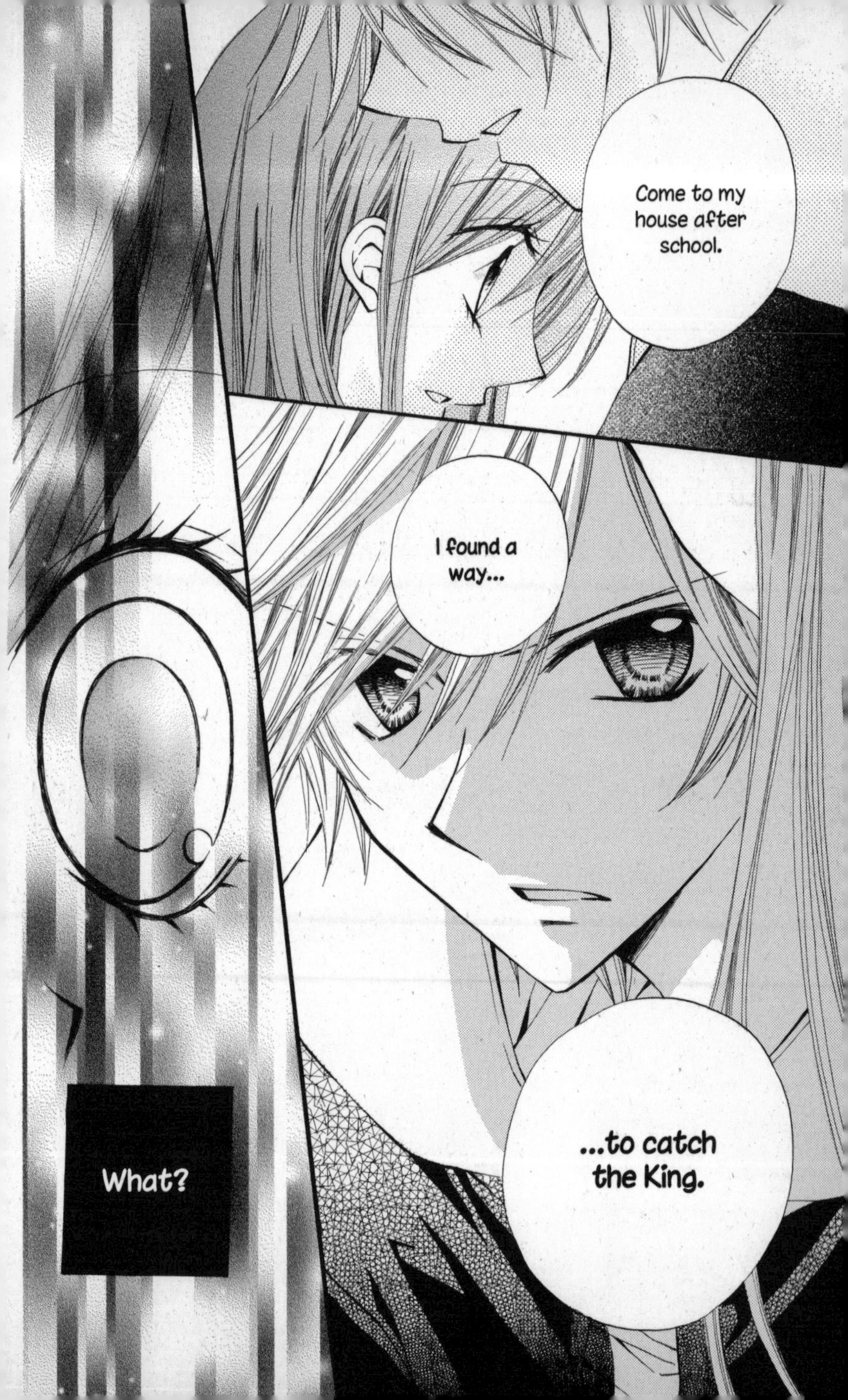
Come to my house after school.
I found a way...
...to catch the King.
What?

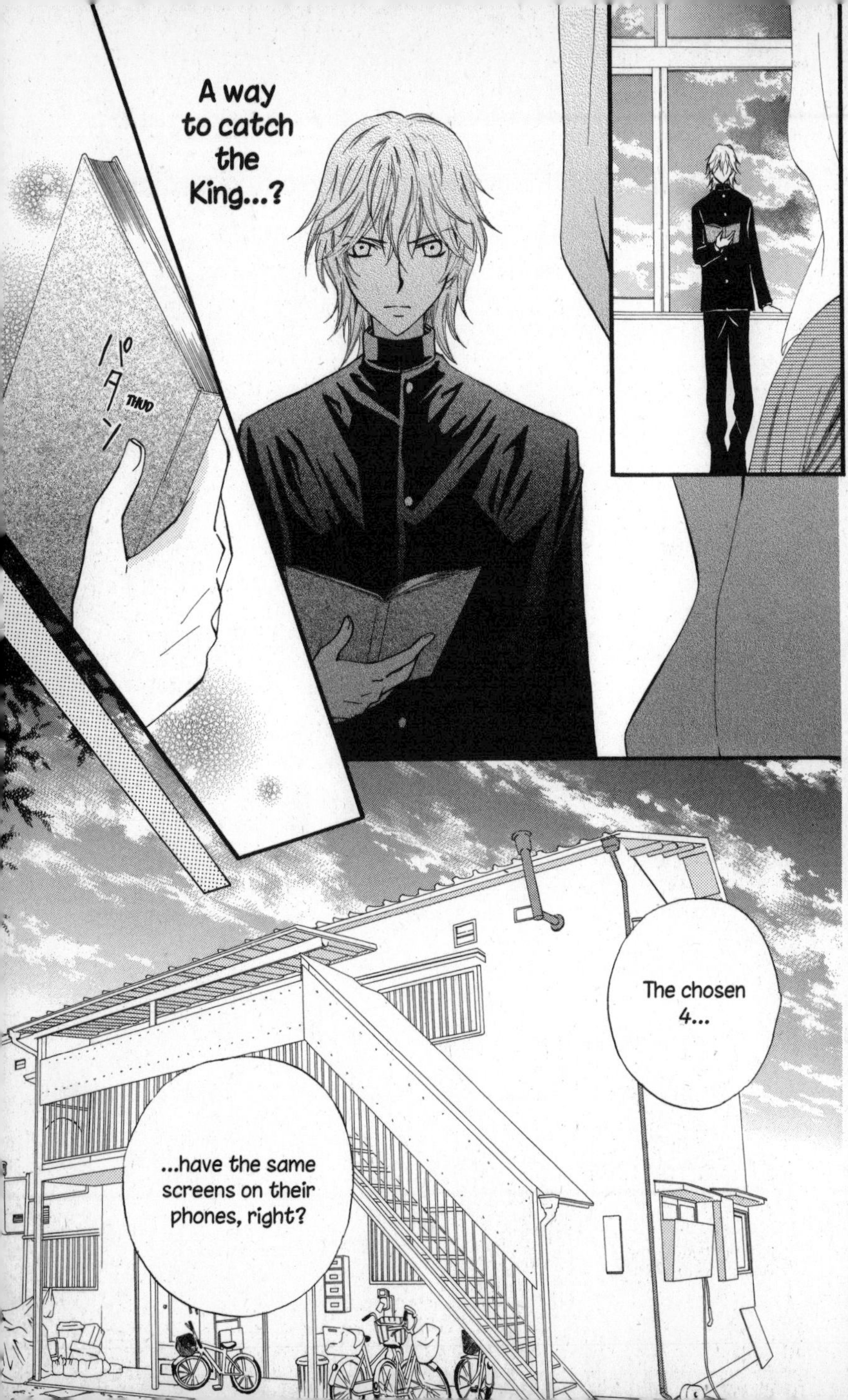
A way to catch the King...?
パタン
THUD
The chosen 4...
...have the same screens on their phones, right?

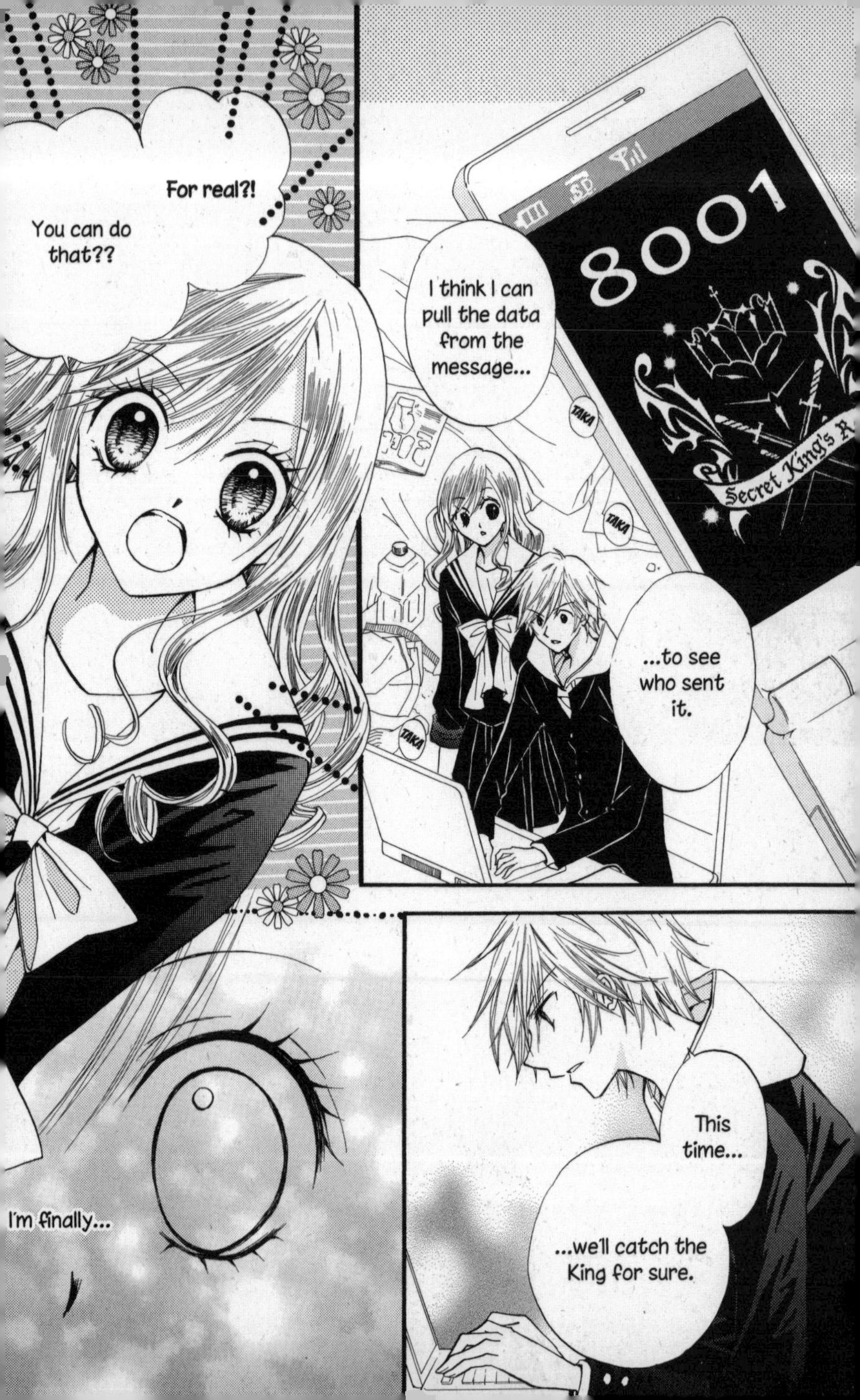
I think I can pull the data from the message...
...to see who sent it.
For real?!
You can do that??
This time...
...we'll catch the King for sure.
I'm finally...

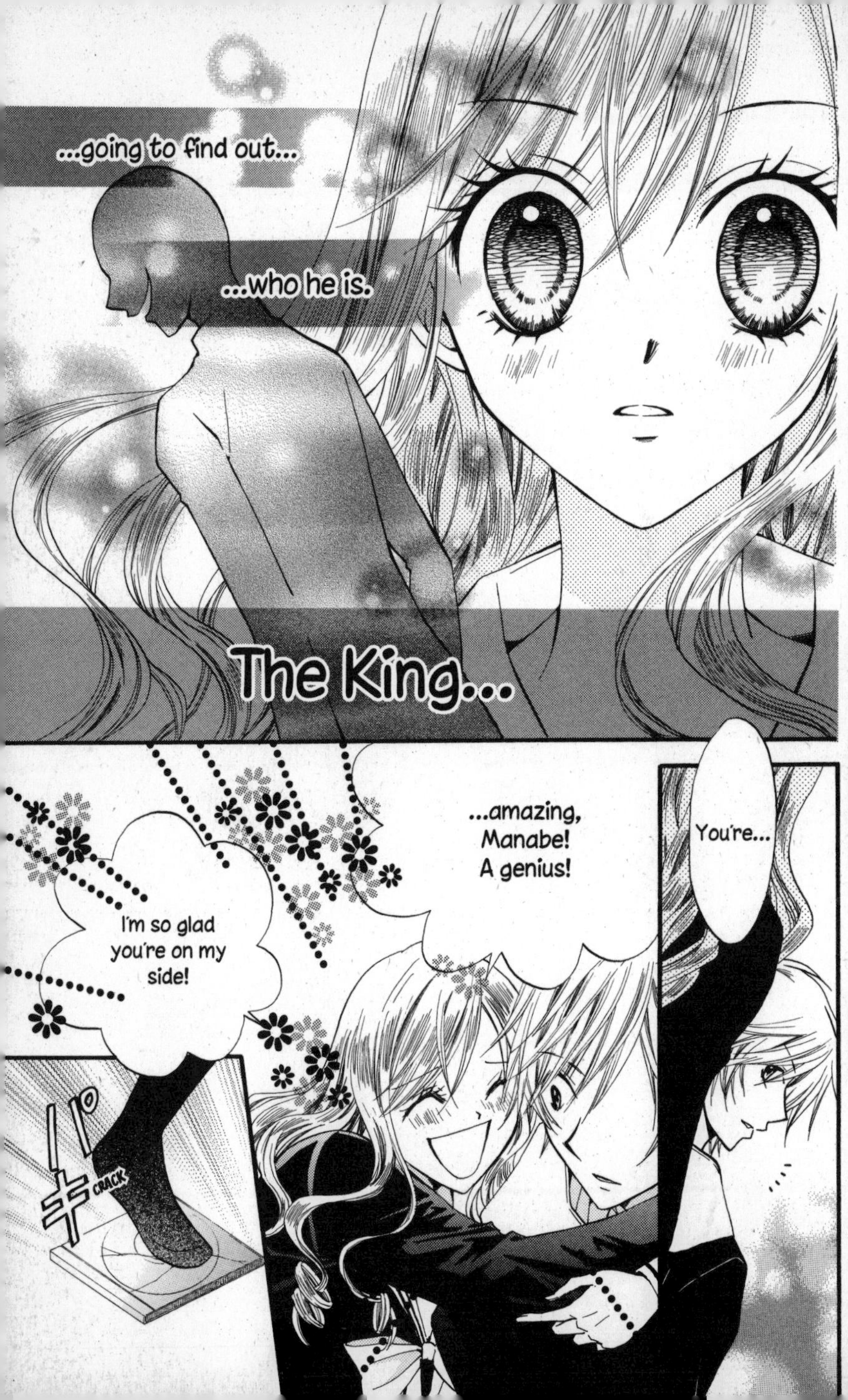
...going to find out...
...who he is.
The King...
You're...
...amazing, Manabe! A genius!
I'm so glad you're on my side!
CRACK

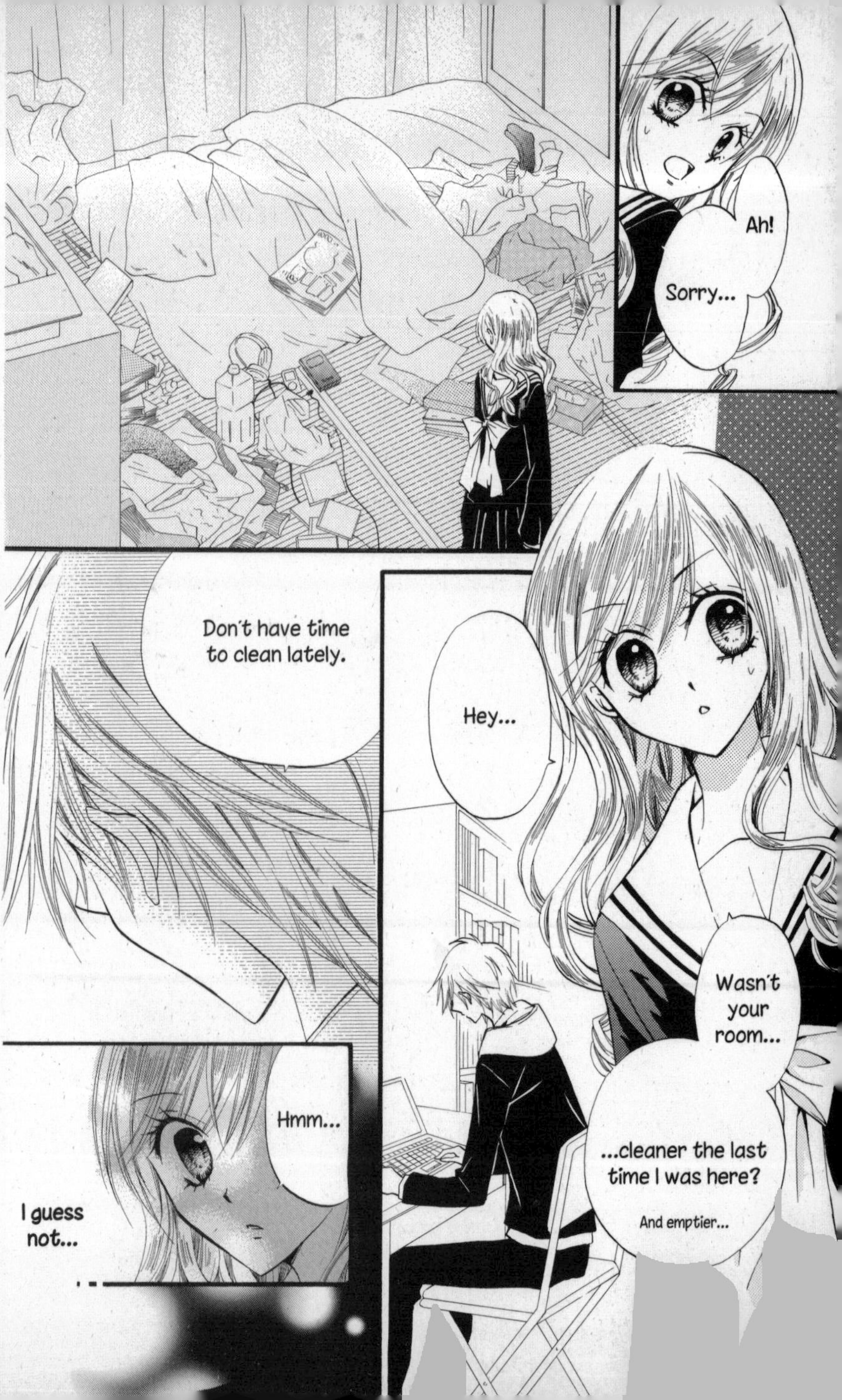
Ah!
Sorry...
Hey...
Wasn't your room...
...cleaner the last time I was here?
And emptier...
Don't have time to clean lately.
Hmm...
I guess not...

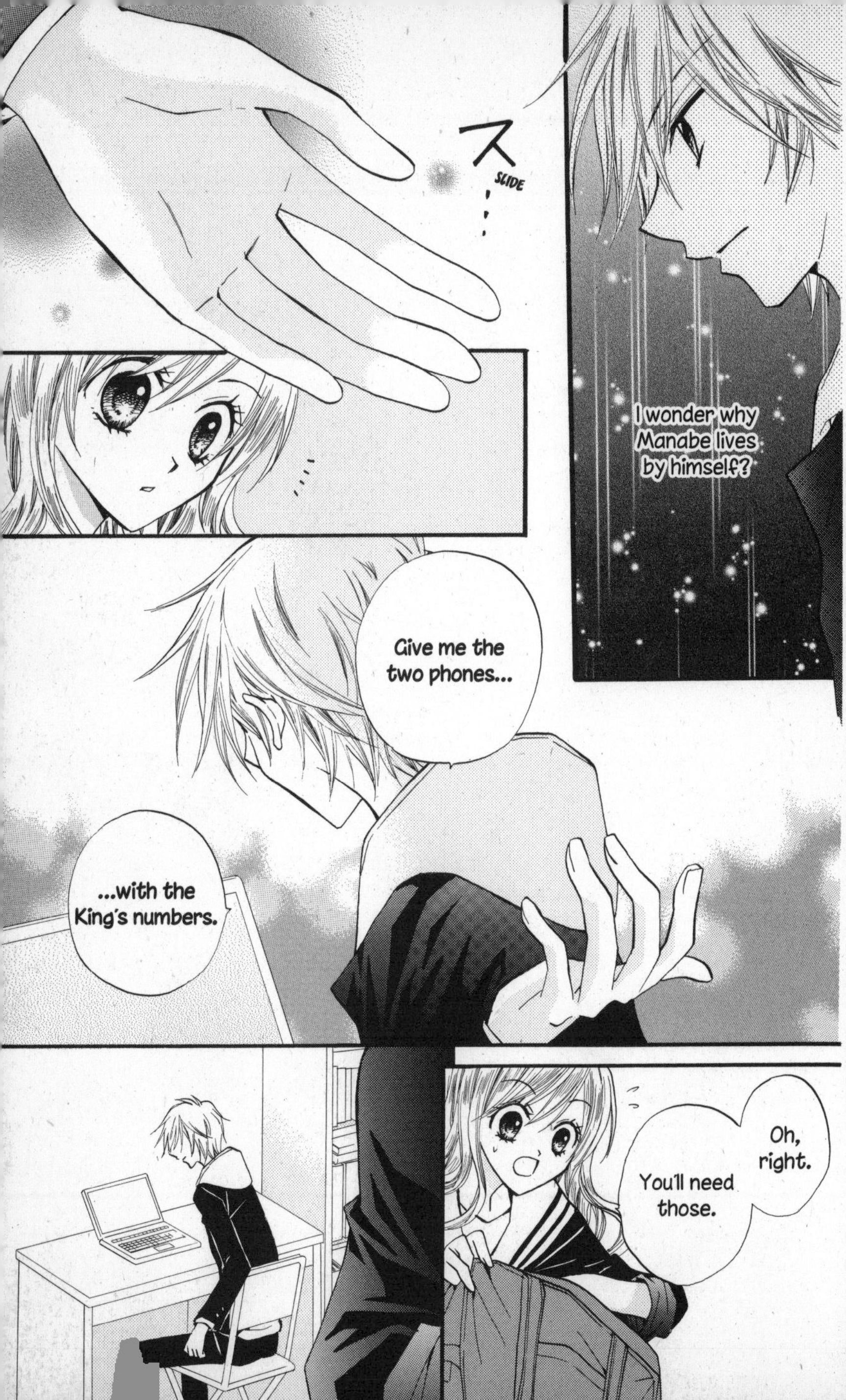
I wonder why Manabe lives by himself?
ス
SLIDE
Give me the two phones...
...with the King's numbers.
Oh, right.
You'll need those.

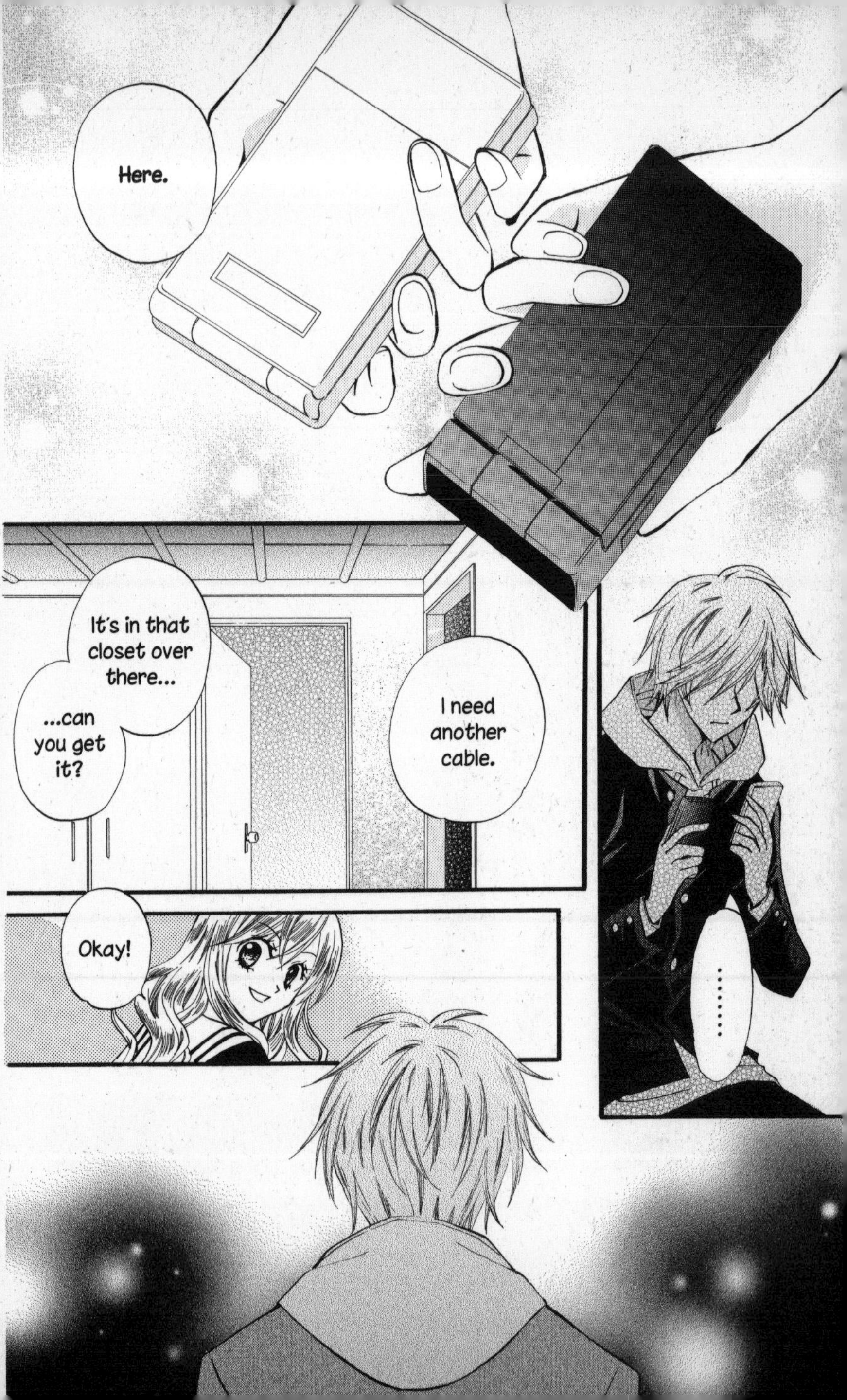
Here.
......
I need another cable.
It's in that closet over there...
...can you get it?
Okay!

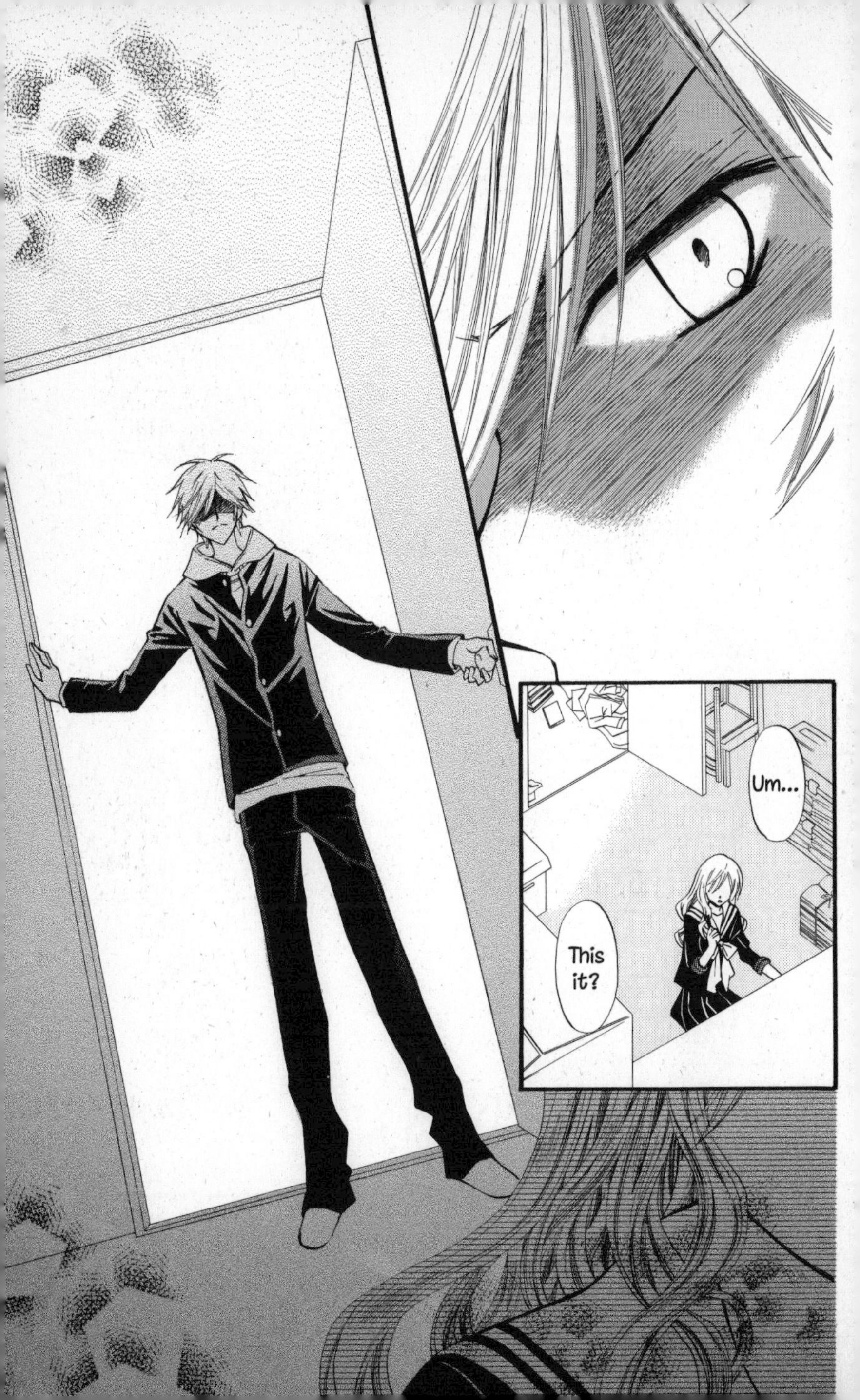
Um...
This it?

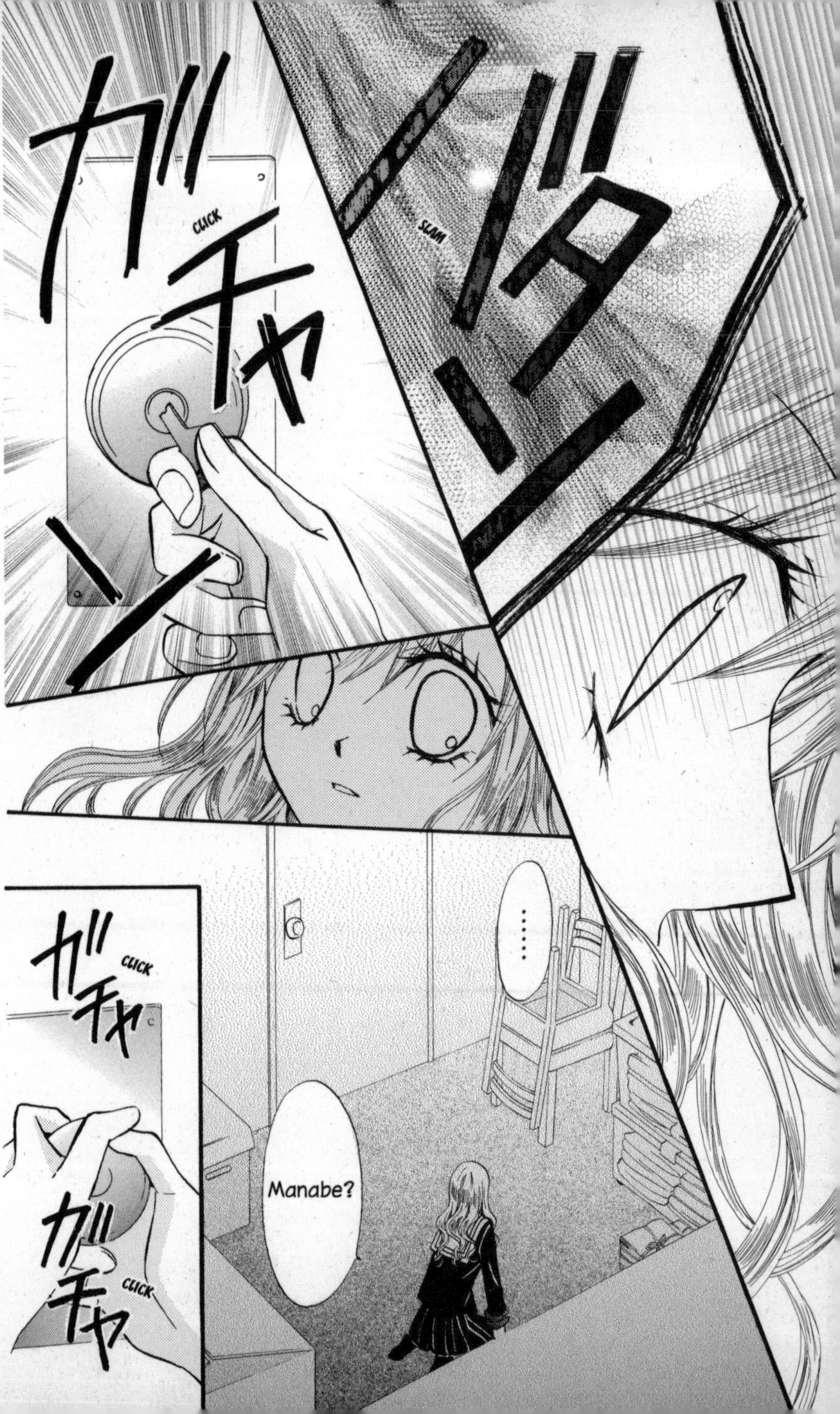
バタン
SLAM
ガチャン
CLICK
……
Manabe?
ガチャ
CLICK
ガチャ
CLICK

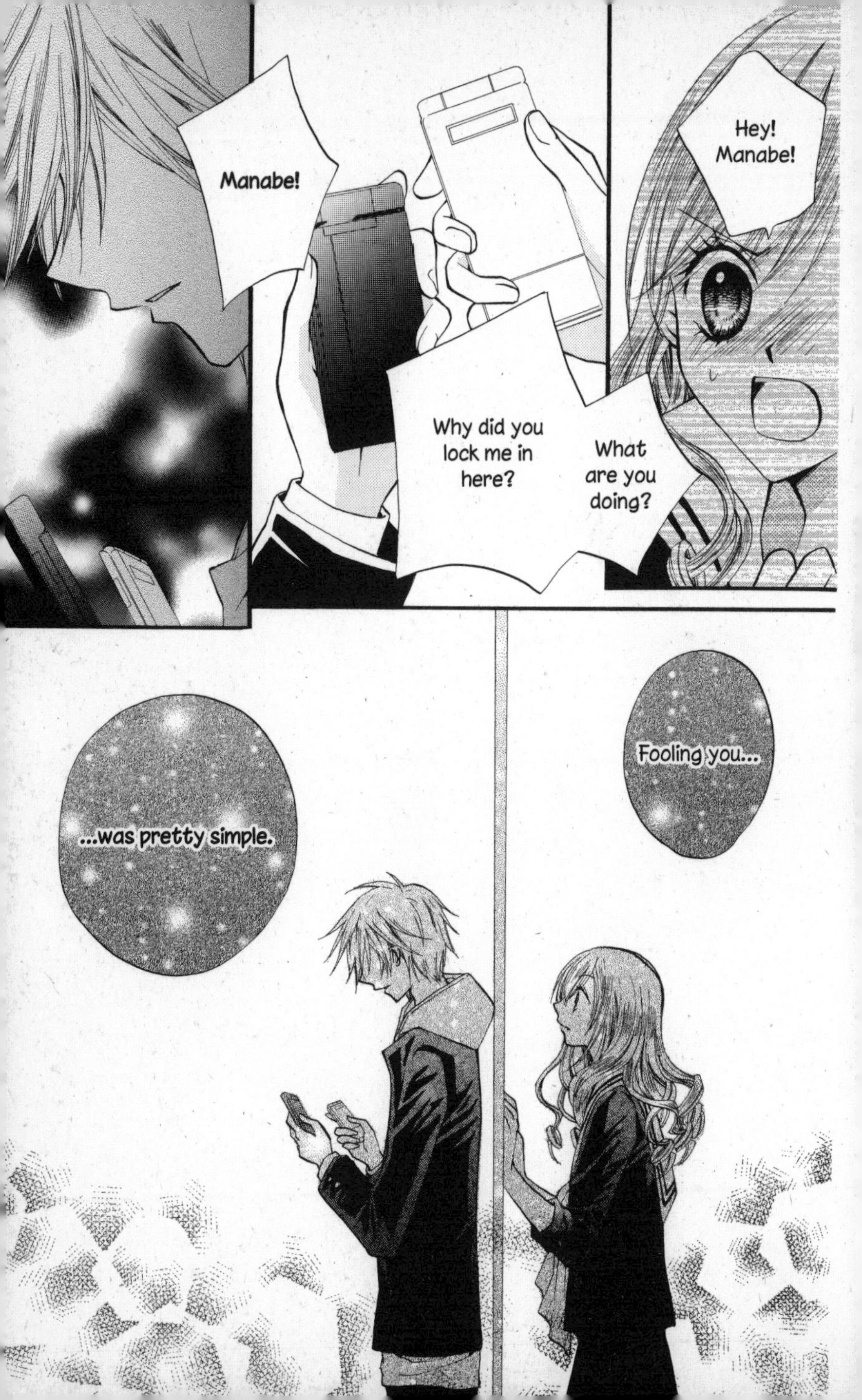
Hey! Manabe!
What are you doing?
Why did you lock me in here?
Manabe!
Fooling you...
...was pretty simple.

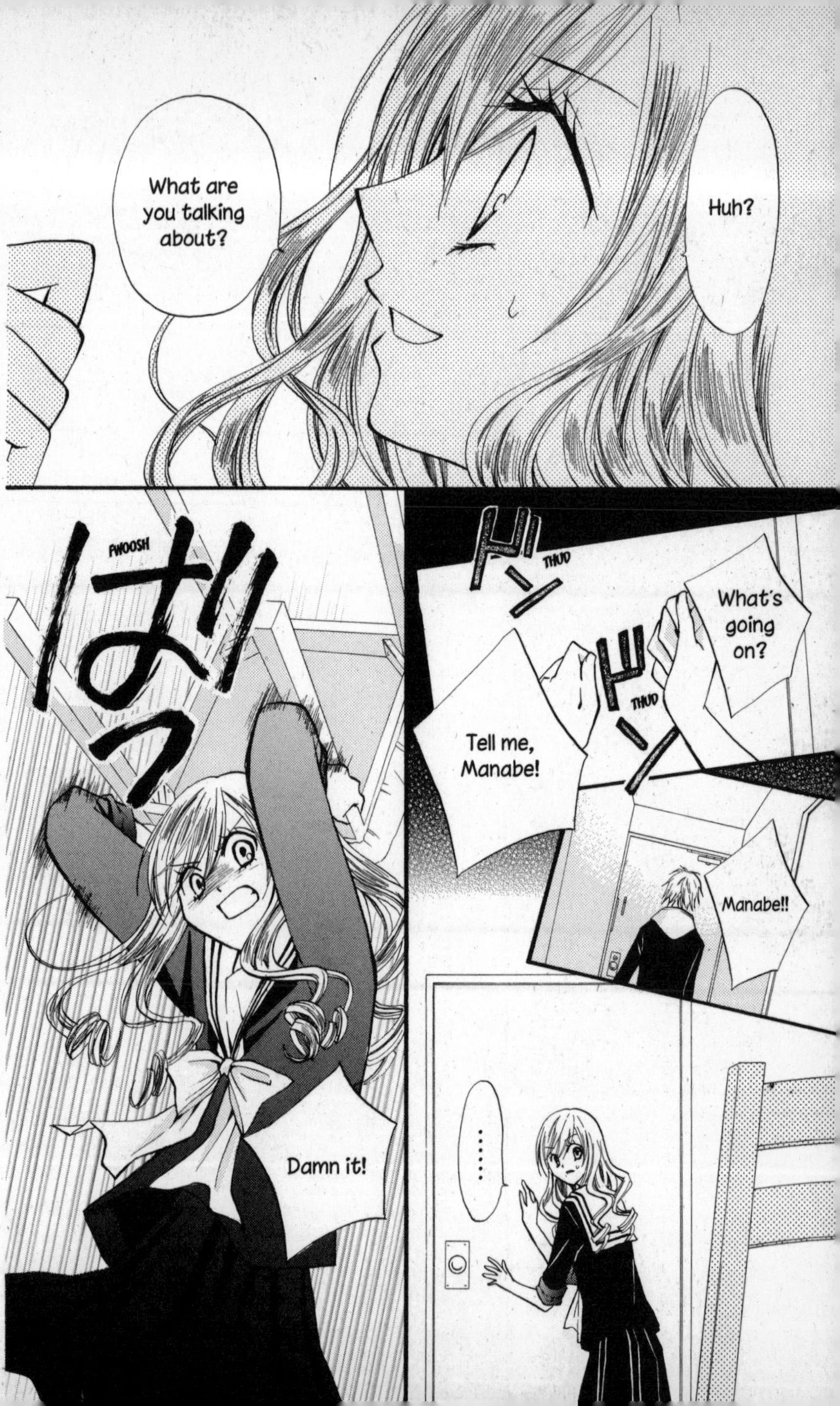
Huh?
What are you talking about?
ドン
THUD
What's going on?
ドン
THUD
Tell me, Manabe!
Manabe!!
……
はっ
FWOOSH
Damn it!

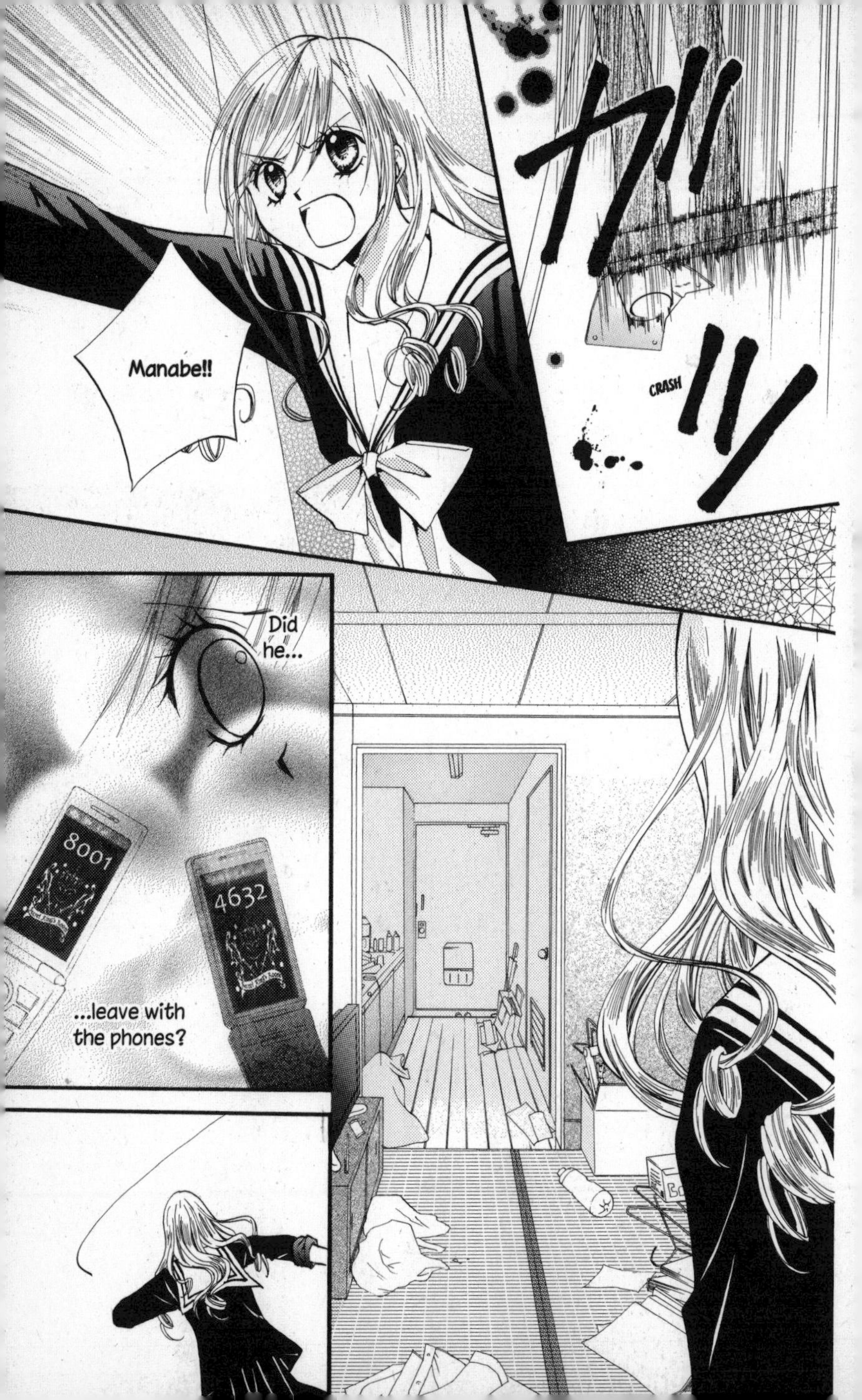
CRASH
Manabe!!
Did he...
8001
4632
...leave with the phones?

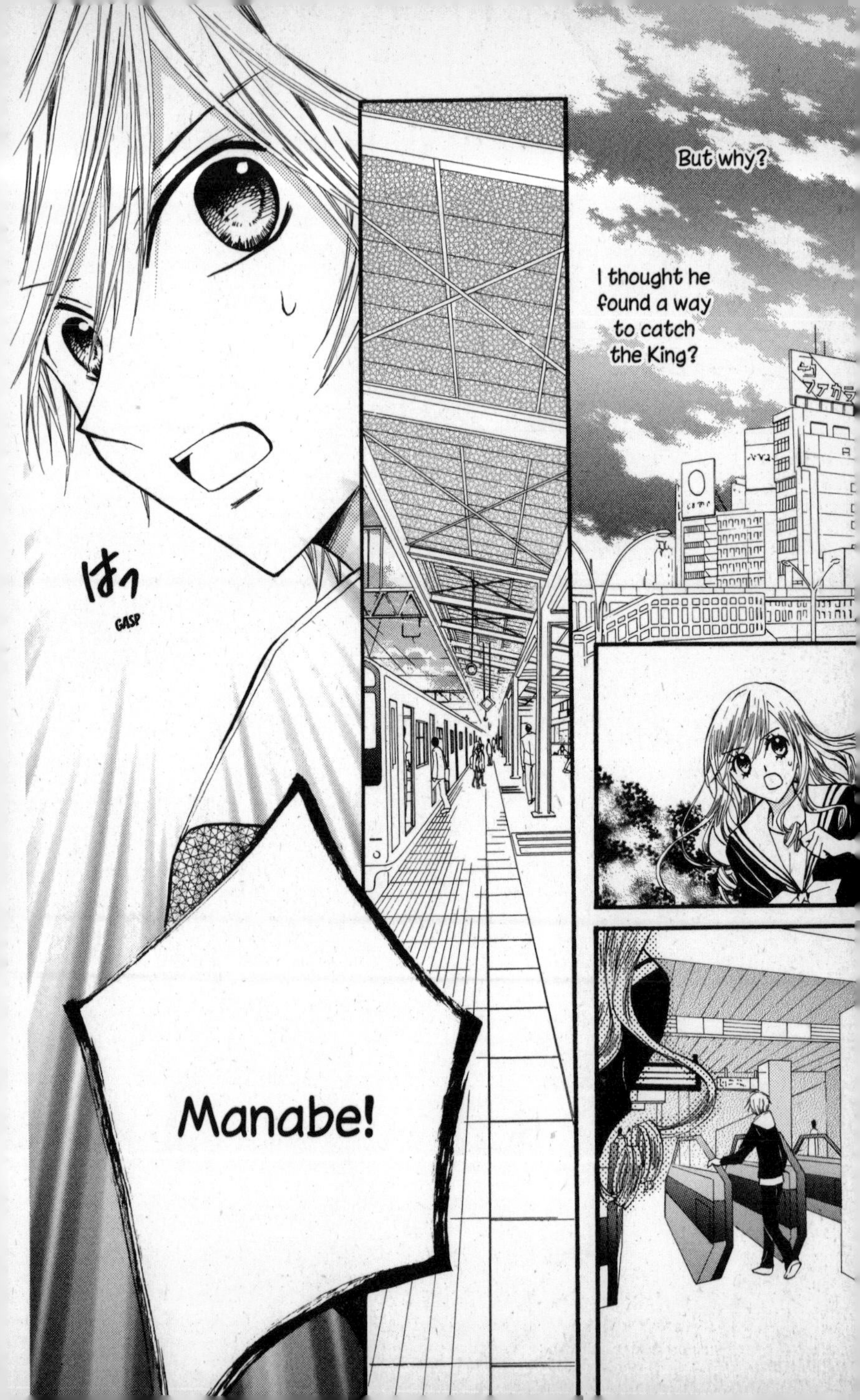
But why?
I thought he found a way to catch the King?
はっ
GASP
Manabe!

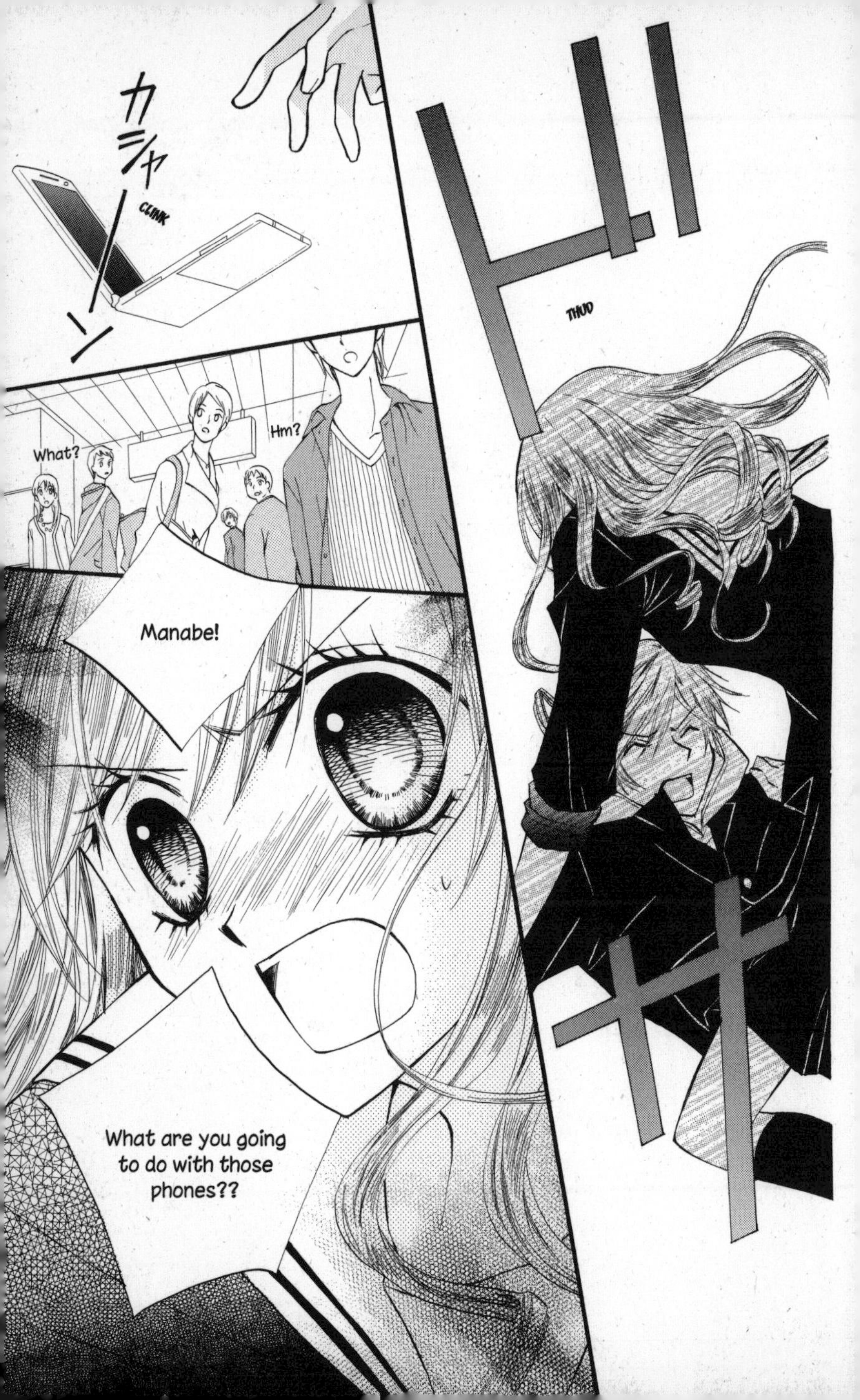
THUD
カシャン
CLINK
Hm?
What?
Manabe!
What are you going to do with those phones??

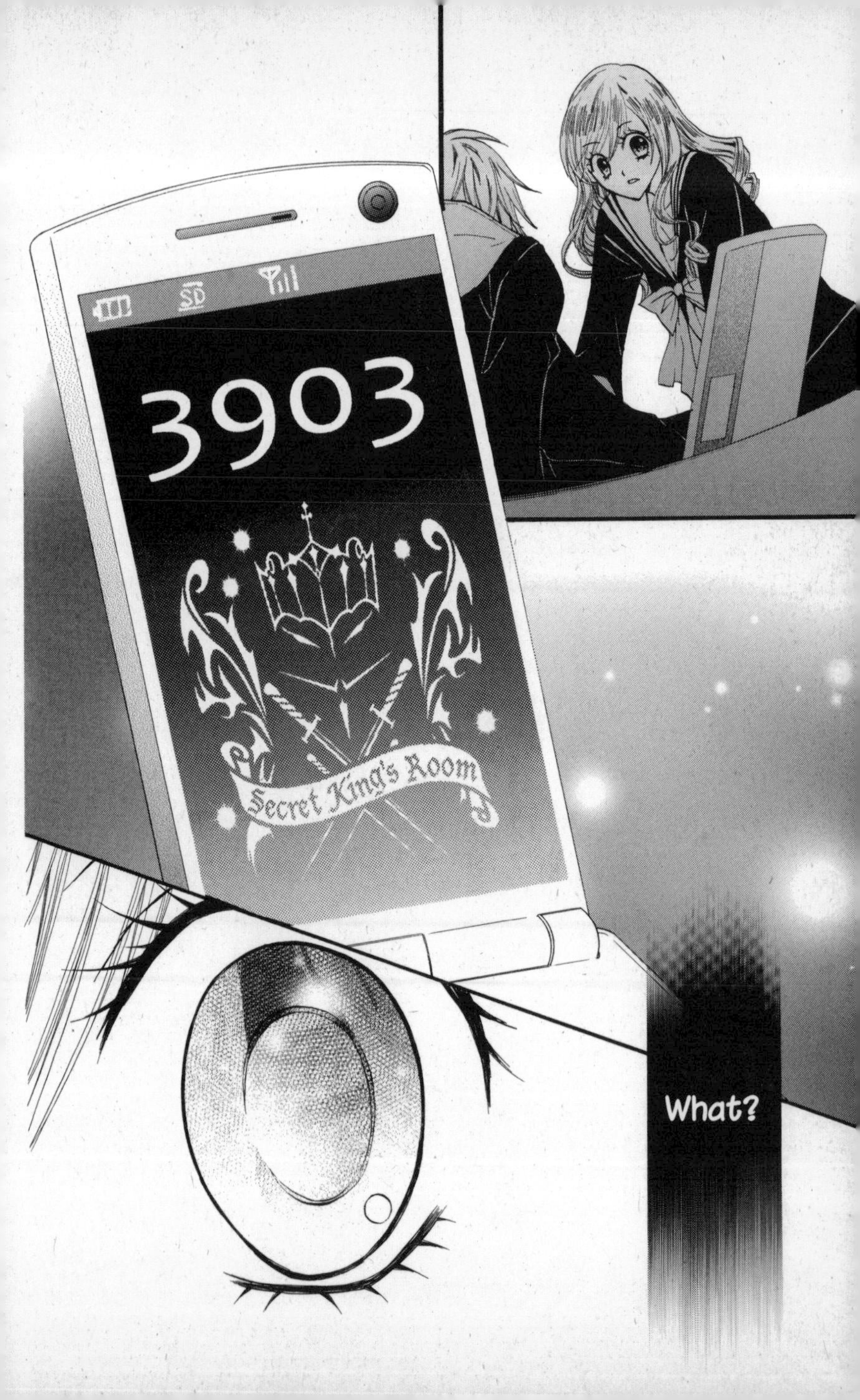
3903
Secret King's Room
What?

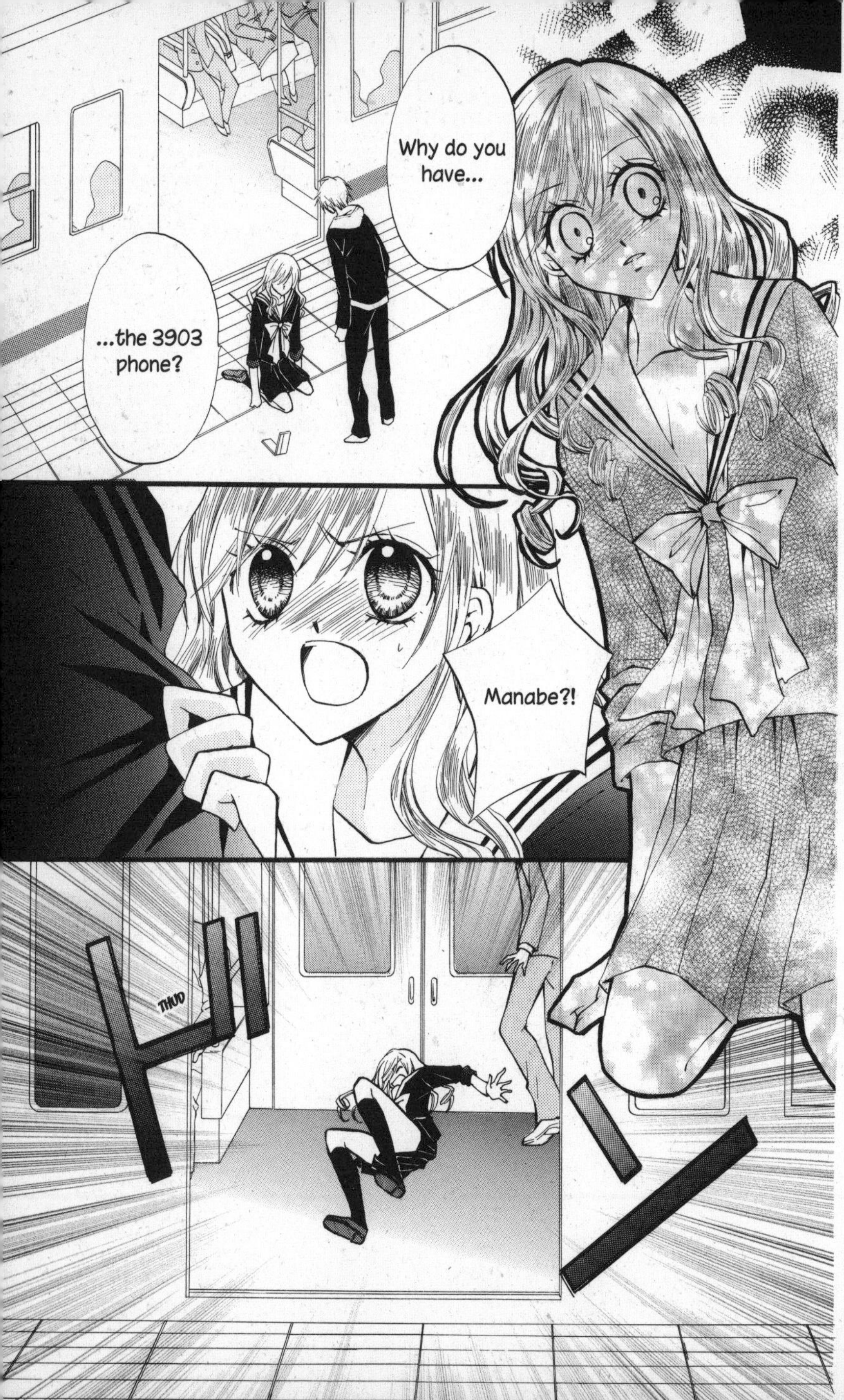
Why do you have...
...the 3903 phone?
Manabe?!
THUD

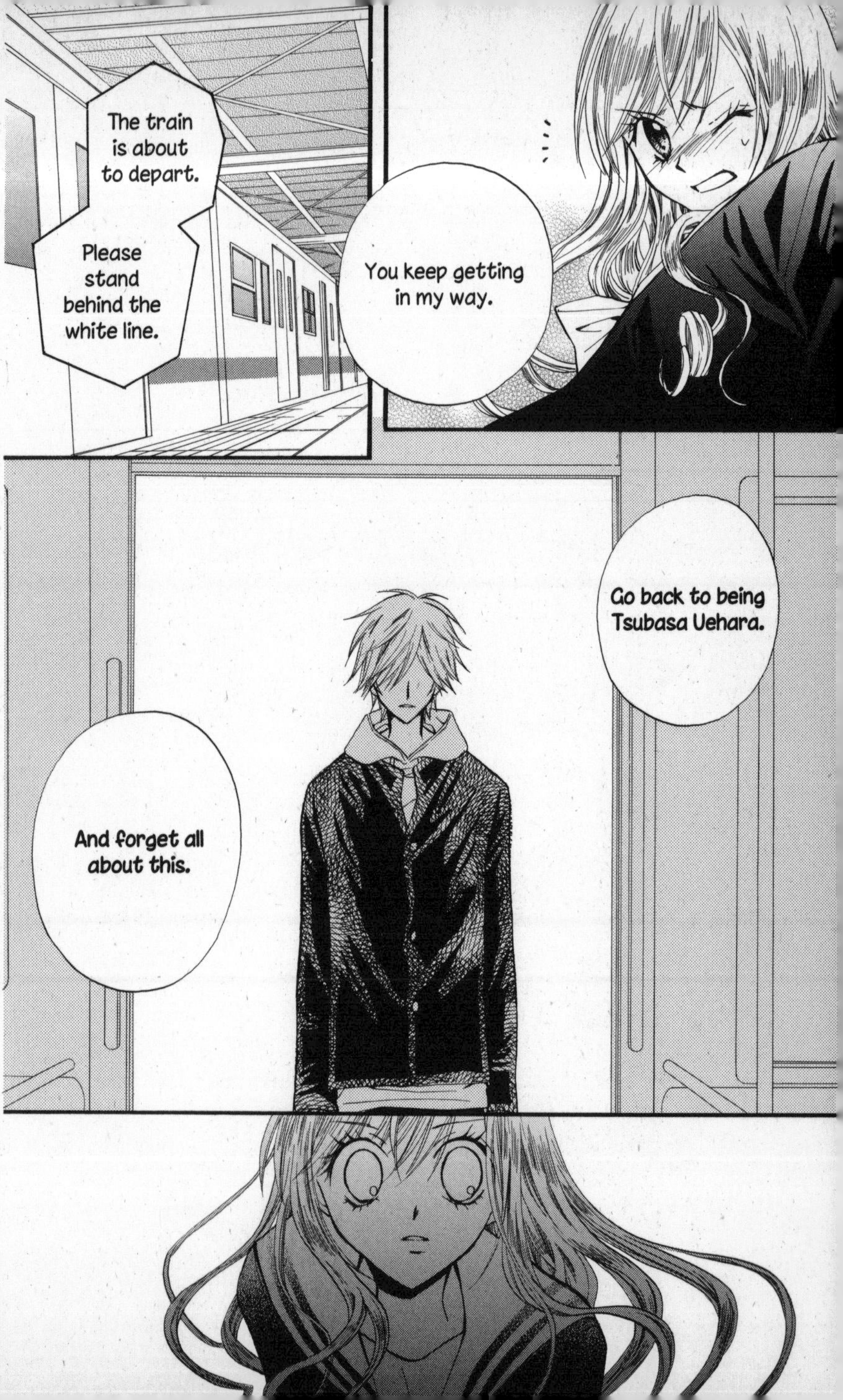
You keep getting in my way.
The train is about to depart.
Please stand behind the white line.
Go back to being Tsubasa Uehara.
And forget all about this.

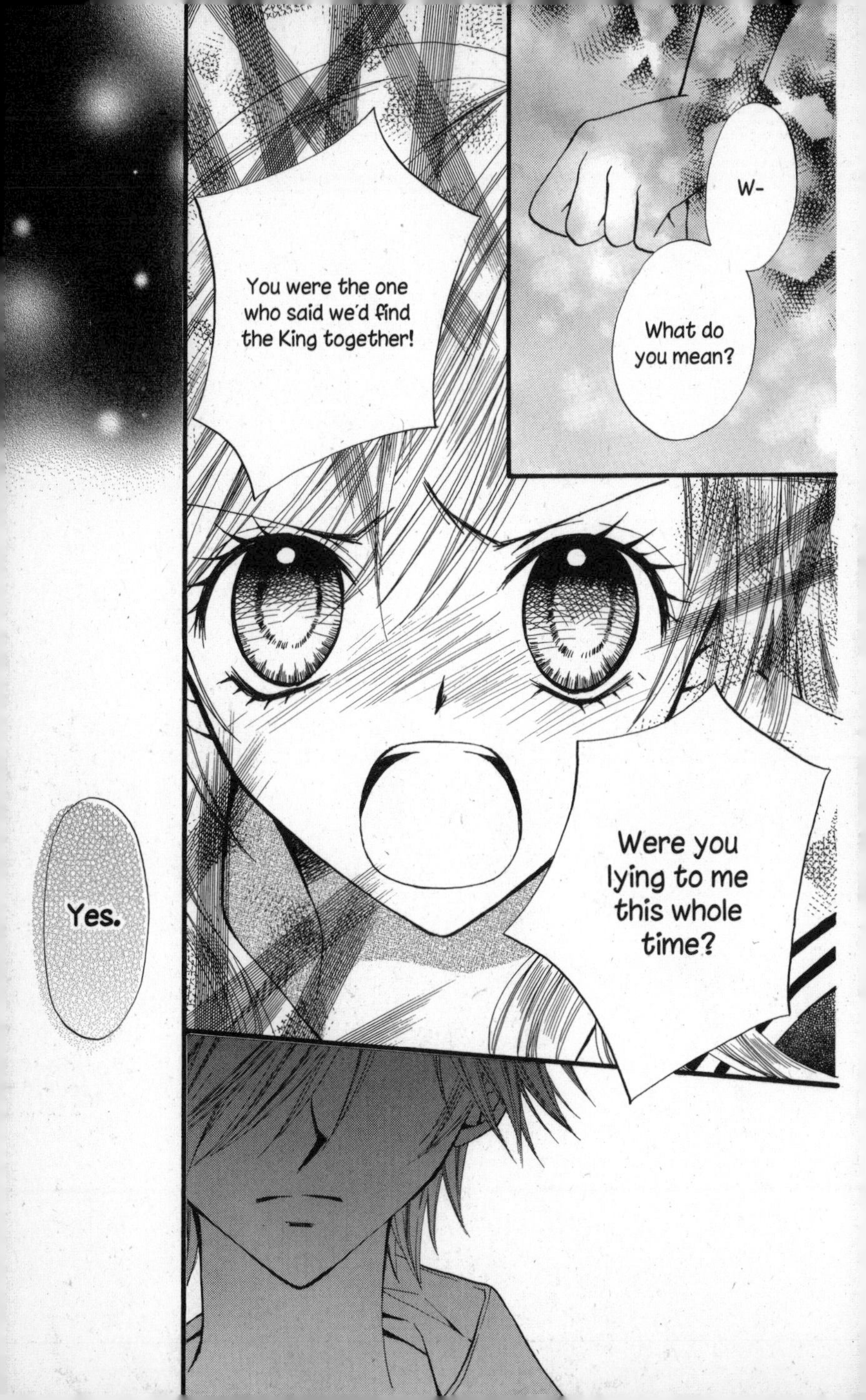
W-
What do you mean?
You were the one who said we'd find the King together!
Were you lying to me this whole time?
Yes.

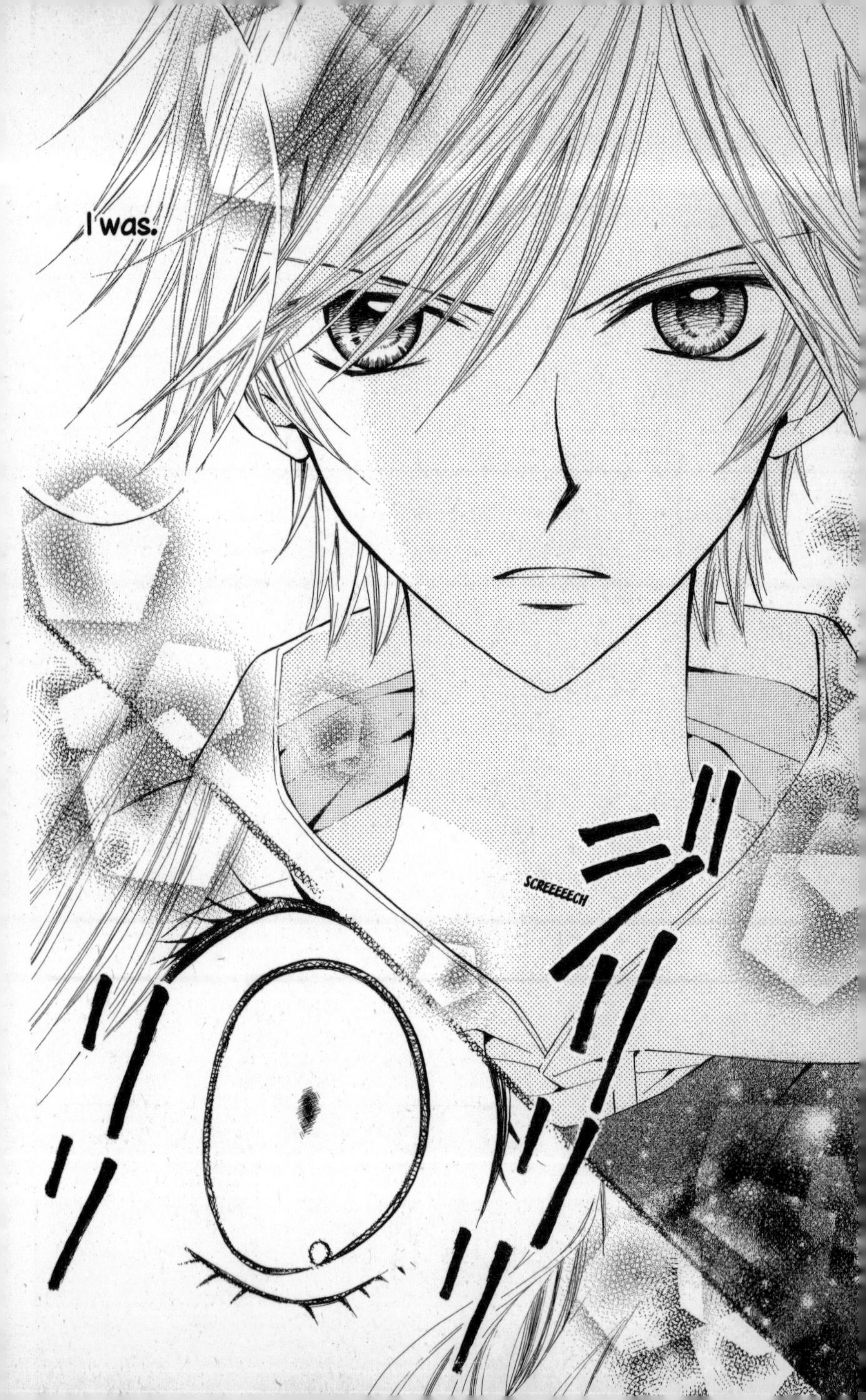
I was.
SCREEEEECH

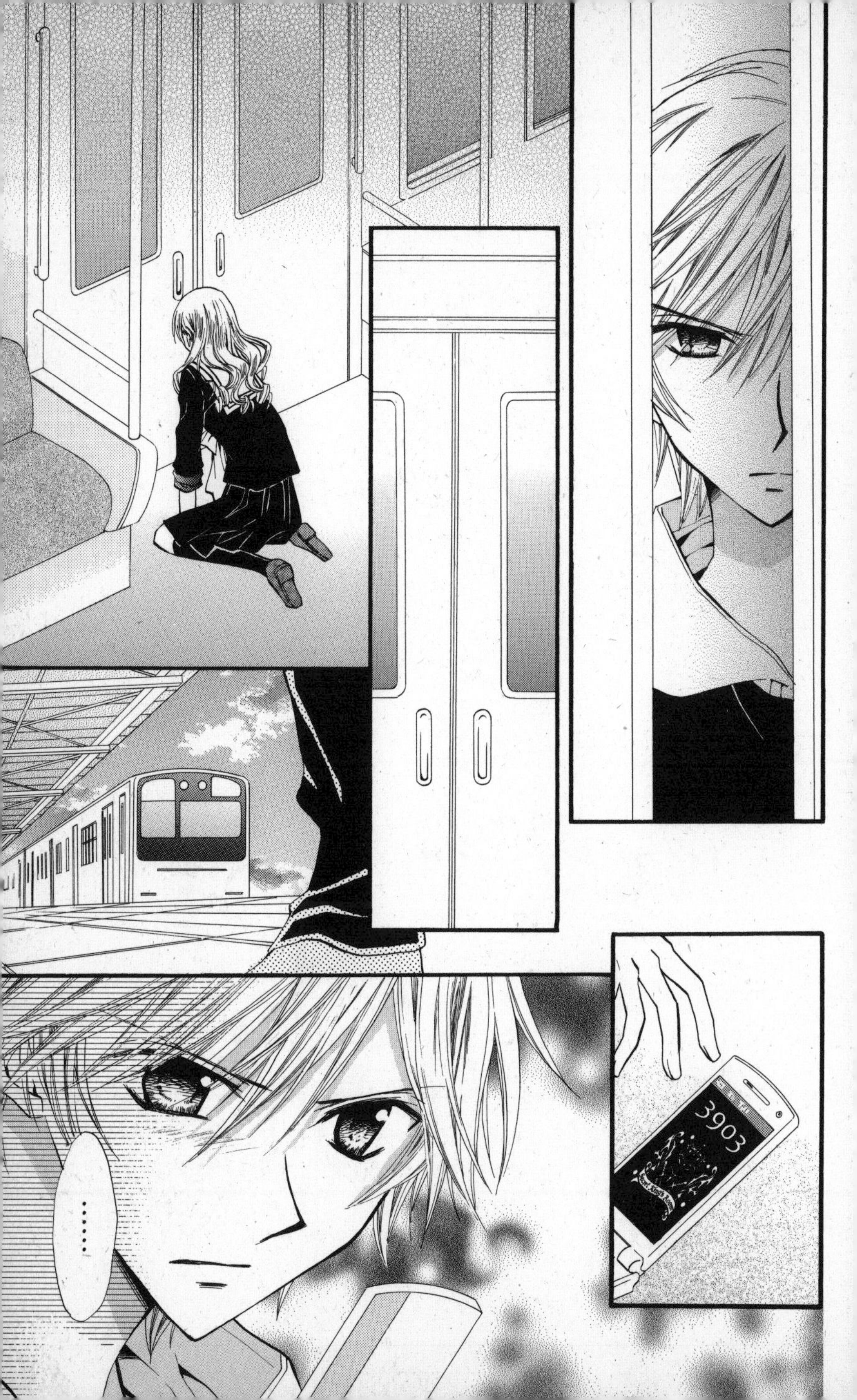
3903
......

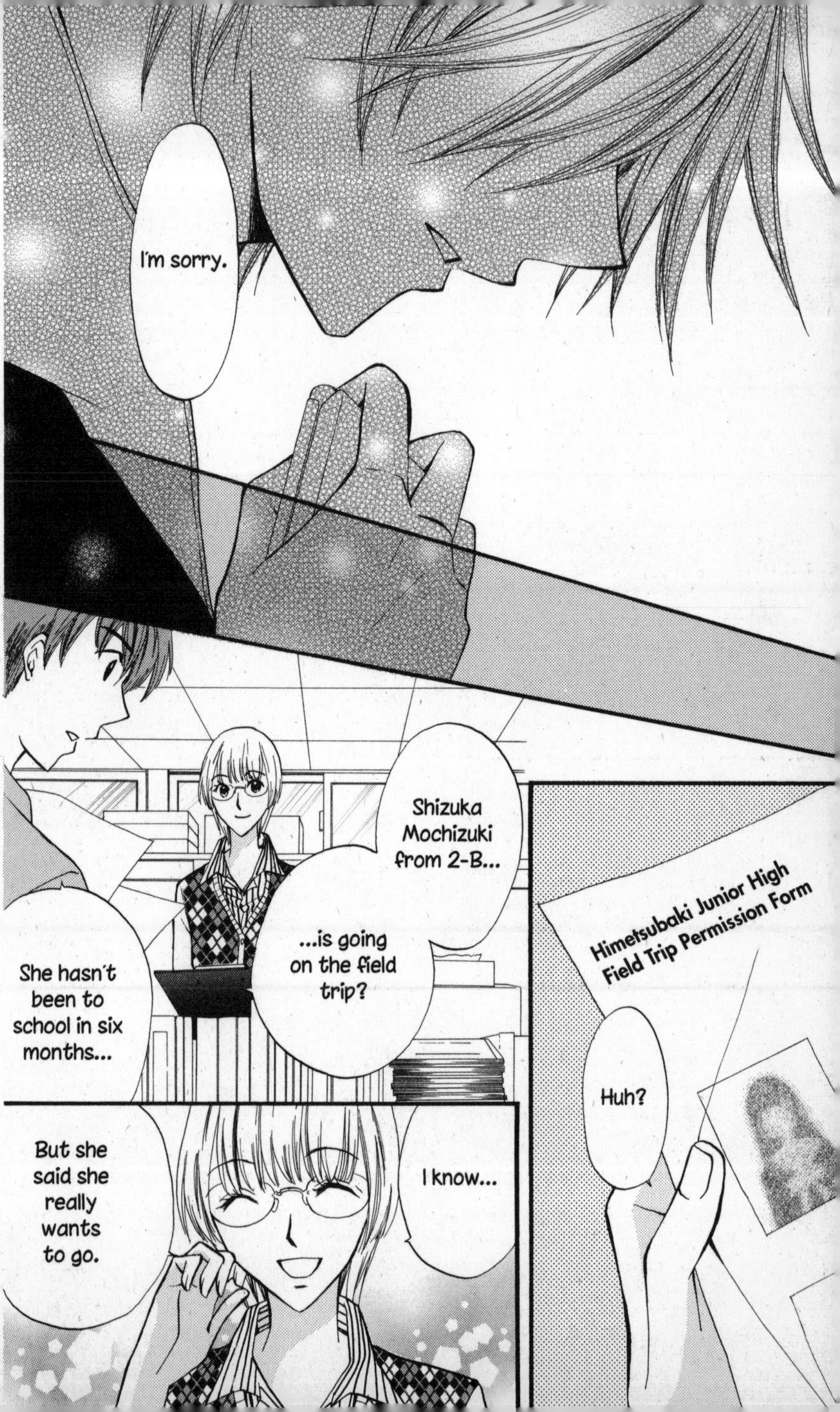
I'm sorry.
Himetsubaki Junior High Field Trip Permission Form
Huh?
Shizuka Mochizuki from 2-B...
...is going on the field trip?
She hasn't been to school in six months...
I know...
But she said she really wants to go.

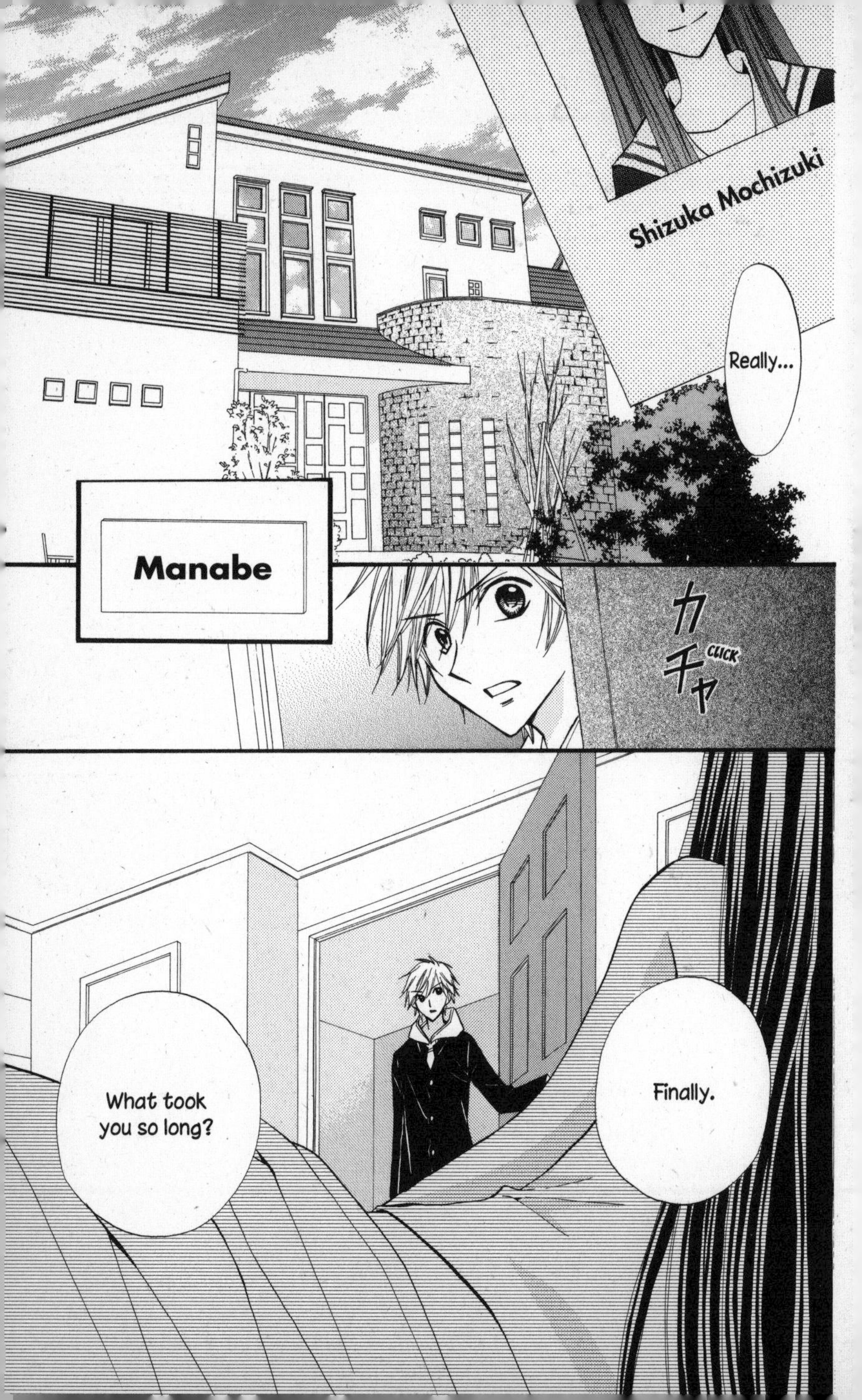
Shizuka Mochizuki
Really...
Manabe
カチャ CLICK
Finally.
What took you so long?

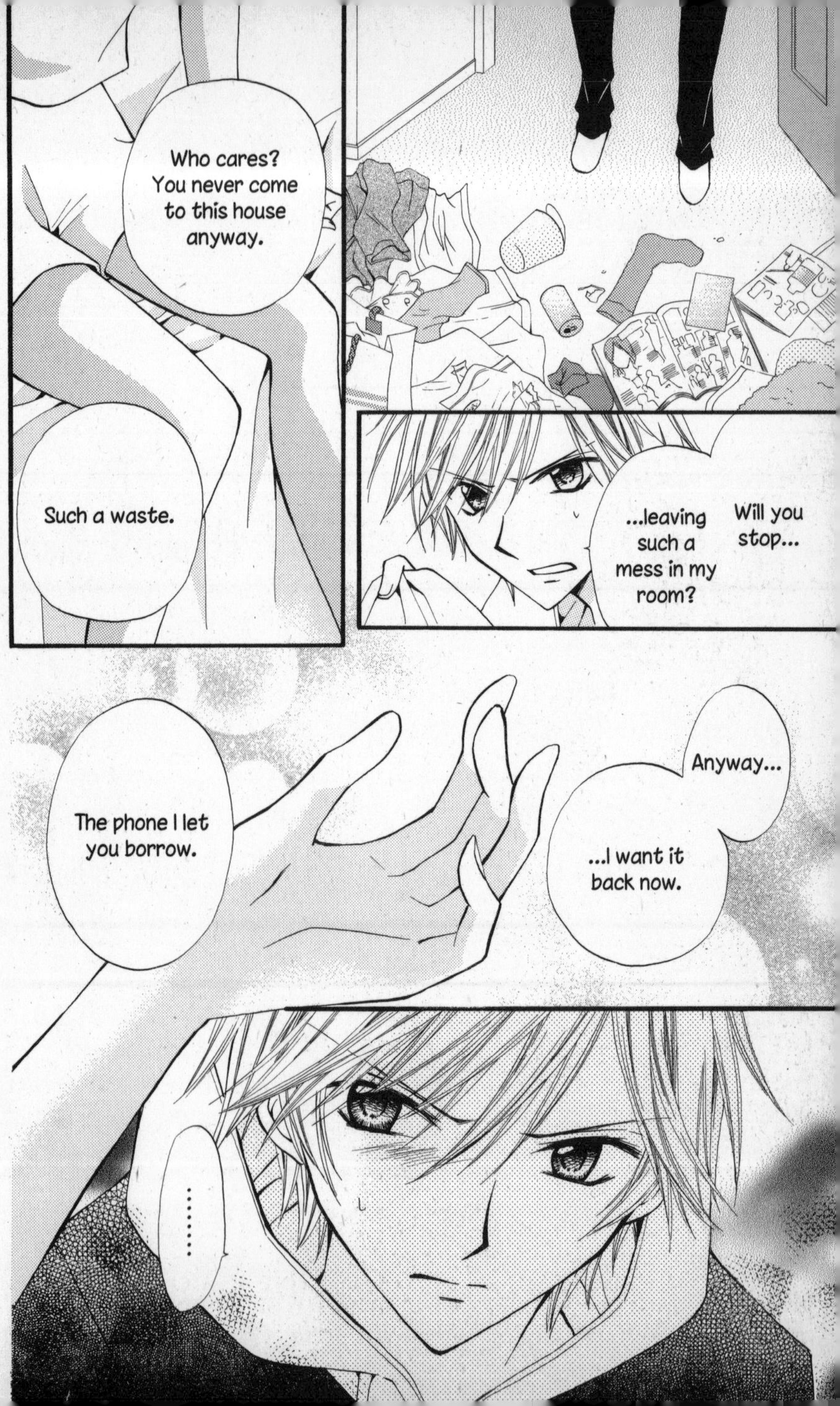
Will you stop...
...leaving such a mess in my room?
Who cares? You never come to this house anyway.
Such a waste.
Anyway...
...I want it back now.
The phone I let you borrow.
......

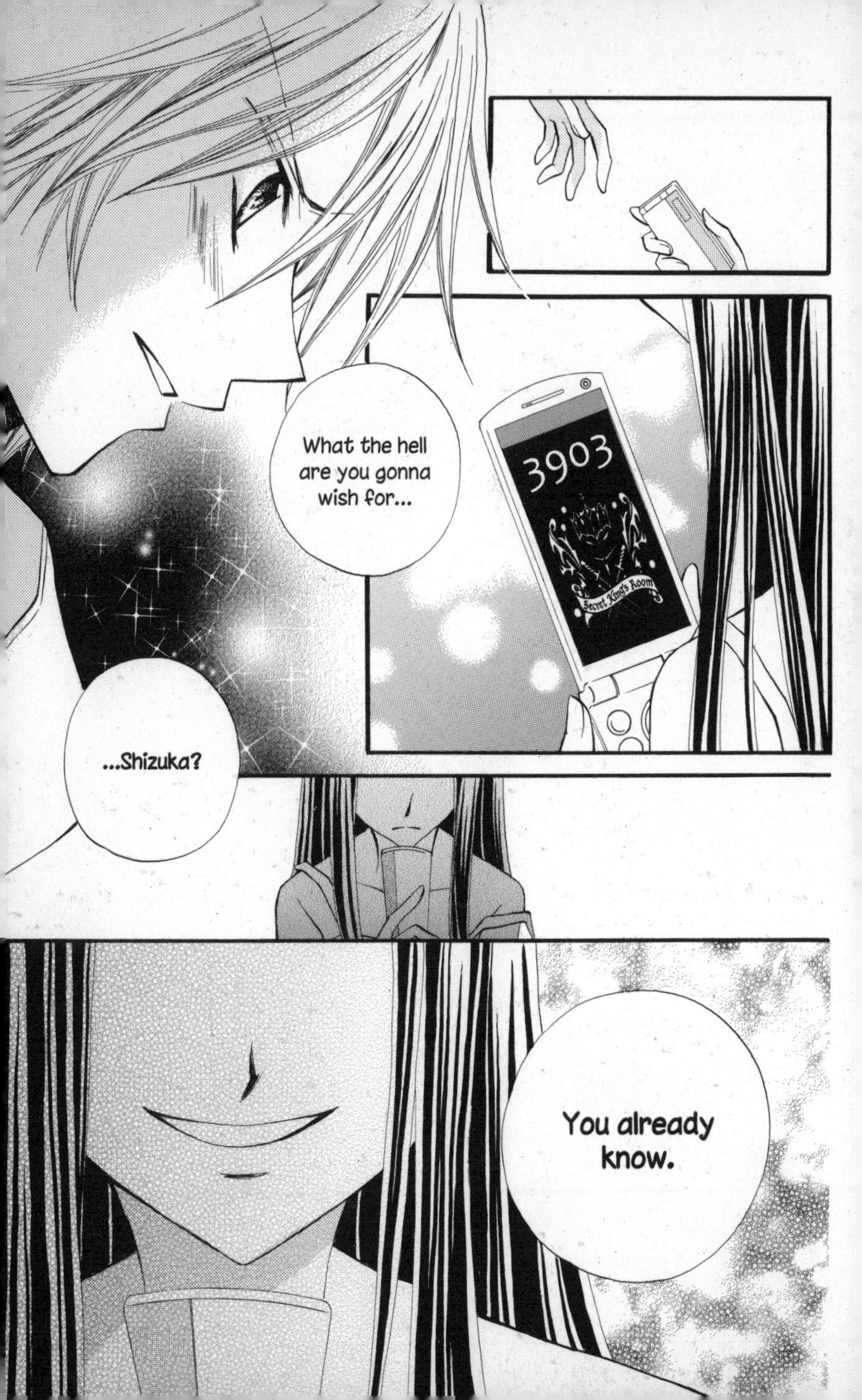
3903
Secret King's Room
What the hell are you gonna wish for...
...Shizuka?
You already know.

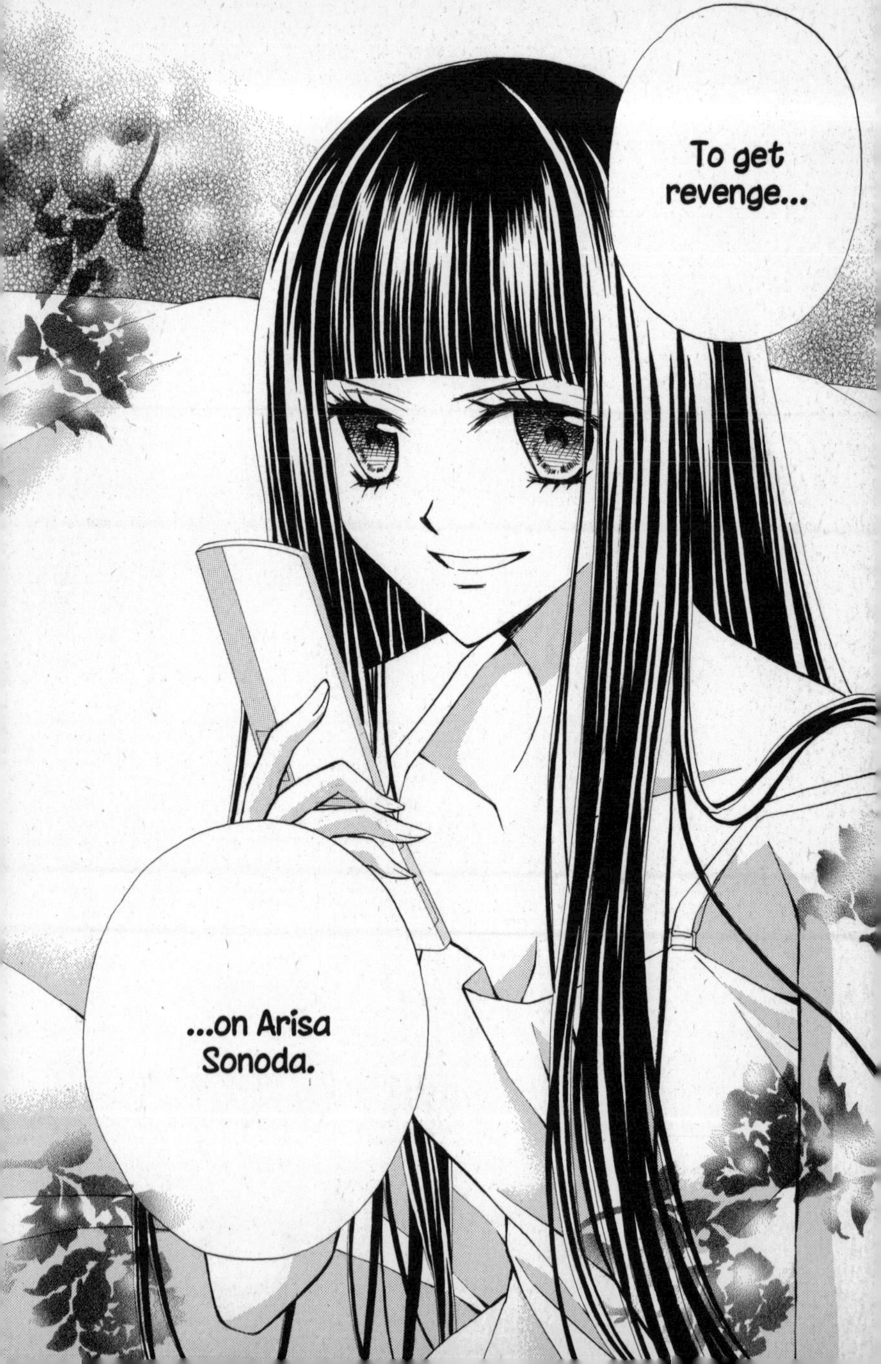
To get revenge...
...on Arisa Sonoda.

ARISA

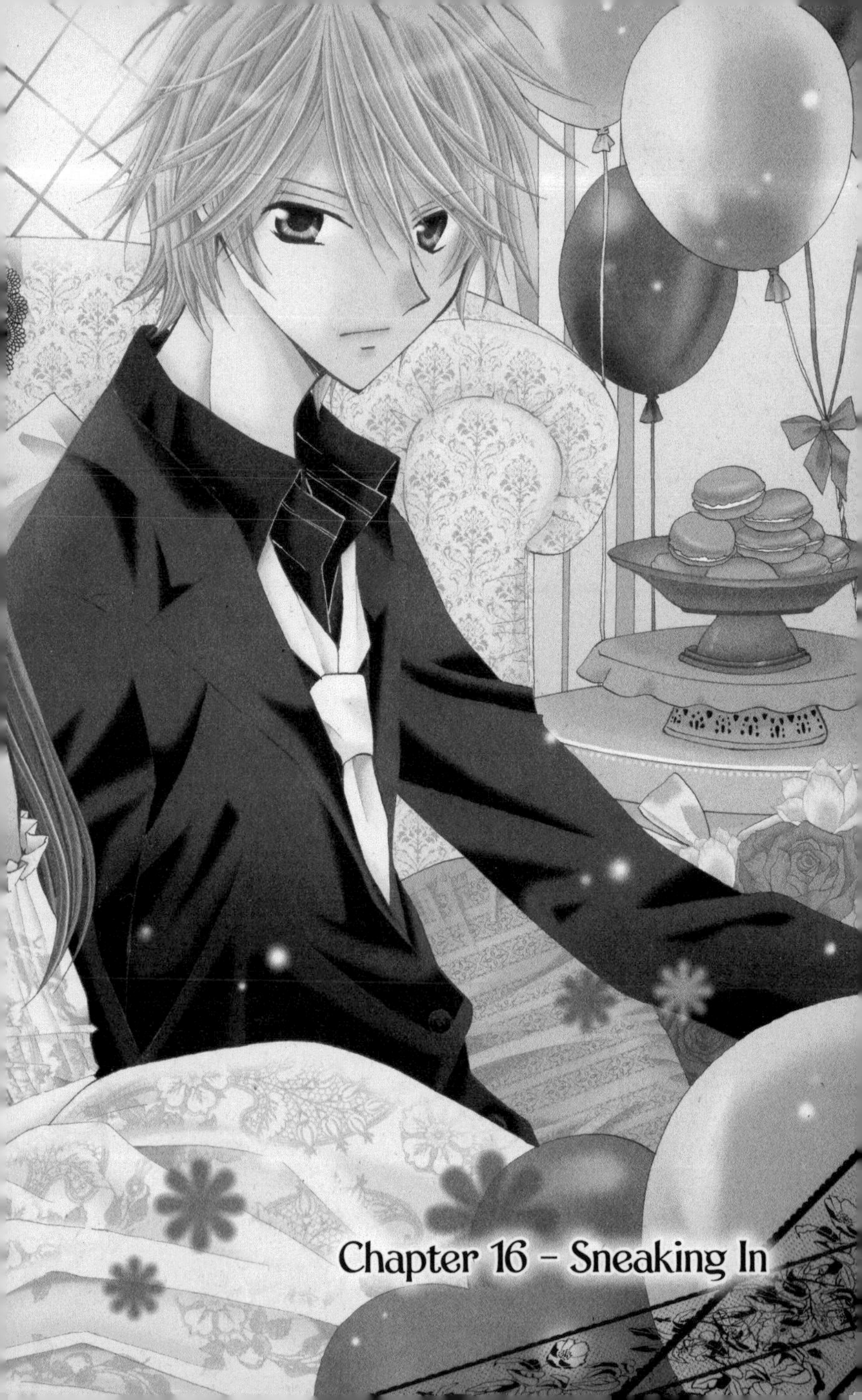
Chapter 16 - Sneaking In

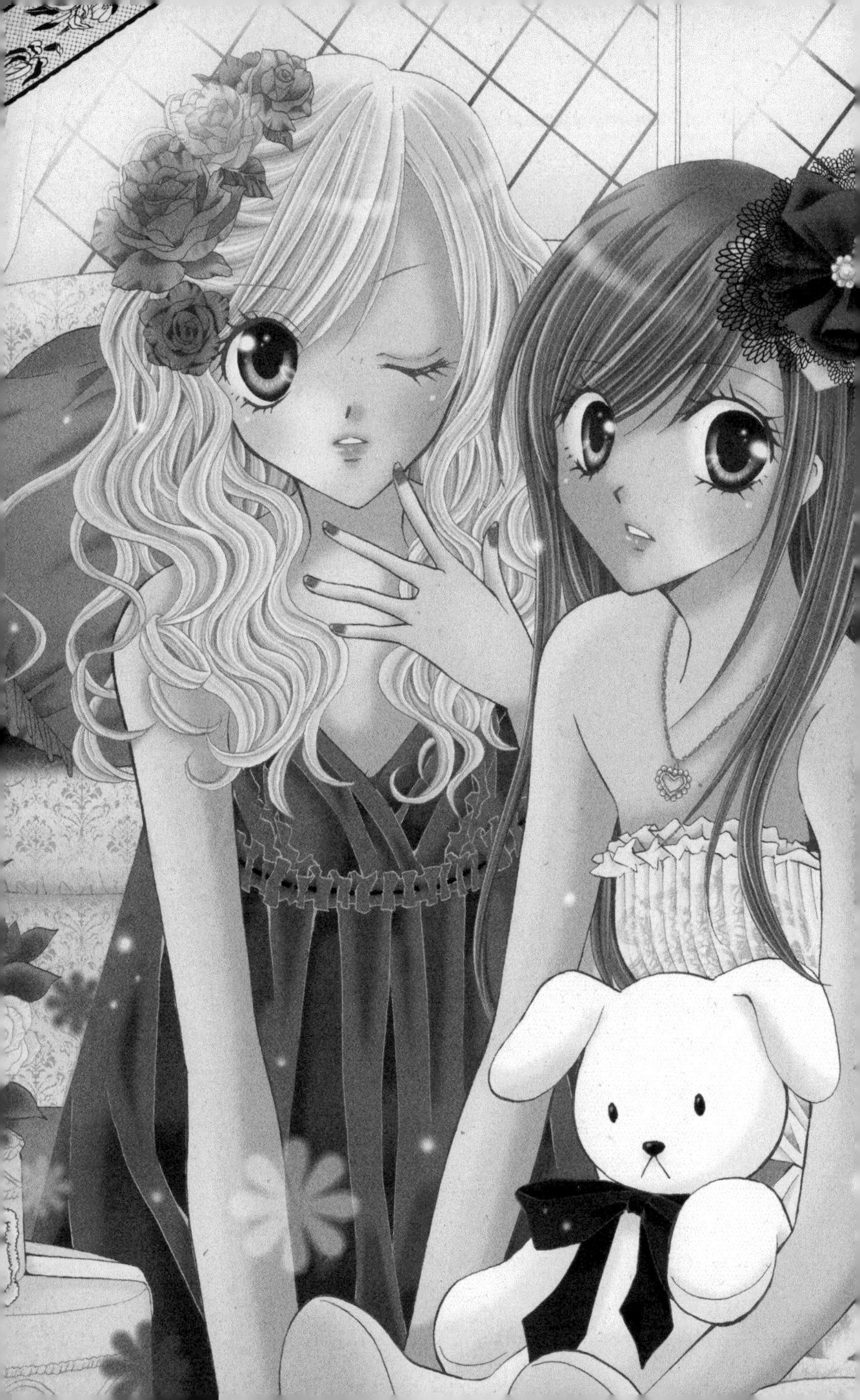

SPECIAL THANKS:

T. Nakamura

H. Kishimoto

M. Nakata

M. Shirasawa &

Nakayoshi Publishing

Takeda-sama &

Red rooster

Takashi
Shimoyama-sama &

GINNANSHA

Toriumi-sama

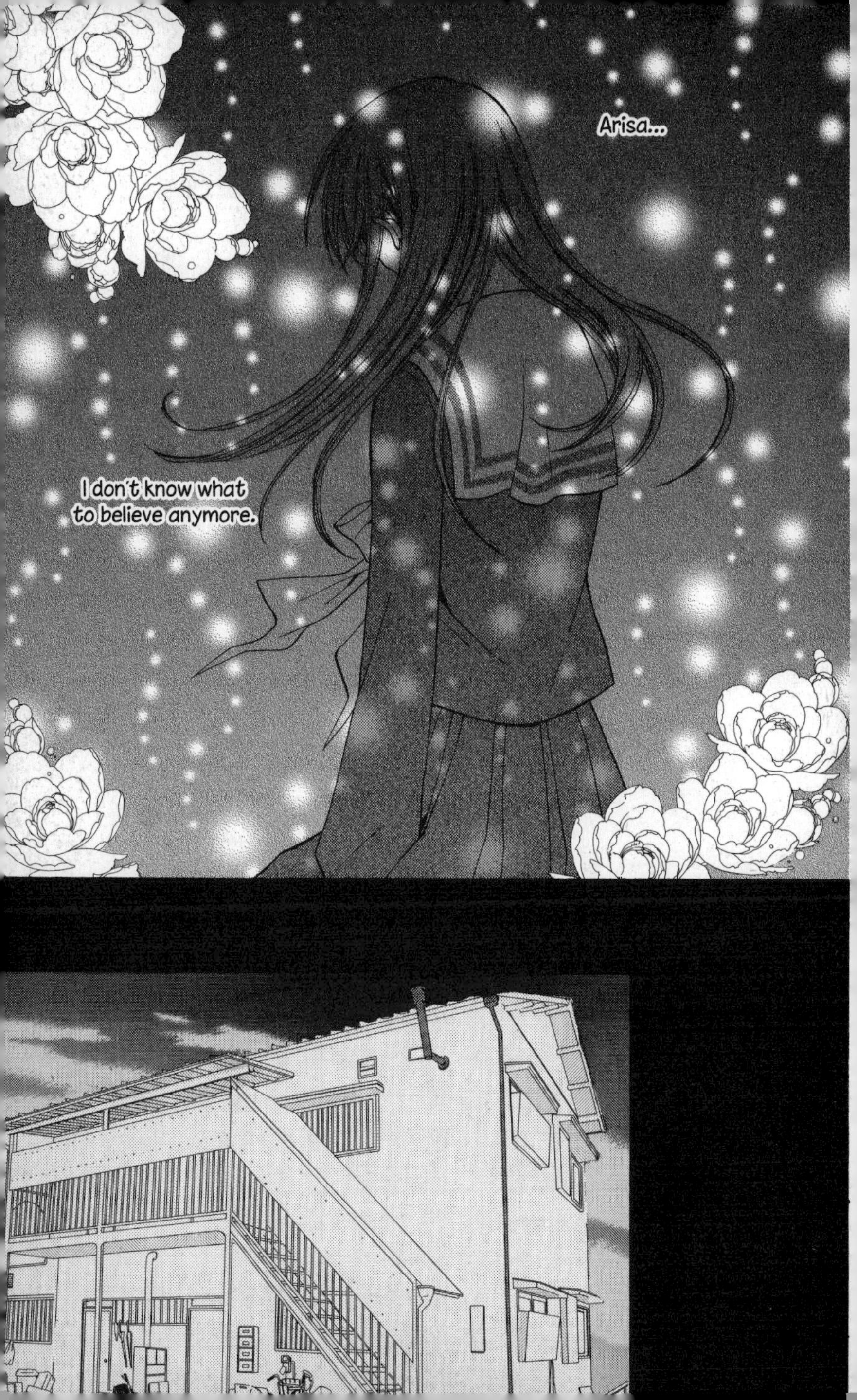
Arisa...
I don't know what to believe anymore.

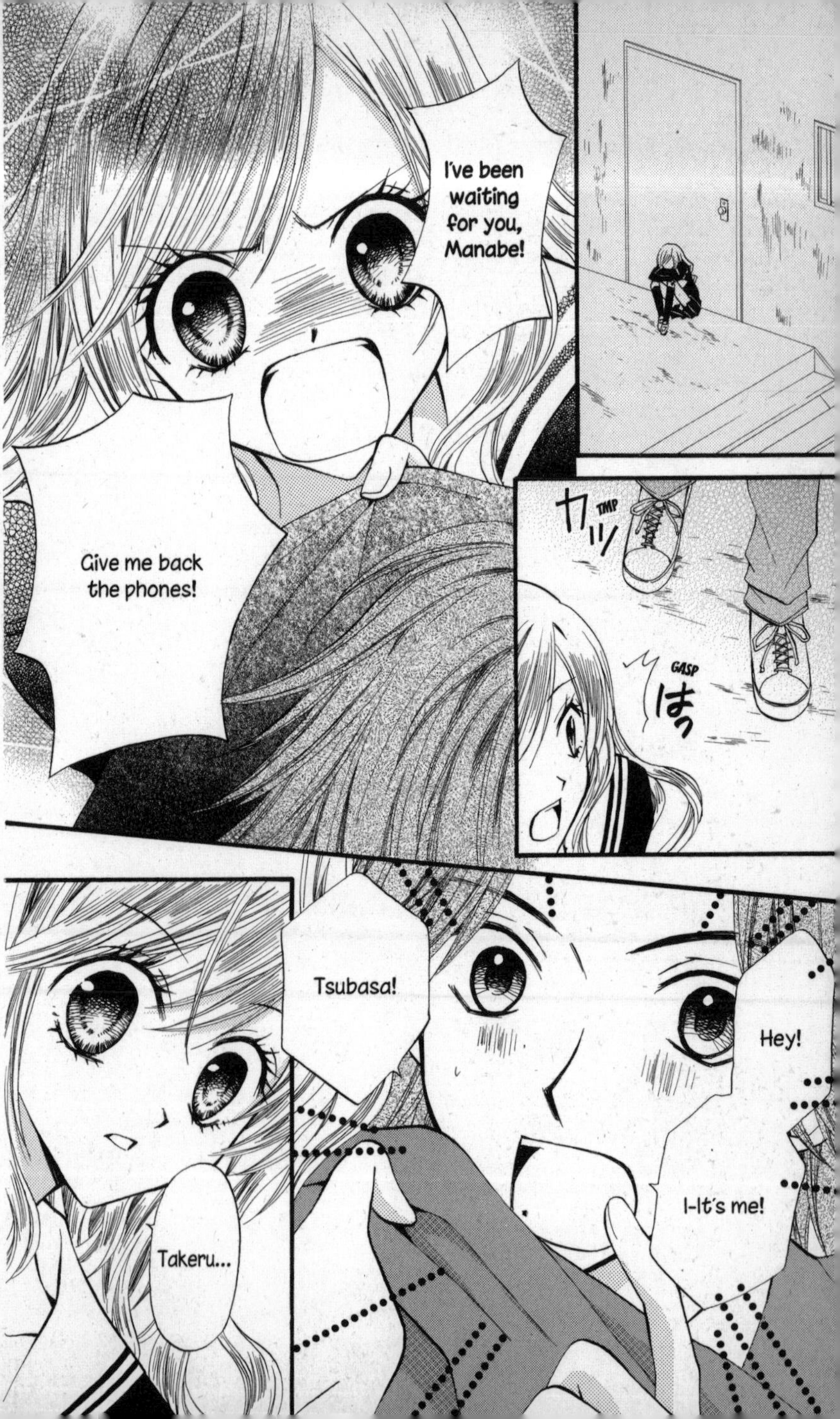
カッ
TMP
はっ
GASP
I've been waiting for you, Manabe!
Give me back the phones!
Tsubasa!
Hey!
I-It's me!
Takeru...

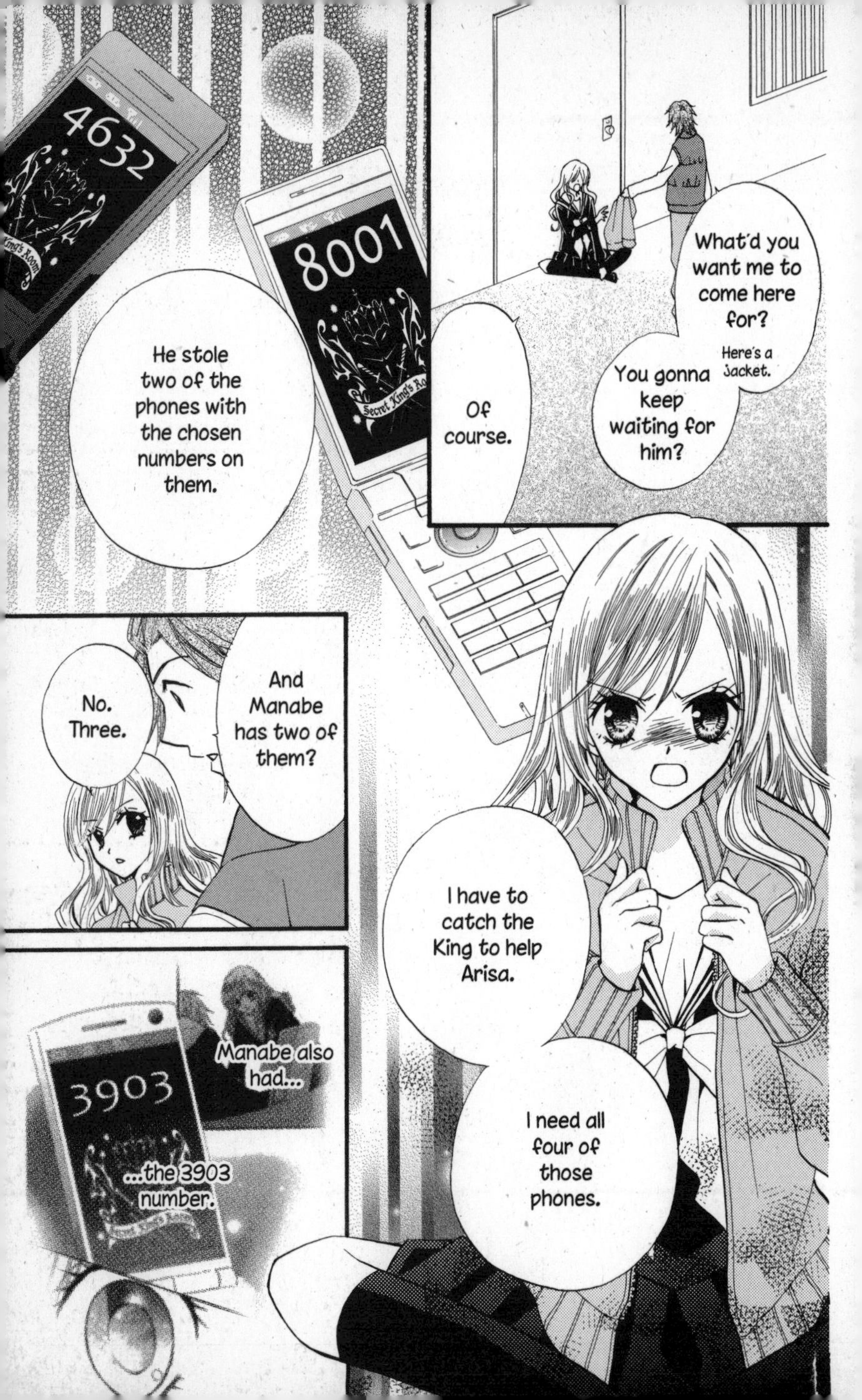
What'd you want me to come here for?
Here's a jacket.
You gonna keep waiting for him?
Of course.
4632
8001
He stole two of the phones with the chosen numbers on them.
I have to catch the King to help Arisa.
I need all four of those phones.
And Manabe has two of them?
No. Three.
3903
Manabe also had...
...the 3903 number.

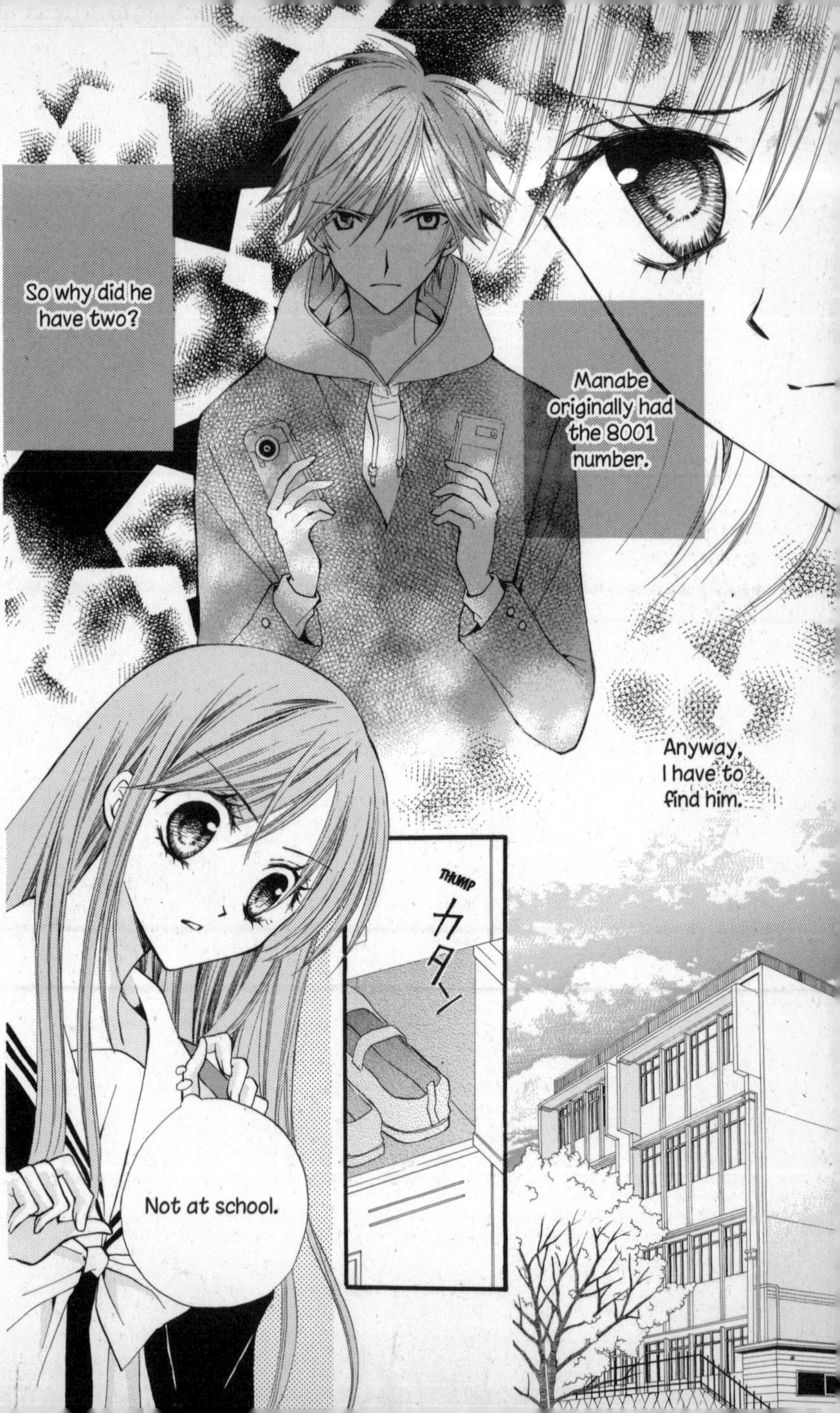
Manabe originally had the 8001 number.
So why did he have two?
Anyway, I have to find him.
THUMP
カタン
Not at school.

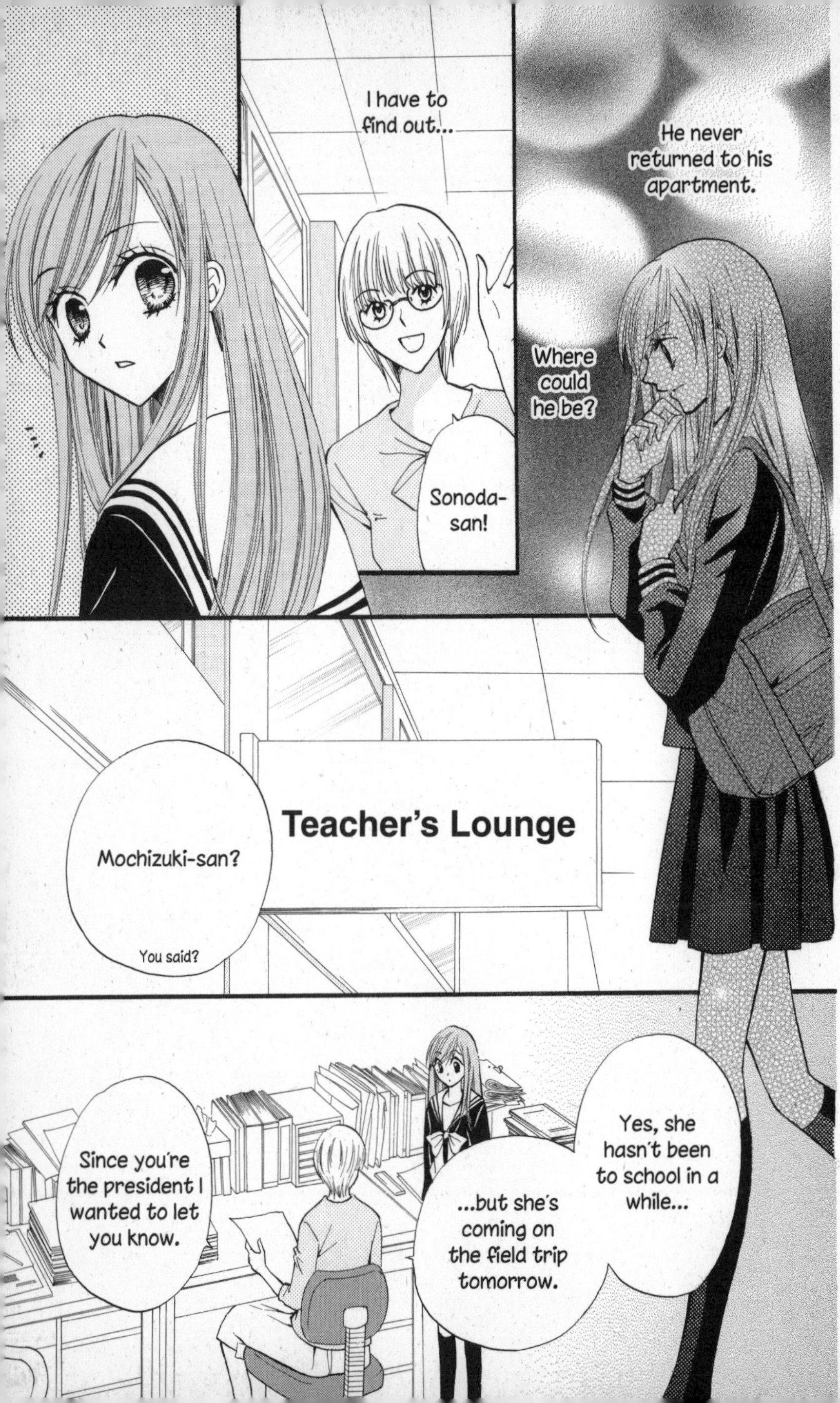
He never returned to his apartment.
Where could he be?
I have to find out...
Sonoda-san!
Teacher's Lounge
Mochizuki-san?
You said?
Yes, she hasn't been to school in a while...
...but she's coming on the field trip tomorrow.
Since you're the president I wanted to let you know.

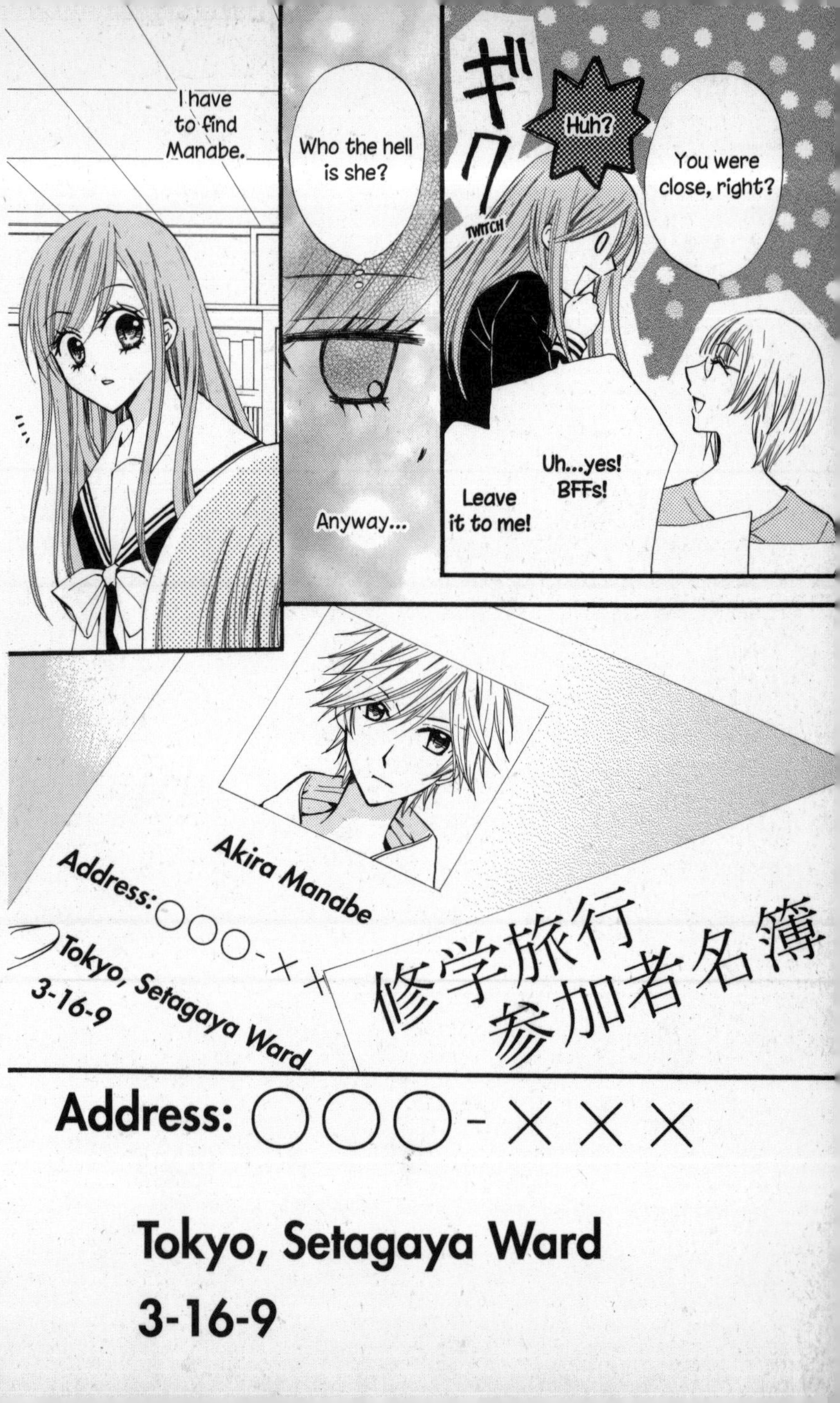
You were close, right?
Huh?
ギク
TWITCH
Uh...yes! BFFs!
Leave it to me!
Who the hell is she?
Anyway...
I have to find Manabe.
修学旅行参加者名簿
Akira Manabe
Address: ○○○-××
Tokyo, Setagaya Ward
3-16-9
Address: ○○○-×××
Tokyo, Setagaya Ward
3-16-9

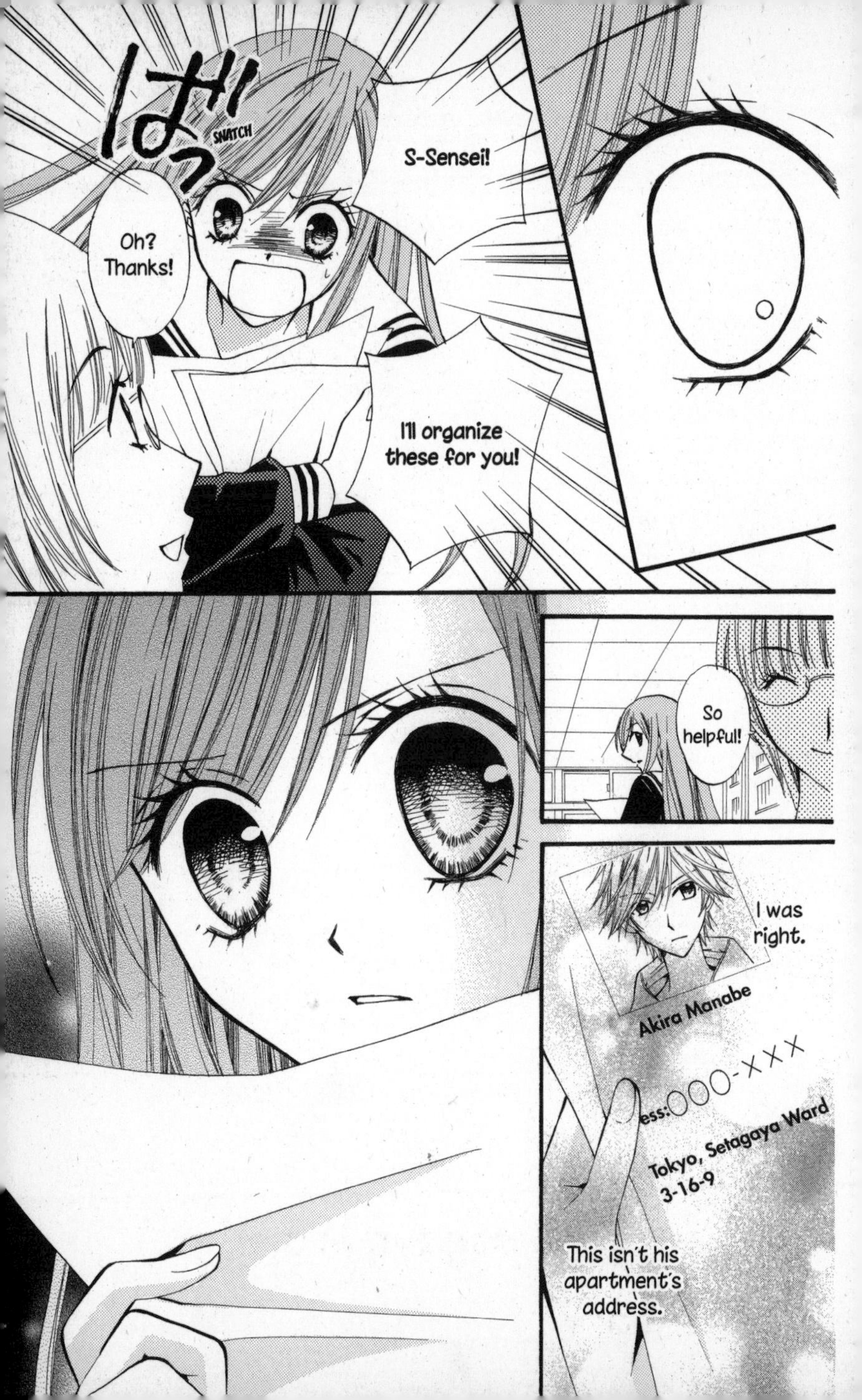
ばっ
SNATCH
S-Sensei!
I'll organize these for you!
Oh? Thanks!
So helpful!
I was right.
Akira Manabe
ess:○○○-×××
Tokyo, Setagaya Ward
3-16-9
This isn't his apartment's address.

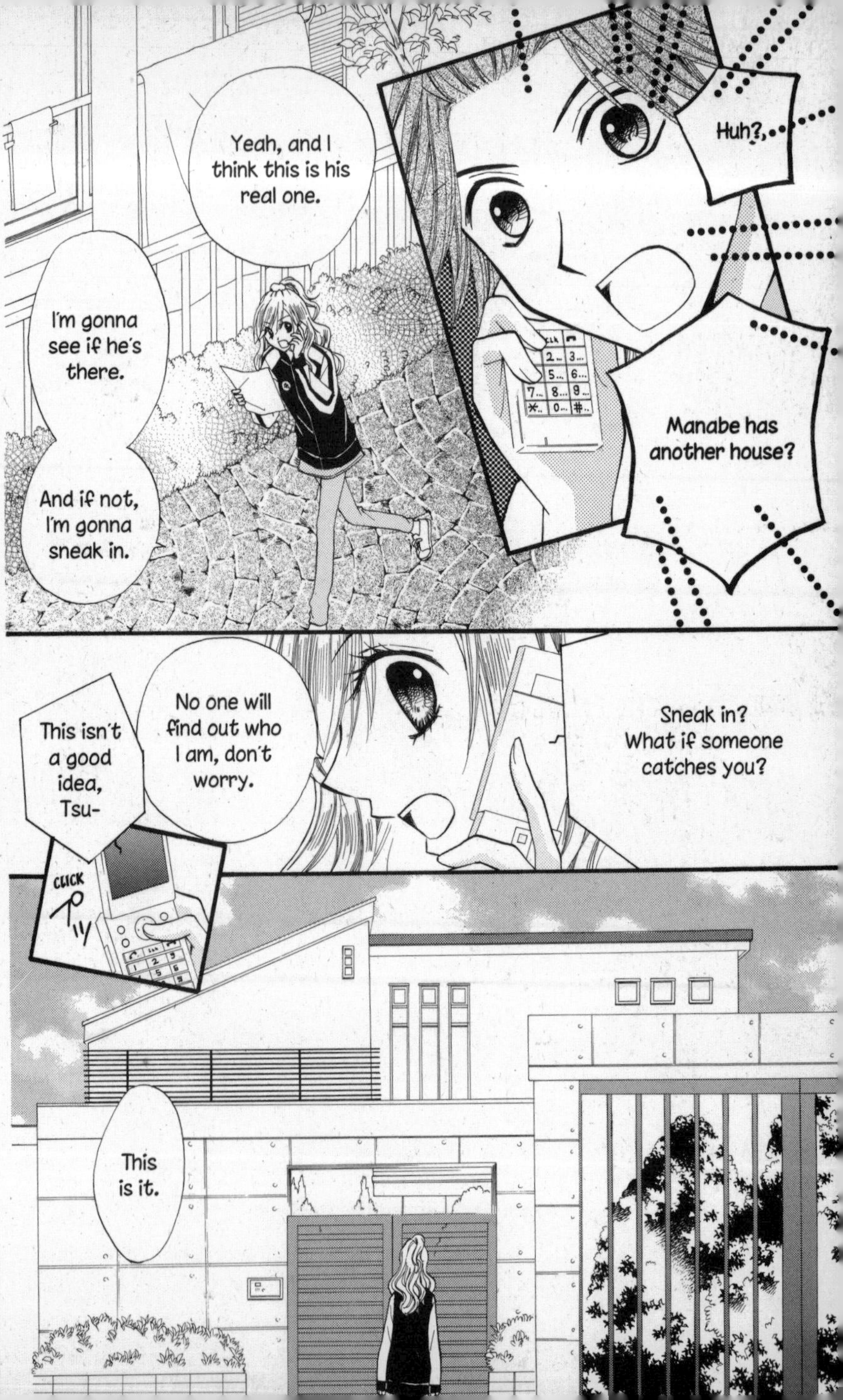
Huh?
Manabe has another house?
Yeah, and I think this is his real one.
I'm gonna see if he's there.
And if not, I'm gonna sneak in.
Sneak in? What if someone catches you?
No one will find out who I am, don't worry.
This isn't a good idea, Tsu-
CLICK
This is it.

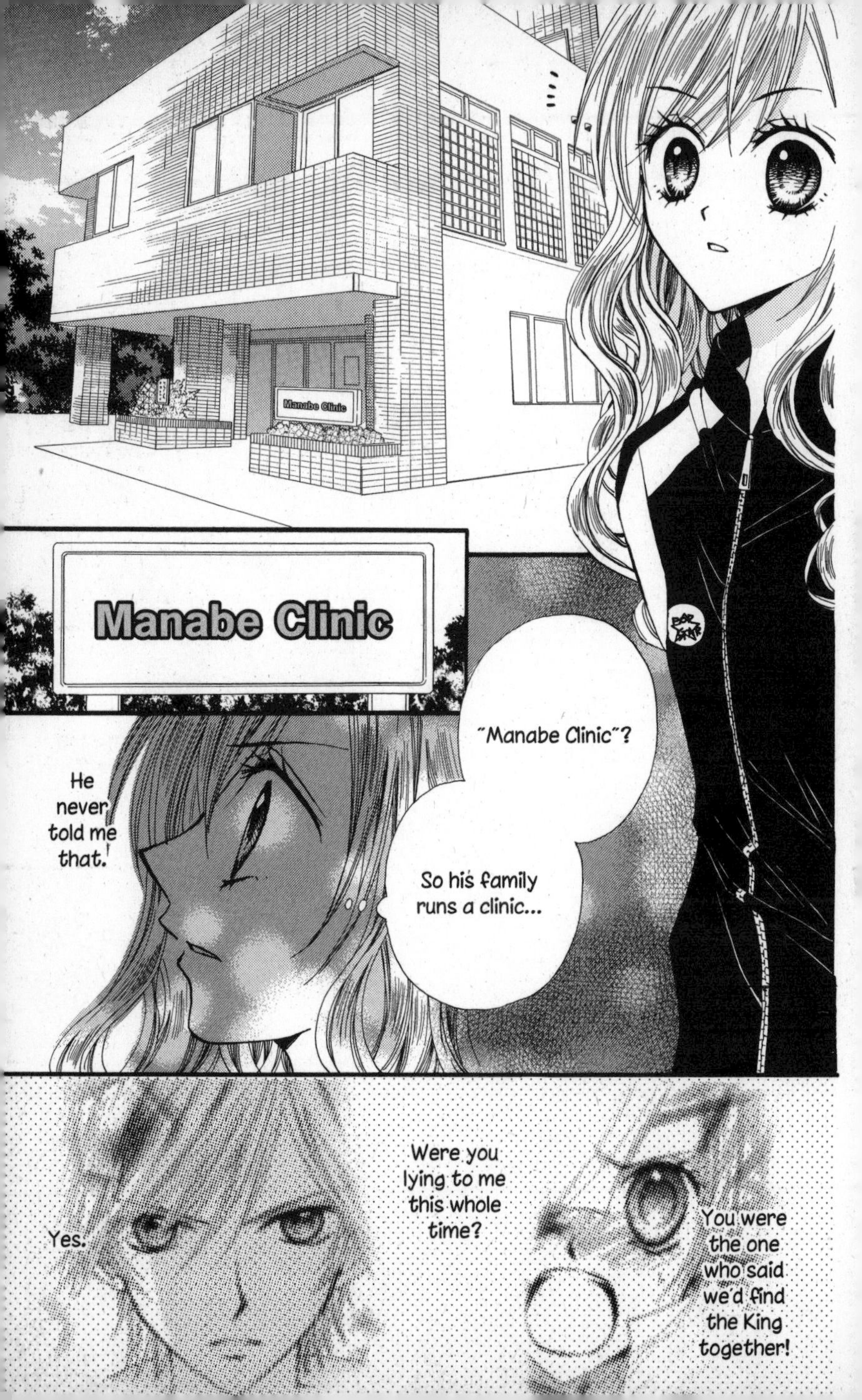
Manabe Clinic
Manabe Clinic
"Manabe Clinic"?
So his family runs a clinic...
He never told me that.
You were the one who said we'd find the King together!
Were you lying to me this whole time?
Yes.

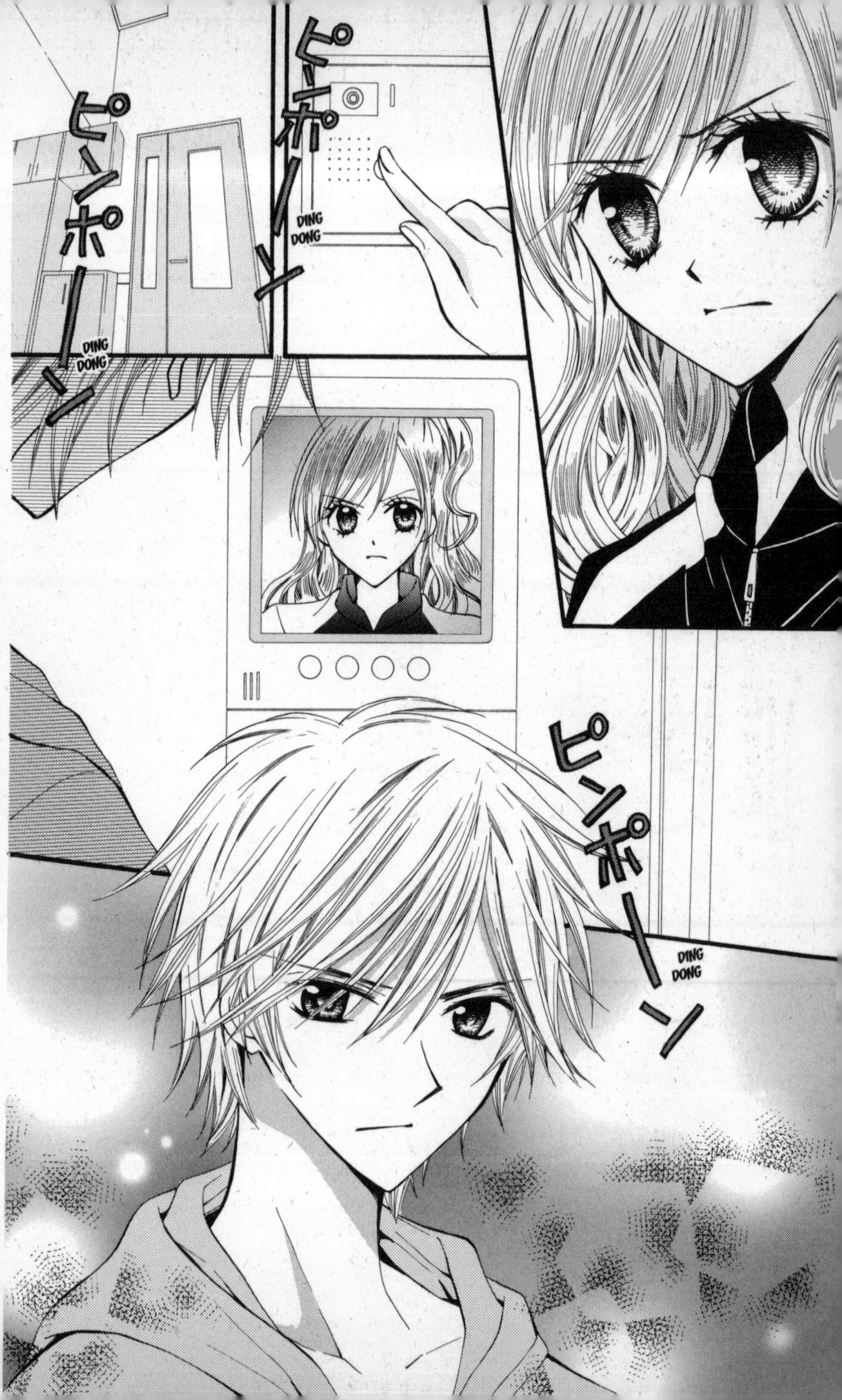
ピーンポーン
DING DONG
ピンポーン
DING DONG
ピンポーン
DING DONG

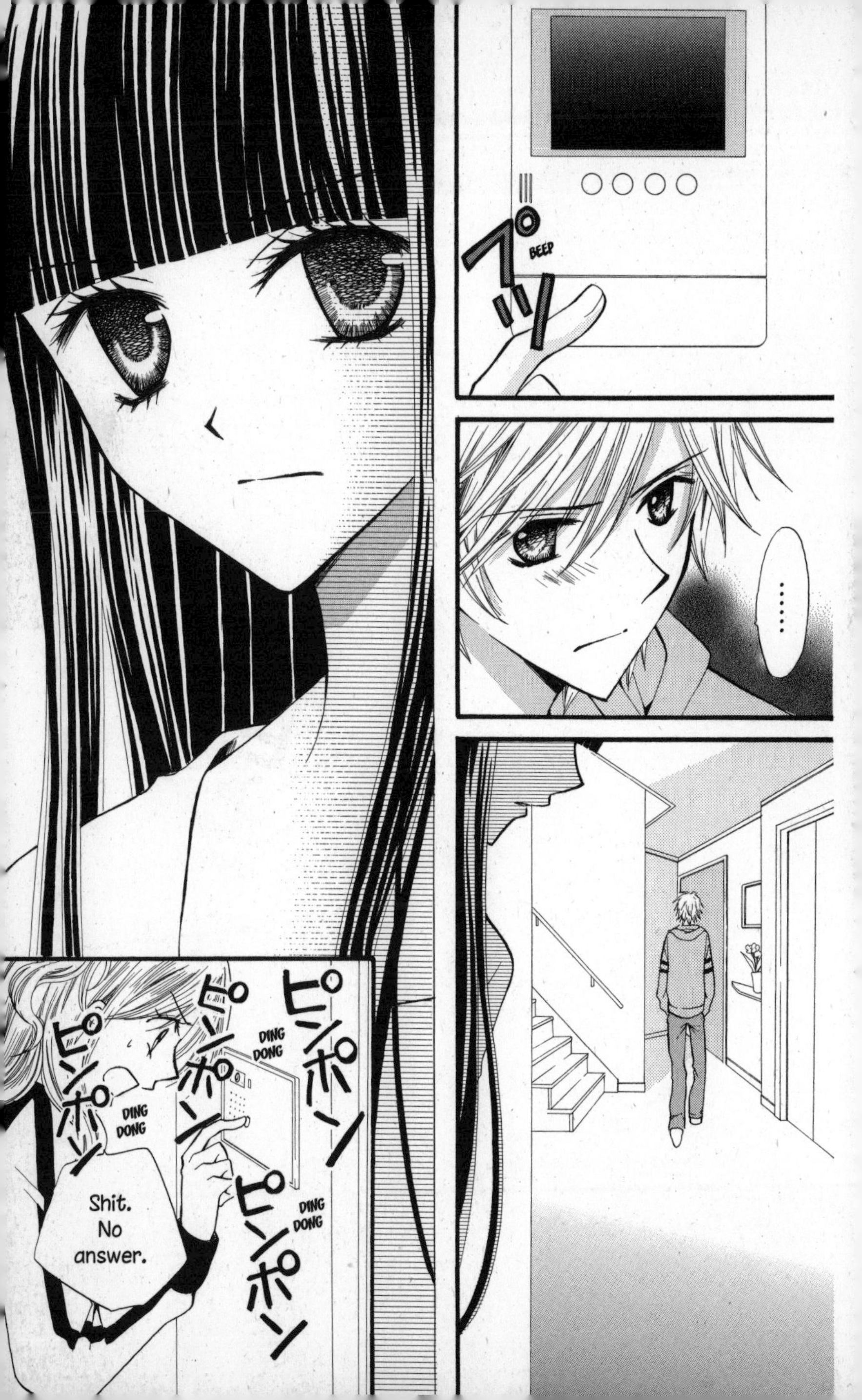
プッ
BEEP
......
ピンポーン
ピンポーン
DING DONG
ピンポーン
DING DONG
ピンポーン
DING DONG
Shit. No answer.

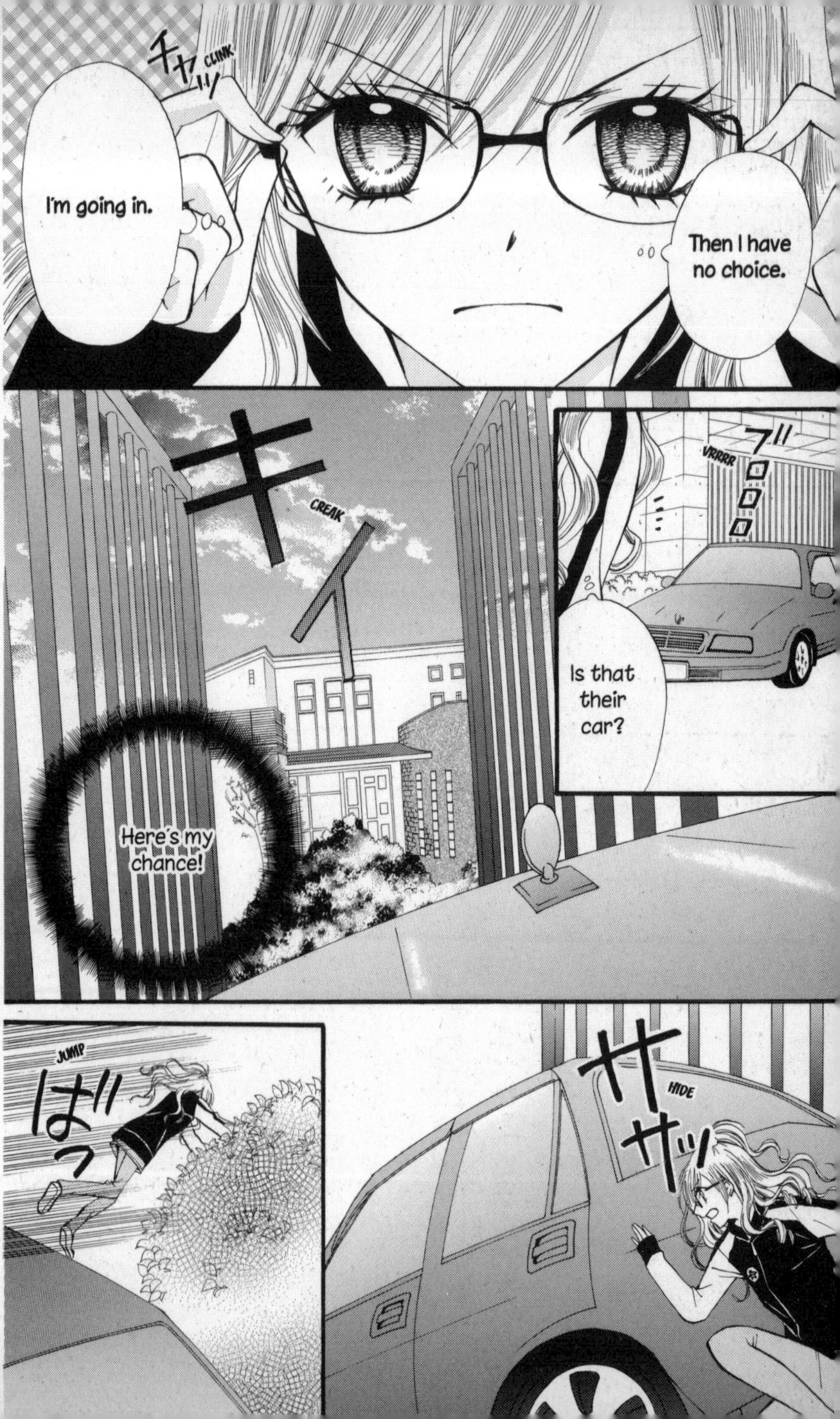
Then I have no choice.
CLINK
I'm going in.
VRRRR
Is that their car?
CREAK
Here's my chance!
HIDE
JUMP

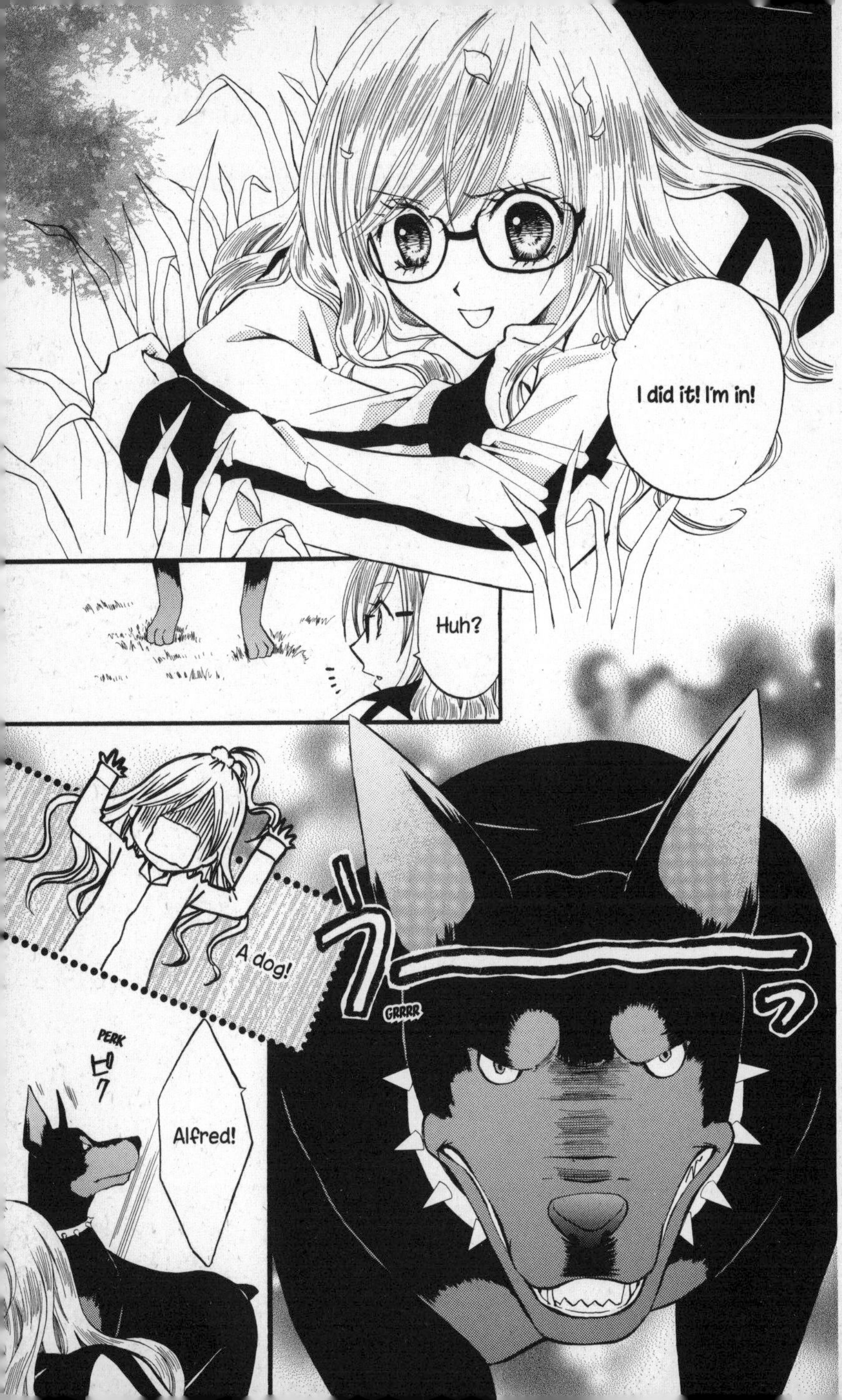

I did it! I'm in!
Huh?
GRRRR
A dog!
PERK
ピク
Alfred!

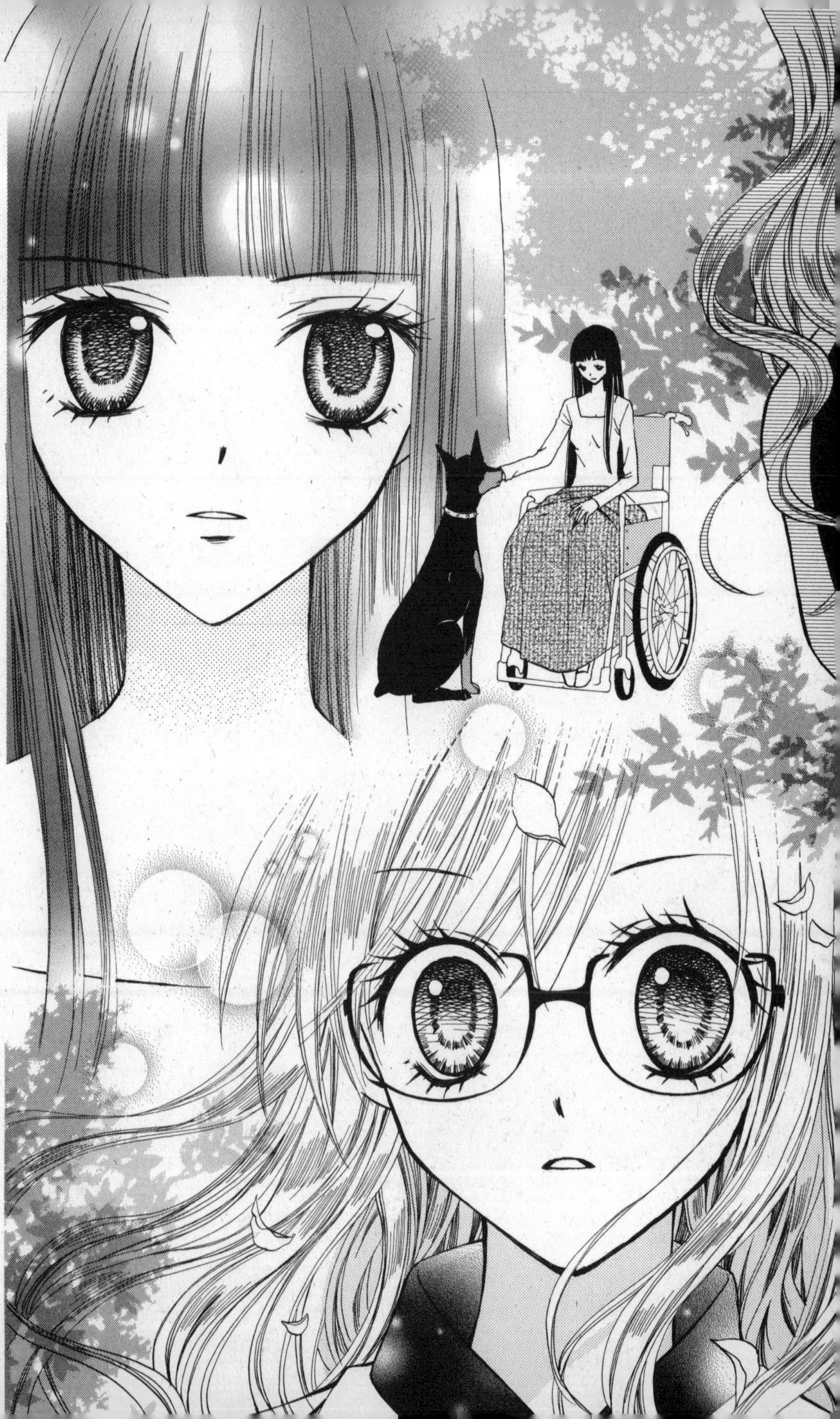

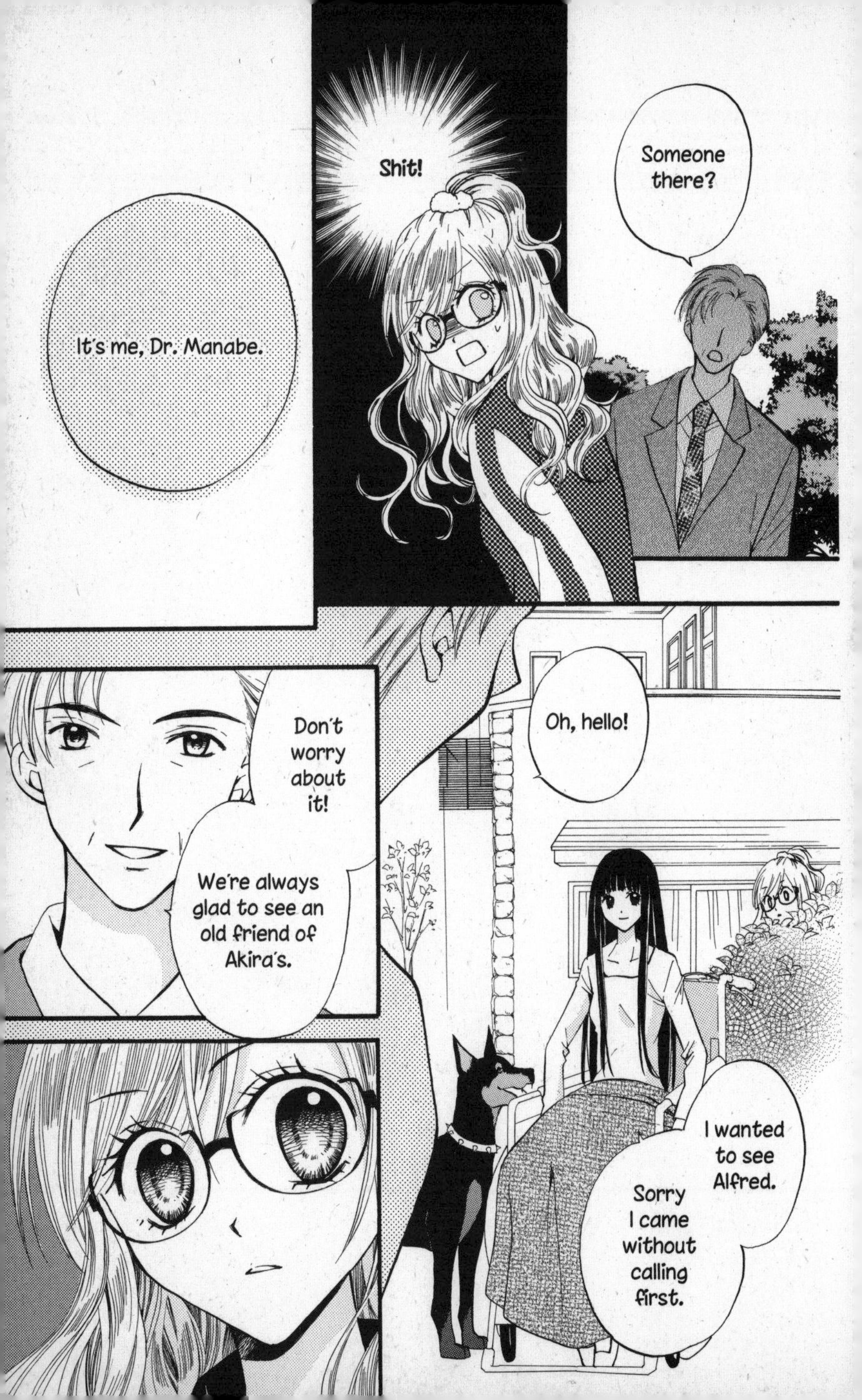
Someone there?
Shit!
It's me, Dr. Manabe.
Oh, hello!
I wanted to see Alfred.
Sorry I came without calling first.
Don't worry about it!
We're always glad to see an old friend of Akira's.

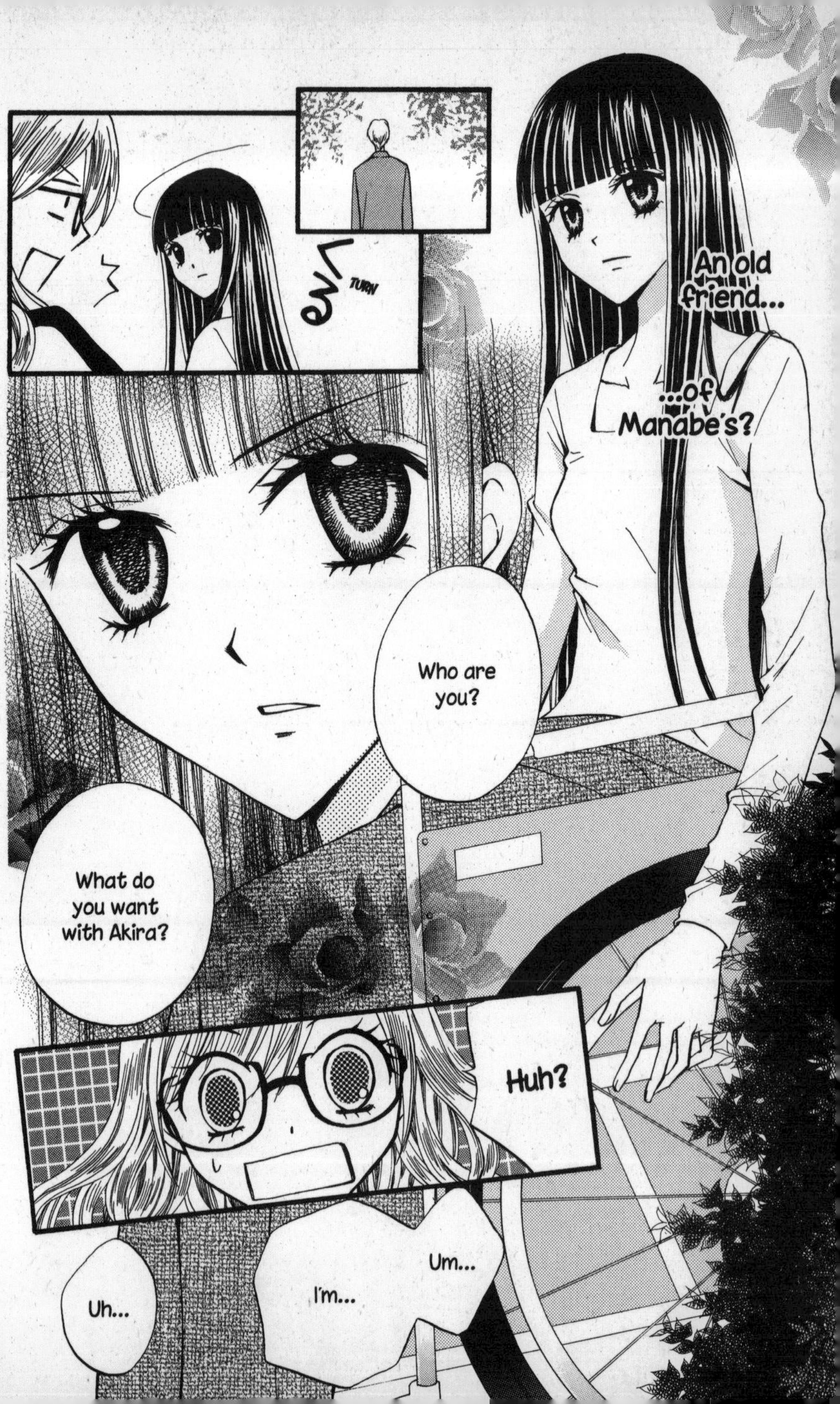
An old friend...
...of Manabe's?
TURN
Who are you?
What do you want with Akira?
Huh?
Um...
I'm...
Uh...

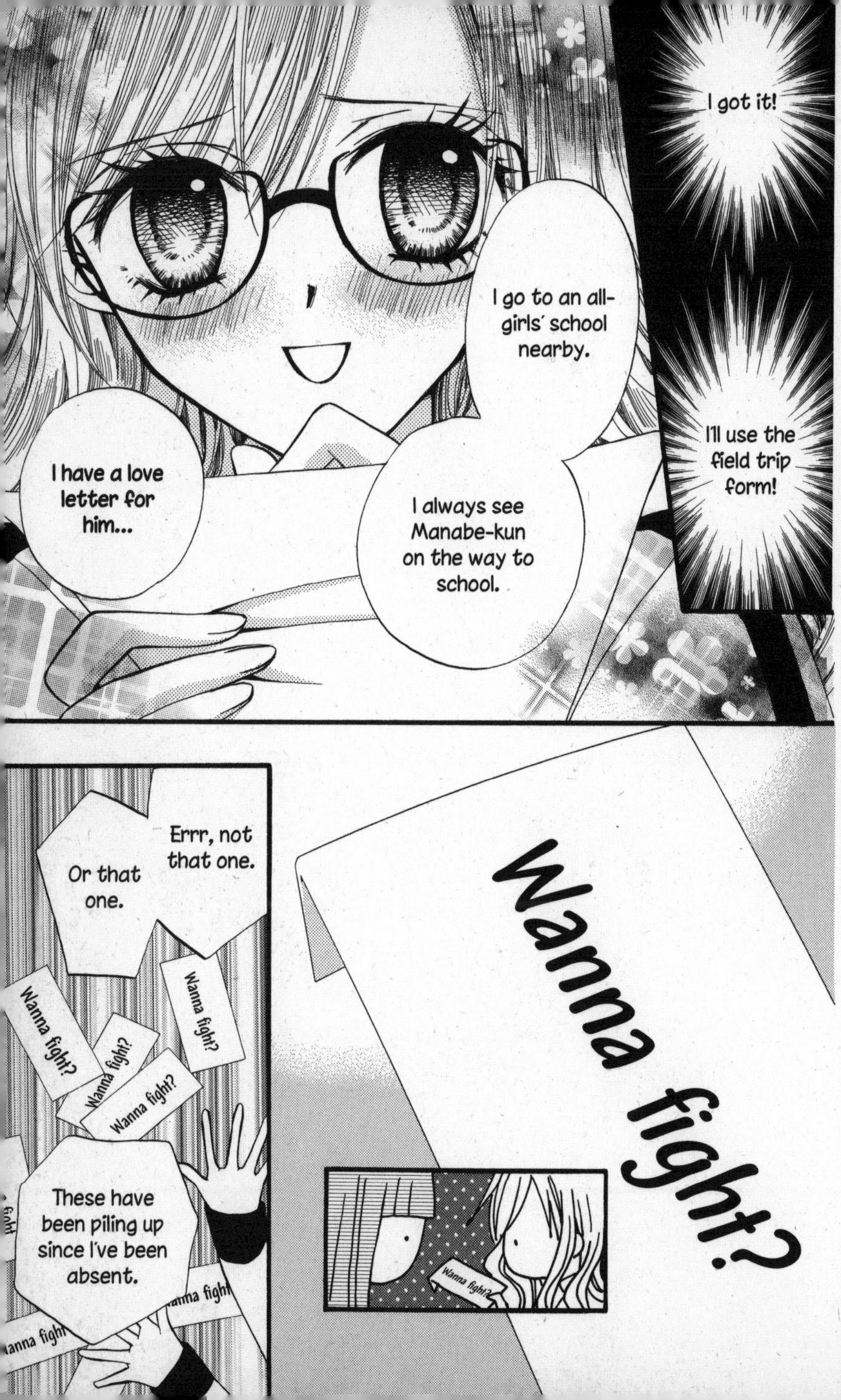

I got it!
I'll use the field trip form!
I go to an all-girls' school nearby.
I always see Manabe-kun on the way to school.
I have a love letter for him...
Wanna fight?
Wanna fight?
Errr, not that one.
Or that one.
Wanna fight?
Wanna fight?
Wanna fight?
Wanna fight?
These have been piling up since I've been absent.

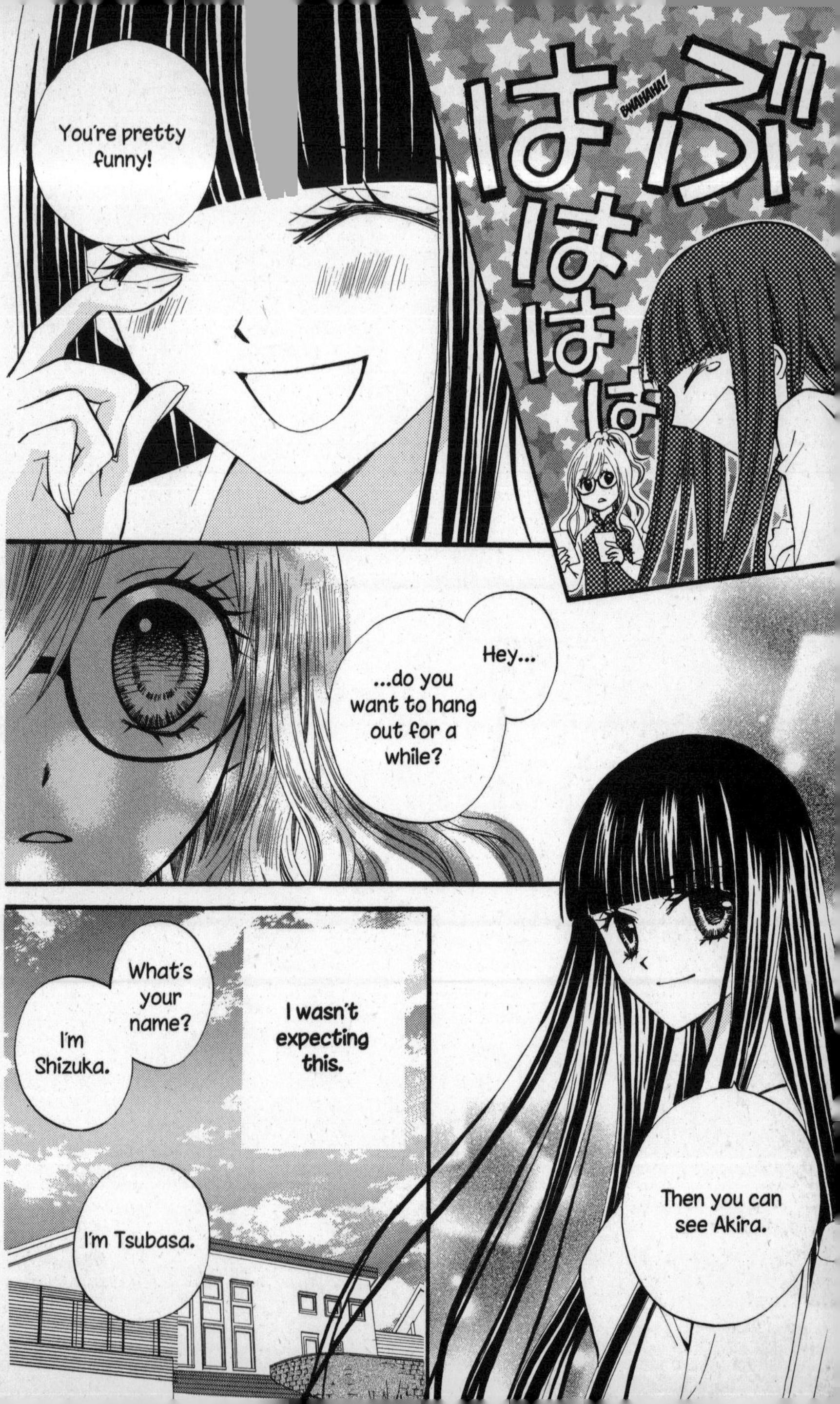

ぶははは
BWAHAHA!
You're pretty funny!
Hey...
...do you want to hang out for a while?
Then you can see Akira.
I wasn't expecting this.
What's your name?
I'm Shizuka.
I'm Tsubasa.

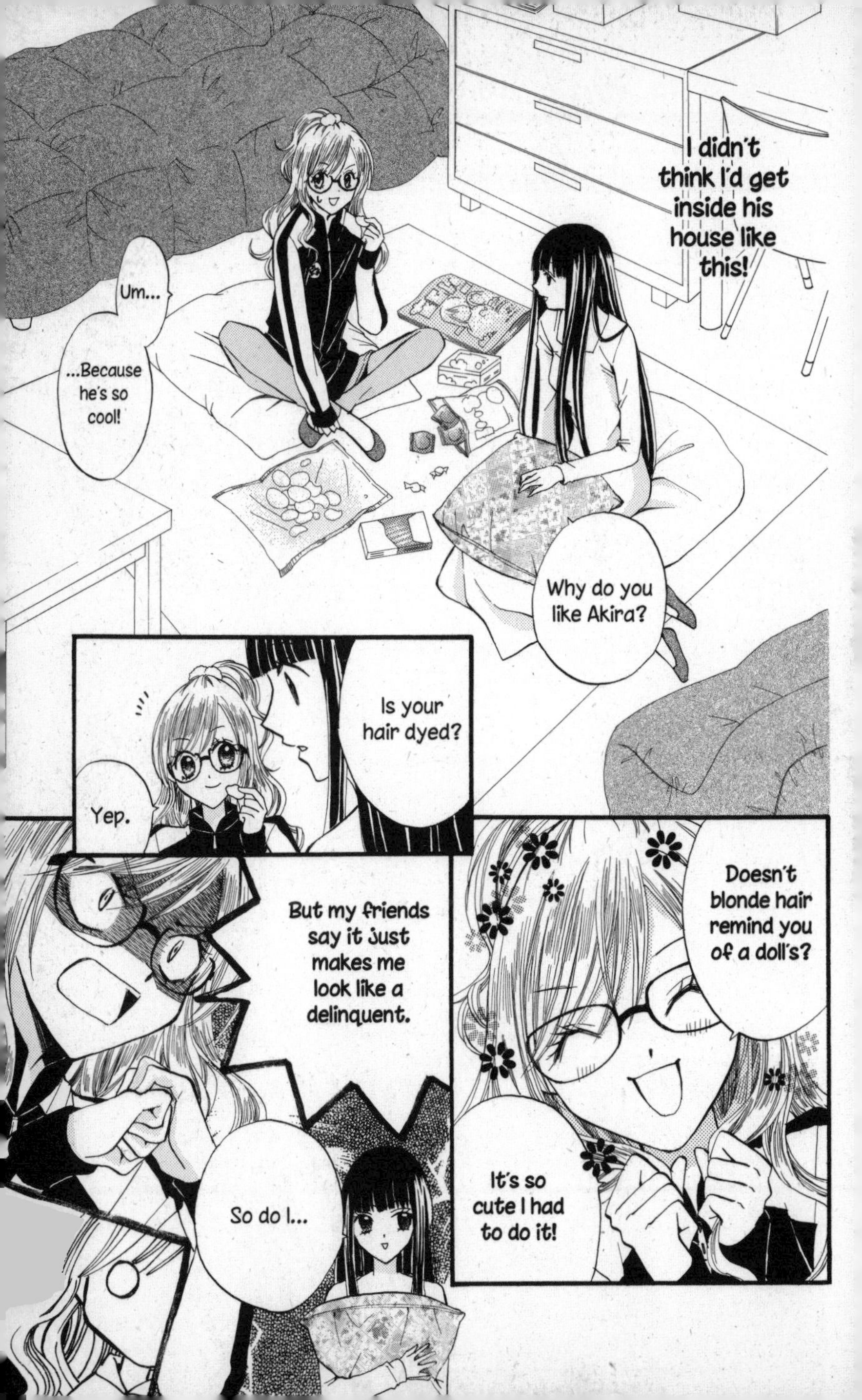
I didn't think I'd get inside his house like this!
Why do you like Akira?
Um...
...Because he's so cool!
Is your hair dyed?
Yep.
Doesn't blonde hair remind you of a doll's?
It's so cute I had to do it!
But my friends say it just makes me look like a delinquent.
So do I...

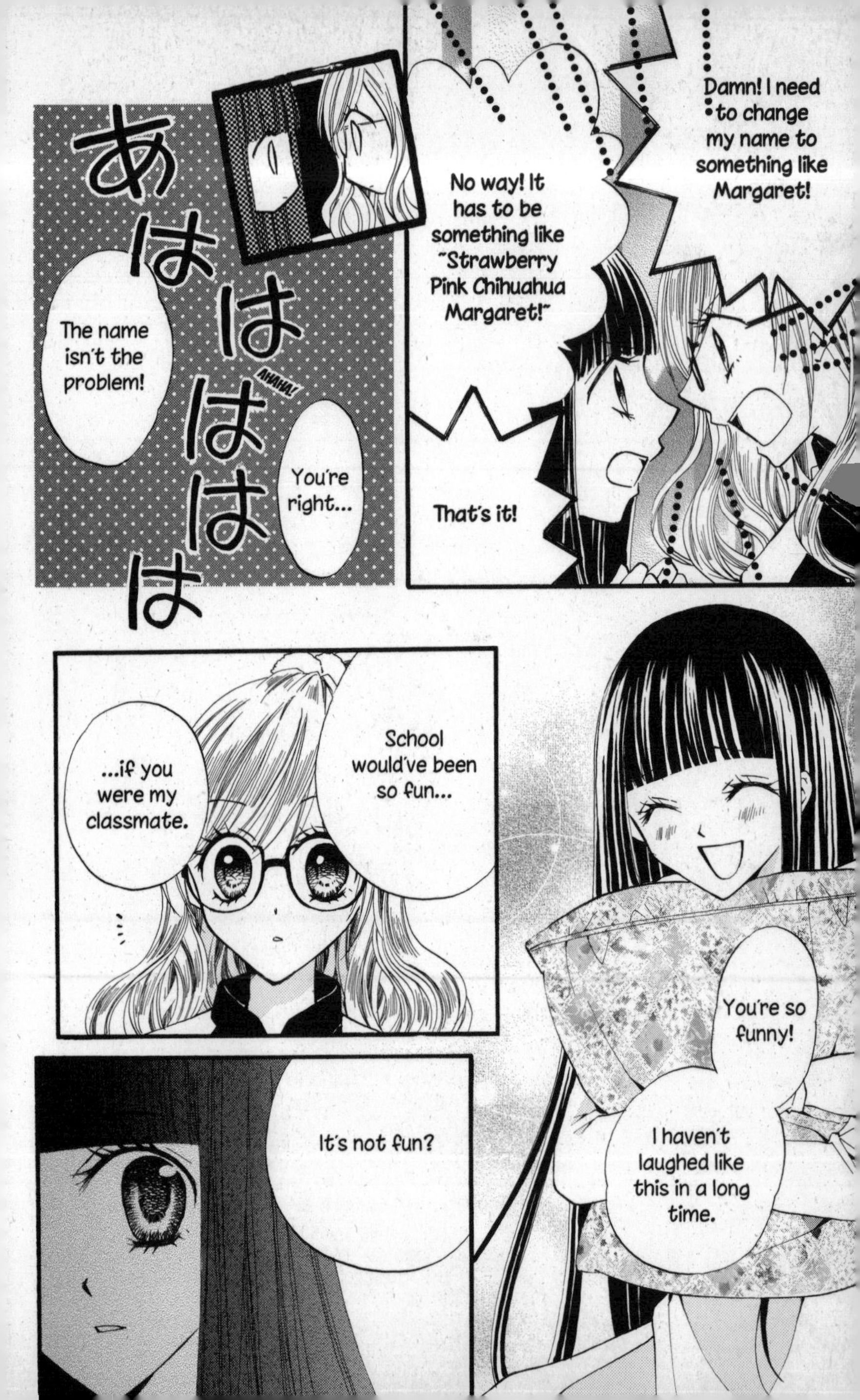
Damn! I need to change my name to something like Margaret!
No way! It has to be something like "Strawberry Pink Chihuahua Margaret!"
That's it!
あははははは
AHAHA!
You're right...
The name isn't the problem!
You're so funny!
I haven't laughed like this in a long time.
School would've been so fun...
...if you were my classmate.
It's not fun?

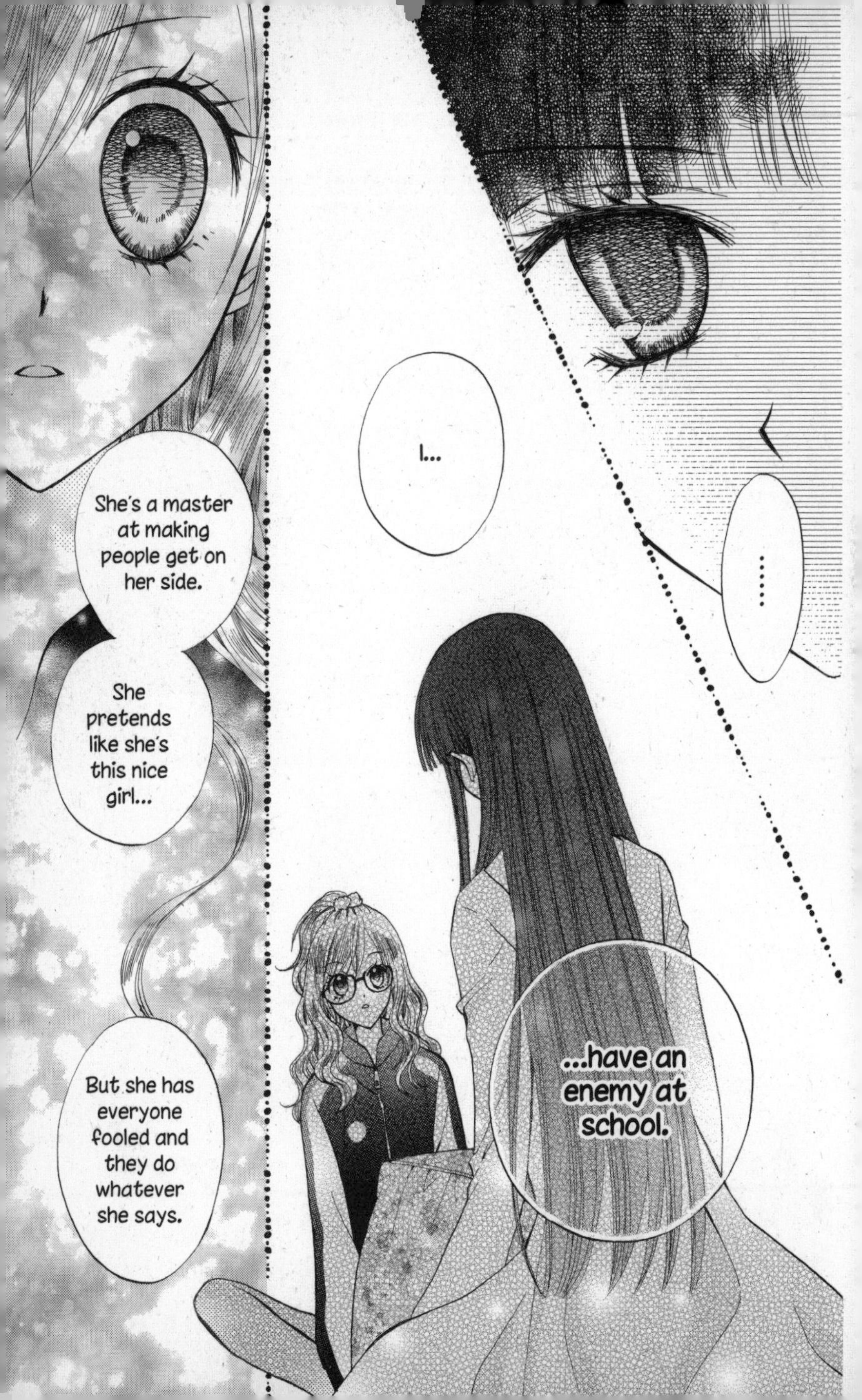
...
I...
...have an enemy at school.
She's a master at making people get on her side.
She pretends like she's this nice girl...
But she has everyone fooled and they do whatever she says.

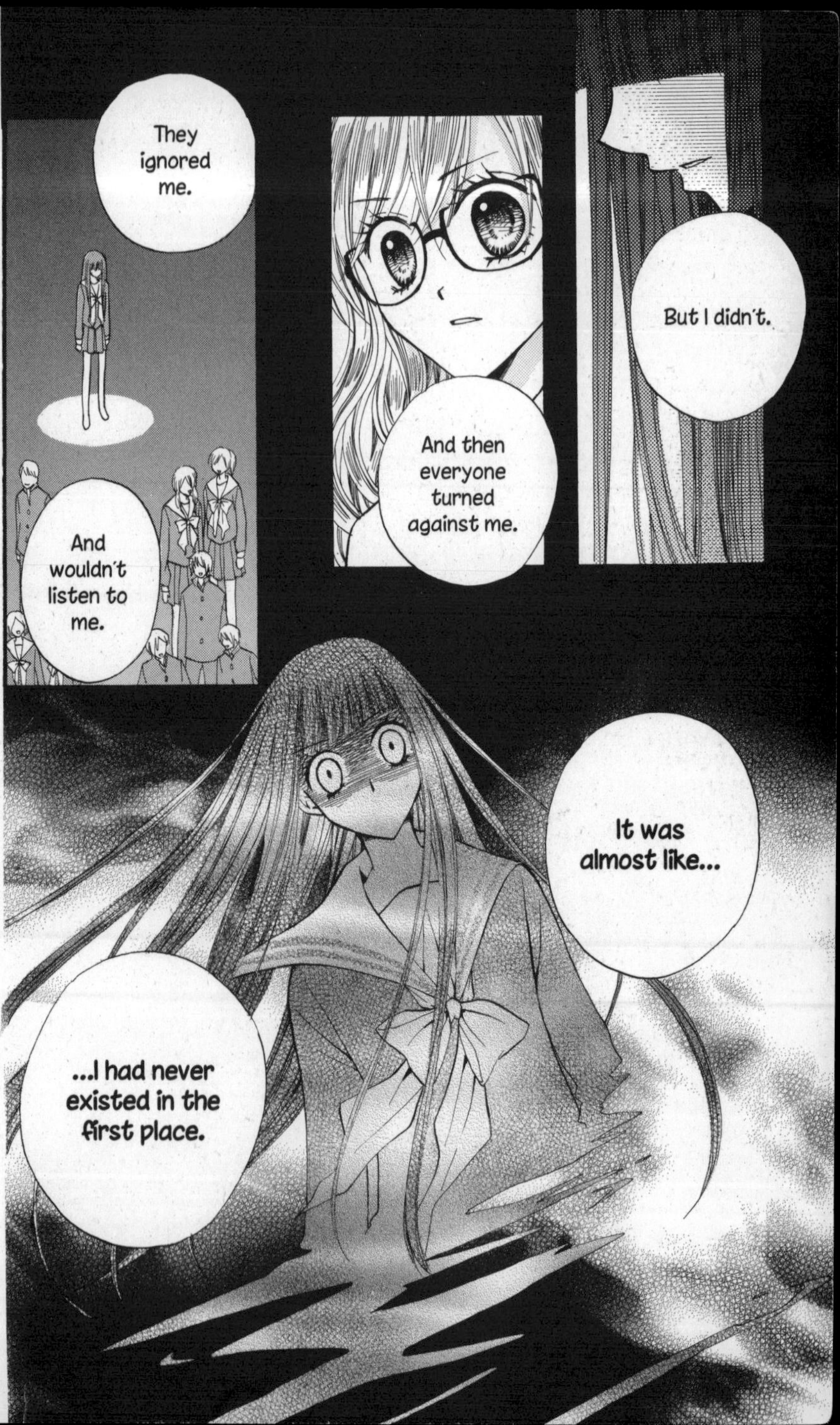
But I didn't.
And then everyone turned against me.
They ignored me.
And wouldn't listen to me.
It was almost like...
...I had never existed in the first place.

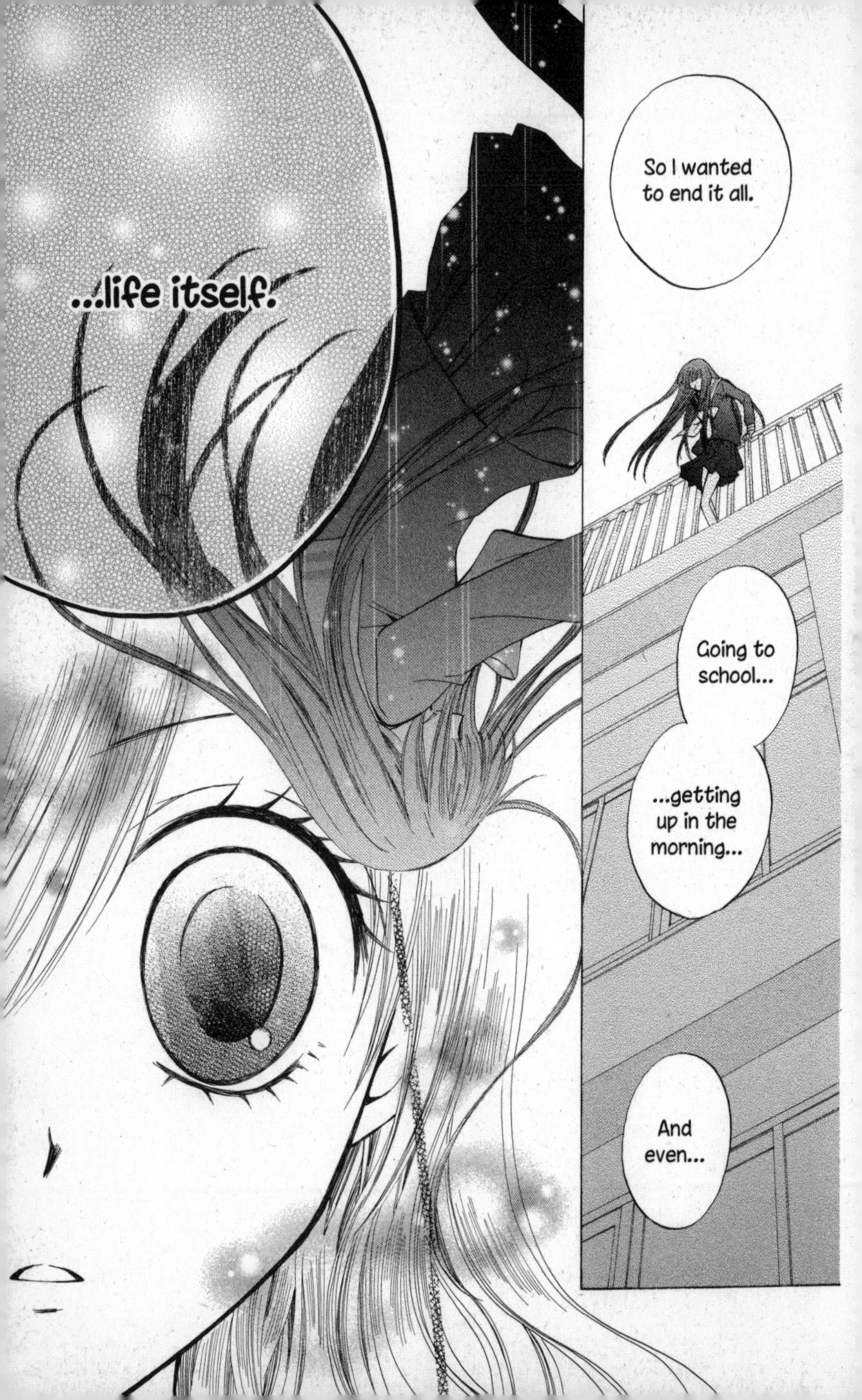
So I wanted to end it all.
Going to school...
...getting up in the morning...
And even...
...life itself.

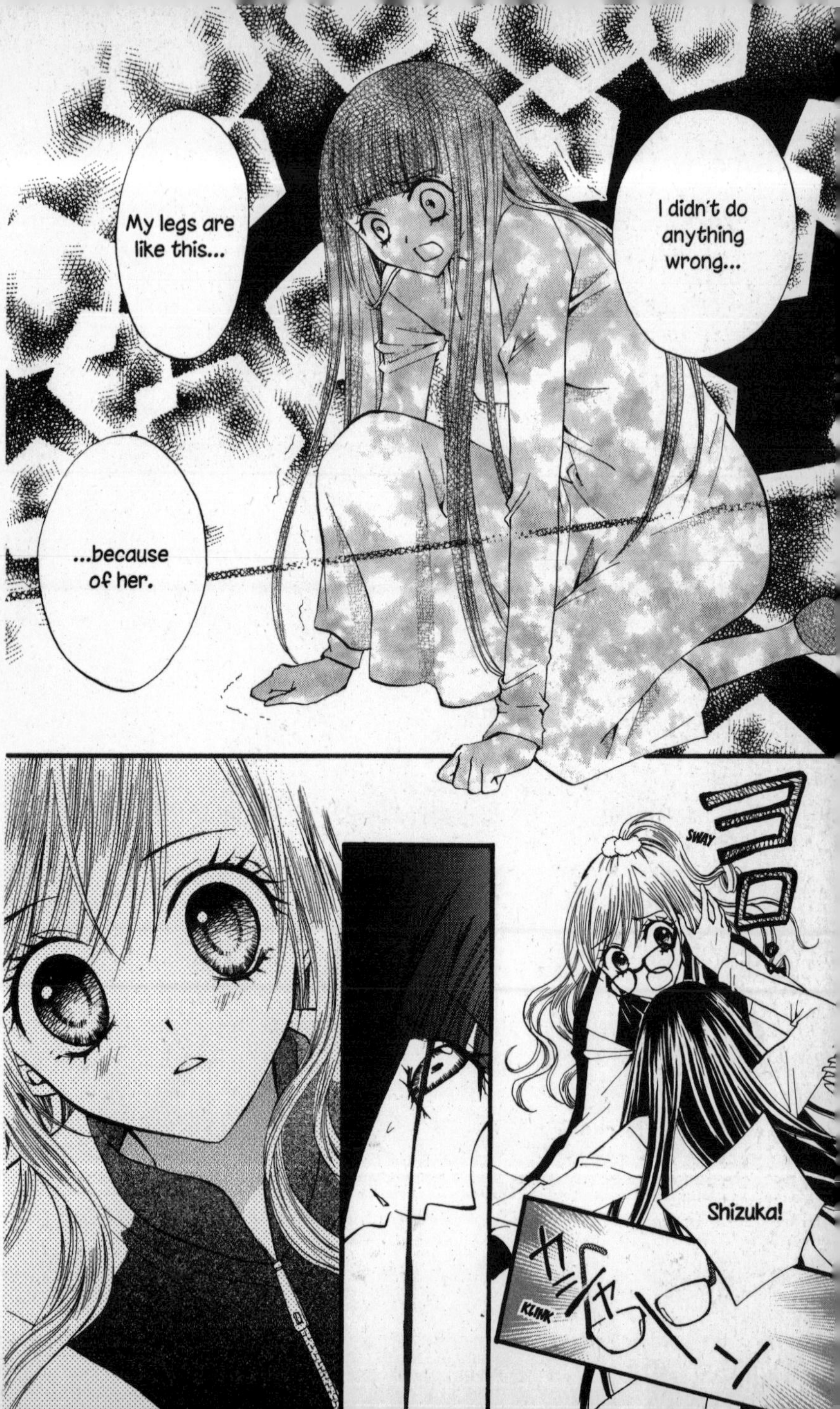
I didn't do anything wrong...
My legs are like this...
...because of her.
SWAY
Shizuka!
KLINK

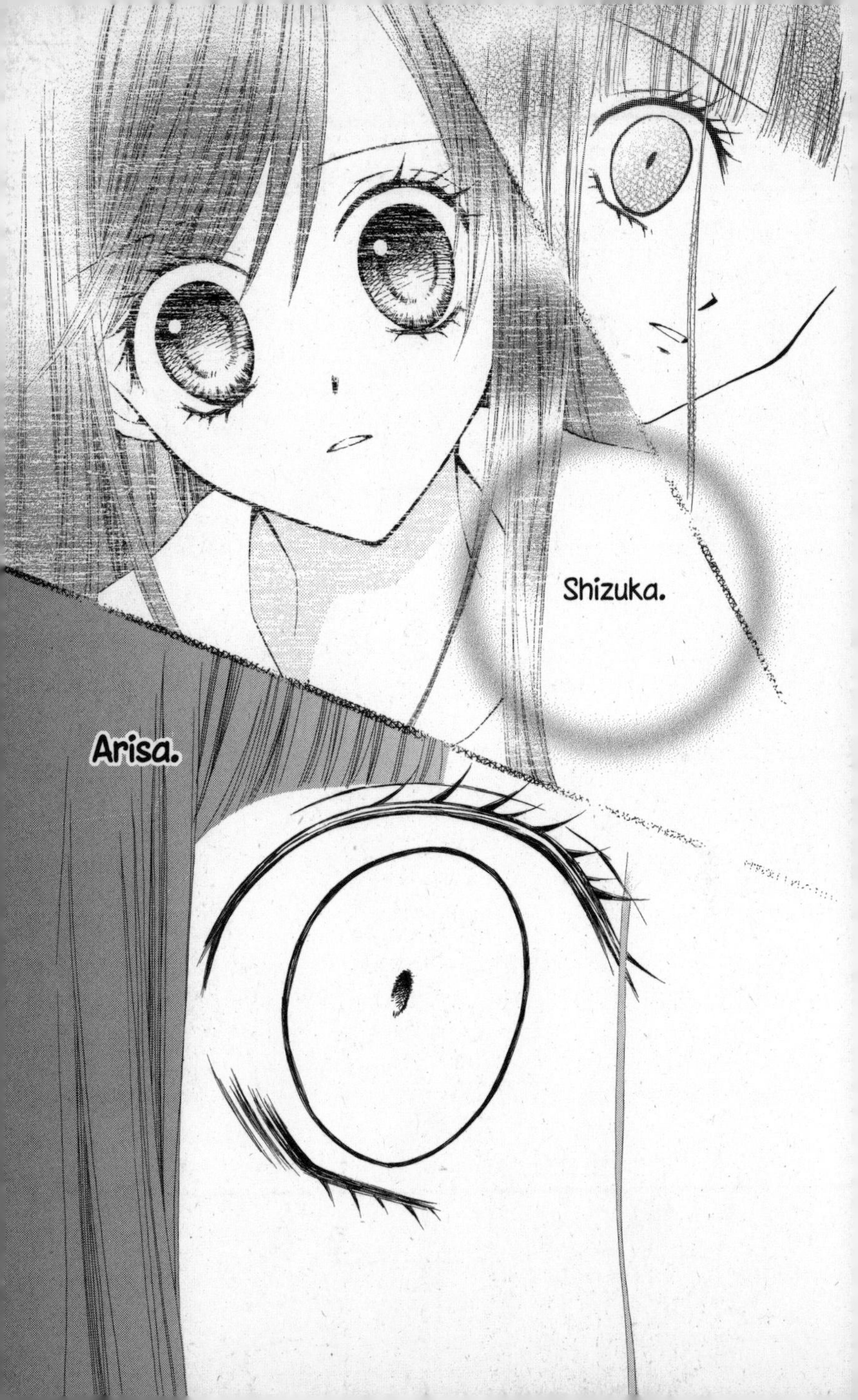
Shizuka.
Arisa.

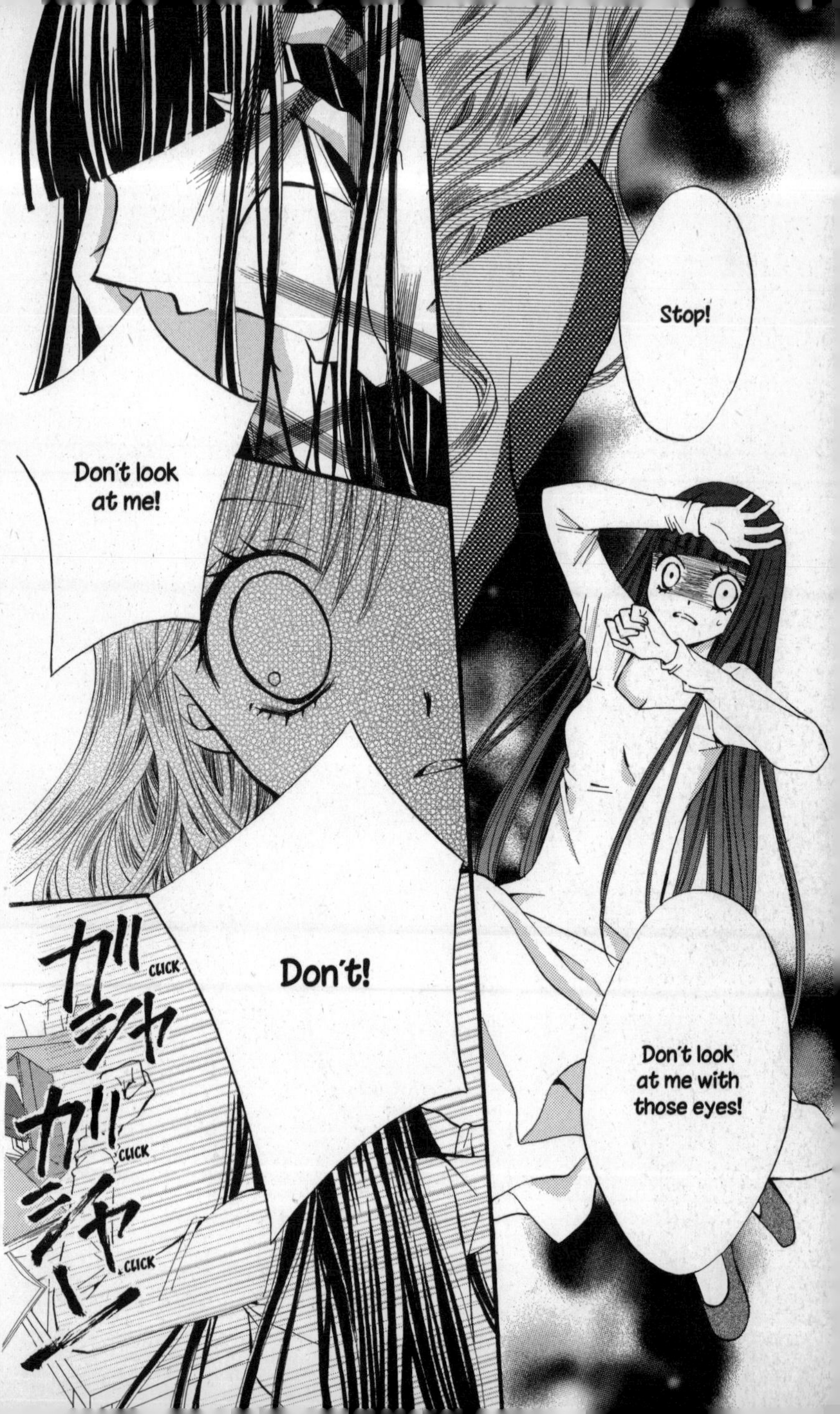

Stop!
Don't look at me with those eyes!
Don't look at me!
Don't!
ガシャ
CLICK
ガシャ
CLICK
ガシャーン
CLICK

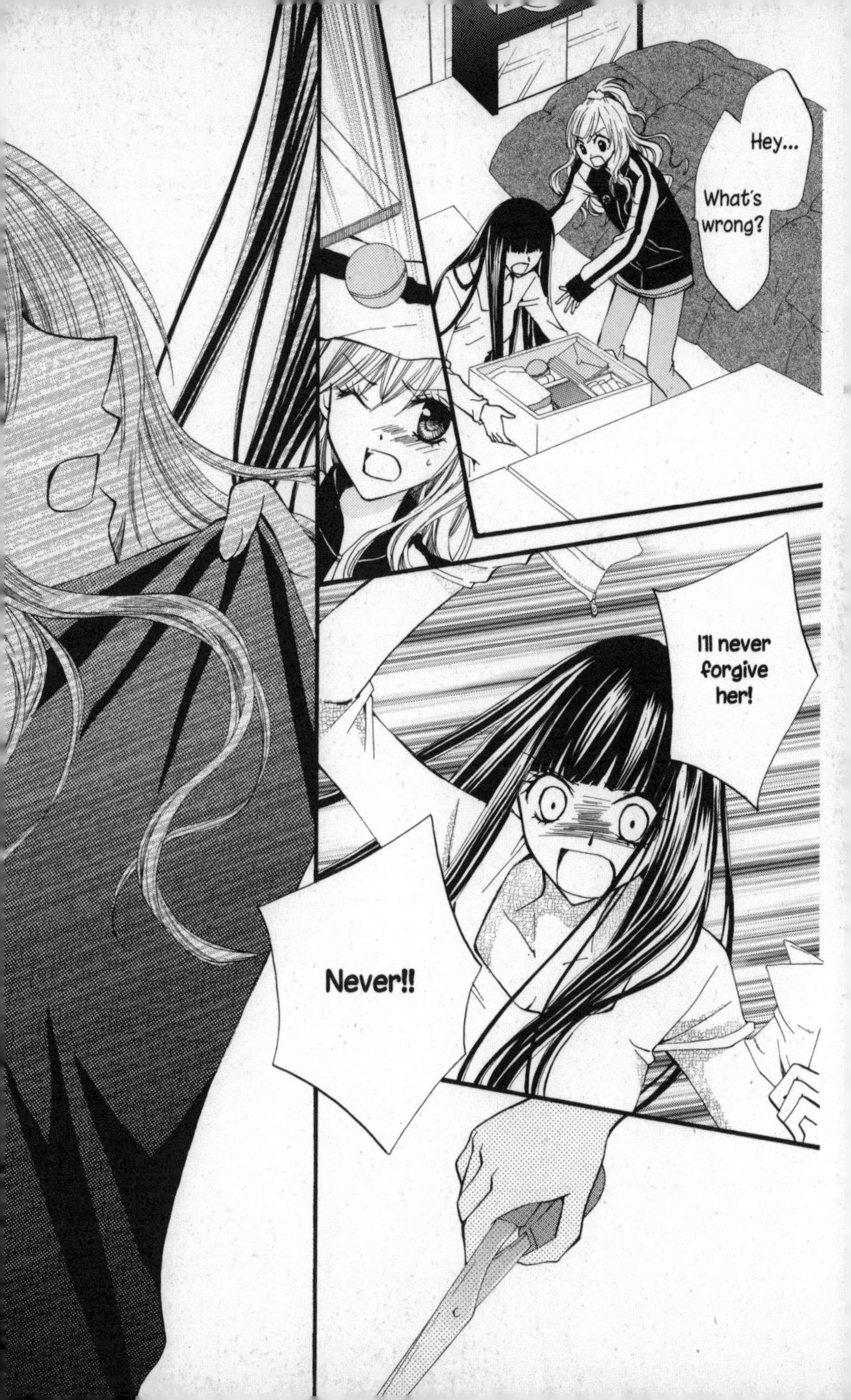
Hey...
What's wrong?
I'll never forgive her!
Never!!

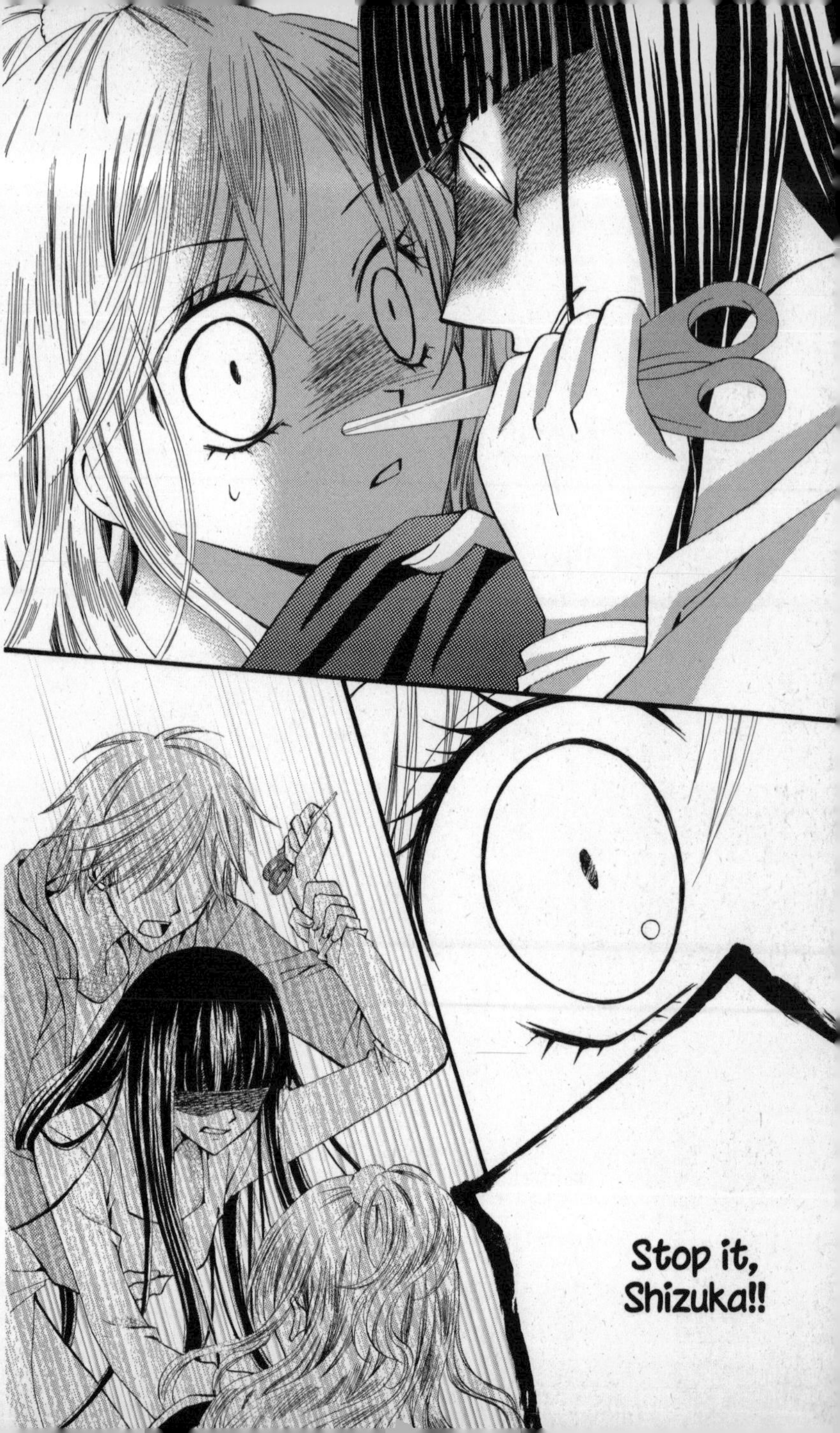
Stop it, Shizuka!!

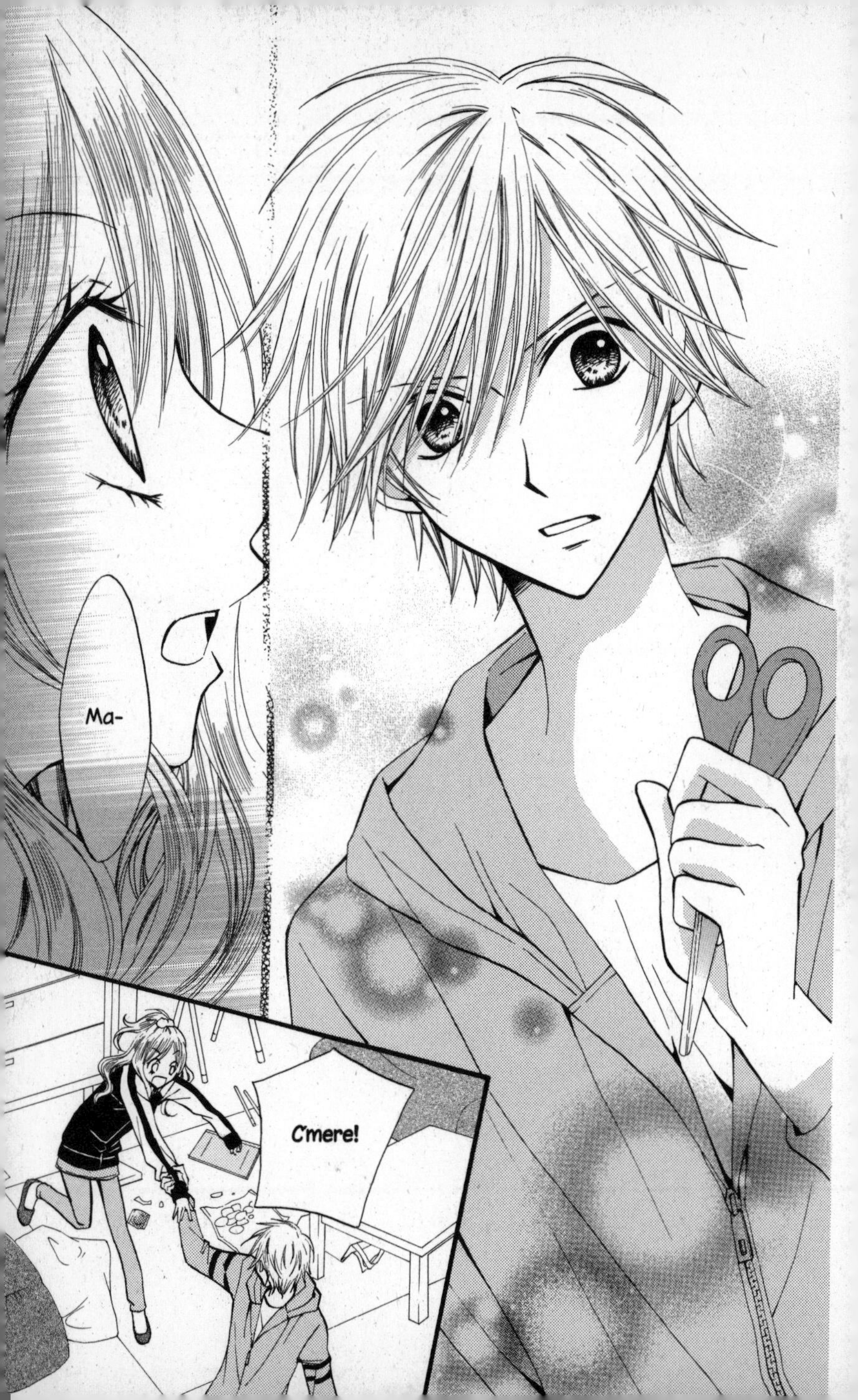
Ma-
C'mere!

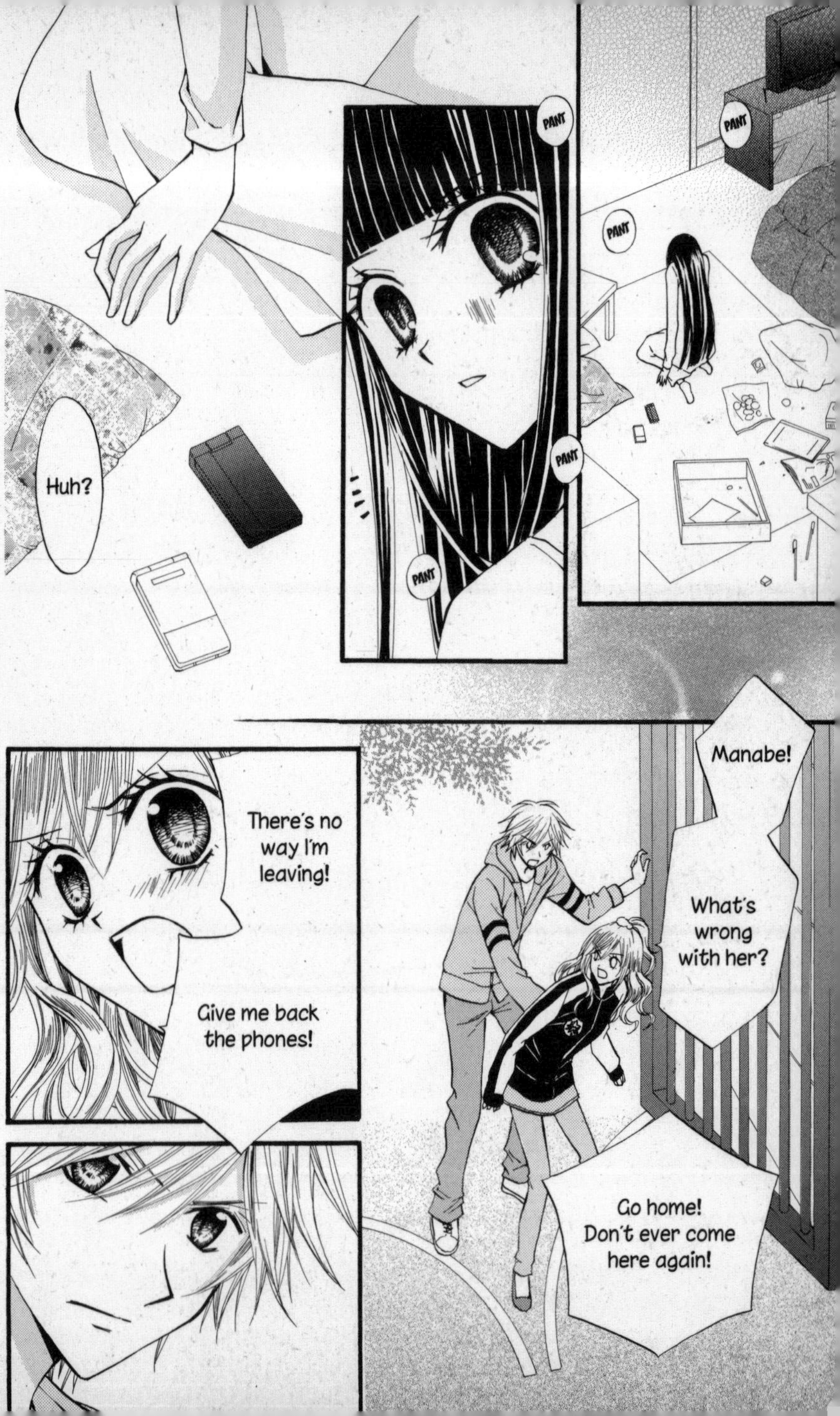
PANT
PANT
PANT
PANT
PANT
Huh?
Manabe!
What's wrong with her?
Go home! Don't ever come here again!
There's no way I'm leaving!
Give me back the phones!

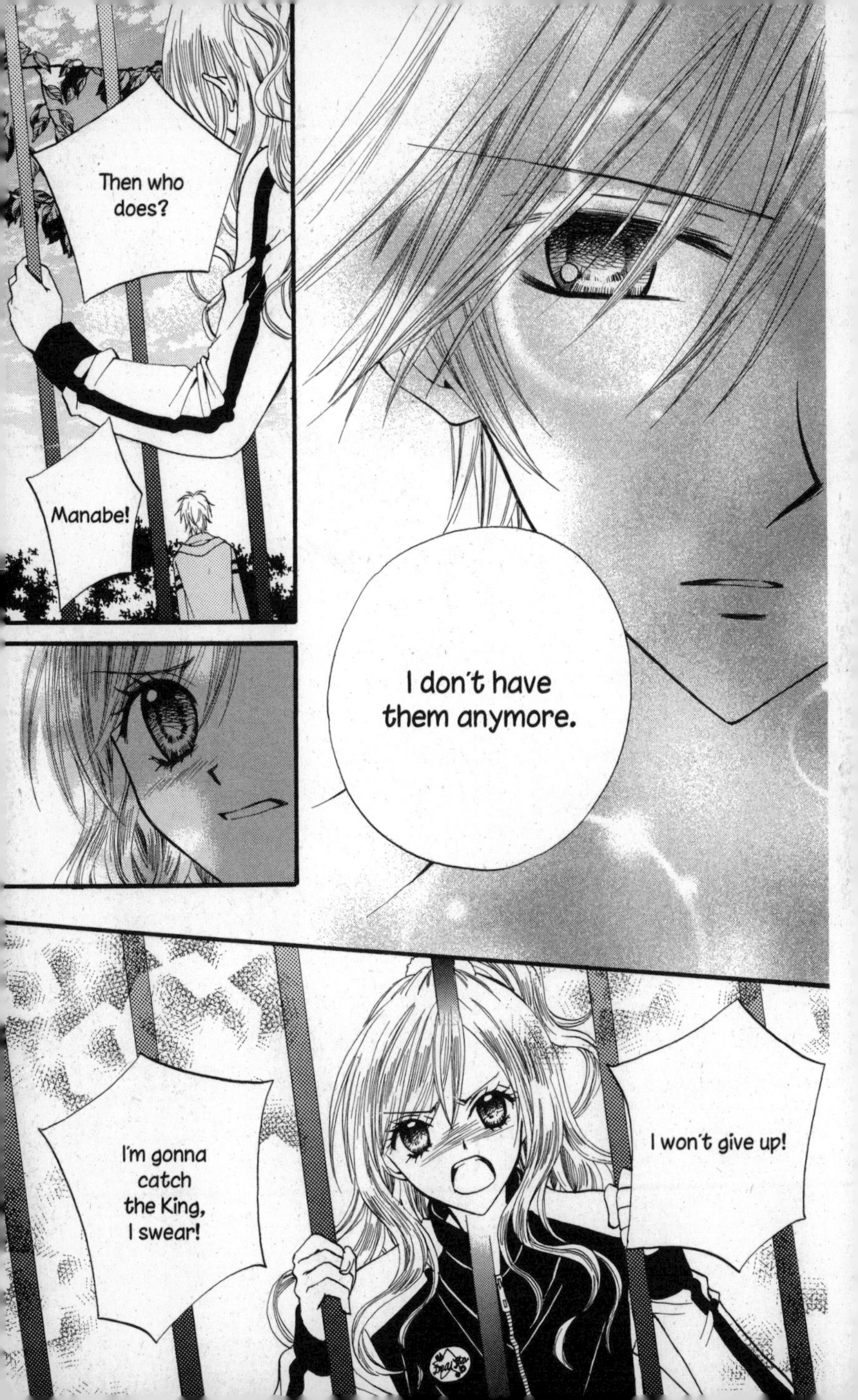
I don't have them anymore.
Then who does?
Manabe!
I won't give up!
I'm gonna catch the King, I swear!

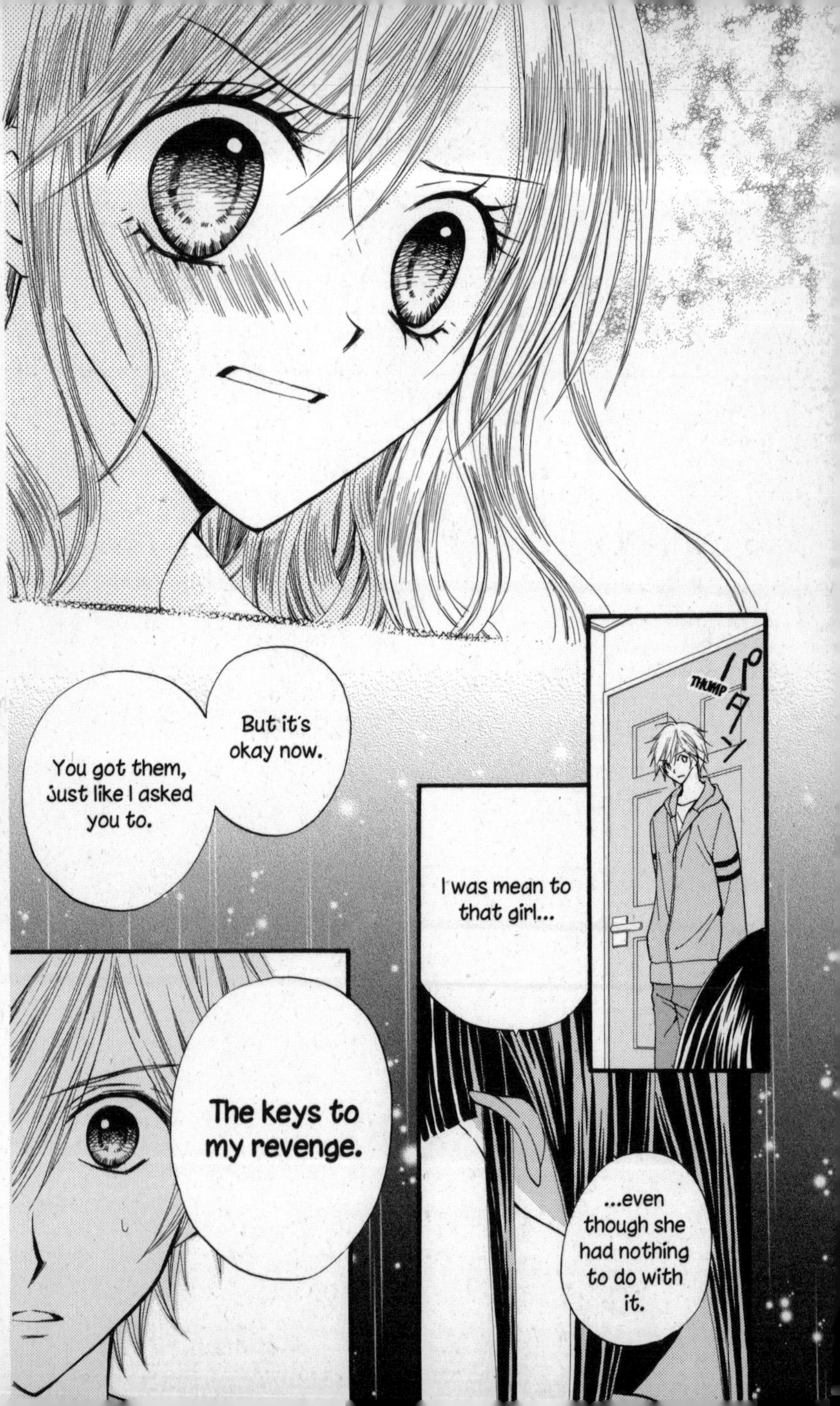
パタン
THUMP
I was mean to that girl...
...even though she had nothing to do with it.
But it's okay now.
You got them, just like I asked you to.
The keys to my revenge.

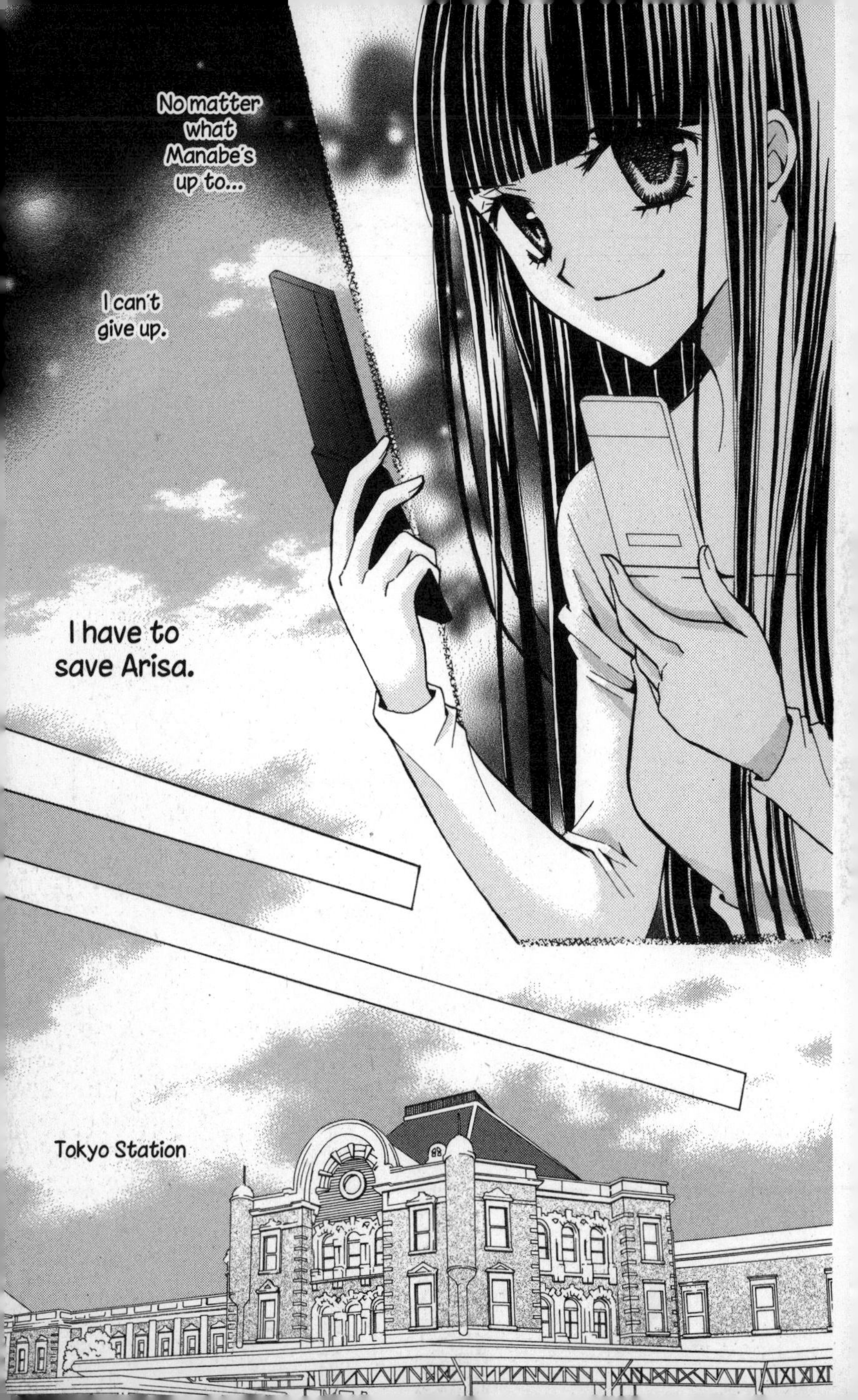
No matter what Manabe's up to...
I can't give up.
I have to save Arisa.
Tokyo Station

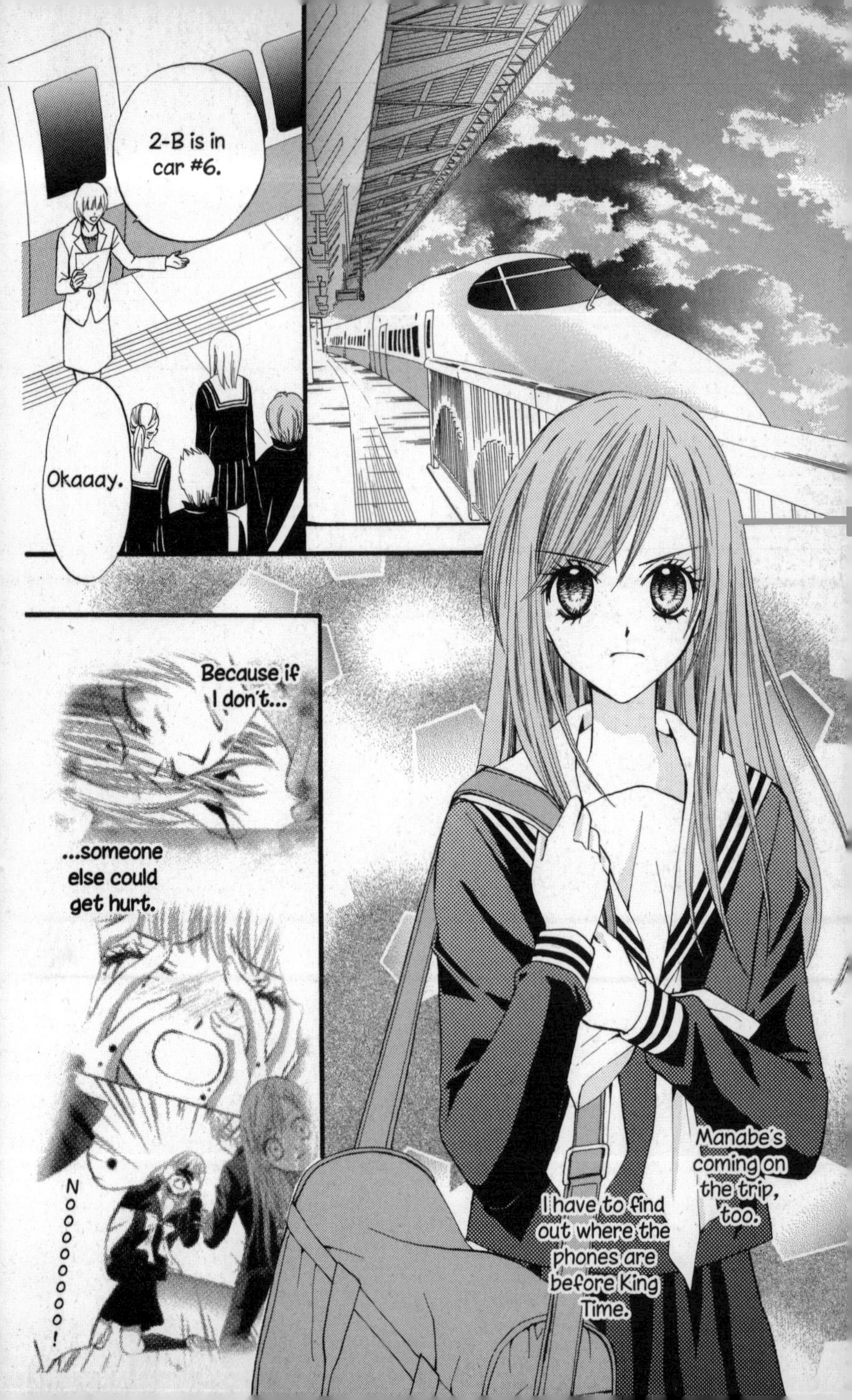
2-B is in car #6.
Okaaay.
Manabe's coming on the trip, too.
I have to find out where the phones are before King Time.
Because if I don't...
...someone else could get hurt.
Noooooooooo!

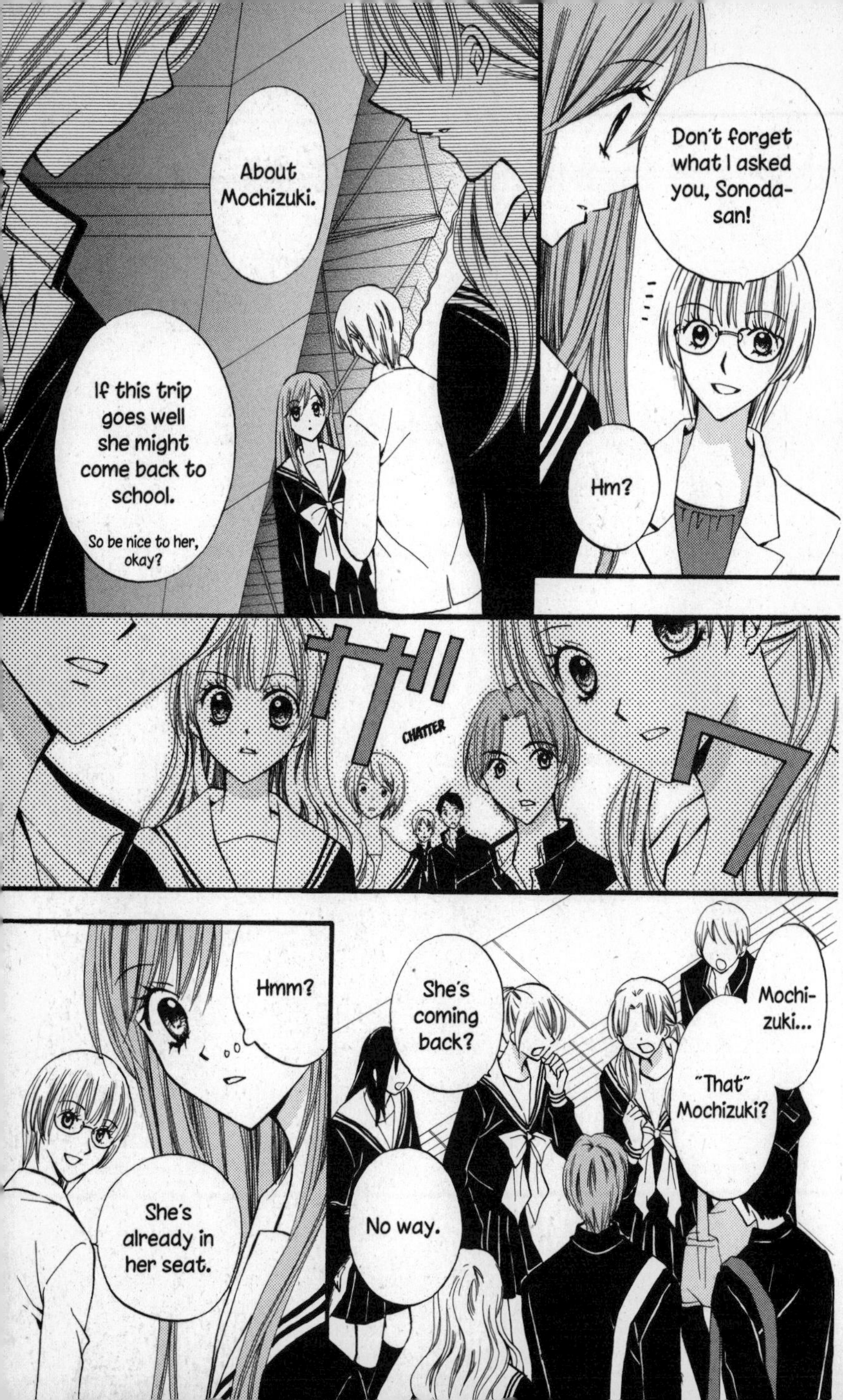
Don't forget what I asked you, Sonoda-san!
Hm?
About Mochizuki.
If this trip goes well she might come back to school.
So be nice to her, okay?
CHATTER
Mochi-zuki...
"That" Mochizuki?
She's coming back?
No way.
Hmm?
She's already in her seat.

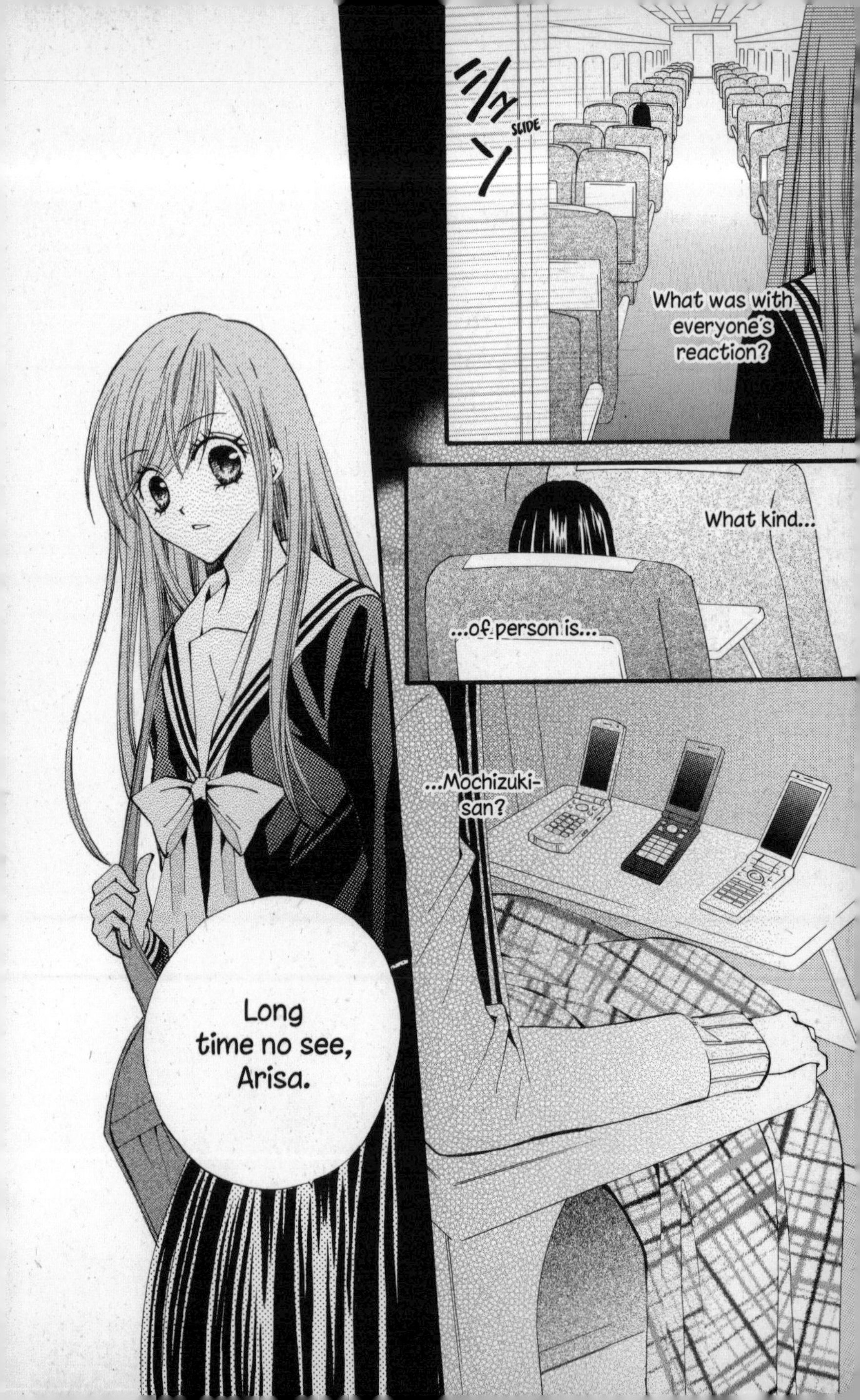
SLIDE
What was with everyone's reaction?
What kind...
...of person is...
...Mochizuki-san?
Long time no see, Arisa.

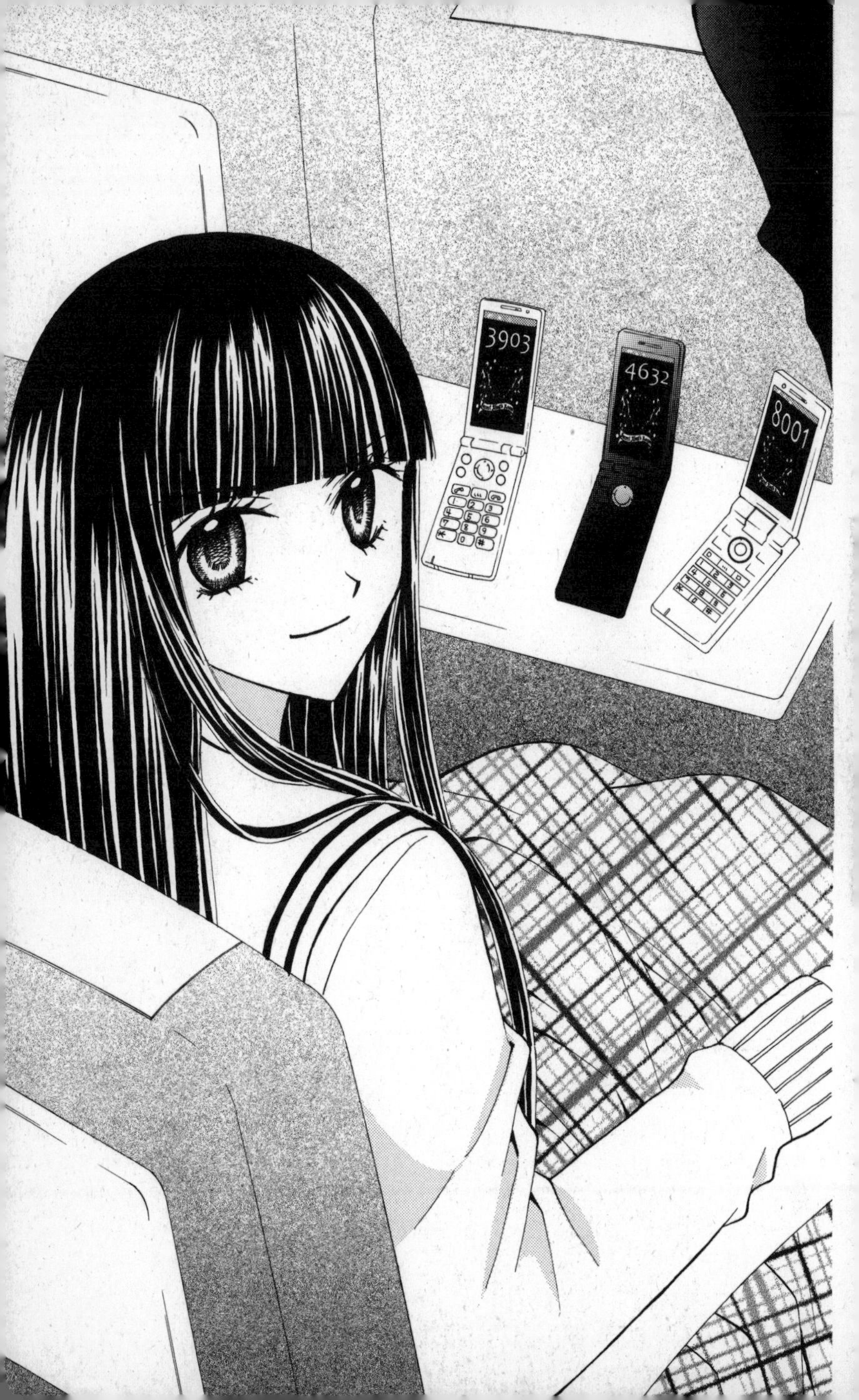
3903
4632
8001

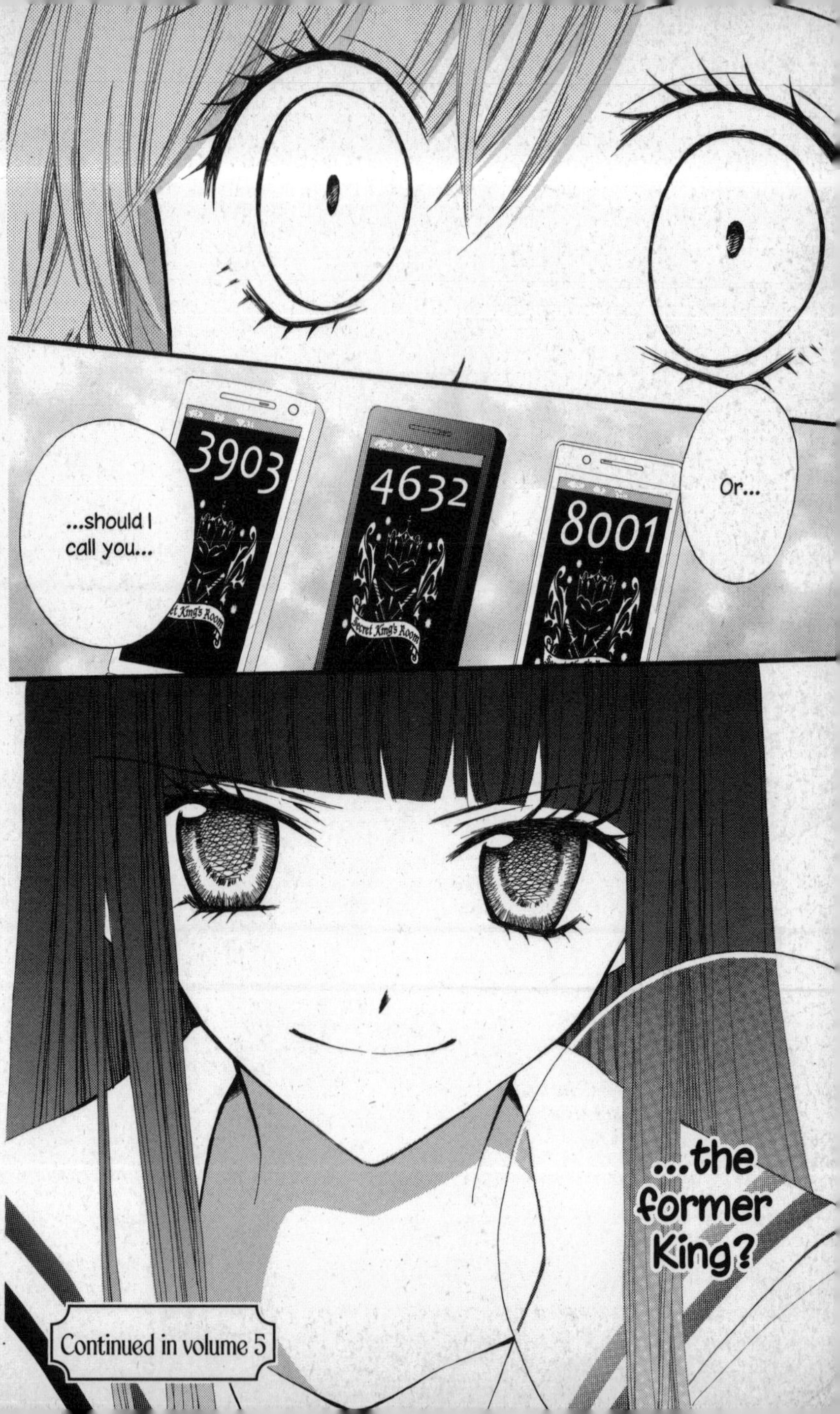
Or...
8001
4632
Secret King's Room
3903
...should I call you...
...the former King?
Continued in volume 5

Please send mail to:
Natsumi Ando c/o
Kodansha Comics
451 Park Ave. South, 7th Fl.
New York, NY 10016

None of the lottery numbers on my New Year's cards were winners again this year.

My friend said, "I've never heard of having no winning numbers!" But I'm unbelievably unlucky...

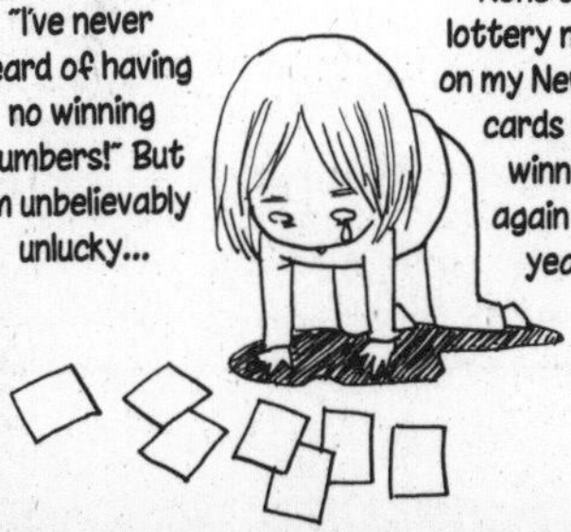

So I'm sending out New Year's cards for replies. ♥

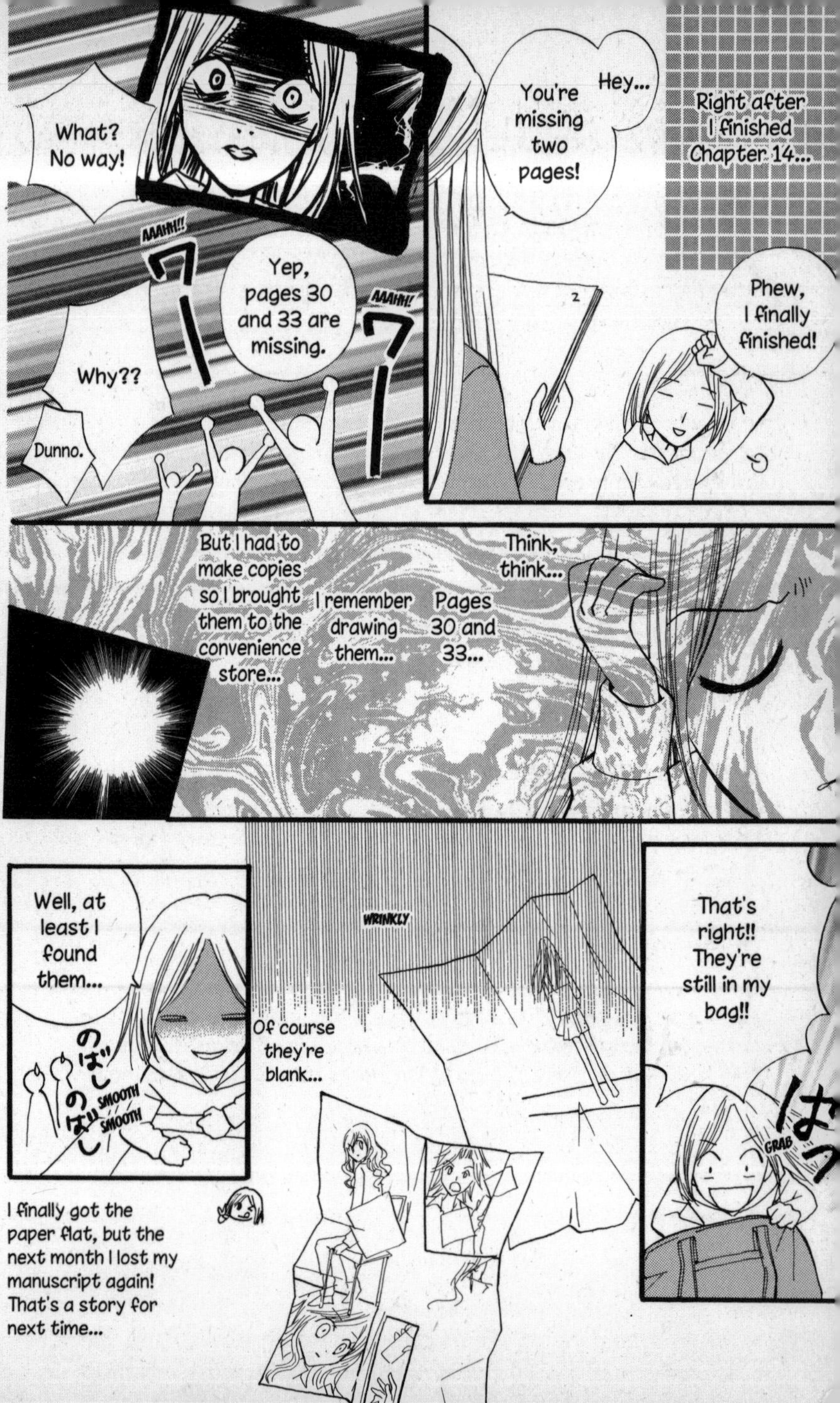
Right after I finished Chapter 14...
Phew, I finally finished!
Hey...
You're missing two pages!
What? No way!
AAAHH!!
Yep, pages 30 and 33 are missing.
AAAHH!
Why??
Dunno.
Think, think...
Pages 30 and 33...
I remember drawing them...
But I had to make copies so I brought them to the convenience store...
That's right!! They're still in my bag!!
はっ
GRAB
WRINKLY
Of course they're blank...
Well, at least I found them...
のばしのばし
SMOOTH SMOOTH
I finally got the paper flat, but the next month I lost my manuscript again! That's a story for next time...

Translation Notes

Japanese is a tricky language for most Westerners, and translation is often more art than science. For your edification and reading pleasure, here are notes on some of the places where we could have gone in a different direction with our translation of the work, or where a Japanese cultural reference is used.

The King

In Japanese, there is no pronoun used to refer to the King. It is not clear in the Japanese whether the King is male or female. This is more difficult in English, so the King is referred to as "he" in this translation. Keep in mind this does not necessarily mean the identity of the King is a male (or isn't).

Arisa, page 70

Tsubasa saying "Arisa" here isn't giving away her identity. It's fairly common in Japanese for young girls to refer to themselves in third person, so Midori wouldn't have been suspicious.

Wanna fight?, page 143

These letters are actually "hatashi-jō." They are basically letters to challenge someone else to a fight. Since Tsubasa has been absent from school so much, they really have been piling up!

New Year's cards, page 165

Sending New Year's cards to friends, family, and co-workers is a very important part of the New Year's celebration in Japan. The cards are usually postcards issued by the Japanese postal service that have a lottery number stamped on the bottom of each one. The lottery isn't for money, but for various household goods.

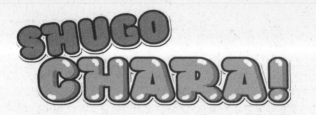

SHUGO CHARA!

PEACH-PIT

CREATORS OF *DEARS* AND *ROZEN MAIDEN*

PEACH-PIT
CREATORS OF DEARS AND ROZEN MAIDEN
SHUGO CHARA!
1

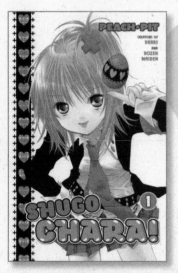

Everybody at Seiyo Elementary thinks that stylish and supercool Amu has it all. But nobody knows the real Amu, a shy girl who wishes she had the courage to truly be herself. Changing Amu's life is going to take more than wishes and dreams—it's going to take a little magic! One morning, Amu finds a surprise in her bed: three strange little eggs. Each egg contains a Guardian Character, an angel-like being who can give her the power to be someone new. With the help of her Guardian Characters, Amu is about to discover that her true self is even more amazing than she ever dreamed.

Special extras in each volume! Read them all!

VISIT WWW.KODANSHACOMICS.COM TO:

- **View release date calendars for upcoming volumes**
- **Find out the latest about new Kodansha Comics series**

KC KODANSHA COMICS

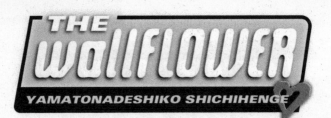

THE wallFLOWER
YAMATONADESHIKO SHICHIHENGE

BY TOMOKO HAYAKAWA

It's a beautiful, expansive mansion, and four handsome, fifteen-year-old friends are allowed to live in it for free! But there is one condition—within three years the young men must take the owner's niece and transform her into a proper lady befitting the palace in which they all live! How hard can it be?

Enter Sunako Nakahara, the horror-movie-loving, pock-faced, frizzy-haired, fashion-illiterate hermit who has a tendency to break into explosive nosebleeds whenever she sees anyone attractive. This project is going to take far more than our four heroes ever expected; it needs a miracle!

1
THE wallFLOWER
YAMATONADESHIKO SHICHIHENGE
TOMOKO HAYAKAWA

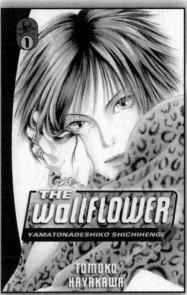

Ages: 16 +

Special extras in each volume! Read them all!

KC KODANSHA COMICS

VISIT WWW.KODANSHACOMICS.COM TO:

- View release date calendars for upcoming volumes
- Find out the latest about new Kodansha Comics series

TOMARE!

[STOP!]

You're going the wrong way!

Manga is a completely
different
type of reading experience.

To start at the *beginning*,
go to the *end*!

That's right! Authentic manga is read the traditional Japanese way—from right to left. Exactly the *opposite* of how American books are read. It's easy to follow: Just go to the other end of the book, and read each page—and each panel—from the right side to the left side, starting at the top right. Now you're experiencing manga as it was meant to be!